ROUTLEDGE LIBRARY EDITIONS:
AGING

Volume 40

PLANNING LOCAL
AUTHORITY SERVICES
FOR THE ELDERLY

PLANNING LOCAL AUTHORITY SERVICES FOR THE ELDERLY

GRETA SUMNER
AND
RANDALL SMITH

Routledge
Taylor & Francis Group

LONDON AND NEW YORK

First published in 1969 by George Allen & Unwin Ltd

This edition first published in 2024
by Routledge
4 Park Square, Milton Park, Abingdon, Oxon OX14 4RN

and by Routledge
605 Third Avenue, New York, NY 10158

Routledge is an imprint of the Taylor & Francis Group, an informa business

British Library Cataloguing in Publication Data
A catalogue record for this book is available from the British Library

ISBN: 978-1-032-67433-9 (Set)
ISBN: 978-1-032-68534-2 (Volume 40) (hbk)
ISBN: 978-1-032-68542-7 (Volume 40) (pbk)
ISBN: 978-1-032-68541-0 (Volume 40) (ebk)

DOI: 10.4324/9781032685410

Publisher's Note
The publisher has gone to great lengths to ensure the quality of this reprint but points out that some imperfections in the original copies may be apparent.

Disclaimer
The publisher has made every effort to trace copyright holders and would welcome correspondence from those they have been unable to trace.

PLANNING LOCAL AUTHORITY SERVICES FOR THE ELDERLY

BY
GRETA SUMNER
AND
RANDALL SMITH

London
GEORGE ALLEN AND UNWIN LTD
RUSKIN HOUSE   MUSEUM STREET

PRINTED IN GREAT BRITAIN
in 10 *on* 11 *point Times type*
BY UNWIN BROTHERS LTD
WOKING AND LONDON

FOREWORD

In 1964 the National Corporation for the Care of Old People, which was interested in the effect of the ten-year plans for local health and welfare services in England and Wales, and in the effect of the lack of such plans in Scotland, made a grant to the Department of Social and Economic Research in the University of Glasgow for a study of the planning of local authority services for the elderly.

The study was carried out by Randall Smith and Greta Sumner under the general supervision of J. B. Cullingworth, now Director of the Centre for Urban and Regional Studies, University of Birmingham. Much of the report was prepared jointly by the research workers, but Randall Smith was particularly concerned with the sections on residential accommodation and finance, and Greta Sumner with those on post-war national policy, housing, staffing, sites and architects' services. She also prepared the basic draft for Part IV of the report.

Many other people have helped in the study and their help is gratefully acknowledged. In particular, we would like to thank Professor W. Ferguson Anderson, Dr E. V. Kuenssberg, Dr W. D. Rees and Dr J. Williamson for their interest and help, and we are grateful for the support and encouragement given to our work by other geriatricians and general practitioners. We would specially like to thank Bleddyn Davies of the London School of Economics, who has influenced our thinking on the planning of social services, and Brian Donald of the University of Southampton, who has generously shared with us the results of his own work on the development of techniques for manpower planning in the health services.

Thanks are due to Professor D. J. Robertson and other colleagues in the Department of Social and Economic Research, University of Glasgow, especially to Janet Sleeman. A special word of thanks is due to Mrs Hilda Walker for her work in typing interview notes and later the report itself. Others who have helped in various ways include a number of civil servants in the Ministry of Health, Ministry of Housing and Local Government, Scottish Development Department and Scottish Home and Health Department.

Our main thanks are reserved for the officers of the local health, welfare, and housing authorities which co-operated in the study, for without their help the study could never have been made. Our debt to them is great indeed.

G.S.
R.S.

CONTENTS

FOREWORD   *page* 7

LIST OF TABLES   11

INTRODUCTION   13

I BACKGROUND TO THE STUDY
  1 Developments in National Policy since 1945   23
  2 Services in 1965—Residential Accommodation   49
  3 Services in 1965—Housing   67
  4 Services in 1965—Domiciliary Services   84

II PROBLEMS OF DEVELOPMENT—
    THE ASSESSMENT OF NEEDS
  5 Residential Accommodation—Planning for   107
    Replacement
  6 Residential Accommodation—The Nature of   113
    Current Need
  7 Residential Accommodation—Estimating Future   122
    Need
  8 Sheltered Housing   134
  9 Local Authority Housing Programmes and Plans   149
    for the Elderly
 10 Domiciliary Services—Planning to Improve Quality   164
 11 Domiciliary Services—Planning for Unmet Needs   181
 12 Domiciliary Services—The Ten-Year Plans   204

III PROBLEMS OF DEVELOPMENT—
    THE MOBILIZATION OF RESOURCES
 13 Staffing—Recruitment Difficulties   215
 14 Staffing—Employment Policies   226
 15 Finance—Capital Projects   247
 16 Finance—Revenue Expenditure   258
 17 Finance—Housing for the Elderly   267
 18 Sites   285
 19 Architectural Services and Building Resources   292
 20 Alternative Suppliers—Other Statutory Bodies   307
 21 Alternative Suppliers—Voluntary Organisations   318
 22 Alternative Suppliers—The Private Sector   332

A*

IV CONCLUSIONS AND RECOMMENDATIONS
    23 Conclusions   347
    24 A Possible Approach to Planning—Recommendations 360

APPENDICES
    1 Suggestions for Overcoming some Current Problems of Administration and Development of Services for the Elderly   375
    2 Home Help Service: Scale for Guidance in Determining the Number of Hours per Week to be Authorized (in use in 1965)   380
    3 Basic Brief agreed between a Welfare Department and an Architect's Department (in use in 1965)   381

SELECTED BIBLIOGRAPHY   385

INDEX   398

LIST OF TABLES

1   Places in Local Authority Accommodation per Thousand   52
    Elderly Population at March 31, 1965 for Local Authori-
    ties in England and Wales

2   Hospital Geriatric Bed Provision (1960) and Places in   54
    Local Authority Part III Accommodation (1965) for 11
    Hospital Regions in England and Wales

3   Hospital Geriatric Bed Provision and Places in Local   55
    Authority Part III Accommodation by Hospital Regions
    in Scotland, 1965

4   Homes for the Elderly in Scotland at March 31, 1965   56

5   Materially Handicapped Elderly Residents as a Percentage   59
    of Total Elderly Residents in Residential Accommodation
    in England and Wales at December 31, 1958–65

6   Materially Handicapped Elderly Residents as a Percentage   60
    of Total Elderly Residents in Residential Accommodation
    in 13 English and Welsh Case Study Authorities at
    December 31, 1958–65

7   Materially Handicapped Elderly Residents as a Percentage   61
    of Total Residents in Residential Accommodation in 16
    English and Welsh Case Study Authorities at December
    31, 1965 by Type of Local Authority

8   Net Expenditure per Thousand Total Population and Cost   63
    per Resident-Week on Residential Accommodation by 140
    Local Welfare Authorities in England and Wales in
    1965–6

9   Net Expenditure per Thousand Total Population and   64
    Expenditure per Resident-Week on Residential Accom-
    modation by 55 Scottish Welfare Authorities in 1965–6

10 Range of Persons per Thousand Elderly Population in   69
    Sheltered Housing in 140 English and Welsh Welfare
    Authorities at March 31, 1965 by Type of Local
    Authority

11 Range of Contributions towards Cost of Special Features   70
    in Housing for the Elderly by 54 English and Welsh
    Counties in the Financial Year 1965–6

12 Domiciliary Services: National Staff Ratios per Thousand   85
    Total Population for England and Wales, and for
    Scotland, at end-1965

11

13 Domiciliary Services: Lowest and Highest Staff Ratios   86
    per Thousand Total Population for Local Authorities in
    England and Wales, and Scotland, at end-1965

14 Distribution of Estimated Health Visitor Staff Ratios per   87
    Thousand Total Population for Local Authorities in
    England and Wales at end-1965

15 Distribution of Home Nurse Staff Ratios per Thousand   88
    Total Population at end-1965 for England and Wales, and
    for Authorities with a separate Home Nursing Service in
    Scotland

16 Distribution of Home Help Staff Ratios per Thousand   89
    Total Population by Type of Local Authority in England
    and Wales, and Scotland, at end-1965

17 Distribution of Estimated Social Worker Staff Ratios per   90
    Thousand Total Population at end-1965 for England and
    Wales

18 Estimated Staffing Levels at December 31, 1965 of Indi-   91
    vidual Local Authorities compared with Ministry
    Recommendations (England and Wales)

19 Elderly Cases as a Percentage of Total Cases for Three   93
    Domiciliary Services in England and Wales, and Scotland,
    1965

20 Range of Elderly Cases as Proportion of Total Cases for   93
    Three Domiciliary Services in 16 Case Study Authorities
    in England and Wales and in 55 Local Authorities in
    Scotland, 1965

21 Comparison between England and Wales, and Scotland,   94
    of the Proportion of Net Expenditure on Local Health
    Services spent on Individual Services in 1965–6

22 Net Expenditure per Thousand Total Population on   95
    Three Domiciliary Services in England and Wales, and
    Scotland, 1965–6

23 Domiciliary Services: Lowest and Highest Net Expendi-   96
    ture per Thousand Total Population by Individual Local
    Authorities in England and Wales, and Scotland, 1965–6

24 New Residents: Incapacity for Self-Care by Type of Home   121
    (Sample of 530 New Residents), England and Wales

25 Dwellings Built by Private Developers as a Percentage of   333
    All Dwellings Built between January 1, 1945 and December
    31, 1965 in 41 Case Study Housing Authorities

INTRODUCTION

In 1965 there were about six and a half million people over the age of sixty-five in Great Britain, just over half a million of these living in Scotland. This is equivalent to 12% of the total population of England and Wales, and 11% of the total population of Scotland. The proportion of old people in the population more than doubled between the 1901 and the 1961 census of population, and this rising trend is expected to continue until the 1980's. Although on the basis of present population projections[1] the proportion of the total population which is in the age group sixty-five and over is expected to fall slightly after about 1980, the proportion in the age group seventy-five and over will continue to rise until about the end of the century. The actual number of people in the age group sixty-five and over is expected to fall slightly by the end of the century, but the actual number in the age group seventy-five and over will still be increasing.

Since 1945 there have been numerous studies of the social, medical and economic circumstances of old people,[2] resulting in an increased understanding of their needs. Many of these studies have revealed deficiencies in the extent of public provision for meeting these needs. In 1962 a survey was carried out by Townsend with the expressed aims of finding out how effective the existing social services for old people were, and of estimating the extent of unmet need.[3] His results confirmed that provision fell short of needs. They also provided a quantitative estimate, at national level, of the size of the deficiency.

There are thus two reasons why services for old people need to be developed, first to make good the deficiencies in present provision, and secondly to cater for the needs of the larger numbers of old people, especially those in the higher age groups, who will be living in Britain during the next thirty years.

The present study is concerned with the local authority services, although these are only some of the services provided for old people

[1] General Register Office, *The Registrar General's Quarterly Return for England and Wales, Births, Deaths and Marriages etc., No. 468*, H.M.S.O.,1966 and *Quarterly Return of the Registrar General for Scotland, Births, Deaths and Marriages, No. 444*, H.M.S.O., 1966.
[2] See P. Townsend and D. Wedderburn, *The Aged in the Welfare State*, G. Bell and Sons Ltd., 1965, Appendix I, for a selected list.
[3] *Ibid.*, Chapter 3.

in Britain by both public and private organizations. Thus retirement incomes, employment, hospital and general medical services are not the direct concern of this study. There are, however, many implications in what follows for the organizations which provide these services. The services provided for the elderly by voluntary organizations occupy a rather special position, since many of them are similar in kind to those which local authorities may provide, and since they are often provided on behalf of, or in close association with, a local authority. For these reasons the role of voluntary organizations, as seen by local authorities, did form an important part of the study.

Local authorities have powers under the National Health Service Acts and National Assistance Acts to provide services such as home nursing, home helps, health visiting, chiropody, laundry, meals and old people's homes, which help to meet the needs of old people. They can also, by the exercise of powers conferred by the Housing Acts, make an important contribution to the well-being of old people by providing good housing conditions.

Local authorities also have powers under the National Assistance Act to provide welfare services for the blind, deaf and other physically handicapped. Many handicapped people, especially the blind, are also elderly. In England and Wales at the end of 1965, 99,807 people were registered as blind, of whom 68,755 (68·9%) were elderly. In addition 27,545 people over the age of sixteeen and not at school were on the register of partially-sighted persons, of whom 18,515 (67·2%) were sixty-five or over. Of the 41,525 on the deaf, deaf and dumb and hard of hearing registers 13,409 (32·3%) were elderly, and there were 148,164 people handicapped in other ways, of whom 54,707 (36·9%) were elderly.[1] In Scotland 73·6% of the 10,261 persons registered as blind at the end of 1965 were over sixty-five.[2] Information about the proportion of elderly people in other classes of the handicapped in Scotland is not available. The present study concentrated on local authority services provided for the elderly rather than on special services provided on account of specific handicaps.

There is considerable variation in the extent to which services for the elderly have been developed by different local authorities. This is partly because some powers are permissive, so that in some areas, for example, there is no laundry or meals-on-wheels service, but

[1] Ministry of Health, *Report for 1965, Cmnd. 3039*, H.M.S.O., 1966, Table 54, pp. 127–30.
[2] Scottish Home and Health Department, *Report for 1965, Cmnd. 2984*, H.M.S.O., 1966, p. 43.

there is wide variation in provision even in the services such as home nursing or old people's homes which local authorities are required to provide. Planned levels of provision also vary considerably between local authorities in England and Wales.[1] Some such variation would be expected, since demographic, economic and social conditions differ from place to place, and these will affect the level of need for services. However, the work of Bleddyn Davies suggests that the highest levels of provision are not necessarily in the areas in which one would expect the greatest needs.[2] This too is understandable since, as Griffith has shown, it is an accepted feature of the relationship between central government departments and local authorities that the latter are responsible for assessing the need for the services in their areas in the light of local circumstances, but there is no general agreement as to how this should be done.[3]

The main purpose of this study was, therefore, to find out how local authorities plan to meet the need for services for the elderly in their areas. The two major issues which face local authorities are the assessment of needs for the services and the mobilization of resources to meet those needs. It is on these two issues that this study is focused.

METHODS OF RESEARCH

The fieldwork for this project was carried out between September 1965 and November 1966 in co-operation with 24 local health and welfare authorities, of which 8 were in Scotland and 16 in England and Wales. By studying 24 areas in some detail it was possible to ensure that a variety of different types of area were included. In addition, in the case study county areas a number of housing authorities were selected, so that in all, housing provision was studied in 41 local authority areas.

As much as possible of the factual background information about services in each area was collected from documents, either from published sources or from reports made available by the local authorities.

The research team then visited each of the health and welfare authorities for about a week, during which they discussed with local

[1] Ministry of Health, *Health and Welfare, The Development of Community Care, Cmnd. 1973*, H.M.S.O., 1962, and subsequent revisions. There is no equivalent publication for Scotland.

[2] B. P. Davies, 'Local Health and Welfare Services', *Local Government Chronicle* No. 5159, January 15, 1966, pp. 97–100.

[3] J. A. G. Griffith, *Central Departments and Local Authorities*, Allen and Unwin, 1966.

authority officials the planning and development of health, welfare and housing services. They did not normally see elected members, since it was not the intention of this project to study directly the part they play in the formulation of policy.

The main discussions were with senior officers[1] in health and welfare departments. There were 8 authorities (4 in Scotland, 4 in England) which formally had combined health and welfare departments, but there was in each case a senior or chief welfare officer who took part in the discussions as well as the medical officer of health. In several cases the chief welfare officer headed a section or division which was barely distinguishable from a separate department, and in one or two cases he was even responsible to a separate welfare committee. In several areas discussions were also held with chief nursing officers and home help organizers. In counties which had a divisional or area structure the research workers saw one or two of the divisional medical officers, nursing officers and welfare officers, and visited two authorities with some delegated health and welfare functions. In most areas visits to two or three welfare homes included a talk with the matron or superintendent. In housing authorities interviews were held with the housing manager if there was one, or if not, with whoever was chiefly concerned with housing. This might be the public health inspector, medical officer of health, engineer and surveyor, clerk, treasurer, or architect; in several cases responsibility for different aspects of housing policy and management was divided between two or more officials. In health and welfare authorities treasurers and architects were also interviewed.

Interview schedules were used as a guide and check list of topics to be covered, but otherwise the interviews were unstructured. With senior officers it was usual to hold one long interview early in the week, with a shorter interview later in the week to clear outstanding topics and ask follow-up questions.

SELECTION OF CASE STUDY AREAS

The areas visited were selected as follows. All local health and welfare authorities except London boroughs[2] were grouped according to certain characteristics. First of these was the type of local authority, county council or county borough in England and Wales, county council, county of city or large burgh in Scotland. The type of local

[1] In a few cases the chief officer was not available at the time of the visit.
[2] Under the London Government Act 1963 health and welfare services became the responsibility of the 32 new London borough councils and the City of London Council. The London borough councils only came into being on April 1, 1965, and were therefore not included in the study.

authority was thought to be important partly because of the different nature of the areas in which county councils are providing services compared with the boroughs, and partly because of certain differences in function, particularly with regard to housing.

Secondly, local authorities were grouped according to size of total population, since it seemed probable that, compared with small authorities, large authorities would have different patterns of administrative organization, more flexibility in the deployment of resources, and some gains from economies of scale. Thirdly, local authorities were grouped according to the proportion of the population which was aged sixty-five and over, on the grounds that local authorities with a higher than average proportion of old people might view matters differently from other authorities. Finally, one local authority was selected from each group, with general regard to the desirability of including areas from different regions of the country. One local authority found itself unable to co-operate, and was replaced by another with broadly similar characteristics.

In England and Wales county boroughs are housing authorities as well as health and welfare authorities, but in counties health and welfare are the responsibility of the county council, while housing is the responsibility of municipal borough, urban and rural district councils. In Scotland, counties of city and large burghs are housing authorities as well as health and welfare authorities, but in counties the county council is the health and welfare authority, while housing is the county's responsibility for the landward area only, and small burghs are responsible for their own housing policy. It was not possible to interview all housing authorities in the counties selected for study, so a small number of housing authorities in each county were invited to co-operate. All those approached willingly agreed to do so. Apart from a general aim of choosing a municipal borough, an urban and a rural district in each county, and one or two small burghs in Scottish counties, there was no special reason why one housing authority was chosen rather than another. The considerations which entered into the selection were the practical ones that the housing authority offices had in most cases to be within reasonable travelling distance of county headquarters, and that quite often they were in a town which also had a welfare home or an area health or welfare office.

THE CHARACTER OF THE CASE STUDY AREAS

The health and welfare authorities selected comprised 7 counties and 9 county boroughs in England and Wales, 4 counties, a county of city and 3 large burghs in Scotland. The total of 41 housing authorities included, as well as the county boroughs, large burghs, the Scottish city and the Scottish counties, 6 municipal boroughs, 5 urban districts, 7 rural districts, and 6 Scottish small burghs.

Four counties and 5 boroughs had a population of less than 100,000. At the other end of the scale 4 counties and 2 boroughs had a population of more than 400,000, including 2 counties with a population of about 1 million. The population of the housing authorities ranged from the 2 boroughs with about half a million, down to about 2,000 in one urban district. The largest municipal borough was larger than the smallest county borough, while the smallest municipal borough was smaller than 2 of the rural district councils.

The proportion of the population aged sixty-five and over was less than 10% in 2 boroughs and 2 counties, and more than 14% in 3 boroughs and 5 counties. The proportion of total households present at the 1961 Census which were one and two person households containing a person of pensionable age ranged from about 18% in 1 county borough and 1 municipal borough to 27% or more in 2 county boroughs and an urban district in England and Wales, and from about 15% in 1 small burgh to 27% or more in 2 other small burghs in Scotland.

In terms of regional representation, 5 case studies were in Northern England, 3 in the Midlands, 2 in Eastern England, 2 in the South-East, 3 in the South-West and one in Wales. Of the Scottish authorities studied 4 were in the Central Belt, and 4 in the Highland or Border areas.

Five county boroughs could best be described as mainly industrial towns, the other four as resorts, administrative or commercial towns.[1] Two Scottish urban authorities were mainly industrial, and two administrative and commercial. The counties are more difficult to typify, as some larger counties include areas vastly different in character, ranging from isolated farms and small villages to large industrial towns. The measure which probably gives the most helpful general indication of whether a county is mainly rural or urban is density of population, which was 0·1 persons per acre or less in the four more rural of the counties studied, over 1·0 persons per acre in two others, and ranged from 0·4 to 0·8 in the remaining five.[2]

The towns classified as resorts, administrative or commercial, and

[1] See C. A. Moser and W. Scott, *British Towns*, Oliver and Boyd, 1961, for a system of classifying towns according to social and economic characteristics.
[2] General Register Office, *Census 1961, County Reports*, H.M.S.O.

the more sparsely populated counties tended to be areas with high proportions of elderly in their population.

Housing conditions varied considerably. Using the percentage of households with exclusive use of four household arrangements (cold and hot water tap, fixed bath and water closet) as a measure[1] the worst conditions in 1961 were in two industrial county boroughs (54%, 56%) and two of the more sparsely populated administrative counties (48%, 56%) in England and Wales, while the best conditions were in two industrial boroughs (81%, 78%) and two of the more densely populated administrative counties (77%, 78%), two of these being in Scotland.[2]

In general, conditions were better in more densely populated counties and worse in more sparsely populated areas, the majority of boroughs coming in between, with the exception of the four already mentioned. However, there were wide variations within administrative counties. For example, in one county with relatively poor conditions (56%) one housing authority visited was a small town with good conditions (81%), and in another county with relatively good conditions (75%) a rural district with poor conditions (53%) was visited. Once again, it was, on the whole, in more sparsely populated areas that conditions were worst, and these were one type of area which tended to have a relatively high proportion of elderly in the population.

STRUCTURE OF THE REPORT

Part I provides a background to the study. Chapter 1 traces the development of national policies for the elderly since 1945. Chapters 2, 3 and 4 outline the level of provision of local authority services at the end of 1965, and show the range of variation between local authorities. The material for these four chapters is drawn from annual reports of central government departments except where otherwise indicated.

Parts II and III are based mainly on discussions held with officials in case study authorities. Although the method of selecting health and welfare authorities for case study was similar to that for selecting

[1] General Register Office, *Census 1961, County Reports* and General Registry Office, Edinburgh, *Census 1961, County Reports*, H.M.S.O.

[2] On this measure, there is no difference between Scottish case study authorities and the English ones, although there is a marked difference if density of persons per room is compared. Only 2 of the 14 Scottish housing authorities visited had, in 1961, an average density of persons per room of less than 0·75, compared with 26 of the 27 housing authorities visited in England and Wales.

a stratified random sample no statistical validity is claimed for the findings. A summary of the main points is provided at the end of each chapter.

Part II is concerned with how the level of need is estimated for residential accommodation, housing and domiciliary services. Part III considers the problems caused for planning by the limited availability of staff, finance, sites and architectural services, and by the existence of alternative suppliers of similar services.

In Part IV the findings are drawn together in a discussion of whether or not the services could be planned more effectively, and the implications for future policy are considered.

The report as a whole is intended to contribute both to the current discussion on the aims, methods and organization of the activity of social planning, and to the furtherance of the relatively new academic subject of social administration. It is hoped that this analysis of planning services for the elderly, and its implications, will be of interest to those concerned with the planning and execution of social policy and also to teachers and students of social administration.

PART I

BACKGROUND TO THE STUDY

CHAPTER 1

DEVELOPMENTS IN NATIONAL POLICY SINCE 1945

Local authorities are granted their statutory powers to provide services by the central government and partly depend on the exchequer for finance for the services. Therefore the development of local authority services for the elderly must be viewed against the backcloth of national policy and national decisions on relative priorities for different services. This chapter outlines the main developments at national level between 1945 and 1965. The material for this chapter is taken from annual reports of central government departments except where otherwise indicated.

THE LEGISLATIVE FRAMEWORK 1945–8

The legislative framework within which health and welfare services for the elderly are provided was established by the National Assistance Act 1948, and the National Health Service Act 1946.[1] In addition local housing authorities can exercise their powers under the Housing Acts to provide housing for the elderly.

In his opening speech on the second reading of the National Assistance Bill in 1947,[2] Aneurin Bevan, then Minister of Health, said: 'There is another category of persons for whom we shall have to accept an even larger measure of responsibility than we have had in the past, and these are old persons . . . We have, of course, gone a long way towards it by making for increased old age pensions,[3] and it is one of the more fortunate and agreeable aspects of this problem that modern medicine and better nutrition enable old people to continue working longer than they formerly did.' Bevan went on to describe the findings of the Nuffield Foundation Survey[4]

[1] For Scotland the relevant statute is the National Health Service (Scotland) Act 1947.

[2] 444 H.C. Deb. 5s., col. 1609 (November 24, 1947).

[3] Bevan was referring to the provisions of the National Insurance Act 1946.

[4] *Old People*, Report of a Survey Committee on the Problems of Ageing and the Care of Old People, Oxford University Press for the Trustees of the Nuffield Foundation, 1947.

that 95% of old people lived independent lives in their own homes or the homes of their children and to stress that old people wanted to be free to lead their own lives with as much independence and privacy as possible. For those old people 'who are still able to look after themselves . . . but who are unable to do the housework, the laundry, cook meals and things of that sort', special homes for 25–30 people were to be provided by local welfare authorities. The old workhouses were to go, and to avoid the stigma attached to the old Poor Law system old people going to live in the new special homes would pay an economic rent for their accommodation. He went on to explain that it would be the duty of the new National Assistance Board to ensure that all old people had sufficient income to be able to pay this rent. Thus the main emphasis was on the provisions for income. If adequate retirement pensions were provided the majority of old people would continue to live independent lives. For those who could not manage to live independently because of physical inability to do housework the emphasis was on the provision of residential care, while safeguarding privacy for the individual as much as possible.

It was not altogether unrecognized that there were other ways of providing for the social needs of the elderly. Alice Bacon, speaking in the same debate, said: 'I hope, too, that these schemes for homes for the aged will be complementary to, and not instead of the very excellent little houses and bungalows which local authorities are building on housing estates, and that the Minister of Health will see to it that where these small houses and bungalows are being built there are available to the old people those hot meals services, and health and nursing services . . . so that as many old people as possible will find it easy to go on living in their own little homes.'[1] However, the powers to provide supportive domiciliary services were incomplete.

The National Health Service Acts created separate statutory authorities to provide other medical services, but required local health authorities to provide for health visiting,[2] for 'the attendance of nurses on persons who require nursing in their own homes',[3] and empowered them 'to make such arrangements as the Minister may approve for providing domestic help for households where such help is required owing to the presence of any person who is ill, lying-in,

[1] 444 H.C. Deb. 5s., cols. 1668–9 (November 24, 1947).
[2] National Health Service Act 1946, Part III, s. 24. National Health Service (Scotland) Act 1947, Part III, s. 24.
[3] National Health Service Act 1946, Part III, s. 25. National Health Service (Scotland) Act 1947, Part III, s. 25.

an expectant mother, mentally defective, aged, or a child not over compulsory school age'.[1] However, it was envisaged that services such as hot meals for elderly people living at home would be provided by voluntary organizations. Local authorities were given powers to make financial contributions to voluntary organizations providing these services.[2] Other services, such as chiropody and laundry, for people living at home came within the general scope of the National Health Service Acts which permitted, subject to Ministerial approval, the making of arrangements for the 'prevention, care or after-care of persons suffering from illness'.[3] These provisions, together with the envisaged extension of the functions of the health visitor from the care of mothers and young children to a concern with 'the health of the household as a whole',[4] created a framework within which domiciliary care for the elderly was a possibility, even allowing for the lack of powers under the National Assistance Act to provide domiciliary services.

THE FIRST TEN YEARS 1948–58

The new health and welfare legislation came into force on July 5, 1948. Services developed gradually during the next ten years, but growth was hampered by shortages of staff, lack of finance and the low priority accorded to the services at national level. These factors affected different services in differing degrees.

(a) *Residential Accommodation*

Progress on provision of small homes was impeded by government restrictions on capital expenditure, and also by shortages of building materials in the years up to 1954. Between the end of the war and 1954, 798 small homes with places for about 23,000 persons were provided in England and Wales, but only 43 homes were new buildings. In Scotland, although local authorities had planned in 1949 to provide an extra 184 homes accommodating 6,000 persons by 1954,[5] only 62 homes with 1,584 places were in fact provided, many of them being adapted premises.

[1] National Health Service Act 1946, Part III, s. 29. National Health Service (Scotland) Act 1947, Part III, s. 28.

[2] National Assistance Act 1948, Part III, s. 31.

[3] National Health Service Act 1946, Part III, s. 28, National Health Service (Scotland) Act 1947, Part III, s. 27.

[4] Ministry of Health, *Circular 118/47.*

[5] Department of Health for Scotland, *The Ageing Population*, H.M.S.O., 1953, p. 9.

By 1953 the disadvantages of caring for the more infirm elderly in adapted premises were becoming apparent, and it was becoming more difficult to obtain properties suitable for conversion. These considerations led to a shift in policy towards the provision of more purpose-built homes. A similar shift in policy took place in Scotland, where by the end of 1955 the number of places to be provided in new buildings under construction exceeded for the first time the number to be provided in acquired premises.

At the same time the Ministry of Health was concerned that standards in some old people's homes were too extravagant, while in others they were inadequate. Therefore, during 1954 a review was undertaken in the Ministry to see what modifications were desirable in the interests of adequate provision for the special needs of the elderly, with due regard to the need for economy in expenditure on construction and maintenance. This led to the recommendation that, especially in heavily populated areas where sites were difficult to acquire and the demand for accommodation was greatest, homes for up to 60 residents should be built.[1] It was also suggested that local authorities might provide more multi-bedded rooms and reduce the size of living rooms, but more ground floor accommodation was said to be desirable. In Scotland, however, the central department continued to encourage local authorities to build homes accommodating 30–35 people, and to provide two storey homes, with a lift if necessary, in preference to single storey accommodation which was thought to be uneconomical both in terms of construction costs and in the use of land.

These shifts in policy were slow to take effect because of the continued severe restrictions in capital expenditure on welfare projects. In the latter part of 1957 some projects for which loan sanction had been promised were postponed by the local authorities themselves after the Chancellor of the Exchequer's statement of September 1957 and the increase of bank rate to 7%.

Meanwhile evidence was accumulating on the inadequacy of the provision for places in residential homes. It had been estimated in 1953 that Scotland had available about 10,000 places (including voluntary and private), but needed places for at least 17,000 on the basis of the central department's suggested target of 2·5 hostel places per hundred old people.[2] A Ministry survey in England and Wales showed that the waiting list for places in homes was 7,354, although it was estimated that only between a quarter and a third

[1] Ministry of Health, *Circular 3/55*.
[2] *The Ageing Population, op. cit.,* p. 9.

of this number were urgent cases.[1] As well as an overall shortage, the available places were not well distributed, and many were in old institutional accommodation or adapted premises.

The shortage of places in residential accommodation heightened the practical difficulties of determining whether the elderly chronic sick were the responsibility of the welfare authority or of the hospital service. The latter also had staff and accommodation problems, and was also subject to government restrictions on capital expenditure. The intention of the post-war legislation was that hospitals should provide for those needing medical and nursing care, while the local authority would provide for those too frail to look after themselves in their own homes and lacking the care and attention they needed. The problems arose over elderly people needing more attention than welfare homes could provide, but whose medical condition was not such as to merit hospital care. The local authorities, through the major local authority associations, pressed the Ministry for a redefinition of responsibilities, as well as for steps to ensure an increase in the number of hospital beds available for the elderly chronic sick.[2]

However, the Ministry attached more weight to the view put forward by the Phillips Committee that it would be inopportune to embark on long-term building plans to increase the number of hospital beds until more was known about how the development of care in geriatric units would affect future need for places for long-term care.[3] Work in the seventy or so geriatric units which had been established in existing hospitals since the war was showing that active medical treatment could restore many old people who had previously been regarded as chronic sick to the independence of home life. The Phillips Committee concluded that: 'Old people should as far as possible continue to live as members of the community. With this end in view, we consider that it is important that special housing of varying types, adapted to the needs of old people but not isolated from the rest of the community, should be provided. The necessary domiciliary services should be developed and co-ordinated both with the general practitioner and geriatric services.'[4] This view was endorsed by the Guillebaud Committee, which

[1] C. A. Boucher, *Survey of Services Available to the Chronic Sick and Elderly in 1954–5*, Reports on Public Health and Medical Subjects No. 98, H.M.S.O., 1957, p. 37.

[2] See J. Parker, *Local Health and Welfare Services*, Allen and Unwin, 1965, pp. 114–17.

[3] *Report of the Committee on the Economic and Financial Problems of the Provision for Old Age, Cmd. 9333*, H.M.S.O., 1954, p. 74.

[4] *Ibid.*, p. 75.

considered that it would be 'a genuine economy measure, and also a humanitarian measure in enabling old people to lead the sort of life they would much prefer'.[1] The Boucher report similarly proclaimed that: 'The key to the problems stemming from an ageing population lies with the preventive and domiciliary services; the extension of communal accommodation, as the only measure, will not prove a solution.'[2] The Ministry signified its general approval of these views to local authorities in a 1957 circular,[3] in which an attempt was made to redefine the respective roles of hospitals and local authorities.

b) *Domiciliary Services*

Some of the domiciliary health services had grown considerably during the first few years after the National Health Service Acts came into operation. The number of patients cared for by home nurses increased from 865,686 to 1,176,549 in England and Wales, and from 139,000 to about 165,000 in Scotland, between 1949 and 1953. Over the same period home help cases increased from 139,816 to 199,033 in England and Wales, and from 11,274 to about 17,500 in Scotland.

Domiciliary services, however, were also suffering from shortages of finance and of staff. Capital expenditure restrictions were of less importance than they were for welfare homes and hospitals, but even so there was some indirect effect, since lack of accommodation for district nurses was one factor contributing to difficulties in recruiting extra staff for this service.

By the end of 1949 all English and Welsh authorities provided a home help service. 35 of the 55 Scottish authorities provided a service by the end of 1948, and all but 3 of the remaining Scottish authorities started a service before 1953. The last Scottish authority to provide the service received approval for its scheme in 1957. The pace of development varied. The coverage of the service in rural areas was sometimes very limited, and some urban areas experienced staffing difficulties. Nevertheless, the service proved to be very much in demand, with many elderly among the clients. By 1950 the Ministry was commenting that: 'Difficulties of recruitment to the home help service were largely overcome during the year, and financial considerations became the chief brake on progress.'[4] A similar situation was developing in Scotland.

[1] *Report of the Committee of Enquiry into the Cost of the National Health Service, Cmd. 9663*, H.M.S.O., 1956, p. 217.
[2] Boucher, *op. cit.*, p. 54.   [3] Ministry of Health, *Circular 14/57*.
[4] Ministry of Health, *Annual Report 1950, Part I, Cmd. 8342*, H.M.S.O., 1951, p. 48.

The concern over the rising cost of domestic help served to highlight the inadequacies of policies for retirement incomes. The National Health Service Acts permitted local authorities to charge for the domestic help service, but it was found that the proportion of the cost recovered in this way was small, since so much of the help was for old people who were able to pay little or nothing towards the cost. The local authority associations took up this problem with the National Assistance Board, arguing that the Board should pay extra grants to people drawing national assistance and needing domestic help to enable them to make a contribution towards the cost.[1] The request of the local authority associations was in keeping with the spirit of the National Assistance Act, if Bevan's words[2] about the intentions of the Act are to be taken literally. However, the opposite view prevailed.

The development of services for the prevention, care and after-care of illness was also restricted by lack of finance. A major consequence of this in England and Wales was the slow development of chiropody services although there was evidence from surveys such as Sheldon's[3] that chiropody would be a boon to many old people and would help to keep them mobile.

Three county councils and one county borough in England and Wales maintained a limited chiropody service at the time of the Ministry survey in 1954[4] but the development of this service was dependent on Ministerial approval. In the fifties the Ministry would not permit the extension of chiropody services by local authorities. In some areas a service was organized by voluntary organizations, and in 1955 the National Corporation for the Care of Old People announced that £60,000 had been set aside to be used over a period of three years for assisting chiropody schemes undertaken by voluntary societies. In spite of the efforts of voluntary organizations the availability of the service remained limited.

In Scotland, however, the central department allowed the service to develop more freely. In March 1952 a clinic for the elderly was opened at Rutherglen, and chiropody treatment was one of the facilities available. Aberdeen Corporation provided a similar service, and two other Scottish authorities sought approval for the payment of contributions to voluntary organizations providing a service. By 1956, the central department reported that: 'While there is not yet a comprehensive service in any area, chiropody provision of some

---

[1] J. Parker, *op. cit.*, pp. 94–5.   [2] See p. 24.
[3] J. H. Sheldon, *The Social Medicine of Old Age*, Oxford University Press for Nuffield Foundation, 1948.
[4] Boucher, *op. cit.*, p. 44.

kind is now available for elderly people in the areas of the 55 local authorities.'[1] 16 authorities provided a direct service, and there were 74 voluntary schemes, although not all of these received financial support from the local authority. Even so, the expansion of directly provided services was limited in view of the general financial stringency.

Other services such as laundry, which theoretically came within the scope of the powers to provide for the prevention, care and after-care of illness, hardly developed at all in the fifties. Only 6 authorities in England and Wales provided a laundry service for the elderly sick by 1953. It seems that elsewhere such help with laundry as was available to the elderly at home was part of the domestic help service. By 1956 a few authorities had set up laundry centres with a view to conserving the energy of the home help for other duties in the home.

According to a survey of meals-on-wheels services carried out in 1958[2] 5 local authorities had obtained special permission from the Ministry to provide a service under section 28 (27 in Scotland) of the National Health Service Acts. These schemes catered for the sick of all ages but the majority of recipients were in fact old people. In 1952, the county borough of Preston took powers under a local Act to provide a direct meals-on-wheels service. With these few exceptions, meals services could only be provided by voluntary organizations, since there were no powers available under the National Assistance Act for local welfare authorities to provide a direct service.

The Ministry had tried to encourage local authorities to use their powers to contribute to the funds of voluntary organizations providing services for the elderly,[3] and to co-operate with old people's welfare committees.[4] Similar encouragement was given in Scotland.[5] Voluntary provision of meals services grew slowly in the early fifties, both in Scotland and in England and Wales. In 1953 the Ministry reported that: 'Meals-on-wheels services have proved difficult to organize economically and are still limited in scope.'[6] In the mid-fifties voluntary bodies also started lunch clubs in some

---

[1] Department of Health for Scotland, *Annual Report, 1956, Cmnd. 140*, H.M.S.O., 1957, p. 54.

[2] A. I. Harris, *Meals on Wheels for Old People*, A Report of an Inquiry by the Government Social Survey, National Corporation for the Care of Old People, 1960.

[3] Ministry of Health, *Circular 51/49*.   [4] Ministry of Health, *Circular 11/50*.

[5] Department of Health for Scotland, *Circular 65/49*.

[6] Ministry of Health, *Annual Report, 1953, Part I, Cmd. 9321*, H.M.S.O., 1954, p. 187.

areas, especially in northern industrial towns. Despite the efforts of voluntary organizations, and renewed encouragement from the Ministry about the value of co-operation between statutory and voluntary bodies,[1] there was concern nationally about the adequacy of provision of meals services. In 1957 the Department of Health for Scotland asked the Scottish Old People's Welfare Committee to provide information about areas with insufficient facilities, while two years later the Ministry considered that in most areas the service still only touched the fringe of the need.

As well as lack of money, and in the case of meals-on-wheels lack of legislative power to provide a direct service, lack of staff affected the development of domiciliary services. There were shortages of domestic helps in some areas and of volunteers in others, but the greatest difficulties were experienced in recruitment of trained staff, especially home nurses and health visitors.

While this was partly a reflection of the shortage of registered nurses which affected hospitals as well as local authorities, the question of special additional training for local authority work was also relevant. Most local health authorities made some provision for training their district nurses, usually under the auspices of the Queen's Institute of District Nursing. However, there was some uncertainty about the need for special training, and so in 1953 the Minister and the Secretary of State for Scotland set up a working party 'to consider what training it is desired that registered nurses and enrolled assistant nurses, respectively, should undertake prior to their employment on home nursing duties, and the means by which such training should be provided'. The working party affirmed[2] that some form of district training was desirable, and recommended that, while the Queen's Institute of District Nursing or local authorities themselves should continue to provide training courses, a central committee should be established to advise the Minister on all matters relating to district training and to set a national standard for training. The Advisory Committee on the training of District Nurses was established in 1957.

Meanwhile, the Ministry had recommended[3] for the consideration of local authorities the Report of the Standing Nursing Advisory Committee on the Position of the Enrolled Assistant Nurse within the National Health Service, which recommended wider use of the services of the assistant nurse, working under the supervision of

---

1 Ministry of Health, *Circular 14/57.*

2 Ministry of Health, Department of Health for Scotland, *Report of the Working Party on the Training of District Nurses,* H.M.S.O., 1955.

3 Ministry of Health, *Circular 25/54.*

the trained district nurse, especially with chronic sick patients requiring chiefly basic nursing care.

Local authorities had even greater difficulty in recruiting trained health visitors. In England and Wales local authorities could not employ unqualified health visitors without obtaining a dispensation from the Minister from the regulation requiring that only qualified health visitors should be appointed.[1] Although dispensations were granted, the existence of the regulation enabled the Ministry to press local authorities to employ qualified staff, and in fact the number employed under dispensation fell from 1,409 in mid-1948 to 938 in 1953. In Scotland the central department encouraged local authorities to employ qualified staff and to arrange for staff to qualify, but there was no formal regulation corresponding to the English one.

The shortage of qualified health visitors was thought to be partly responsible for the uneven progress made towards the extension of health visitors' duties envisaged by the National Health Service Acts. In 1953 a committee was appointed to enquire into 'the field of work, training and recruitment of health visitors'. The report[2] proposed modifications in the arrangements for training health visitors. It was estimated that in the ensuing ten years an additional 3,500 health visitors would need to be recruited in Great Britain in order to extend the service into fields other than the traditional one of welfare of mothers and children. As one example of the way the service could develop the report outlined the scope for health visitors to assist in ascertainment of social needs of the aged, and close co-operation with general practitioners was also recommended.

One feature of the development of health visiting in the fifties was the increase in social work as opposed to medical and nursing content of the job. Other social workers were employed in local authority health and welfare services, although on a very small scale and many had little or no training. In 1955 another working party was set up to consider the field of work, recruitment and training of all social workers in local authority health and welfare services, and in particular whether there was a place for a general purpose social worker with an in-service training as a basic grade. This working party recommended[3] that a two-year training leading

1 *Statutory Instrument No. 1415*, 1948.
2 Ministry of Health, Department of Health for Scotland, Ministry of Education, *An Inquiry into Health Visiting*, (Jameson Report), H.M.S.O., 1956.
3 Ministry of Health, Department of Health for Scotland, *Report of the Working Party on Social Workers in Local Authority Health and Welfare Services*, (Younghusband Report), H.M.S.O., 1959.

to a national certificate in social work should be established. It was envisaged that social workers with university and professional training would in future act in a supervisory and advisory capacity, and deal with more difficult cases. The two-year trained staff would undertake the main range of social work, and welfare assistants with an in-service training would undertake straightforward visiting and simple duties under the supervision of trained staff. Only by providing professional training and status for the general social worker was it likely that an adequate supply of staff for the services could be ensured. The working party estimated that the services needed an increase of about 2,500 staff (for Great Britain) with a general training in social work, and that to achieve this over a decade would require an average annual recruitment of about 500. Of these, about 80 a year would be staff recruited for services concerned mainly with the elderly. In addition the report suggested that at least 200 welfare assistants should be recruited annually for five years.[1]

Thus by 1959 there was ample evidence of major shortcomings in the provision of domiciliary services. The number of patients cared for by home nurses in England and Wales actually fell slightly between 1953 and 1958, although the number of visits rose, and it was estimated that 60% of visits were to elderly patients compared with about 44% in 1953. The coverage of the home help service increased during the fifties, from 199,033 cases in 1953 to 271,968 cases in 1958, and the proportion of cases who were elderly or chronic sick increased from 58% in 1953 to 73% in 1958. The trends in Scotland were apparently similar, although national figures on he proportion of elderly and chronic sick cases were not regularly reported. In spite of these increases the services were still thought to be inadequate in some areas, if not in all. Lunch clubs and meals services were patchy, while laundry and chiropody services hardly existed at all in England and Wales, although chiropody was somewhat better developed in Scotland. Local authorities had very limited numbers of social work and welfare staff, and health visitors still worked mainly with children in many areas. Thus home visiting services for the elderly were left almost entirely to voluntary bodies, but the coverage of such services was thought to be inadequate and was under consideration by the National Old People's Welfare Council.

---

[1] Ministry of Health, Department of Health for Scotland, *Report of the Working Party on Social Workers in Local Authority Health and Welfare Services*, (Younghusband Report), H.M.S.O., 1959, pp. 221–9.

(c) *Housing*

By the late fifties an increasingly important contribution to the well-being of the elderly in their own homes was being made by housing authorities.

After the 1949 Housing Act the local authorities' powers were no longer restricted to provision of houses only for the working classes.

Some authorities built specially designed dwellings for the elderly, and the central housing departments issued advice on design and layout of housing for old people.[1,2] Nevertheless, total housing progress was at first affected by building restrictions and rationing of building materials, and needs for rehousing were perceived by the central housing advisory committees in terms of families who were overcrowded, suffering from ill-health or lacking a separate home. In Scotland the emphasis was on priority for families whose housing conditions were unsatisfactory, and on housing for essential workers in agriculture or industry.[3]

In 1947 the Nuffield Foundation Survey had concluded that the housing conditions of old people were not, on average, worse than housing conditions generally.[4] This view was challenged by an analysis of 1951 census data, which revealed that proportionately more elderly people living alone were without basic household amenities such as piped water, cooking stoves and w.c.s than were others in the population.[5]

In 1954 there was a shift in housing policy in England and Wales. The most pressing needs resulting from the war had been met, and local authorities were urged to resume slum clearance which the war had interrupted.[6] The Housing Repairs and Rents Act 1954 also provided a new standard of fitness for human habitation in place of the provision in section 188(4) of the Housing Act 1936. The greater emphasis on slum clearance was reflected in the new pattern of subsidies set up by the Housing Subsidies Act 1956. The principal purpose was to abolish general needs subsidies and to encourage local authorities to concentrate on particular aspects of

[1] Ministry of Housing and Local Government, Central Housing Advisory Committee, *Housing for Special Purposes*, 1st Supplement to the Housing Manual, H.M.S.O., 1951.

[2] Department of Health for Scotland, Scottish Housing Advisory Committee, *Housing of Special Groups*, H.M.S.O., 1952.

[3] D. V. Donnison, *Housing Policy since the War*, Codicote Press, 1960, p. 21.

[4] *Old People, op. cit.*, p. 37.

[5] National Corporation for the Care of Old People, *Seventh Annual Report, 1954*, p. 11.

[6] Ministry of Housing and Local Government, *Circular 30/54*.

housing, principally on clearance of slums and building of houses in overspill areas. However, a reduced general needs subsidy of £10 per house was retained for one bedroom dwellings so as to encourage local authorities to build more homes for elderly and single people. In addition, the Minister of Housing announced in the House of Commons on May 1, 1956, that he had decided to inquire into whether old people were receiving a reasonable share of the accommodation provided by local authorities, and whether it was of a kind suited to their physical needs and financial circumstances. Subsequently the Minister asked local authorities and certain voluntary organizations to supply information about the amount and types of accommodation they provided for old people.[1] The inquiry led to a relaxation in the conditions required to qualify for subsidy, such that new dwellings for the elderly need not be fully self-contained, and could provide for shared sanitary facilities, as long as the standard of provision conformed broadly to the standard required to qualify for improvement grants. The standard for conversions was similarly relaxed towards the standard for hostels.[2] Later in 1956 the Minister recommended that local authorities, when reviewing their housing programmes for 1958 in the light of the recently introduced capital investment restrictions, should give special thought to making adequate provision for the elderly, including those who might be affected by the decontrol provisions of the 1957 Rent Act. At the same time local authorities were urged to use their powers to make improvement grants and loans to encourage private owners and housing associations to undertake conversions of suitable property, and to purchase by agreement large houses belonging to elderly people who would like to become tenants of small council dwellings. The local authority could then use the larger houses to accommodate large families on the waiting list.[3]

In Scotland, events took a slightly different course. The nature of the housing problem was different in some respects from that in England, and so the new subsidy structure introduced under the Housing and Town Development (Scotland) Act 1957, provided for continued payment of a general needs subsidy of £24 per house for houses built to relieve overcrowding, for families sharing a house, or for old people. Greater emphasis was placed on slum clearance programmes from 1958 onwards.[4] However, before this, Scottish

---

[1] Ministry of Housing and Local Government, *Circular 32/56.*
[2] Ministry of Housing and Local Government, *Circular 18/57.*
[3] Ministry of Housing and Local Government, *Circular 55/57.*
[4] Department of Health for Scotland, *Circular 75/58.*

local authorities were reminded of the need to keep the housing needs of older people under regular review, and urged to plan housing schemes so as to include a proportion of smaller houses suitable for older people.[1]

The results of this greater emphasis on the needs of the elderly began to show in England and Wales in 1957, when more one bedroom houses and flats were completed during the year than in any preceding year since the war. One bedroom dwellings formed 13% of all local authority housing for the year. By 1959 the proportion had risen to about 20%, and of tenders approved in 1959, 27% were for one bedroom dwellings. In Scotland the trend towards smaller houses was less marked, but in 1959 15% of tenders approved were for houses with one or two rooms, compared with an average of under 3% for the years 1945–54.

A small part of the increase in housing provision for the elderly in England and Wales was due to the growth of sheltered housing, broadly defined as a group of dwellings with a warden to keep a friendly eye on tenants and to give help when necessary. A few housing authorities in South-West England had built sheltered housing schemes in the early fifties, and a problem arose because the county welfare authorities wished to make a financial contribution towards the cost of the warden and other welfare facilities in the schemes. The Ministry of Health considered that a county had no power under the National Assistance Act to make a financial contribution to a district council for welfare purposes, but referred the problem to the Ministry of Housing and Local Government who agreed to approve contributions under section 126 of the Local Government Act 1948.[2] After 1958 the power to make such contributions was derived, in England and Wales, from section 56 of the Local Government Act 1958, and exercise of the power was no longer subject to Ministerial approval. Scotland as yet lacked similar powers.

The Ministry of Housing and Local Government commended the idea of sheltered housing schemes to local authorities in 1957, and also offered further advice on design of housing for the elderly.[3] Yet more advice was contained in handbooks published in 1958[4] and 1960.[5] Other valuable advice on layout and design, and also on

[1] Department of Health for Scotland, *Circular 88/57*.
[2] J. A. G. Griffith, *Central Departments and Local Authorities*, Allen and Unwin, 1966, p. 457.
[3] Ministry of Housing and Local Government, *Circular 55/57*.
[4] Ministry of Housing and Local Government, *Flatlets for Old People*, H.M.S.O., 1958.
[5] Ministry of Housing and Local Government, *More Flatlets for Old People*, H.M.S.O., 1960.

management, and on the estimation of the housing needs of the elderly was contained in a Memorandum published by the Institute of Housing in 1958.

DEVELOPMENTS 1959–65

The Local Government Act 1958 was designed to give local authorities greater independence and freedom from detailed central control. These aims were to be achieved, first by the replacement of specific grants by the general grant, and secondly by ceasing to require Ministerial approval for the exercise of certain powers. The Act also allowed delegation of most health and welfare services in counties in England and Wales to county districts with a population of 60,000 or more, and delegation schemes were approved for 29 county districts.

Increased support for the ideal of community care was given by the recommendations on the care of the mentally ill,[1] and various developments in national policy made the realization of community care for the elderly more of a practical possibility than it had been in the early fifties. Moreover, the early sixties saw the introduction of forward planning for health, welfare and housing services.

(a) Domiciliary Services

In March 1959 the Minister of Health announced that the time had come when he could agree to the extension of chiropody services, and a circular was issued to local authorities suggesting various ways in which the service could be provided.[2] By the end of 1960, approval had been given to the 108 schemes of which 35 were for a service to be run directly by the local authority and 73 were for services provided partly by the local authority but supplemented by voluntary schemes.

In November 1959 the Minister of Health announced proposals for legislation on services for old people, including power for local authorities themselves to provide meals. This power was eventually given to local authorities by the National Assistance Act 1948 (Amendment) Act 1962, which also widened the powers of local authorities to assist voluntary organizations through help with vehicles and equipment, premises and staff as well as through

[1] *Royal Commission on the Law Relating to Mental Illness and Mental Deficiency, Cmnd. 169*, H.M.S.O., 1957, p. 207.
[2] Ministry of Health, *Circular 11/59*.

financial contributions. It was also stressed that the term 'recreation' in section 31 of the National Assistance Act covered 'work centres' or 'occupation centres' for the elderly.[1]

In 1962 the Health Visiting and Social Work (Training) Act set up the Council for the Training of Health Visitors and the Council for Training in Social Work, each with functions extending over the United Kingdom. The Act was based on the recommendations of the working party reports of the fifties.

Developments on the ground were slow in coming. The number of centres in England and Wales providing training courses for health visitors remained at 23 (which it had been for many years), and the number of available places decreased between 1962 and 1964. However, the number of places filled had always been consistently well below the number of places available. By 1965 there were signs that development might be under way. One new training course became available in 1965, and four more in 1966, although the number of places filled was still only the same in 1966 as in 1963 and 1964. New training rules came into operation in 1964, prescribing the new health visitors' certificate as a qualification for employment, and removing the Minister's former powers of dispensation with regard to employment of unqualified persons.[2] These rules were revised in 1965. In Scotland, regulations governing qualifications of health visitors came into operation for the first time in 1965, barring unqualified staff from appointment as health visitors unless the Secretary of State grants a dispensation.[3]

Rather more immediate progress resulted from the creation of the general training courses for the certificate in social work. Three courses in England and Wales, plus one in Scotland, had started in 1961 in anticipation of the Act. In England and Wales the number of courses increased from four (153 students) in 1962, to sixteen (387 students) at the end of 1965. At the same time the one year courses for experienced officers increased from one in 1962 to four in 1965. In Scotland, the Scottish College of Commerce (later Strathclyde University), provided a two year course until the 1965 intake, after which this course ceased. A two year course started at Moray House College of Education in Edinburgh in 1965, and a one year course for experienced officers started there in 1966.

There were changes in general nurse training also. From July 1, 1962, candidates had to satisfy the minimum educational requirements laid down by the General Nursing Council. It was hoped to reduce wastage during training by this change in selection procedure.

[1] Ministry of Health, *Circular 12/62.*   [2] *Statutory Instrument No. 1099*, 1964.
[3] *Statutory Instrument No. 1490 (s. 80)*, 1964.

Other changes designed to improve quality of training came into operation in 1964. Some smaller hospitals which could not meet the new conditions of approval for training courses changed to training state enrolled nurses. These changes had implications for the supply of trained staff for the home nursing service, although the full effect would hardly be felt by 1965.

One other development on professional training which affected local authority services was the gradual introduction of regulations under the Professions Supplementary to Medicine Act 1960. Under this Act machinery was set up for the registration of chiropodists (among others), and state registration was added to the chiropody qualifications required since 1954 for employment in the National Health Service.[1] These regulations came into force in October 1962, and the Chiropodists' Board accepted applications for registration from January 1963. This step was also aimed at maintaining professional standards.

(b) *Housing*

Housing authorities continued to develop housing for the elderly, although the general needs subsidy for one bedroom housing in England and Wales was abolished by the 1961 Housing Act. Instead, all houses qualified for subsidy at one of two basic rates, £24 per house or £8 per house according to whether or not the housing authority satisfied a test of financial need based on an annual examination of its housing revenue account. However, local authorities were again encouraged to improve their arrangements for the elderly, and a joint circular was issued by the Ministry of Health and the Ministry of Housing and Local Government suggesting ways in which existing arrangements could be improved, and stressing the desirability of co-operation between health and welfare authorities, housing authorities and voluntary organizations.[2] In addition the Ministry of Housing and Local Government published two design bulletins in 1962.[3,4] A further bulletin in this series appeared in 1966.[5]

1 *Statutory Instrument No. 2033,* 1962 (replacing *Statutory Instrument No. 55,* 1954).

2 Ministry of Health, *Circular 12/61.* (Ministry of Housing and Local Government, *Circular 10/61*).

3 Ministry of Housing and Local Government, *Some Aspects of Designing for Old People,* Design Bulletin No. 1, H.M.S.O., 1962.

4 Ministry of Housing and Local Government, *Grouped Flatlets for Old People,* Design Bulletin No. 2, H.M.S.O., 1962.

5 Ministry of Housing and Local Government, *Old People's Flatlets at Stevenage,* Design Bulletin No. 11, H.M.S.O., 1966.

In Scotland, the Secretary of State convened a conference in May 1961, to which fourteen local authorities and representatives of some voluntary organizations were invited, to discuss achievements and plans for provision of housing for the elderly. Two study groups were set up, and their decision that more information was needed about existing provision led to a request to local authorities to supply facts about the number and types of accommodation suitable for, and occupied by, old people in their areas.[1] It should be noted that housing became the concern of the new Scottish Development Department after 1962.

Two changes in Scottish legislation helped to bring housing powers into line with those in England and Wales. The Housing (Scotland) Act 1962 broadened the definition of a 'house' for purposes of subsidy to include accommodation with separate cooking facilities but with other facilities, such as bathrooms and toilets, shared. This gave local authorities the opportunity to build blocks of flatlets for old people. Secondly, section 101 of the Housing Act 1964 empowered welfare authorities in Scotland to contribute to expenditure incurred by housing authorities in providing accommodation for elderly or handicapped persons by meeting the cost of call-bell systems, or other welfare features.

As well as encouraging local authority housing, it was part of national policy to encourage provision for the elderly by housing associations. In 1957 local authorities were given permissive powers to assist housing associations by helping in the acquisition of land, by making loans of up to 100% towards capital expenditure, by passing on certain Exchequer grants and subsidies, and by supplementing these grants either with a local rate subsidy or with a welfare grant towards the cost of welfare facilities such as a warden.[2] Loans and grants could also be made for acquisition, improvement and conversion of existing buildings. Ministry circulars in 1962[3] and 1964[4] encouraged local authorities to use these powers as widely as possible. The change in policy on subsidies under the 1961 Housing Act meant that housing associations building for the elderly qualified for Exchequer subsidy at the rate of £24 per house per annum. The Scottish housing legislation made similar provisions, although the basic subsidy was higher (£32 per house per annum) than in England.

Part I of the 1961 Housing Act established an Exchequer fund of £25 million from which loans could be given to housing associations

---

[1] Scottish Development Department, *Circular 31/63.*
[2] Housing Act, 1957, ss. 119 and 120.
[3] Ministry of Housing and Local Government, *Circular 12/62.*
[4] Ministry of Housing and Local Government, *Circular 41/64.*

building for people who were ready and able to pay the full (i.e. unsubsidized) cost of their housing, but unable or unwilling to buy. Similarly a fund of £3 million was set up for Scotland under section 11 of the Housing (Scotland) Act 1962. The 1964 Act provided for the appointment of a Housing Corporation with access to up to £100 million of Exchequer money to use for lending to housing *societies* building for letting at cost-rents without profit and without subsidy, or on the basis of collective ownership. The earlier provisions relating to housing *associations* building dwellings which qualify for subsidy for groups such as the elderly remained in force.[1]

(c) *Residential Accommodation*

In England and Wales, the provision of welfare homes for the elderly accelerated after 1959, because of a relaxation of capital restrictions on health and welfare projects. In November 1958, it was announced that the government wished to bring forward into the following twelve months some capital expenditure which would otherwise have to be incurred later.[2] Local authorities were invited to consider projects which could be submitted for loan sanction within three months (later extended to six months) and which could be completed by the end of 1959. This move led to the approval of additional capital expenditure amounting to £3·6 million, divided roughly equally between health and welfare. Loan sanctions for welfare homes in England and Wales totalled £5·5 million in 1959–60, £8·2 million in 1960–1, and £9 million in 1961–2. This compares with an average of £4·2 million for health and welfare projects together in the five years preceding 1959–60. Moreover, policy swung back towards favouring the 30–35 bed home. Information about loan sanctions for welfare projects in Scotland is not readily available, but judging from the numbers of homes opened each year the trend seems to have been in the opposite direction. 6 homes were opened in each year from 1957 to 1959, 3 in 1960, 3 in 1961, 7 in 1962 and 2 in 1963.

The Mental Health Act 1959 and the Mental Health (Scotland) Act 1960 gave powers to local authorities to provide residential accommodation for the mentally infirm, including the elderly mentally infirm. The intention here was to provide care for those who did not need the facilities of a mental hospital all the time,

---

[1] For further details see *A guide to the formation, constitution and purpose of Housing Associations and Societies*, Revised Edition, November 1964, published by the National Federation of Housing Societies.

[2] Ministry of Housing and Local Government, *Circular 60/58.*

and who could, it was thought, live in close association with the community.

In 1962 the policy of providing communal homes for the elderly was attacked by Townsend, who proposed that the number of communal homes should be progressively reduced, starting with the closing of former workhouses. They would be replaced partly by providing more sheltered housing, and partly by a slight extension of the hospital service. In addition he proposed that domiciliary services should be greatly expanded.[1]

However, while the policy of community care was firmly reiterated in 1962, there is still some confusion as to what this means. Sometimes it seems to relate to services to keep people out of hospital, while at other times it seems to relate to services to keep people in their own homes as long as possible. Thus residential accommodation is sometimes part of community care, and sometimes not.

The issue of who is to provide continuous nursing care for those who need this but not necessarily medical care as well is equally undecided. Since the late fifties there had been increasing emphasis on the needs of the very frail elderly, some of whom were being cared for in welfare homes. The needs of these people raised issues about the employment of nursing staff, and of night attendants, and it was partly because of disquiet over this that the National Council of Social Service agreed in October 1962, to promote an investigation into the staffing of residential establishments—the Williams Committee.[2] The hospital service had developed day hospitals in many areas, which made some contribution to the solution of the problem.[3] Similarly, private nursing homes make an important contribution, although standards are not always satisfactory, and the regulations providing for registration and inspection by public authorities can be difficult to enforce.[4] The Nursing Homes Act 1963 and Regulations made under it were aimed at strengthening the powers of the public authorities to ensure satisfactory standards.

(d) *Long-Term Planning*

Further impetus to the development of community care came from the

[1] P. Townsend, *The Last Refuge*, Routledge and Kegan Paul, 1962, Chapters 16 and 17.

[2] The Committee reported in 1967 under the title *Caring for People*, Allen and Unwin.

[3] J. Farndale, *The Day Hospital Movement in Great Britain*, Pergamon Press, 1961.

[4] C. Woodroffe and P. Townsend, *Nursing Homes in England and Wales*, National Corporation for the Care of Old People, 1961.

move towards long-term planning, which started in the hospital field as a result of the increase in capital sums available for hospital building. Schemes of major reconstruction and new building became possible for the first time in the history of the National Health Service in 1955. Capital expenditure on hospital building increased from £10·6 million in 1955–6 to £17·2 million in 1957–8 and £23·7 million in 1960–1, and the increase was expected to continue for the next decade. In January 1961 regional hospital boards were asked to formulate long-term building programmes, and in January 1962 the first ten-year plans for development of the hospital service in England and Wales were published.[1] At the same time the Minister of Health sent a circular[2] to local health and welfare authorities drawing their attention to the section in the hospital plans which emphasizes that: 'The plan for the development of the hospital service is therefore complementary to the expected development of the services for prevention and for care in the community and a continued expansion of these services has been assumed in the assessment of the hospital provision to be aimed at. It follows that the local authority services need to be planned for the same period ahead as the hospital service.' Therefore local authorities were asked to review their health and welfare services and to draw up a plan for developing them over the next 10 years.

Guidance as to what factors a local authority should take into account when drawing up plans was, for the most part, given only in very general terms. On the elderly the Ministry advised that: 'Services for the elderly should be designed to help them to remain in their own homes as long as possible. For this purpose adequate supporting services must be available, including home nurses, domestic help, chiropody and temporary residential care. These supporting services will also often be needed for those who live in special housing where there is a resident warden. Residential homes are required for those who, for some reason, short of a need for hospital care, cannot manage on their own, even in special housing with a resident warden.' The Ministry of Health, and to a lesser extent the Scottish Home and Health Department, did urge that former public assistance institutions should be replaced within 10 years, but for the most part the decision as to what constitutes an *adequate* service, and as to the relative needs for different types of provision, was left to the individual local authority.

[1] Ministry of Health, National Health Service, *A Hospital Plan for England and Wales, Cmnd. 1604*, H.M.S.O., 1962.
[2] Ministry of Health, *Development of Local Authority Health and Welfare Services, Circular 2/62*.

Some guidance was given in the circular about the rate of growth of both capital and current expenditure which would be tolerable at national level in relation to the national economic situation, but the answer to the question about how financial resources should be allocated between local authorities was left to emerge from statements local authorities made about the rate of development of services required in their area. For the first ten-year plans the Ministry asked for estimates of how many staff in the main grades of trained staff would be required in each of the first 5 years and at the end of the tenth year. No guidance seems to have been given on whether local authorities should take account of recruitment difficulties. The plans were revised annually, and in the request for the 1965 revisions[1] the Ministry did advise local authorities that estimates of staff needed for the first 3 years should be based on expected recruitment, but that estimates for later years should take no account of possible recruitment difficulties.

Publication of the first ten-year plans gave local authorities a basis for comparison between their own proposals and those of other local authorities. Information supplied on the present level of services was also used by the Ministry as a basis for a tentative statement of what seemed to be an adequate level for the various services.[2] For the revisions, therefore, local authorities had the previous versions as a guide, although not necessarily a very helpful guide. The chief welfare officer of Bromley criticized the publication of the first revision on the grounds that: 'These consisted of a mass of statistics, not always presented to make comparison easy, and contained no further comment upon the principles hesitatingly advanced when the plans were first published in 1963. The exercise appeared to deteriorate into an "averaging operation" both at the Ministry and local authority level.'[3]

In Scotland, a ten-year plan for hospitals was published in 1962.[4] While the plan refers to interdependence between hospital services and local authority health and welfare services the Department of Health for Scotland did not ask Scottish local health and welfare authorities to prepare ten-year plans. Nevertheless, in March 1962 local authorities were asked 'to review each service so as to ensure that it was adapted to meet tomorrow's needs rather than yester-

[1] Ministry of Health, *Circular 14/65.*

[2] Ministry of Health, *The Development of Community Care, Cmnd. 1973,* H.M.S.O., 1963, paras. 24, 57, 60, 115.

[3] J. Hanson, 'Challenge in the Welfare Services', *Municipal Review,* Vol. 36, No. 431, November 1965, p. 666.

[4] Department of Health for Scotland, *Hospital Plan for Scotland, Cmnd. 1602,* H.M.S.O., 1962.

day's, and to harmonize with the hospital ten-year plan and developments elsewhere in the Health Service'.[1] On the question of standards for the services the Secretary to what was then the Department of Health for Scotland had stated on July 9, 1961, when speaking of the home help service, that: 'Detailed appraisals of services in different areas operating at different intensities are probably the only reliable way of making progress towards the establishment of standards.'[2] The Department's preference for this approach was apparent in the agreement reached with the local authority associations in June 1962 that 'longer term planning would be assisted by a series of detailed studies of individual services. These studies . . . would seek to discover what the role of each of the services should be in the future'.[3]

In England and Wales the Ministry had always stressed the need for plans for future development of local authority services to take account of what was happening in related fields, and urged that hospital authorities, local executive councils and local medical committees, voluntary organizations and housing authorities should be consulted when plans were being prepared.[4]

For the first and second revisions local health and welfare authorities were asked to submit information about special housing (the term sheltered housing is used in this study, for reasons explained in Chapter 3) provided or planned by housing authorities or housing societies.[5] Plans for housing were for a 5-year period only.

The Ministry of Housing and Local Government later introduced its own 5-year programmes for housing authorities. Apart from slum clearance programmes, which local housing authorities were required to submit to the Ministry under the Housing Repairs and Rents Act 1954, building programmes were authorized on an annual basis until 1965, when local housing authorities were asked to prepare programmes for the next 4 years.[6] It was recognized that techniques for estimating housing needs, both in terms of the total number in particular areas and of the house types required, were inadequate.

[1] Scottish Home and Health Department, *Annual Report for 1962, Cmnd. 1996,* H.M.S.O., 1963, p. 39.

[2] See T. D. Haddow, 'The Future of Local Authority Health Services' (talk at the Annual Summer School of the County Borough Group of the Society of Medical Officers of Health), *Health Bulletin (issued by the Chief Medical Officer of the Department of Health for Scotland),* Vol. XX, No. 1, January 1962, p. 7.

[3] *Cmnd. 1996, op. cit.,* p. 39.   [4] Ministry of Health, *Circular 2/62.*

[5] Since 1964 the term *housing societies* has the special meaning explained on p. 41. *Housing associations* is now the appropriate term. The request for information did not cover almshouses or other housing provided by voluntary organizations not registered as housing associations.

[6] Ministry of Housing and Local Government, *Circular 21/65.*

The Ministry was working on this problem, but in the meantime local authorities were advised to do the best they could by sifting information on their waiting lists, analysing the demands made on them from outside their areas and applying the lessons of the census to their particular conditions. Plans were to include proposals for houses for old people. The Minister hoped that local authorities would put to him only programmes which were realistic in terms of their capacity to build, as decided by the local authority.

Following the White Paper[1] of November 1965, Scottish local authorities were also asked to prepare advance housing programmes for 5 years.[2]

To enable local authorities to embark on a rising housing programme the structure of housing subsidies in Scotland was to be revised to provide a basic subsidy related to costs, with additional subsidies for authorities with especially low rating resources, for high flats, expensive land, and for houses built for overspill and industrial needs. The Housing Subsidies Act 1967 introduced basic subsidies related to costs for England and Wales also.[3]

THE POSITION IN THE MID-SIXTIES

Thus by the mid-sixties all types of local authority were being encouraged to plan ahead, both for provision of housing and for development of health and welfare services to make community care a reality. As well as the variations in present provision revealed by the ten-year plans in England and Wales, independent research studies were providing evidence of the inadequacy of domiciliary services,[4] and suggesting that sheltered housing could provide an alternative to residential accommodation.[5]

At the same time there was renewed concern nationally about the income levels of the elderly. In 1954 the Phillips Committee, having concluded that the elderly often lived on or near the borderline of poverty,[6] had recommended extension of occupational pensions as the solution to the problem of financial provision for old age. The

[1] Scottish Development Department, *The Scottish Housing Programme 1965–1970*, Cmnd. 2837, H.M.S.O., 1965.
[2] Scottish Development Department, *Circular 68/65*.
[3] See Ministry of Housing and Local Government, *Housing Subsidies Manual*, H.M.S.O., 1967.
[4] See P. Townsend and D. Wedderburn, *The Aged in the Welfare State*, G. Bell and Sons, 1965.
[5] P. Townsend, *The Last Refuge, op. cit.*, Chapters 16 and 17.
[6] *Cmd. 9333, op. cit.*, p. 29.

National Insurance Act 1959 aimed at encouraging the development of occupational schemes, and providing for employed persons who could not be covered by an appropriate occupational scheme to obtain some pension benefits related to earnings. However, these were long-term solutions.

A study of financial circumstances of old people carried out in 1959–60 indicated that as many as a quarter were living at or below National Assistance Board levels, and that over 12% of elderly households were currently entitled to receive help from the National Assistance Board but were not receiving it.[1]

An analysis of the Ministry of Labour survey of household expenditures for 1960 showed that 35% of persons in low-income households were old people with pensions as their primary source of income. There were about one million retired people not receiving national assistance who had a *prima facie* case which might have allowed them to qualify for supplementary help from the National Assistance Board.[2] In 1965 the Ministry of Pensions and National Insurance and National Assistance Board conducted their own enquiry, and estimated that about 700,000 pensioner households (about 850,000 pensioners) could have received assistance if they had applied.[3] In November 1966 the Ministry of Social Security replaced the Ministry of Pensions and National Insurance and National Assistance Board. A major aim of the reorganization was to try to see that those entitled to supplementary income did in fact receive it.

Nevertheless, the issue of what level of retirement income is appropriate to underpin the policy of helping old people to live at home is still open. The Travel Concessions Act 1964 facilitated the granting of cheap fares on municipal transport for the elderly and some of the handicapped. At the end of 1965 local health authorities were asked not to charge for home help provided to persons in receipt of national assistance or at that level of income.[4] The Rating Act 1966 introduced a nation-wide system of rate rebates for domestic ratepayers with low incomes. These measures do not support the principle of enabling the elderly to pay for the services they need. The issue is of even greater importance in relation to

[1] D. Cole and J. E. G. Utting, *The Economic Circumstances of Old People*, Codicote Press, 1962, pp. 69, 98.

[2] B. Abel-Smith and P. Townsend, *The Poor and the Poorest*, G. Bell and Sons, 1965, p. 49.

[3] Ministry of Pensions and National Insurance, *Financial and Other Circumstances of Retirement Pensioners*, H.M.S.O., 1966.

[4] Ministry of Health, *Circular 25/65*.

rents, with housing authorities being encouraged to charge higher rents but with rebate schemes for low-income households.[1]

The present study took place, therefore, at a time when it was hoped that long-term planning would help to make community care for the elderly more of a reality. At the same time there was renewed concern about the financial circumstances of the elderly living at home. Nevertheless, the general economic situation continued to work against large scale expansion of social services.

Note: Between the beginning of this study and the completion of the report, some changes took place in the organization of central government departments. In 1966 the Ministry of Pensions and National Insurance and the National Assistance Board merged into the Ministry of Social Security. The functions of the National Assistance Board were taken over by the Supplementary Benefits Commission. In 1968 the Ministry of Health and the Ministry of Social Security combined to form the Department of Health and Social Security.

[1] Ministry of Housing and Local Government. *Housing Programme 1965–1970, Cmnd. 2838*, H.M.S.O., 1966.

CHAPTER 2

SERVICES IN 1965—
RESIDENTIAL ACCOMMODATION

The remaining chapters of Part I are intended to give the reader an overall picture of services for the elderly in Britain. A considerable amount of information is supplied annually by local authorities to central departments and professional associations. The quality of this data is not uniform, which makes for difficulties in interpretation. In this and the following two chapters, an attempt has been made to present the data for 1965. When information for all local authorities was not readily available, figures from case study authorities only have been used. Readers who are already familiar with the services may wish to go straight to the body of the report beginning in Part II.

Chapter 2 summarizes available data on the extent of national provision of residential accommodation for the elderly, and the extent of provision by individual local authorities is compared with the standards for provision suggested by the Ministry of Health. The range of variation in provision between local authorities is then studied in relation to voluntary provision and hospital bed provision. Available information on size and type of home is summarized, together with information on residents in different types of home and trends in the proportion of residents who were 'materially handicapped'. Finally, limited data on the staffing of residential accommodation, and figures on expenditure on this service are presented.

NATIONAL PROVISION

At the end of 1965 in England and Wales[1] there were 90,004 elderly people in accommodation provided under Part III of the National Assistance Act, including 3,970 in premises vested in the Minister of Health as hospitals, and 11,075 in homes provided on behalf of local councils by voluntary organizations. Including the 11,075 places occupied by people financed by local authorities there were 40,554

[1] Ministry of Health, *Annual Report for 1965*, Cmnd. 3039, H.M.S.O., 1966, Table 52, p. 124. Most of the national figures in this section are taken from the Ministry's annual reports.

49

places available in voluntary and private homes registered under section 37 of the National Assistance Act. There were also a few premises exempt from registration because they were set up by Royal Charter or through special Act of Parliament. These were mainly run by long-established religious foundations catering for relatively large numbers of people. Accurate recent information about this kind of accommodation is not easily available but Townsend[1] estimated that at the end of 1959 there were about 40 such homes.

Part III residential accommodation also caters for the physically disabled, not all of whom are elderly. In England and Wales at the end of 1965 there were 10,374 non-elderly residents.

In Scotland, at March 31, 1965,[2] there were 7,489 places in residential accommodation provided by local authorities, and 5,421 places in 188 private and voluntary homes. From an analysis of an unpublished document provided by the Scottish Home and Health Department it appears that in Scotland 7,148 places in 179 local authority homes and 4,658 places in 170 other premises (including homes exempt from registration) were provided for the elderly (rather than the disabled, homeless or any other group) on March 31, 1965.

Comparing the ratios of places per thousand elderly population,[3] local authority provision in England and Wales appeared to be rather higher (15·6)[4] than in Scotland (12·4).[5] However, voluntary provision was more extensive in Scotland than in England and Wales, and also, the English and Welsh figure included provision for the physically handicapped, so the comparison should not be pressed too far.

STANDARDS FOR PROVISION

In the commentary accompanying the publication of the original ten-year plans the Ministry of Health guardedly remarked that,

[1] P. Townsend, *The Last Refuge*, Routledge and Kegan Paul, 1962, p. 40. The number of places is not noted.
[2] Scottish Home and Health Department, *Annual Report for 1965, Cmnd. 2984*, H.M.S.O., 1966, Table 11, p. 41.
[3] 'Elderly population' in the ratios given in this chapter means population aged sixty-five and over, since this is the definition used in the ten-year plans.
[4] Ministry of Health, *Development of Community Care, Revision to 1975-6, Cmnd. 3022*, H.M.S.O., 1966, Appendix B, p. 412.
[5] Calculated on the assumption of a mid-1965 elderly population of 576,000 taken from General Register Office (Scotland), *Quarterly Return of the Registrar General for Scotland, Births, Deaths and Marriages, No. 444*, H.M.S.O., 1966, p. 33.

where domiciliary services were well developed and hospital services adequate, local authorities were probably 'achieving appropriate provision with something in the range of 18–22 places for every thousand persons aged 65 or over'.[1] Even more guardedly in the published second revision[2] the Ministry stated that 'knowledge is still too limited to enable standard ratios of places to population to be laid down, and local conditions must in any event call for different levels . . . Meanwhile experience so far would suggest that most authorities would find a ratio of between 15 and 25 places per thousand population aged sixty-five or over appropriate to their areas'. On March 31, 1965,[3] 77 of 140 English and Welsh welfare authorities (excluding the Greater London area and the Isles of Scilly) had *under* 18 places per thousand population aged sixty-five or over, including 44 with less than 15 places. 31 of the 140 had over 22 places, including 15 with over 25.[4]

In Scotland the recommended standard of *total* provision was 25 beds per thousand elderly people.[5] On March 31, 1965, 40 of the 55 welfare authorities had less than this, even *including* the voluntary and private provision within their boundaries.[6] 34 had less than the recommended lower limit in England and Wales of 15 local authority places per thousand elderly population.

RANGE OF PROVISION BETWEEN LOCAL AUTHORITIES

The range of provision by individual local authorities in England and Wales (excluding the new welfare authorities in Greater London, and the Scilly Isles) was from 7·6 places per thousand elderly population in Blackpool to 32·1 in Middlesbrough. Table 1 shows the distribution of levels of provision by type of local authority.

Variation in provision may be partly explained by the extent of private and voluntary accommodation. There are no recent published figures on this for individual authorities, but in the sixteen case study authorities the gap between the lowest and highest provider widened when voluntary and private provision was included.

[1] Ministry of Health, *The Development of Community Care*, Cmnd. 1973 H.M.S.O., 1963, p. 21.

[2] *Cmnd. 3022, op. cit.*, pp. 22–3.

[3] *Cmnd. 3022, op. cit.*, Appendix A.

[4] 7 of the 16 case study authorities had less than 18 places and 6 less than 15. 5 had more than 22 places and 3 over 25.

[5] See *Cmnd. 2984, op. cit.*, pp. 32, 41. The current national provision was said to be 23·5 beds per thousand elderly population but this included beds for non-elderly.

[6] 5 of the 8 Scottish case study authorities were below this level.

TABLE 1

PLACES IN LOCAL AUTHORITY ACCOMMODATION PER
THOUSAND ELDERLY POPULATION AT MARCH 31, 1965 FOR
LOCAL AUTHORITIES IN ENGLAND AND WALES

Level of Provision	County Boroughs		Counties	
	No.	%	No.	%
Less than 12·0	2	(2)	12	(21)
12·0–14·9	13	(16)	17	(29)
15·0–17·9	16	(20)	17	(29)
18·0–20·9	20	(24)	8	(14)
21·0–23·9	13	(16)	2	(3)
24·0–26·9	13	(16)	1	(2)
27·0 and over	5	(6)	1	(2)
Total	82	(100)	58	(100)

Source: *Derived from The Development of Community Care, Revision to 1975–6 Cmnd. 3022.*

Local authority provision ranged from 10·3 to 26·2 places per 1,000 elderly population. Total provision ranged from 12·0 to 34·4. Case study authorities with high local authority provision tended to have little voluntary or private provision within their boundaries. Average providers of local authority places tended to have a lot of voluntary provision if the authority was in a retirement area. Low providers of local authority places tended to have relatively high levels of non-local authority provision if the area was a retirement area, such as some rural counties in the more prosperous parts of Britain.

In Scotland, 11 local authority hostels providing 900 of the total 7,148 places were shared by more than one authority. In order to compare levels of provision by individual local authorities, these places were allocated to authorities according to a formula drawn up by the authorities involved or, failing that, according to the actual number of residents for whom each authority had financial responsibility on March 31, 1965, or nearest date for which information was available.

Provision of local authority places on this basis ranged from 2·4 per thousand elderly population[1] in Clackmannan County (which had only a one-sixth share in one former institution of 60 places and nothing more at that date) to 29·0 in Orkney. The range of *total* provision (including voluntary and private homes) by all Scottish

[1] Mid-1966 estimate by the Registrar General for Scotland.

authorities was from 5·5 in Clydebank, which had about a quarter share in one former institution and no voluntary or private homes within its boundaries, to 48·8 in Selkirk County, which had considerable statutory and voluntary provision in relation to the sparse population of its small area. The range of provision of places between Scottish local authorities is *increased*, just as in England and Wales, when voluntary and private homes are included.

The example given illustrates one of the difficulties of making inter-area comparisons. Voluntary provision in Selkirk County is not reserved for people from that county, and the smaller the local authority area the more likely it is that the voluntary body provides accommodation for people from beyond the boundaries of that area. This is possibly the explanation for the finding of the Royal College of Physicians (Edinburgh), that, contrary to expectation, it was not generally the case that areas with low welfare bed ratios had relatively high voluntary bed ratios.[1]

The availability of hospital beds may also be related to the level of places in homes for the elderly. As shown in Table 2, in 1960 the level of geriatric bed provision in England and Wales averaged 1·3 per thousand population (a total of 59,069) but varied from 1·0 in the Newcastle Region to 1·7 in the Leeds, East Anglian and South-Western Regions. In the Newcastle Region there are 13 local health authorities, and on March 31, 1965, 8 of them had more Part III beds than the national average of 15·6 per thousand elderly population. In crude terms, it could be suggested that the higher than average local authority provision in a majority of the authorities in the region was offsetting the low provision of hospital geriatric beds.

However, this offsetting did not operate in reverse for authorities in hospital regions with a high level of geriatric bed provision. Thus, in the Leeds Region, 8 of the 10 local authorities had more than the national average of 15·6 (7 of the 8 having 22·0 or more) Part III places per thousand elderly population; in the East Anglia Region, 6 of the 8 authorities were above average; and in the South-Western Region 5 of the 9 authorities were above average. Oxford and Manchester Regions also had above average hospital bed provision, and a clear majority of local authorities in these regions also had above average provision of Part III accommodation.

For any one local authority area the number of available geriatric beds might appear much smaller or larger than these extremes, though the availability of hospital beds is often difficult to measure properly in relation to individual local authority areas. A county

[1] Royal College of Physicians (Edinburgh), *The Care of the Elderly in Scotland*, 1963, p. 30.

TABLE 2

HOSPITAL GERIATRIC BED PROVISION (1960) AND PLACES IN
LOCAL AUTHORITY PART III ACCOMMODATION (1965) FOR 11
HOSPITAL REGIONS IN ENGLAND AND WALES*

Hospital Region	Geriatric Beds per thousand population	Number of Local Authorities with Total Part III Places	
		Below National Average	Above National Average
Newcastle	1·0	5	8
Wales	1·1	9	8
Sheffield	1·2	6	10
Liverpool	1·2	3	5
Birmingham	1·3	5	11
Wessex	1·4	3	3
Oxford	1·5	3	5
Manchester	1·5	5	11
Leeds	1·7	2	8
East Anglia	1·7	2	6
South-Western	1·7	4	5
National Average	1·3*	15·6*	

Source: *For local authorities, the data is derived from Cmnd. 3022, second revision of the ten-year plans. Information for hospital regions is taken from Ministry of Health, A Hospital Plan for England and Wales, Cmnd. 1604, Appendix B, p. 274. This information is rather old but the total number and distribution of beds had probably not changed markedly by 1965. In comparison with 59,069 beds in 1960, there were 58,701 geriatric beds on December 31, 1964. See Ministry of Health, Annual Report for 1964, Cmnd. 2688,* H.M.S.O., *1965, Table 61, Part 2, p. 138.*
* The four Metropolitan Regions, and constituent local authorities, are excluded from the body of the Table but included in the national averages.

welfare officer from one of the case studies commented on the distance between hospital beds and the population served in his area: 'The beds for A are in B which means someone has to pay 4s 8d on bus fares to see an old person in hospital, and they spend a total of three hours in travelling.'

Hospital bed provision also varied from area to area in Scotland. The hospital plan for Scotland stated that the need for beds for old people had been calculated at 15 per thousand elderly population,[1] equivalent, in 1961, to a ratio of 1·65 beds per thousand *total*

[1] Department of Health for Scotland, *Hospital Plan for Scotland, Cmnd. 1602,* H.M.S.O., 1962, p. 17.

population. The plan also commented that a committee of the Scottish Health Services Council recommended that this level should be raised to 2 beds per thousand total population. On September 30, 1965, the approved complement of chronic sick and geriatric assessment beds was 7,087, a ratio of 1·36 per thousand population. The range of provision between regions was rather wider than in England. In Table 3 hospital bed provision is compared with the number of local authorities with levels of provision of Part III accommodation above and below the national average.

TABLE 3

HOSPITAL GERIATRIC BED PROVISION AND PLACES IN LOCAL AUTHORITY PART III ACCOMMODATION BY HOSPITAL REGIONS IN SCOTLAND, 1965

Hospital Region	Geriatric and Chronic Sick Beds per thousand population	Number of Local Authorities with Total Part III Places	
		Below Average	Above average
Northern	1·43	2	3
North-Eastern	1·91	1	6
Eastern	2·05	1	4
South-Eastern	1·06	6	5
Western	1·29	14	13
National Average	1·36	12·4	

Source: *For hospital beds, derived from Scottish Home and Health Department, Scottish Health Statistics, 1965, Section VII, Table 5, and for local authority places in Part III accommodation from information made available by the Scottish Home and Health Department.*

The method of comparison is crude, but suggests that regions with higher provision of geriatric beds may also have higher provision of Part III accommodation, rather than low provision of one being offset by high provision of the other.

SIZE AND TYPE OF HOME

In England and Wales the total number of residents in Part III accommodation were housed in 1,843 homes (excluding those run by voluntary bodies), of which 71 were located within hospitals. There were 716 small homes with less than 35 places, 890 of medium size with 35–70 places, and 166 large premises with over 70 places. 17·8% of the residents were in the small homes, 41·6% in the medium-sized, 23·9% in the large homes, 4·4% in hospital-run premises and 12·3% in accommodation provided on behalf of local councils by voluntary organizations. The 40,554 places available in non-local authority homes for old, and old and disabled, persons were in 2,254 homes.

In Scotland the proportion of small homes was relatively higher than in England and Wales, as Table 4 shows.

TABLE 4

HOMES FOR THE ELDERLY IN SCOTLAND AT MARCH 31, 1965

	Local Authority Provision			Other Provision		
Size of Home	Number of Homes	Number of Places	Proportion of Total Local Authority Places	Number of Homes	Number of Places	Proportion of Total 'Other' Places
			%			%
Less than 35	123	2,775	38·8	124	2,081	44·7
35–70	44	1,963	27·5	41	1,768	38·0
Over 70	12	2,410	33·7	5	809	17·4
Total	179	7,148	100	170	4,658	100

Source: *Compiled from information made available by the Scottish Home and Health Department.*

Seven of the 123 small Scottish local authority homes were in fact located in premises vested in the Secretary of State as hospitals and contained 115 of the 2,775 places. 2 of the medium-sized homes (110 places) and 3 of the large homes (368 places) were also in hospital premises. Thus, of the total of 7,148 local authority places, 593 were in hospital premises, 3,353 in premises provided under the National Assistance Act 1948, and 3,202 in premises existing prior to 1948 but not transferred to the Regional Hospital Boards. Over half of the total 7,489 places (including places for non-elderly residents) in Scotland were located in 59 former poor law institutions and the remainder in 127 other local authority homes.

In England and Wales it is Ministry of Health policy to urge the closure of former public assistance institutions as soon as possible, but the information required by the central department from local authorities does not now distinguish between these institutions, converted premises and purpose-built homes for the elderly. However, a few small homes, many of the larger homes and all the hospital premises are probably former public assistance institutions, so that there were well over 200 such premises still in use in 1965, providing accommodation for 'an estimated 27,000 persons',[1] which was over a quarter of all people in Part III accommodation. 23·9% of elderly residents were in homes of over 70 places.

Only 3 county boroughs of the 16 case study authorities in England and Wales had no residents in former public assistance institutions at the end of 1965. In all 3, the local authority had not become responsible for such buildings in 1948. In one case there were also no Part III residents in joint-user institutions in 1948. The other 2 local authorities withdrew from joint-user arrangements with hospitals during the fifties. At the end of 1965, 5 other case study authorities had nobody in homes of over 70 places. In 2 counties and one county borough the former public assistance institutions were vested in the Minister as hospitals and the local authority remained the junior partner in the arrangement. In one county the former public assistance institution contained less than 70 places. The fifth case—a county borough—extended its boundaries in 1966, and as a result became responsible for people in a former institution.

The proportion of elderly residents in large homes (over 70 places) to total elderly residents thus ranged from none in half the case studies to over 85% in one northern industrial county borough. In the 8 case study local authorities with large homes of over 70 places the proportion of all male residents in local authority homes in each area who were in the large homes ranged from 0% to 73·2%. For female residents the range was from 8·4% to 94·5%[2].

The Scottish Home and Health Department has also exhorted local authorities to replace or improve old establishments, but has not adopted the same uncompromising policy as the Ministry of Health in England. 'Many welfare homes, and particularly those provided under the old Poor Law, fall short of modern standards in spite of the thought and expenditure which have been devoted to their improvement. 12 homes built before 1948 are to be replaced during the next few years, several more are to be extensively modernized; most of the others are already of a satisfactory standard.'[3]

[1] *Cmnd. 3039, op. cit.*, p. 28.
[2] Information derived from Form H4 returns to the Ministry of Health.
[3] *Cmnd. 2984, op. cit.*, p. 42.

Moreover, the Birsay report[1] recommended that existing welfare homes in the crofting counties should be expanded by adding some beds under the control of local general practitioners for patients who would ordinarily have to be admitted to hospital at some distance. Similarly, the addition of a welfare wing at some hospitals is suggested.

Of the 8 Scottish local authorities studied in detail none have entirely dispensed with the former poor law institution, although the premises are vested in the hospital board in 2 cases, in a joint committee of local authorities in 4, and directly controlled by the individual local authority in only 2 cases.

The policy of replacement of former public assistance institutions in the case study authorities is discussed in Chapter 5.

RESIDENTS IN DIFFERENT TYPES OF HOME

Just over a third of the 90,000 elderly residents in residential accommodation in England and Wales at the end of 1965 were men.[2] They occupied roughly a third of places in the small and medium-sized homes, over two-fifths of the places in large homes and over a half of the places in hospital premises. Just over a quarter of places in homes run by voluntary organizations were occupied by men.

Although local authorities in Scotland make regular returns on Forms N.A.1 and N.A.2, information on the number and sex of Residents in Scottish homes has not been published since 1963,[3] when of the total 7,956 residents for whom local authorities were responsible, 3,539 (44·5%) were men—a markedly higher proportion than in England and Wales. Men formed 46% of the residents in premises managed by local authorities and 38·4% of residents in accommodation provided by voluntary organizations by arrangement with local authorities.

National figures for England and Wales indicate that the proportions of elderly men and women in small and medium-sized homes were near the average for residents in all kinds of homes. However, in the case study authorities the percentage of men in small homes ranged from 12·9% to 79·4% and in medium-sized

---

[1] Scottish Home and Health Department, *General Medical Services in the Highlands and Islands, Cmnd. 3257*, H.M.S.O., 1967, pp. 61–2.

[2] Derived from *Cmnd. 3039, op. cit.*, Table 52, p. 124.

[3] Scottish Home and Health Department, *Report for 1963, Cmnd. 2359*, H.M.S.O., 1964, Appendix 3, p. 95.

homes from 19·5% to 64·9%.[1] Men were to be found more than proportionately in hospital-run joint-user institutions and markedly less than proportionately in accommodation provided for local authorities by voluntary organizations. In the case study authorities the percentage of men in hospital premises (in 7 of the 16 authorities) ranged from 28·0% to 60·9% (national average 51·0%); in voluntary homes it ranged from 4·3% (one man among 23 residents) to 44·7% (national average 26·0%). There were no elderly residents financed by the local authority in voluntary homes in one borough; only one elderly woman in voluntary accommodation in a rural Welsh county; only 4 people (3 men) in voluntary accommodation in a second borough; and 5 people (2 men and 3 women) in a third borough. 3 of these 4 authorities with few or no residents in voluntary accommodation had a markedly higher than average provision of Part III accommodation.

PROPORTION OF 'MATERIALLY HANDICAPPED' RESIDENTS

The proportion of residents officially designated 'materially handicapped' in English and Welsh local authority homes or in other homes in which the residents are the responsibility of the local authority is shown for 8 recent years in Table 5. Comparisons with

TABLE 5

MATERIALLY HANDICAPPED ELDERLY RESIDENTS AS A PERCENTAGE OF TOTAL ELDERLY RESIDENTS IN RESIDENTIAL ACCOMMODATION IN ENGLAND AND WALES AT DECEMBER 31, 1958–65

Year	Percentage of Elderly Residents Materially Handicapped
1958	43·0
1959	42·1
1960	41·8
1961	41·7
1962	41·8
1963	42·1
1964	41·9
1965	42·3

Source: *Annual Returns (Form H4) to Ministry of Health.*

[1] Derived from annual returns to Ministry of Health, (Form H4).

earlier years are not possible because the information provided in annual returns from local authorities in earlier years is ambiguous, but there appears to have been no marked shift in the percentage of elderly handicapped residents between 1958 and 1965 for the country as a whole.

However, there was a widening of the range in the proportion of handicapped residents in the 13 English and Welsh case studies for which the data seemed reliable, as shown in Table 6. In 9 of these

TABLE 6

MATERIALLY HANDICAPPED ELDERLY RESIDENTS AS A
PERCENTAGE OF TOTAL ELDERLY RESIDENTS IN RESIDENTIAL
ACCOMMODATION IN 13* ENGLISH AND WELSH CASE STUDY
AUTHORITIES AT DECEMBER 31, 1958–65

Year	Percentage of Elderly Handicapped Residents	
	Lowest	Highest
1958	27	64
1959	23	67
1960	18	71
1961	22	74
1962	22	74
1963	22	73
1964	22	69
1965	18	71

Source: *Annual Returns (Form H4) to Ministry of Health.*

* The other three authorities—all county boroughs—showed such marked internal inconsistencies in their returns over this period that they could not be included.

authorities the proportion of handicapped residents increased between 1958 and 1965, in 5 cases markedly. In 4 it decreased, in one case markedly. Table 7 shows the range of provision in 1965 in all 16 English and Welsh case study authorities.

Very broadly, county boroughs appeared to have a higher proportion of 'materially handicapped' residents than counties. This could be because their accommodation is suitable for the handicapped (see Chapter 5) or because it is easier to provide effective domiciliary services for the mildly handicapped in their own homes in more densely populated areas. The development of sheltered housing (see Chapter 3) may also have an effect on the degree of handicap of applicants for residential accommodation, especially in county areas where sheltered housing is more developed. However, it is too early to assess the overall impact of sheltered housing, still a relatively new service, on other services for the elderly.

TABLE 7

MATERIALLY HANDICAPPED ELDERLY RESIDENTS AS A
PERCENTAGE OF TOTAL RESIDENTS IN RESIDENTIAL
ACCOMMODATION IN 16 ENGLISH AND WELSH CASE STUDY
AUTHORITIES AT DECEMBER 31, 1965 BY TYPE OF LOCAL
AUTHORITY

Percentage of Elderly Handicapped Residents	County Boroughs	Counties
Less than 25%	1	1
25–34%	1	2
35–44%	1	2
45–54%	3	1
55–64%	1	1
65% and over	2	0

Source: *Annual Returns (Form H4) to Ministry of Health.*

Information is not available for Scotland except for June 30, 1958,[1] when the proportion of handicapped residents (both elderly and non-elderly) to total residents for whom local authorities were financially responsible was 54·2%, and for December 16, 1963,[2] when the proportion of handicapped to total residents was 60%. These percentages were markedly higher than those for England and Wales, even allowing that the populations were not strictly comparable and that the categories of residents were ambiguous. As there were very few sheltered housing schemes in Scotland it cannot be that the higher proportion of handicapped residents was due to sheltered housing providing alternative accommodation for those less handicapped.

[1] Department of Health for Scotland, *Scottish Health Statistics, 1958*, H.M.S.O., 1959, Section XIII, p. 205.
[2] Scottish Home and Health Department, *Report for 1963, Cmnd. 2359*, H.M.S.O., 1964, Appendix 3, p. 95.

STAFFING OF RESIDENTIAL ACCOMMODATION

The available information on the staffing of residential accommodation is limited.[1] The Ministry of Health began to collect statistics of staffing in residential homes only in 1966. At September 30, 1966[2] there was a total whole-time equivalent of 31,970 staff in post, comprising 2,359 matrons or wardens, 1,554 deputies, 12,286 attendants, and 14,976 manual or domestic staff. Altogether, 37,132 people were involved in staffing the homes. Parallel statistics are not published for Scotland but there was an estimated whole-time equivalent of 2,339 staff working in Part III accommodation (including temporary accommodation) in the local financial year 1965–6.[3] The main categories were: supervisory nursing—166; nursing—344; medical auxiliaries—179; administrative and clerical—166; domestic, etc.—1,283; and others—130.

NET EXPENDITURE ON RESIDENTIAL ACCOMMODATION

Revenue account expenditure (net of income from residents) on Part III accommodation by local welfare authorities in England and Wales in the financial year 1965–6 was £33·2 million[4] or £695 per thousand population.[5] The range of net expenditure per thousand population was from £248 in Hampshire to £1,222 in Oxford City and the cost per resident-week ranged from 122s 0d in Montgomeryshire to 232s 5d in Glamorgan.[6] Table 8 groups 140 local authorities according to net expenditure per thousand population, and cost per

[1] Considerable detail on the staffing of residential accommodation for the elderly at November 30, 1963, can be obtained from the statistical tables prepared for the Williams Committee. Only some of the data is published (*Caring for People*, National Institute for Social Work Training Series No. 11, Allen and Unwin, 1967), but more detailed tables are available from the National Council of Social Service or the National Institute for Social Work Training.

[2] Ministry of Health, *Annual Report for 1966, Cmnd. 3326*, H.M.S.O., 1967, Table 51, p. 133.

[3] Returns to the Scottish Development Department, *Form RSG7A (1967–9), Part III*, p. 3.

[4] *Cmnd. 3326, op. cit.*, Table 57, p. 144.

[5] Assuming a mid-1965 population for England and Wales of 47,762,800. See *Cmnd. 3022, op. cit.*, p. 412.

[6] Institute of Municipal Treasurers and Accountants, *Welfare Services Statistics, 1965–6*, December 1966, Columns 17 and 66. This publication does not cover all local authorities because of late returns and the information it provides is not strictly comparable with the national figures. Table 8 excludes the London Boroughs and the Scilly Isles.

resident-week, by type of local authority. The possible reasons for the range of costs are many and sometimes puzzling even within a single local authority. A treasurer from a case study county said: 'We are often a little disturbed by differences in cost between homes, but you can make statistics say what you want them to say. What is the cause of the range of costs? Is variation in feeding costs due to good housekeeping, the Oliver Twist mentality or the three or four star hotel mentality?' A county borough welfare officer, comparing his costs with those of a neighbouring county, said that the standard charge for the county homes was higher because the homes were newer and larger, and the county paid more in wages because they had a higher staff ratio.

TABLE 8

NET EXPENDITURE PER THOUSAND TOTAL POPULATION AND COST PER RESIDENT-WEEK ON RESIDENTIAL ACCOMMODATION BY 140 LOCAL WELFARE AUTHORITIES IN ENGLAND AND WALES IN 1965-6

Net Expenditure per Thousand Total Population	County Boroughs		Counties		Cost per Resident-Week	County Boroughs		Counties	
	No.	%	No.	%		No.	%	No.	%
Less than £400	4	(5)	11	(19)	Less than 140/-	4	(5)	3	(5)
£400–499	13	(16)	18	(31)	140–149/-	12	(15)	5	(9)
£500–599	16	(20)	12	(21)	150–159/-	12	(15)	5	(9)
£600–699	20	(24)	12	(21)	160–169/-	14	(17)	15	(26)
£700–799	11	(13)	2	(3)	170–179/-	11	(13)	6	(10)
£800–899	14	(17)	0	(0)	180–189/-	14	(17)	9	(16)
£900 and over	4	(5)	1	(2)	190–199/-	8	(10)	7	(12)
Not known	0	(0)	2	(3)	200 and over	7	(9)	6	(10)
					Not known	0	(0)	2	(3)
Total	82	(100)	58	(100)		82	(100)	58	(100)

Source: *I.M.T.A., Welfare Services Statistics, 1965-6.*

Net expenditure by Scottish welfare authorities on residential accommodation in the financial year 1965–6 was £2·1 million or

£404 per thousand population,[1] a sum considerably lower than the national average of £695 in England and Wales. Excluding Clackmannan County,[2] expenditure ranged from £92 per thousand in

TABLE 9

NET EXPENDITURE PER THOUSAND TOTAL POPULATION AND EXPENDITURE PER RESIDENT-WEEK ON RESIDENTIAL ACCOMMODATION BY 55 SCOTTISH WELFARE AUTHORITIES IN 1965–6

Net Ex-penditure	Large Burghs	Counties of Cities	Counties	Expen-diture per Resi-dent-Week	Large Burghs	Counties of Cities	Counties
Less than £150	1	0	2*	Less than 100/-	1	0	2*
£150–299	6	0	8	100–129/-	2	0	3
£300–449	6	2	10	130–159/-	3	1	6
£450–599	4	2	3	160–189/-	7	1	7
£600 and over	3	0	8	190–219/-	5	1	9
				220–249/-	2	0	4
				250/- and over	0	1	0
Total	20	4	31		20	4	31

Source: *I.M.T.A. (Scottish Branch), Rating Review, 1965–6.*
* Including Clackmannan County (see footnote 2 on this page).

[1] Taken from Institute of Municipal Treasurers and Accountants (Scottish Branch), *Rating Review 1965–6*, March 1967, Part 7, Columns 7 and 10, and Column 9.

[2] According to the *Rating Review* Clackmannan County had 'nil' expenditure or income for residential accommodation. This county had no home of its own, but only a proportion of the places in a former poor law institution. It may also be financially responsible for some residents in voluntary homes or in the homes of other local authorities. This suggests that money is expended on the service but is not shown as a direct burden on the welfare services account. Therefore Columns 7 and 10 in the *Rating Review* may not be providing information that makes inter-authority comparison helpful. For this reason the figures in Table 9 should be treated with caution.

Perth and Kinross County (markedly lower than the lowest local authority in England and Wales) to £1,140 in Orkney, and expenditure per resident-week ranged from 67s 6d in Perth and Kinross County to 261s 5d in Edinburgh. Table 9 groups the 55 Scottish welfare authorities according to net expenditure per thousand population, and expenditure per resident-week, by type of local authority.

SUMMARY

About 120,000 elderly people were accommodated in nearly 4,500 homes for the elderly in Britain in 1965.

Nearly a third of the local welfare authorities in England and Wales (excluding the Greater London area) had less than the Ministry of Health's recommended lower limit of 15 local authority places per thousand elderly population. The proportion of counties below this minimum standard was one half. In Scotland about two-thirds of the authorities were below this level.

There was considerable variation between local authorities. Voluntary and private accommodation tended to compensate for low levels of local authority residential accommodation, but this was particularly marked in areas said to be favoured by the elderly for migration after retirement. The extent of hospital provision for geriatric and chronic sick patients did not always seem to be closely associated with the level of provision of places in residential accommodation, since hospital regions with more generous provision of geriatric beds tended also to encompass local authorities with a high level of provision.

About a quarter of local authority places in England and Wales were in large premises of over 70 places, and just over a third in Scotland, where the policy of replacing the former poor law institution was not so uncompromising as in England.

A third of the residents in Part III accommodation in England and Wales were men, but a higher proportion than this was to be found in both large premises and in hospital-run premises. Well over two-fifths of the residents in Scotland were men.

The proportion of elderly residents who were 'materially handicapped' appeared to be higher in Scotland than in England and Wales. For England and Wales as a whole the proportion of 'materially handicapped' residents apparently did not increase between 1958 and 1965, although the proportion did increase in 9 of the 16 English case study authorities, while in 4 it decreased.

Published information on the staffing of residential accommodation is limited, although the Ministry of Health began to collect regular statistics in 1966.

Net expenditure per thousand population on residential accommodation, and cost per resident-week appeared to vary considerably between local authorities.

CHAPTER 3

SERVICES IN 1965—HOUSING

It is not easy to provide a clear picture of housing provision for the elderly in Britain in the mid-sixties. Local authorities provide housing for old people in various ways and the statistical information available about the extent of provision at national level is difficult to interpret. In this chapter the problem of definitions of different types of housing for the elderly is discussed. The available national figures on sheltered housing and on small housing generally are summarized, and compared with estimates of required provision made by research studies. The available national figures on the private and voluntary sectors are also summarized. Examples from the housing case study authorities are given to illustrate the range of variation in provision between authorities.

DEFINITIONS OF OLD PEOPLE'S HOUSING

The lack of agreed definitions of the different types of housing makes inter-authority comparisons difficult. In the ten-year plans for local authority health and welfare services[1] the Ministry of Health refers to warden-scheme housing as 'special housing', which is the term often used by local authorities to denote housing specially designed for old people, rather than a warden-scheme as such. Some local authorities build houses specially for old people, but with no special features in design compared with other small dwellings. Other local authorities reserve a proportion of existing dwellings for allocation to old people, and in most areas there are some people who have grown old in ordinary council houses.

A further source of confusion is that some local authorities regard only bungalows as old people's dwellings, whereas others include flats or houses. A few authorities think of warden-schemes solely as grouped flatlets with some shared facilities.

In Scotland the Scottish Development Department asked local

[1] Ministry of Health, *The Development of Community Care, Revision to 1975–6*, Cmnd. 3022, H.M.S.O., 1966, p. 19.

authorities to submit information about the extent to which they had housing which was both suitable for and occupied by old people.[1] The central department defined as 'suitable' for old people (aged sixty and over) dwellings of one, two or three apartments (that is up to two bedrooms), situated on either ground or first floor, or in a multi-storey block with lifts, and with separate cooking facilities, but in the case of flatlets, bathrooms or w.c.'s may be shared. While there is scope for disagreement about what constitutes suitable accommodation for old people, the concept of suitability is useful because it is independent of whether or not houses are intended for occupation by old people at the time they are built.

In this study the following definitions are used. *Sheltered housing* includes bungalows, houses, flats or flatlets which are under the overall responsibility of a warden. The dwellings need not be grouped. *Special housing* includes all dwellings specially designed and built for old people. *Reserved housing* includes dwellings which are allocated only to old people even though not specially designed for them. The concept of suitability is used loosely, but for Scottish authorities the term 'suitable' is used only in the sense defined by the Scottish Development Department.

SHELTERED HOUSING

Bearing in mind the difficulties in interpreting published information which is not based on agreed definitions, it seems there were 63,541 old people (10·9 per thousand elderly population) living in sheltered housing in England and Wales at the end of March 1965.[2] The proportion of elderly in sheltered housing ranged from none at all in 20 county boroughs and 4 counties to 42·2 persons per thousand elderly population in Burton-upon-Trent, 42·8 in Manchester, 54·4 in the county of Rutland and 69·3 in the West Riding of Yorkshire. Table 10 shows the range of provision in English and Welsh local authorities (excluding London).

The commentary in the ten-year plans suggests that 'in general the tendency appears to be for special housing to be provided more widely . . . in the counties, and the reverse in the boroughs'.[3] This

---

[1] This information is not available in published form but the authors had access to it by courtesy of the Scottish Development Department. It appears that about a seventh of local authority dwellings suitable for the elderly are not occupied by the elderly.

[2] *Cmnd. 3022, op. cit.*, Appendix B, Table 1(d) ,p. 412.

[3] *Cmnd. 3022, op. cit.*, p. 19.

SERVICES IN 1965—HOUSING

TABLE 10

RANGE OF PERSONS PER THOUSAND ELDERLY POPULATION IN
SHELTERED HOUSING* IN 140 ENGLISH AND WELSH WELFARE
AUTHORITIES AT MARCH 31, 1965 BY TYPE OF LOCAL
AUTHORITY

Persons per Thousand Elderly Population	County Boroughs		Counties	
	No.	%	No.	%
0	20	(24)	4	(7)
0·1–5·0	30	(37)	11	(19)
5·1–10·0	14	(17)	13	(22)
10·1–15·0	11	(13)	16	(28)
15·1–20·0	3	(4)	7	(12)
20·1–25·0	2	(2)	2	(3)
25·1 and over	2	(2)	5	(9)
Total	82	(100)	58	(100)

Source: *Derived from The Development of Community Care, Revision to 1975–6, Cmnd. 3022.*
* The General Notes introducing the ten-year plans state that accommodation provided by Housing Societies is included in addition to local authority provision, *Cmnd. 3022, op. cit.,* p. 29.

view is supported by investigations in Manchester Regional Hospital Board area.[1] Thus the evidence suggests that the fact that housing and welfare are the responsibility of different local authorities in the counties does not impede the development of sheltered housing. Indeed, the reverse seems to be true.

Further evidence is given by figures computed by the Institute of Municipal Treasurers and Accountants to show the cost per thousand total population of the provision of special features in housing for the elderly for counties making contributions to housing authorities within their boundaries. In the financial year 1965–6 the total number of dwelling units for which contributions were paid was nearly 47,000. The range of average contributions per unit is shown in Table 11.

The contributions do not necessarily cover the whole cost of special features, but the fact that 54 out of 56 English and Welsh counties were making contributions, and that the Ministry of

[1] See comment by S. K. Ruck in National Old People's Welfare Council, *Putting Planning into Practice,* Report of the 13th National Conference on the Care of the Elderly, National Council of Social Service, 1966, p. 85.

69

TABLE 11

RANGE OF CONTRIBUTIONS TOWARDS COST OF SPECIAL
FEATURES IN HOUSING FOR THE ELDERLY BY 54 ENGLISH AND
WELSH COUNTIES IN THE FINANCIAL YEAR 1965–6

Average Contribution	Number of Counties	Number of Dwellings
Less than £15	5	16,694
£15–19	8	9,633
£20–24	6	5,317
£25–29	8	4,348
£30–34	14	5,615
£35–39	6	1,909
£40 and over	7	3,431
Total	54	46,947

Source: *Derived from Institute of Municipal Treasurers and Accountants, Welfare Services Statistics 1965–6, Columns 13a and 13b, pp. 20, 24.*

Health commented that financial arrangements of this kind were more often found between housing and welfare authorities in counties than between housing and welfare departments in county boroughs shows that authorities *do* co-operate in order to develop services. Evidence on how case study housing and welfare authorities co-operated to develop sheltered housing is given in Chapter 17.

In Scotland sheltered housing has not been developed as much as in England, which may be partly due to the differences in the legislative framework described in Chapter 1. Scottish welfare authorities were not empowered to make financial contributions to housing authorities for sheltered housing until 1964, although it must be remembered that only the small burghs, which in 1965 owned about a fifth of the local authority dwellings in Scotland, are not welfare authorities as well as housing authorities.[1] The fact that in Scotland flatlets with shared facilities did not qualify for subsidy until the definition of a dwelling was widened in 1962 may also have affected the development of newly built warden-schemes. The tender for the first purpose-built flats scheme was approved towards the end of 1964.[2]

[1] Scottish Development Department, *Rents of Houses Owned by Local Authorities in Scotland, 1965, Cmnd. 2907*, H.M.S.O., 1966, Table 6, pp. 13, 15. The total excludes dwellings provided by the Scottish Special Housing Association and the New Town Development Corporations.

[2] Scottish Development Department, *Report for 1964, Cmnd. 2635*, H.M.S.O., 1965, pp. 31–2.

SERVICES IN 1965—HOUSING

In April 1966 it was emphasized again that few sheltered housing schemes had been built in Scotland compared with England. Only one county, 10 large burghs, and 6 small burghs had sheltered housing schemes in 1964, and although 3 of the 4 cities had schemes the total number of dwellings in them was quite small. In total, Scottish sheltered housing schemes contained less than a thousand dwellings, of which over a fifth were provided by voluntary organizations. There were 279 self-contained one apartment dwellings and 252 two apartment dwellings in housing schemes with a warden or caretaker, or associated with a welfare home. In addition there were 205 one apartment units and 3 two apartment units in hostels.[1]

STANDARDS FOR PROVISION OF SHELTERED HOUSING

No official suggestions have been made about the appropriate level of provision. In England and Wales it has been stated simply that 'it is clear that the need for special (sheltered) housing is large and will grow with the growing numbers of old people'.[2] Reid, referring to an estimate by Townsend, said that Scotland's target is for 25,000 places in sheltered housing.[3]

Townsend, while admitting that the calculation of the level of need for sheltered housing is a complex matter, suggests that provision of this kind should be made in Great Britain for 300,000 old people, or about 5% of the elderly population. This figure is based on the proportion of persons in his sample who lived alone, had no children living within ten minutes' journey, and were moderately or severely incapacitated.[4] Earlier, Townsend had suggested that all housing authorities, in partnership with local voluntary associations, should aim to provide at least 50 dwellings per thousand elderly population in sheltered schemes within ten years. 'An average of nearly 30,000 dwellings a year would be required for England and Wales, some of which would be in converted property.'[5] A similar conclusion resulted from a survey of a random sample of 5% of those over seventy-five in Cumberland (443 out of a total of 8,800), which showed that the probable need for what the working party called 'supported independency' schemes was about 1,300

[1] E. Neil Reid, 'Housing Policy for the Elderly II', in *The Elderly: Priorities*, Scottish Council of Social Service, 1966, pp. 69–84.
[2] *Cmnd. 3022, op. cit.*, p. 19.
[3] Reid, *op. cit.*, p. 78.
[4] P. Townsend and D. Wedderburn, *The Aged in the Welfare State*, G. Bell and Sons Ltd., 1965, pp. 65, 67.
[5] P. Townsend, *The Last Refuge*, Routledge and Kegan Paul, 1962, p. 404.

places,[1] enough for 4·9% of the elderly population of 26,720 (according to mid-1965 estimate). Most local authorities were well short of these standards. Three authorities were not far below, and the 2 counties of Rutland and the West Riding of Yorkshire were actually above this level of provision, although the figures for counties may have concealed wide variations between individual housing authorities.

SMALL DWELLINGS FOR THE ELDERLY

Many local authorities have provided other types of small dwellings for old people. According to the ten-year plans,[2] about 360,000 post-war one bedroom (or bed sittingroom) dwellings had been provided by local housing authorities in England and Wales by 1965, bringing the stock of one bedroom dwellings to 410,000. This total presumably includes one bedroom sheltered housing. According to the Ministry of Housing and Local Government[3] there were 351,994 completed local authority post-war one bedroom dwellings (presumably also including one bedroom sheltered housing) by the end of 1965. This is equivalent to 13·7% of the total number of local authority post-war dwellings built. In recent years the proportion of one bedroom dwellings completed each year has increased markedly from an average of 9·2% in the period 1951–7[4] to 27·3% in 1965[5] (when a total of 36,351 dwellings was completed).

The national proportion of one bedroom dwellings actually occupied by elderly people is not known. Ruck, in a study of 12 authorities in Greater London[6] reported that the percentage of ordinary local authority one bedroom dwellings occupied by old people ranged from 33% (757 dwellings) in East Ham to 100% (346 dwellings) in Ilford, but Ilford was the lower provider of dwellings per thousand population.[7] Ilford was providing for 60% one bedroom dwellings in its current housing programme and East

[1] Cumberland County Council, *The Needs of the Aged in Cumberland*, Report of the Second Working Party, 1966, p. 12.

[2] *Cmnd. 3022, op. cit.*, p. 19.

[3] Ministry of Housing and Local Government, *Housing Return for England and Wales, 30th September, 1966, Cmnd. 3124*, H.M.S.O., 1966, Table 4, p. 4.

[4] Ministry of Housing and Local Government, *Housing Return for England and Wales, 31st December, 1962, Cmnd. 1939*, H.M.S.O., 1963, Table IV, p. 4.

[5] *Cmnd. 3124, ibid.*

[6] S. K. Ruck, *London Government and the Welfare Services*, Routledge and Kegan Paul, 1963, Table XVI, p. 100.

[7] Both these authorities were also low providers of sheltered housing (20 and 84 units respectively) and both had waiting lists of over 300 old people.

Ham for 25%. Ruck reported that of the 13,000 post-war one bedroom dwellings built by the London County Council about 60% were occupied by the elderly.[1] These figures indicate, as Ruck points out, that the number of one bedroom dwellings is an unreliable index of the amount of housing provided for the elderly, unless supplemented by information about allocation.

The number of local authority post-war two bedroom dwellings at the end of 1965[2] was 780,266, providing another 30·4% of the total post-war local authority housing stock. The proportion of two bedroom dwellings built each year has remained fairly constant at something over a third since the early fifties.

Some housing authorities do not build dwellings with less than two bedrooms. The clerk of a Welsh rural district council visited in the course of this study explained: 'We have built our old people's dwellings with two bedrooms because the council take the view that one bedroom is a bad economic proposition. It is wrong that there is nowhere to put one of a couple when one is sick, and it is also desirable to have a room for a relative to sleep in when they are looking after a sick person.' According to Sir Keith Joseph, the policy of not building less than two bedroom dwellings is common among Welsh authorities.[3] However, it is again difficult to judge the adequacy of provision without knowing what proportion of two bedroom units are actually allocated to the elderly.

In Scotland, from 1945–58, the average proportion of approved tenders which were for local authority (including New Town Development Corporation and Scottish Special Housing Association) one or two apartment dwellings (equivalent to bed sittingrooms and one bedroom in England and Wales) was 5·1%. This percentage has since risen steadily. In 1965, 7,333 dwellings (23·1%) of the 31,676 houses approved were either one or two apartment.[4]

The trend is thus similar to that for England and Wales. The fact that the actual proportion of small dwellings built has throughout the period been somewhat lower in Scotland may be partly because Scotland has many older small houses.[5] In 1965 the Scottish Develop-

[1] Ruck, *op. cit.*, p. 103.

[2] *Cmnd. 3124, ibid.*

[3] Sir Keith Joseph, 'Housing Needs and the Ten-Year Plan', in *Planning for Ageing*, Report of the 12th National Conference on the Care of the Elderly, National Council of Social Service, 1964, p. 30.

[4] Scottish Development Department, *Housing Return for Scotland 31st December, 1965, Cmnd. 2885*, H.M.S.O., 1966, Table 6, p. 6.

[5] Between a fifth and a quarter of all Scottish dwellings existing in 1965 and built before 1919 consisted of three rooms or less. See J. B. Cullingworth, *Scottish Housing in 1965*, Government Social Survey, 1967, Table 2, p. 4.

ment Department stated: 'In most areas houses suitable for old people do not yet form as high a proportion of local authority houses as the number of elderly households in the population appears to warrant, even when account is taken of the fact that not all of these households require the assistance of subsidized housing.'[1] Of all approved local authority post-war dwellings to the end of 1965 10·5% were one or two apartment and 46·5% were three apartment dwellings. The proportion of three apartment dwellings approved remained fairly constant at something over 50% in the sixties, though it had been higher—occasionally nearly 60%—in the late fifties, and lower—nearer 40%—in the early fifties.[2]

STANDARDS FOR PROVISION OF SMALL HOUSING

There are no official recommendations about how the level of provision of small housing should be estimated by individual authorities, although local housing authorities have several times been urged to consider the needs of the elderly.[3]

There have been various estimates of the national requirements for small housing for the elderly. The National Labour Women's Advisory Committee[4] stated that on the basis of 5% of all housing being reserved for the elderly, 750,000 units would be required. At the end of 1965 the number of one bedroom dwellings was still considerably short of this target. The National Corporation for the Care of Old People estimated—conservatively—that a minimum of 50,000 dwellings a year was required each year for twenty years.[5] However, the Corporation believed that estimates of national requirements were of limited value and that it was more important for individual local housing authorities to calculate the needs of old people in their own areas. 'The Corporation has the impression that this is seldom done and that the number of dwellings provided for the old is dictated more often by factors less relevant than actual need.'[6] If two bedroom houses were regarded as suitable for the elderly, and were allocated to the elderly, there would not, on the

[1] Scottish Development Department, *Report for 1965*, *Cmnd. 2948*, H.M.S.O., 1966, p. 27.
[2] *Cmnd. 2885, ibid.*
[3] See Chapter 1.
[4] National Labour Women's Advisory Committee, *National Survey into Care of the Elderly*, First Interim Report, 1964, p. 4.
[5] National Corporation for the Care of Old People, *Annual Report for the year ended 30th September, 1964*, p. 20.
[6] National Corporation for the Care of Old People, *op. cit.*, p. 21.

standards suggested, be a national shortage, although the distribution of one and two bedroom houses over the country might well not match the needs of local areas. Furthermore, the needs of non-elderly small households must be taken into account.

In Scotland, according to Reid, the present number of one and two apartment dwellings is approximately half of the requirements. 3 counties, a county of city, 7 large burghs and 38 small burghs have provided more than half of their requirements. If three apartment dwellings are included, there are still at least 16 counties, 2 counties of cities, 4 large burghs and 54 small burghs providing less than half of the requirements.[1]

PRIVATE SECTOR HOUSING

In the private sector in England and Wales 18,988 one bedroom dwellings were completed in the years 1961–5[2]—only $2 \cdot 1\%$ of the total; and 289,162 two bedroom dwellings—$31 \cdot 4\%$ of the total. Griffith suggests that the contrast in the provision of one bedroom dwellings by public authorities and private enterprise may not be meaningful in the way the figures suggest, because 'many old people (especially those with some means) may prefer two bedroom houses built by private enterprise'.[3] However, he claims that the figures of increasing local authority provision of one bedroom dwellings underline the Ministry policy of getting local authorities to do those things private builders are unable or unwilling to do.

Recent housing surveys have provided information on the tenure pattern of elderly households. In 1962 it was estimated that in England the housewife was aged sixty or over in more than a quarter of all households. She was over sixty in about a fifth of council property, a quarter of owner-occupied properties, and a third of privately rented unfurnished accommodation.[4] 'These are the people whose crucial housing decisions were made 30 or 40 years ago, when the housing shortage was considerably more acute than it is today, when owner-occupation was less widespread, and when council housing was in its infancy. As a result a large proportion of

[1] Reid, *op. cit.*, pp. 78, 81. This information should be treated with caution, as the City of Glasgow, one large burgh and about 20 small burghs are excluded.

[2] Information is not available for earlier years, and not at all for Scotland.

[3] J. A. G. Griffith, *Central Departments and Local Authorities*, Allen and Unwin, 1966, p. 247.

[4] J. B. Cullingworth, *English Housing Trends*, G. Bell and Sons Ltd., 1965, Table 5, p. 25.

them now live in privately rented property.'[1] Of all housewives aged sixty or over, three-twentieths lived in council dwellings, more than two-fifths in owner-occupied property, and two-fifths in privately rented unfurnished accommodation.[2] Very few lived in property with a 'below standard' number of bedrooms.[3]

In Scotland, also in 1965[4] the housewife was aged sixty or more in over a quarter of all households. She was over sixty in a quarter of council property, three-tenths of owner-occupied properties, and a little under two-fifths of privately rented unfurnished accommodation. Of all housewives aged sixty or over, over two-fifths were in council property, over a quarter in owner-occupied dwellings and three-twentieths in privately rented unfurnished accommodation.[5] Under a tenth of them lived in property with a 'below standard' number of bedrooms.[6]

Thus a higher proportion of the elderly are housed in the private sector in England and Wales than in Scotland, but this is not to say that they are suitably housed. On the contrary, Cullingworth found that although the older small households were generally well housed in terms of space they were in a relatively poor position with regard to household amenities.[7]

HOUSING PROVIDED BY VOLUNTARY ORGANIZATIONS

Voluntary bodies are thought to make 'a big contribution' to the provision of housing for the elderly.[8] In Britain at the end of 1965 401 (including 17 in Scotland) of the housing associations affiliated to the National Federation of Housing Societies were providing for old people.[9] This figure had increased from 222 at the end of

[1] J. B. Cullingworth, *Housing and Local Government*, Allen and Unwin, 1966, p. 255.

[2] *English Housing Trends*, Table 11, p. 34.

[3] *Ibid.*, Table 13, p. 38. For a description of the standard see P. G. Gray and R. Russell. *The Housing Situation in 1960*, Government Social Survey, 1962 or *English Housing Trends*, pp. 36–7.

[4] *Scottish Housing in 1965*, *op. cit.*, Appendix II, Table A, p. 72.

[5] Obtained by derivation from unpublished table of Scottish housing characteristics in 1965. (See footnote [4] above.)

[6] Obtained from unpublished table of Scottish housing characteristics in 1965. (See footnote [4] above).

[7] *English Housing Trends*, Table 15, p. 40.

[8] Ministry of Health, *The Development of Community Care*, Cmnd. 1973, H.M.S.O., 1963, p. 16.

[9] National Federation of Housing Societies, *Annual Report, 1965*, p. 18.

1960.[1] Of the 120,652 dwellings in Britain provided by those associations affiliated to the Federation which made returns in 1965 (299 out of 401), 11,541 were designated for old people. In Scotland 498 dwellings for the elderly had been completed by housing associations by the end of 1965.

In total, nearly 60,000 new dwellings in England and Wales,[2] and nearly 2,000 in Scotland,[3] were completed by housing associations between 1945 and 1965. In recent years the numbers completed have been rising as a result of the legislative changes in the early sixties. At least 88 schemes involving 5,754 dwellings in England and Wales had been approved under section 7 of the 1961 Housing Act, and 9 schemes involving 563 dwellings in Scotland under section 11 of the 1962 Housing (Scotland) Act, by 1966.[4]

Housing societies as defined under the 1964 Housing Act are confined to cost-rent and co-ownership societies. It is not clear how many such societies provide for the elderly, although some are building small dwellings. Of the 68 completed schemes in England and Wales listed in the Housing Corporation's April 1967 directory of approved cost-rent housing, all but 8 included some accommodation with less than three bedrooms.[5] 44 of the 68 completed schemes had more than one type or size of accommodation. In Scotland there were 4 completed schemes, 3 under construction and one in preparation. There were 214 cost-rent societies (10 in Scotland), and 45 co-ownership societies (2 in Scotland) registered with the Housing Corporation by March 31, 1966, and at the same date 90 cost-rent schemes (none in Scotland) for the construction of 4,800 dwellings, and 24 co-ownership schemes comprising 480 dwellings (including one in Scotland of 35 dwellings) had been approved. A year later 507 societies had registered and 330 had schemes approved. The Scottish figures were 30 and 6 respectively.[6]

In addition to housing associations, and perhaps some housing societies, housing for the elderly is provided by private charitable trusts and almshouses. Comprehensive information is not always available, but the National Association of Almshouses estimated that in 1957 there were about 2,500 separate groups of almshouses with accommodation for at least 35,000 people in England.[7]

[1] National Federation of Housing Societies, *Annual Report, 1961*, p. 16.
[2] *Cmnd. 3124, op. cit.*, Table 3, p. 3.   [3] *Cmnd. 2885, op. cit.*, Table 2, p. 4.
[4] National Federation of Housing Societies, *Annual Report, 1966*, p. 6.
[5] The Housing Corporation, *Are You Looking for a Modern Home? A Directory of Cost-Rent and Co-Ownership Housing*, April 1967, pp. 2–17.
[6] The Housing Corporation, *3rd Report, year ending 31st March, 1967, House of Commons Paper 550*, H.M.S.O., 1967.
[7] National Association of Almshouses, *An Account of Almshouses*, 1957, p. 7.

HOUSING FOR THE ELDERLY IN THE CASE STUDY AUTHORITIES

It is clear from the preceding sections that national figures on the extent of total housing provision for the elderly are incomplete and that much of the available information is difficult to interpret. Complete information was not always available in the local housing authorities studied for this research project, especially about housing in the private and voluntary sectors. However, the case studies did provide data which help in the construction of a picture of housing for the elderly in local areas.

In English and Welsh case study authorities, local authority provision of sheltered housing ranged, for the 9 county boroughs, from 0 to 6·3, and for the 18 housing authorities visited in counties, from 0 to 110·3 per thousand elderly population. In Scotland the provision of sheltered housing was, as might be expected, very limited. One county had 2 small schemes in its landward area, but none of the other Scottish housing authorities visited had a warden-scheme so-called, although 2 had schemes with caretakers.

23 of the 41 housing authorities had at least one person called a warden employed to be responsible for general oversight of a group of old people. The most common arrangement was that the warden lived close to a group of old people's dwellings and was responsible for seeing that residents obtained help whenever the need arose. There were several other arrangements, some serving the same purpose but not called warden-schemes. This topic is discussed in more detail in Chapter 8.

All the housing authorities visited had provided some dwellings for old people. Measuring the extent of housing provision in this wider sense was more difficult than for warden-scheme sheltered housing.

In Scottish case study areas, suitable houses of up to two apartments occupied by old people formed in 1965 anything from 0 to 22·6% of all local authority houses (one authority could not provide figures), but if three apartment houses are also included the range was from 5 to 34%. Yet these figures mean little unless account is taken of the fact that local authority housing is a much higher percentage of all housing in some areas than in others. Thus, for one small burgh the figure of 29% of its housing suitable for, and occupied by, old people loses some significance when one allows that less than 5% of the housing in that area is local authority housing.

Expressing the number of suitable houses as a rate per thousand elderly population, the range is from 5 to 675. This measure also has defects, since the rate of suitable houses per thousand elderly population conceals possible differences in the proportion of elderly households containing more than one person. Furthermore, it tells one nothing about the suitability of housing for old people in the private sector.

For case study housing authorities in England and Wales the Institute of Municipal Treasurers and Accountants' statistics for 1964-5[1] show that for 22 of the 27 authorities, the proportion of one bedroom local authority housing ranged from 3% to 23% and of one and two bedroom housing, from 19% to 59%. As county boroughs make relatively little provision of sheltered housing (see above) it is particularly interesting to note that in 5 of the 9 county boroughs over 50% of the local authority dwellings were one and two bedroom, and in 2 other county boroughs the proportion was only slightly below 50%. In the other housing authorities the proportion of one and two bedroom housing ranged from 19% to 42%, both the extremes being in municipal boroughs. Some of the local authorities did not have readily available figures to show the proportion of their dwellings occupied by old people, but one or two examples can be quoted.

A county borough with 79 units of sheltered housing, or 2·7 units per thousand elderly population, provided in total 979 bed sitting-rooms or one bedroom flats for old people, or 33·8 per thousand elderly population. There was also an unknown number of elderly tenants in other council dwellings.

Another county borough with 5·7 units of sheltered housing per thousand elderly population had in total 1,657 old people's dwellings (bungalows, two storey flats, and multi-storey flats) or 99·9 per thousand elderly population.

A municipal borough with one new block of 30 units of sheltered housing (5·5 per thousand elderly population) also had 222 one and two bedroom prefabs and bungalows which were allocated to old people if there were no steps, and 324 one bedroom flats on the ground floor of two storey buildings which were allocated to the elderly or the handicapped. Thus, for all types of provision this authority had approximately 102 units per thousand elderly population. On housing criteria its record compared well with another municipal borough which had 50·2 units of sheltered housing per thousand elderly population but a smaller number of other dwellings for old people, and was considerably better than the record of a

[1] Institute of Municipal Treasurers and Accountants, *Housing Statistics* (*England and Wales*), *1964-5*, March 1966, Columns 5 and 6.

third municipal borough with 8·6 units of sheltered housing, but only about 15·4 per thousand in total.

An urban district with no sheltered housing provided 40·0 bunga-lows per thousand elderly population, and thus, on housing criteria was not very different from an urban district which had 36 units of sheltered housing per thousand elderly population plus an unknown, but probably fairly small, number of elderly people living in other council houses.

A rural district with 14 units of sheltered housing (6·5 per thousand elderly population) had in total 28 one bedroom and 126 two bedroom bungalows for old people, as well as 60 three bedroom pre-war bungalows reserved for letting to old people. This amounted to 99·3 units per thousand elderly population compared with another rural district with little provision for old people other than its 20·6 units of sheltered housing per thousand elderly population (60 dwellings).

Thus, if other types of local authority housing for old people are taken into account the picture is rather different from that obtained from figures for sheltered housing only. There are still variations in the extent of provision, but the housing authorities with low provision of one type may be average or high in the rank order if all types are included. It could be that the overall variation would be less, but from the incomplete information available, and from the limited number of housing authorities visited, it is not possible to judge. It must again be emphasized that comparisons between local authorities on housing provision must be set against the different patterns of housing tenure in different areas.

Although old people's housing in the form of bungalows is more extensive in rural districts than in other housing authorities, almost all the authorities have some bungalows. Similarly, although it is in county boroughs that housing provision most commonly takes the form of small flats, almost all housing authorities have some flats. The only type of provision peculiar to more densely populated areas is the small flat in a multi-storey block.

Some local authorities use prefabs for old people, since these houses are small, and all on the ground floor. It is now part of national housing policy that these temporary houses should be replaced, and this will involve rehousing their present tenants.

All the case study county boroughs and larger Scottish urban authorities had some housing provision made by voluntary organ-izations, charitable trusts or housing associations, but only about a third of the municipal boroughs and district councils and only one of the smaller Scottish housing authorities visited had such provision within their boundaries. Sometimes, of course, there were housing associations and voluntary organizations operating in parts of the county which were not visited.

The type of provision varied considerably. Two Scottish authorities, 2 county boroughs and a municipal borough had Abbeyfield Societies providing 5 to 7 bed sittingrooms in converted houses, and catering both for old people of limited means and for the better off. These schemes are similar to sheltered housing, as there are resident housekeepers who help those residents who need it, and who also provide some meals. In four of the larger cities the Women's Royal Voluntary Service and the local authority had co-operated to provide flatlet accommodation, usually in converted large terrace houses. Two county boroughs had similar accommodation provided by Church Army Housing Limited.

Two case studies had schemes built by Hanover Housing Association, set up in 1963 at the initiative of the National Corporation for the Care of Old People to provide housing for old people, especially for those such as owner-occupiers of large houses who would not normally qualify for local authority housing. The Association is experimenting with new ideas for housing the elderly, for example by co-operating with private developers to enable the parents of younger families buying houses to live independently but nearby. The earlier schemes, however, are simply small groups of bungalows or flats.

Two county boroughs had flats and bungalows provided by the Sutton Dwellings Trust, established in 1900 under the will of William Sutton, a London Carrier, to provide model low-rented dwellings for occupation by the poor of London and other towns and populous places in England. From the outset the trustees have, wherever possible, included special accommodation for old people in their schemes.

All these organizations operate on a nation-wide basis, and except for the Sutton Dwellings Trust, their activities extend to Scotland. Other organizations operating on a more limited basis in particular localities include housing associations set up by religious groups or others interested in social welfare, and local charitable trusts. Some accommodation provided by the latter is in small groups of perhaps only four dwellings, but nevertheless it makes a contribution. Schemes built with memorial funds included one in Scotland, where 24 dwellings are grouped with an old people's home, and 3 in county boroughs where a local authority scheme of grouped dwellings for old people was partly financed by money from the Lord Mayor's Fund. A few authorities had almshouses, some of which are very old, but in several cases they had been modernized to provide good standard accommodation.

The extent of voluntary housing for the elderly in the case study authorities varied considerably. In one county borough there were about 575 dwellings for old people provided by trusts, housing associations and voluntary bodies (33·6 per thousand elderly population), and 3 other county boroughs had a substantial number. The two other areas where an important contribution was being made by this kind of provision were a municipal borough with 93 almshouses (33·8 dwellings per thousand elderly population) and a Scottish small burgh with 24 almshouses (13·0 per thousand elderly population). In other areas with some voluntary provision the contribution was relatively slight.

SUMMARY

The lack of commonly understood definitions of different types of provision and gaps or overlapping in statistics made it difficult to provide a complete picture of housing for the elderly in Britain. Information was particularly slight for the private sector, and it is not known whether or not the figures for provision by voluntary organizations were comprehensive.

Sheltered housing had been developed more by housing authorities within counties than by county boroughs. In Scotland there was little sheltered housing by 1965.

There are no officially recognized standards for adequate provision, but if estimates made by research studies, that sheltered housing should be provided for about 5% of the elderly population, are accepted as a guide, three English authorities had in 1965 almost this level of provision, and the averages for housing authorities in two counties exceeded it.

Information about other types of housing suitable for the elderly is difficult to interpret. Clearly, in the public sector, a higher proportion of one bedroom dwellings has been provided in recent years. This is not an accurate index of local authority housing provided for the elderly, as the proportion of one bedroom dwellings allocated to the elderly varied between authorities.

Two bedroom houses constituted almost a third of the post-war local authority housing stock in England and Wales, and almost a half of that in Scotland. Some local authorities, especially in Wales, did not build houses with less than two bedrooms. The proportion of two bedroom houses occupied by old people is unknown.

There is no officially recognized standard for the provision of small housing. Estimates have suggested that there was less than half the requirement if one bedroom dwellings only were counted. If two bedroom dwellings were included, and all allocated to the elderly, there would not have been a national shortage in 1965, although the distribution of small housing might not have corresponded to the distribution of needs.

Housing associations are making a small but increasingly important contribution to housing the elderly.

Finally, data from case study housing authorities illustrate the variation in provision of small housing between authorities, and show that a picture different from that given by figures for sheltered housing alone emerged if all types of local authority housing for the elderly were included.

Information from case study authorities also shows that although most of the larger urban authorities had some housing provision made by voluntary organizations, charitable trusts or housing associations, two-thirds of the other authorities had none. The extent of the voluntary housing contribution varied. It was considerable in 4 out of 9 county boroughs and in 2 other authorities. Elsewhere the contribution was relatively slight.

CHAPTER 4

SERVICES IN 1965—
DOMICILIARY SERVICES

A great deal of statistical information is available about the basic domiciliary services which contribute to the care of the elderly in their own homes, but much less is known about newer or less well developed services. In this chapter national staffing levels in 1965 for health visiting, home nursing, home help and social workers in England and Wales are compared, where possible, with those in Scotland. The range of variation in staff ratios for these services in individual local authorities is shown, and the ratios compared with the tentative standards for staff ratios suggested by the Ministry of Health. Other aspects of variation between local authorities for which figures are summarized are in the proportion of cases receiving the services who are elderly, and in net expenditure per thousand total population on the services. Finally, the available information on a number of newer or less well developed services is presented.

NATIONAL STAFFING LEVELS

The main categories of staff involved in care of the elderly and for which national figures are available are health visitors, home nurses, home helps and social workers. The figures given below are, or should be, inclusive of staff employed by voluntary organizations acting as agents for local authorities.

At the end of 1965 local authorities in England and Wales employed the whole-time equivalent of 5,238 health visitors (plus 289 tuberculosis visitors), 8,151 home nurses, 29,039 home helps, and 820 home help organizers.[1] They expected to employ by the end of 1965 1,606 mental health social workers and 2,408 other social workers, a total of 4,014 social workers.[2] These estimates were

[1] Ministry of Health, *Annual Report for the year 1965*, Cmnd. *3039*, H.M.S.O., 1966, Tables 46–48, pp. 118–19.

[2] See Ministry of Health, *The Development of Community Care, Revision to 1975–6*, Cmnd. *3022*, H.M.S.O., 1966, Appendix B, Table V, pp. 414–15.

over-optimistic, since by September 1966 there were only 1,571 mental health social workers,[1] although the number of other social workers at this date is not given.

At the end of 1965 Scottish local authorities employed the whole-time equivalent of 1,274 health visitors, 785 home nurses, and 4,535 home helps.[2] It is not clear how many social workers were employed in the welfare services in Scotland, but returns submitted to the Scottish Development Department in connection with the rate support grant show that there were the whole-time equivalent of $51 \cdot 6$ welfare officers, $27 \cdot 7$ home teachers of the blind, $24 \cdot 6$ occupational therapists and $51 \cdot 6$ administrative and clerical staff providing services for all classes of handicapped, many of whom would be elderly, at the end of the Scottish financial year 1965–6.[3]

Table 12 compares national staff ratios for England and Wales with those for Scotland.

TABLE 12

DOMICILIARY SERVICES: NATIONAL STAFF RATIOS* PER THOUSAND TOTAL POPULATION FOR ENGLAND AND WALES AND FOR SCOTLAND AT END-1965

Service	England and Wales	Scotland
Health Visiting	$0 \cdot 12$	$0 \cdot 24$
Home Nursing	$0 \cdot 18$	$0 \cdot 15$
Home Help	$0 \cdot 63$	$0 \cdot 87$
Social Work	$0 \cdot 08$	Not available

Source: *The Development of Community Care, Revision to 1975–6, Cmnd. 3022 for England and Wales; derived from Scottish Home and Health Department Report for 1965, Cmnd. 2984 for Scotland.*

* The ratios for England and Wales are based on estimated numbers of staff, those for Scotland on actual numbers.

[1] Ministry of Health, *Annual Report for the Year 1966, Cmnd. 3326,* H.M.S.O., 1967, Table 47, Part 4, p. 126 and Table 46, Part 1, p. 124.

[2] Scottish Home and Health Department, *Health and Welfare Services in Scotland, Report for 1965, Cmnd. 2984,* H.M.S.O., 1966, p. 38. The number of home helps is given as 4,642 in the report but this includes organizers and night attendants.

[3] *Rate Support Grant Form (RSG 7B) 1967–9, Part III* made available by the Scottish Development Department. It is not clear whether all local authorities had filled in the form in the same way. For instance, 9 large burghs, a county of city and 11 counties put in a nil return—some of them referring to voluntary provision.

The national staff ratio for health visiting for Scotland appears to have been twice that for England and Wales, but part of the explanation is that the Scottish figures include health visiting time spent on school work whereas the English figures do not. The ratio for home nurses appears to have been slightly lower in Scotland, but this may be because of differences in how staff in combined duty posts are allocated between services. This point is explained more fully later. The ratio for the Scottish home help service was considerably higher than that for England and Wales, probably because of the larger number of areas with a scattered population in Scotland. Wales and Monmouthshire are also areas with a relatively scattered population, and the ratio for them was higher (0·70 per thousand population) than that for England and Wales together.

VARIATION IN STAFF RATIOS BETWEEN LOCAL AUTHORITIES

Staff ratios for individual local authorities varied markedly for each of the services. Table 13 shows the lowest and highest ratios.

TABLE 13

DOMICILIARY SERVICES: LOWEST AND HIGHEST STAFF RATIOS* PER THOUSAND TOTAL POPULATION FOR LOCAL AUTHORITIES IN ENGLAND AND WALES, AND SCOTLAND, AT END-1965

Service	England and Wales		Scotland	
	Lowest Ratio	Highest Ratio	Lowest Ratio	Highest Ratio
Health Visiting	0·03	0·21	0·13†	0·43†
Home Nursing	0·08	0·56	0·08‡	0·21‡
Home Help	0·23	1·39	0·20	4·30
Social Work	0·03	0·22	Not Available	

Source: *The Development of Community Care, Revision to 1975–6, Cmnd. 3022 for England and Wales, and derived from annual returns (Form 15) to Scottish Home and Health Department for Scotland.*

* The ratios for England and Wales are based on estimated numbers of staff' those for Scotland on actual numbers.

† The 24 Scottish authorities with a separately staffed health visiting service only. These figures also include school work.

‡ For the 13 Scottish authorities with a separately staffed home nursing service only.

For health visiting the figures for England and Wales are not strictly comparable with those for Scotland, but within each country the range between the lowest and the highest is considerable. For home nursing the range appears to have been much wider in England and Wales, probably because counties could not be included for Scotland. For home help the range was much wider in Scotland than in England and Wales.

Table 14 shows the frequency distribution of health visitor staff ratios for English and Welsh authorities. It suggests that county boroughs were rather better staffed than counties. Table 15 shows the frequency distribution of home nurse staff ratios for English and Welsh authorities, and for the 13 Scottish authorities with a separately staffed home nursing service.

TABLE 14

DISTRIBUTION OF ESTIMATED HEALTH VISITOR STAFF RATIOS PER THOUSAND TOTAL POPULATION FOR LOCAL AUTHORITIES IN ENGLAND AND WALES AT END-1965

Ratios	County Boroughs		Counties	
	No.	%	No.	%
0·00–0·04	1	(1)	0	—
0·05–0·09	11	(13)	11	(19)
0·10–0·14	49	(60)	36	(62)
0·15–0·19	19	(23)	9	(16)
0·20 and over	2	(2)	2	(3)
Total	82	(100)	58	(100)

Source: *Derived from Development of Community Care, Revision to 1975–6, Cmnd. 3022.*

The Scottish urban authorities included in the table had lower home nurse staff ratios than most English county boroughs. Compared with county boroughs, a larger proportion of counties had staff ratios above 0·20 per thousand population. The highest ratios in England and Wales were, for both county boroughs and counties, mainly in retirement areas or rural counties.

However, too much reliance should not be placed on staff ratios for either health visiting or home nursing in counties. Many counties employ nurses on combined duties, and the validity of staff ratios for individual services depends on the accuracy with which staff are allocated between the services. For annual returns the Ministry of

Health asks English and Welsh local authorities with combined duty services to show staff as 'part-time' and 'whole-time equivalent' against each of the duties normally performed. For the ten-year plans local authorities are requested to divide staff into different categories by working hours. Thus the figures for English and Welsh counties taken from the ten-year plans for the tables in this chapter ought to

TABLE 15

DISTRIBUTION OF HOME NURSE STAFF RATIOS* PER
THOUSAND TOTAL POPULATION AT END-1965 FOR ENGLAND
AND WALES, AND FOR AUTHORITIES WITH A SEPARATE HOME
NURSING SERVICE IN SCOTLAND

Ratios	England and Wales County Boroughs		Counties		Scotland 3 Cities and 10 Large Burghs
	No.	%	No.	%	No.
0·05–0·09	1	(1)	0	—	2
0·10–0·14	14	(17)	8	(14)	6
0·15–0·19	44	(54)	26	(45)	4
0·20–0·24	18	(22)	15	(26)	1
0·25 and over	5	(6)	9	(15)	0
Total	82	(100)	58	(100)	13†

Source: *Derived from Development of Community Care, Revision to 1975–6, Cmnd. 3022 for England and Wales; from annual returns (Form 15) to the central Department in Scotland.*

* Ratios for England and Wales are based on estimated numbers of staff, those for Scotland on actual figures.
† Percentages not calculated because of small numbers.

be reasonably reliable. However, it is laborious, if not actually impossible, for a local authority to allocate the working hours of combined duty nurses accurately between services, so comparisons involving counties should not be pressed too far.

In Scotland it is not clear how staff on combined duties are allocated between services in the annual returns to the central department. For this reason it was impossible to include Scottish counties, and for home nursing some of the large burghs and counties of cities, in Tables 13 and 15. The additional problem of allocating health visitors between health visiting and school work meant that no Scottish authorities could be included in Table 14.[1]

[1] In Scotland, 28 of the 55 health authorities had combined duty nurses for health visiting, home nursing and domiciliary midwifery, 22 had them for home

For home helps comparisons between local authorities give a rather more reliable indication of variations in staff ratios. Table 16 shows the distribution of home help staff ratios.

TABLE 16

DISTRIBUTION OF HOME HELP STAFF RATIOS* PER THOUSAND TOTAL POPULATION BY TYPE OF LOCAL AUTHORITY IN ENGLAND AND WALES, AND SCOTLAND, AT END-1965

Ratios	England and Wales				Scotland	
	County Boroughs		Counties		Large Burghs	Cities	Counties
	No.	%	No.	%	No.	No.	No.
Less than 0·30	0	—	1	(2)	1	0	3
0·30–0·49	17	(21)	23	(40)	3	0	6
0·50–0·69	33	(40)	21	(36)	4	1	2
0·70–0·89	20	(24)	6	(10)	5	0	5
0·90–1·09	8	(10)	2	(3)	3	1	5
1·10 and over	4	(5)	5	(9)	4	2	10
Total	82	(100)	58	(100)	20†	4†	31†

Source: *Derived from The Development of Community Care, Revision to 1975–6, Cmnd. 3022 for England and Wales; from annual returns (Form 15) to Scottish Home and Health Department for Scotland.*

* Ratios for England and Wales are based on estimated numbers of staff, those for Scotland on actual numbers.

† Percentages not calculated because of small numbers.

Comparing Scottish burghs and cities with English and Welsh county boroughs, proportionately more of the former had high rather than medium staff ratios, although about a fifth of the urban health authorities in each country had low ratios. Comparing Scottish counties with English and Welsh counties, almost half of the Scottish ones had high staff ratios but only one eighth of the English and Welsh ones. However, 5 of the 7 highest staff ratios for English and Welsh counties were in fact in sparsely populated

nursing and midwifery, and 5 had them for other combinations of duties. At the same time 39 authorities had some staff working only on health visiting, and 25 had some staff working only on home nursing. The categories are not exclusive, as some authorities had both combined duty nurses and separate health visitors or home nurses, and this explains why the total of authorities comes to more than 55.

Welsh counties, and the high ratios in Scotland were mainly in sparsely populated counties also. A high staff ratio is needed to provide a service in a sparsely populated area because of the distances between cases, and sparsely populated counties also tend to have a higher than average proportion of old people in the population, and thus a greater potential need for the service.

The distribution of staff ratios for social workers in local health and welfare services in England and Wales is shown in Table 17. As already explained, it is not clear how many social workers were employed in these services in Scotland. It appears that use of social workers was more extensive in county boroughs than in counties, but there were again wide differences between individual county boroughs and between individual counties.

TABLE 17

DISTRIBUTION OF ESTIMATED SOCIAL WORKER STAFF
RATIOS PER THOUSAND TOTAL POPULATION AT END-1965
FOR ENGLAND AND WALES

Ratios	County Boroughs		Counties	
	No.	%	No.	%
0·00–0·04	2	(2)	4	(7)
0·05–0·09	41	(50)	45	(78)
0·10–0·14	31	(38)	7	(12)
0·15–0·19	7	(9)	1	(2)
0·20 and over	1	(1)	1	(2)
Total	82	(100)	58	(100)

Source: *Derived from The Development of Community Care, Revision to 1975–6, Cmnd. 3022.*

Therefore, in spite of incomplete and sometimes unreliable data, and in spite of the fairly obvious reasons for high staff ratios for home nursing and home help in sparsely populated counties in Scotland and Wales, there were considerable variations between local authorities in staff ratios for all the four services so far considered. In particular, there was for each service a small number of authorities with apparently very low staff ratios indeed.

STANDARDS FOR STAFF RATIOS

When the original ten-year plans for England and Wales were published the Ministry of Health made a tentative effort to establish minimum standards for staffing, referring to staffing levels in authorities where the service was well developed and where there were also no special features such as a marked skew in the age structure of the population.[1] For both home helps and social workers these standards were revised upwards in the published second revision of these plans. The Ministry referred to studies, particularly the report on *The Aged in the Welfare State* by Townsend and Wedderburn published in 1965, which suggested that the home help service was 'not meeting reasonable requirements'. Therefore they undertook their own study of 10 authorities with a high ratio of home helps per thousand population and another 10 authorities with a low ratio and concluded that 'the size of the service provided is sometimes determined without full knowledge of the extent of local need'. The Ministry also noted that local authority forecasts of requirements for social workers had markedly increased over the numbers given in the earlier revision of the ten-year plans and believed that the

TABLE 18

ESTIMATED STAFFING LEVELS AT DECEMBER 31, 1965
OF INDIVIDUAL LOCAL AUTHORITIES COMPARED
WITH MINISTRY RECOMMENDATIONS (ENGLAND AND
WALES)

Service	1963 Standard	1966 Revised Standard	Number and Percentage of 140 Local Authorities expected to be at or above 1963 Standard at 31.12.1965		Number and Percentage of 140 Local Authorities expected to be at or above 1966 Standard at 31.12.1965	
			No.	%	No.	%
Health Visitors (including T.B. Visitors)	0·17	—	14	(10)	—	—
Home Nurses	0·18	—	17	(55)	—	—
Home Helps	0·73	1·00	43	(31)	13	(9)
Social Workers	0·11	0·12	36	(26)	26	(19)

Source: *Derived from The Development of Community Care and the Second Revision, Cmnd. 1973 and Cmnd. 3022.*

[1] Ministry of Health, *The Development of Community Care*, Cmnd. 1973, H.M.S.O., 1963, pp. 8, 17, 18, 33.

working party on social workers in the local authority health and welfare services 'if they were writing their report (the Younghusband Report was published in 1959) today, might well have envisaged a ratio higher than 0·11'.[1]

Table 18 shows the number and proportion of local authorities whose level of staffing at the end of 1965 reached or exceeded the recommended ratios for each service.

By 1965, the proportion of local authorities exceeding the 1963 Ministry standard was over half for home nursing, about a third for home help, a quarter for social work, and only a tenth for health visiting. The proportion of authorities exceeding the revised 1966 Ministry standard was barely a tenth for home help, but almost a fifth for social work.

As explained in Chapter 1 Scottish health and welfare authorities were not required to submit forward plans except for rate support grant purposes, though the Home and Health Department drew attention to the ten-year plan for the Scottish hospital service and to the staffing level recommended by the Jameson report on health visiting. National figures for this service in the year after the publication of that report were below the recommended level. At the end of 1965 a third of the 24 large burghs and counties of cities had a staff ratio equal to or above 0·23 per thousand population.

There was in 1965 no Scottish equivalent to the Ministry standards for home nursing and home help, but if the staff ratios of Scottish local authorities are set against English standards the following picture emerges. At the end of 1965, 3 of the 13 local authorities with a separate home nursing service had a staff ratio equal to or above the standard of 0·18 per thousand population, and 32 of all 55 local health authorities had a home help staff ratio equal to or above the 1963 standard of 0·73 per thousand population, while 20 were at or above the 1966 standard of 1·00 per thousand population. By the Ministry standards, therefore, it looked as though Scottish local authorities came nearer to providing an adequate home help service.

PROPORTION OF THE SERVICES DEVOTED TO THE ELDERLY

Domiciliary services care for other groups in the population, not only for the elderly. Some information is available on the proportion of total cases who were elderly, and this is shown for 1965 in Table 19.

Thus, for all three services, elderly people formed a higher propor-

[1] *Cmnd. 3022, op. cit.*, pp. 13, 14.

TABLE 19

ELDERLY CASES AS A PERCENTAGE OF TOTAL CASES FOR
FOR THREE DOMICILIARY SERVICES IN ENGLAND AND
WALES, AND SCOTLAND, 1965

Service	England and Wales	Scotland
	%	%
Health Visiting	6·9	3·5
Home Nursing	52·6	41·7
Home Help	77·2	66·4

Source: *Ministry of Health Report for 1965 for England and Wales; annual returns (Form 15) to Scottish Home and Health Department for Scotland.*

tion of cases in England and Wales than in Scotland. In neither country does it appear that health visiting was making a major contribution to care of the elderly.

Published figures are not available to show the variation in the proportion of elderly cases between individual local authorities, but some indication of this variation can be given from data collected for this study. The lowest and highest proportion of elderly cases in the 16 English and Welsh case studies, and in all Scottish health authorities, is shown in Table 20.

TABLE 20

RANGE OF ELDERLY CASES AS PROPORTION OF TOTAL CASES
FOR THREE DOMICILIARY SERVICES IN 16 CASE STUDY
AUTHORITIES IN ENGLAND AND WALES AND IN 55 LOCAL
AUTHORITIES IN SCOTLAND, 1965

Service	England and Wales Case Study Authorities Only		Scotland All Local Health Authorities	
	Lowest Proportion of Elderly Cases	Highest Proportion of Elderly Cases	Lowest Proportion of Elderly Cases	Highest Proportion of Elderly Cases
	%	%	%	%
Health Visiting	0·3	24·1	Nil	18·1
Home Nursing	41·3	67·6	16·6	83·3
Home Help	9·1	92·7	28·4	93·0

Source: *Annual Returns to Ministry of Health (LHS 27) and Scottish Home and Health Department (Form 15).*

PLANNING LOCAL AUTHORITY SERVICES FOR THE ELDERLY

It is not clear how a local authority with a combined duty nursing service counts, for the central department return, a case described as a 'person aged sixty-five and over' visited by a health visitor and a 'person aged sixty-five or over at the time of the first visit' nursed by a home nurse, when both services are provided at one visit. The figures for individual authorities have been accepted, but this fact of the triple duty nursing service may explain at least some of the apparent variation in provision. Explanations for the extreme variation in the extent of provision for the elderly in these domiciliary services are linked not only with the organization of the services but also with problems of recruitment and with the use of alternative suppliers such as voluntary organizations. Further evidence on these issues is given in Chapters 10, 11, 13, 21 and 22.

EXPENDITURE ON LOCAL AUTHORITY HEALTH SERVICES

Expenditure, net of income from charges, on local health services in 1965-6 was about £109·2 million in England and Wales, and

TABLE 21

COMPARISON BETWEEN ENGLAND AND WALES, AND SCOTLAND, OF THE PROPORTION OF NET EXPENDITURE ON LOCAL HEALTH SERVICES SPENT ON INDIVIDUAL SERVICES IN 1965-6

Service	England and Wales*		Scotland	
	£m.	%	£m.	%
Health Visiting	7·0	8	0·9	10
Home Nursing	12·0	14	1·5	17
Domestic Help	15·4	18	1·7	19
Prevention of Illness	4·5	5	0·5	6
Domiciliary Midwifery	9·4	11	0·6	7
Mother and Child Welfare	13·2	15	1·8	20
Mental Health	13·9	16	0·6	7
Administration	9·4	11	0·9	10
Other	1·6	2	0·4	4
Total	86·4	100	8·9	100

Source: *Derived from Annual Reports of Ministry of Health for England and Wales, 1966 (Table 56, p. 144) and Scottish Home and Health Department 1966 (Figure 2, p. 54).*
 * To enable comparisons to be made, expenditure on the ambulance service is excluded here, as it is not a local authority function in Scotland.

94

about £9 million in Scotland. Table 21 shows that the proportions spent on health visiting and home nursing are slightly higher in Scotland than in England and Wales. This may be partly because of the way expenditure on combined duty nursing is allocated, since the proportion spent on domiciliary midwifery is slightly lower in Scotland. The proportion spent on domestic help is slightly higher in Scotland, and in both countries this service accounts for about a fifth of all expenditure on local health services. The most striking differences shown by the Table are, however, the high proportion spent on mother and child welfare in Scotland compared with England (which may again be partly due to differences in definition of categories), and the low proportion spent on mental health in Scotland compared with England.

Table 22 shows that net expenditure per thousand population appears to be higher in Scotland for all three services. However, the problems of interpreting figures relating to the nursing services described earlier in this chapter account for some of the difference. The figures for the home help service are not so divergent, which at first sight seems inconsistent with the higher staff ratio for this service in Scotland. However, data on income from charges for this service for the case study authorities suggest that Scottish authorities tended to recover a higher proportion of the cost of this servce in charges, often because of arrangements with the (then) National Assistance Board.[1]

TABLE 22

NET EXPENDITURE PER THOUSAND TOTAL POPULATION ON THREE DOMICILIARY SERVICES IN ENGLAND AND WALES, AND SCOTLAND, 1965–6

Service	England and Wales	Scotland
	£	£
Health Visiting	147	172
Home Nursing	251	282
Home Help	322	333

Source: *Annual Reports (1966) of the Ministry of Health and Scottish Home and Health Department.*

The range of net expenditure per thousand population between individual local authorities is wide, as shown in Table 23.

[1] Charging policy in the case studies is discussed in Chapter 11.

TABLE 23

DOMICILIARY SERVICES: LOWEST AND HIGHEST NET
EXPENDITURE PER THOUSAND TOTAL POPULATION BY
INDIVIDUAL LOCAL AUTHORITIES IN ENGLAND AND WALES,
AND SCOTLAND, 1965–6

Service	England and Wales		Scotland	
	Lowest	Highest	Lowest	Highest
	£	£	£	£
Health Visiting	46	292	61	497
Home Nursing	112	638	30	1,714
Domestic Help	122	711	42	1,045

Source: *Institute of Municipal Treasurers and Accountants, Local Health Statistics, 1965–6 for England and Wales, and derived from returns (RSG5 1967–9 Part II) to the Scottish Development Department for Scotland.*[1]

For all three services there was considerable variation between authorities. For health visiting, 43% of English counties spent less than £120 per thousand population compared with 33% of county boroughs. In Scotland, the tendency was apparently the opposite, as 11 out of 24 urban authorities spent less than this, compared with 5 out of 31 counties, while 15 counties spent £201 or more per thousand population. However, whether all authorities with combined nursing services allocate expenditure on the same basis is doubtful. A county medical officer of health in one of the case study authorities said, referring to IMTA statistics: 'Each local authority submits its figures in its own way. Our health visiting compared badly with other local authorities until we found we were allocating 50% of our health visiting to schools, whereas other local

[1] For England and Wales there may be slight differences in the way IMTA figures are calculated as compared with the national figures used in Table 22, but it is thought that the differences are slight. The Scottish Branch of IMTA has not published figures for local health services since the late fifties, but relevant expenditure by each local authority is returned for purposes of calculating the rate support grant. Total relevant expenditure for 1965–6 according to these returns (taken from Scottish Development Department *Form RSG5 (1967–9) Part II*) is a little different from the published figures in the Annual Report for 1966 which refers to expenditure by local health authorities of £8,964,000 (Figure 2, p. 54). Total relevant expenditure according to the returns amounted to £8,400,237, including £853,833 on health visiting (10·2%), £1,403,084 on home nursing (16·7%) and £1,646,691 on the home help service (19·6%). The notes accompanying the form ask that expenditure on nursing services where there are double and triple duty services should be allocated over the services concerned 'on the best practicable basis'.

authorities were allocating less. Therefore, we changed it and now it shows up better in the league table.'

For home nursing expenditure per thousand population was generally higher in counties than in urban authorities. In England and Wales, 49 % of counties, compared with 32% of county boroughs, spent more than £250 per thousand population. In Scotland, 26 of the 31 counties had expenditure above this level compared with 4 of the 24 urban authorities. Variation in expenditure on home nursing is caused partly by the high *per capita* cost of providing services in sparsely populated areas. These areas also have higher than average proportions of elderly in the population so that demand for this service is higher than in other areas.[1] It is again not clear whether different local authorities allocate expenditure on combined duty nursing services in the same way.

For home help the distribution of net expenditure per thousand population was fairly evenly dispersed for boroughs in both England and Scotland. English counties, however, tended to be in the lower to middle range, but Welsh counties and a third of Scottish counties were at the top end of the range. Variation in expenditure on home help is also partly accounted for by the high *per capita* cost of providing a service in rural areas. Variation may also be due to differences in the range of duties which home helps perform in different areas, the proportion of part-time to whole-time staff, and the availability of alternative services provided privately or by voluntary organizations. These influences are discussed in relation to the case study authorities in Chapters 10, 13, 21 and 22.

OTHER SERVICES FOR THE ELDERLY

(a) *Meals-on-Wheels*

Local authorities provide or finance other domiciliary services for the elderly, but national information is not always available or is incomplete in its coverage. However, in England and Wales 62,000 old people were receiving meals-on-wheels at the end of 1965. In that year, the WRVS delivered 6·3 million meals, and provided just over a million more in lunch clubs.[2] Local old people's welfare

---

[1] See Scottish Home and Health Department, *Gene. al Medical Services in the Highlands and Islands, Cmnd. 3257*, H.M.S.O., 1967, especially Chapters 9 and 10. A similar situation obtains in some Welsh counties.

[2] *Cmnd. 3039, op. cit.*, p. 30. (These figures do not seem to tie in very closely with the WRVS figure of 8 million meals given in the National Old People's Welfare Council annual report for the year ended March 31, 1966, but it is possible that the latter includes figures for Scotland as well.)

committees, the Red Cross, other voluntary bodies and some local authorities also provided meals for a large number of people although exact figures were not published. It is estimated that an eighth of the meals-on-wheels schemes in 1963–4 were run directly by local authorities.[1] In 1967 the Ministry of Health requested English and Welsh local authorities to collect information about all meals services in their areas for a return at the end of that year.

In Scotland in 1965 the WRVS delivered 432,494 meals, and old people's welfare committees were operating 58 lunch clubs.[2] Only one Scottish local authority had elected, by 1964, to use its powers to provide a direct meals service. According to the Scottish Old People's Welfare Committee, at the end of 1964 meals were being provided in two-thirds of the 90 affiliated old people's welfare committees responding to the questionnaire (77% response rate).[3] At least 2,300 old people were receiving the services, 4 of which operated once a week, 25 twice a week, 18 three times, 3 four times, 6 five times and 1 six times. The frequency is not known for 4 services.

(b) Chiropody

On September 30, 1966,[4] local authorities employed the whole-time equivalent of 602 chiropodists, 332 being full-time employees and the remainder working on a sessional basis. Voluntary organizations acting as agents for local authorities employed a whole-time equivalent of 121 chiropodists, 20 being full-time employees and the rest working on a sessional basis. There were also 1,606 chiropodists paid on a fee-for-treatment basis either by a local authority or a voluntary organization. (Some of these chiropodists may also have worked on a sessional basis.) In the last quarter of 1966,[5] 103 local authorities provided a direct service, 64 provided a service both directly and through voluntary organizations, and 4 through voluntary organizations only. The service was available in clinics in 152 authorities, in patients' own houses in 154, in old people's homes in 133, and

[1] National Labour Women's Advisory Committee, *Care of the Elderly*, Second Interim and Final Report, August 1964, p. 9.

[2] *Cmnd. 2984, op. cit.*, p. 42.

[3] Scottish Old People's Welfare Committee, *Summary of Services provided by Old People's Welfare Committees in Scottish Counties, 1965*, Scottish Council of Social Service, undated.

[4] Ministry of Health, *Report for 1966*, Cmnd. 3326, H.M.S.O., 1967. This was the first time statistics on chiropody services were published.

[5] *Cmnd. 3326, op. cit.*, Table 46, Part 2, p. 125.

in chiropodists' surgeries in 76.[1] In the same quarter, 525,923 (95%) of the 553,856 people who received treatment were elderly.[2]

In July 1966 in Scotland, 63 full-time and 57 part-time chiropodists were employed directly in at least 19 local authorities and probably more.[3] This appears to add up to more than the whole-time equivalent of 72·9 chiropodists mentioned on rate support grant forms submitted to the Scottish Development Department, unless the part-timers worked the equivalent of only one day a week. The Royal College of Physicians' report suggested that one chiropodist per hundred thousand population is essential in a big town and a higher ratio in rural areas where more time is spent travelling.[4] By this standard Scotland, with a mid-1965 population of 5,203,900, is over-provided with chiropodists in its local health services.

In July 1966, 20 Scottish authorities were running a direct service, 25 an indirect service and 4 had both. 31 provided a clinic-based service, 10 a service based on private practitioners' surgeries and 37 ran a domiciliary service. In 1965, 220,316 treatments were given, of which 61% (134,256) were in clinics or hostels, 14% (29,926) in private surgeries, and 25% (56,134) in patients' own homes.

(c) *Night-sitter and Good Neighbour Schemes*

Annual returns to the Ministry of Health (Form LHS 27) and the ten-year plan forms do not allow for entries under good neighbour or night-sitter services. In 1965 there were said to be about 8 large-scale paid good neighbour schemes and night-sitter services 'in some areas'.[5] In other areas these services were part of the home help service.

(d) *Marie Curie Schemes*

The Marie Curie Memorial Foundation provides terminal nursing care for cancer patients, many of whom are elderly. The 8 nursing homes (285 places) in England and Wales took 1,439 patients in

---

[1] A number of authorities provide more than one type of service, so that the total number of services is higher than the number of local health authorities.

[2] *Cmnd. 3326, op. cit.*, p. 26.

[3] For Scotland, information based on the results of a survey of chiropody services in all local health authorities in the United Kingdom (published in *The Chiropodist*, February 1967) was made available by the Society of Chiropodists.

[4] Royal College of Physicians (Edinburgh) *The Care of the Elderly in Scotland*, 1963, p. 43.

[5] National Old People's Welfare Council, *Annual Report for the year ended 31st March, 1965*, p. 19.

1965-6. The Foundation also finances a domiciliary nursing service staffed by part-time nurses and operated on behalf of the Foundation by local health authorities. In the year ended June 30, 1966, 1,568 patients received domiciliary care in England, Wales and Northern Ireland. The Foundation also has three homes in Scotland (101 places), and in 1965-6, 312 people were admitted. Over the same period 336 patients in Scotland received domiciliary nursing care.[1]

(e) *Laundry*

In 1962 48 English and Welsh local health authorities provided a laundry service.[2] The National Old People's Welfare Council reported in 1965 that less than a quarter of the areas replying to their questionnaire had laundry services. In only about 40% of these areas was the service provided by the local authority (just over 70 authorities).[3] Laundry services were provided in parts of 7 Scottish counties at the end of 1964,[4] in two cases by the local authority, in one by a voluntary organization, in one by both, and in three by the operation of reduced charges by commercial laundries. 4 large burghs operated a direct service, reduced fees operated in one city, and there was a launderette in a club in another city. In an August 1963 survey of need for this service for the incontinent elderly,[5] the Scottish Old People's Welfare Committee reported that in 41 areas plastic draw-sheets were available and in 49 areas disposable pads were prescribed. In 58 areas the report stated that the service was desirable and in some cases urgently required.

Laundry services are difficult to categorize, and the information available about the extent of services is hard to interpret. In some areas home helps do laundry work, and laundry or launderette con-

[1] Marie Curie Memorial Foundation, *Annual Report 1965-6*, pp. 17, 19, 21.

[2] *Cmnd. 1973, op. cit.*, p. 19.

[3] National Old People's Welfare Council, *Survey of Services for the Elderly provided by Voluntary Organisations, 1965*, National Council of Social Service, no date, p. 14. Only half of the questionnaires sent out were returned in time for analysis (748 replies).

[4] Scottish Old People's Welfare Committee, *Summary of Services provided by Old People's Welfare Committees in Scottish Counties 1965*, Scottish Council of Social Service, no date.

[5] Scottish Old People's Welfare Committee, *Report of an Enquiry into the Need for Laundry Services for Incontinent Old People Living at Home in Scotland, August 1963*, (duplicated), undated. The Committee received replies from 71 of their affiliated committees (a 63% response rate) and replies from a few county branches of the British Red Cross Society were incorporated in the survey, making a total of 75 areas. The survey material is not very well organized and has not been properly analysed. For instance, the report does not indicate whether a laundry service as such was available at the time of the survey.

cession schemes are sometimes available. The (former) National Assistance Board also used to pay a discretionary supplementary benefit for laundry for some old people.

(f) *Social Centres*

On March 31, 1965,[1] there were 115 social centres for the elderly provided by English and Welsh local authorities, catering mainly for the frail elderly who might otherwise have been housebound and isolated. There were also over 7,000 social clubs provided by voluntary organizations.

On December 31, 1964,[2] 15 out of 90 Scottish local old people's welfare committees reported no social clubs operating. In the other 75 areas there was a total of 69 clubs open at least six days a week (in 40 areas), 201 weekly clubs (in 44 areas) and 127 open less frequently than once a week (in 26 areas). 80 of the 127 were in one area—Glasgow.

(g) *Advisory Health Clinics*

A small number of advisory health clinics for the elderly have been set up, for example, the one at Twickenham which is run in conjunction with the hospital and general practitioner services.

The Royal College of Physicians reported only two health clinics for the elderly in Scotland in 1962, one being the justly famous pioneer centre at Rutherglen opened in 1952. The report stated that 'one reason why more of these centres have not been set up has been that consultant geriatric facilities have not always been available for the purpose'.[3]

(h) *Boarding-Out Schemes*

By 1965 there were at least 12 well established schemes for boarding-out or helping elderly people to find suitable accommodation, 9 of which were organized by voluntary bodies and the others by local authorities.[4]

[1] *Cmnd. 3022, op. cit.*, Appendix B, p. 412.

[2] *Summary of Services provided by Old People's Welfare Committees in Scottish Counties 1965, op. cit.*

[3] Royal College of Physicians (Edinburgh), *op. cit.*, pp. 32–3.

[4] National Old People's Welfare Council, *Annual Report for the year ended 31st March, 1965*, p. 17. See the Council's publication *Boarding-Out Schemes for Elderly People*, revised edition, April 1966, for more details about such schemes. In contrast to these small numbers the Council's 1965 *Survey of Services for the Elderly* provided by voluntary organizations in Britain claims that 50 respondent committees had some sort of boarding-out scheme (see p. 11 of the report).

(i) *Visiting Schemes*

By 1965 a voluntary visiting service existed in over 80% of the 748 areas covered by the National Old People's Welfare Council survey.[1] There were 615 areas with a service in England and Wales, and over 70 in Scotland. The extent and nature of the work in individual areas varied. Some services operated seasonally, some were restricted to the sick or the housebound, others were brought into operation 'as need arises' or only occasionally, were undertaken mainly or solely by committee members, or were 'unorganized'. For many areas in Scotland no details could be given about number of visitors, frequency of visiting, and number of old people visited. However, the number of visitors was at least 1,500 and the number visited at least 4,000.

(j) *Holiday Schemes*

There were about 480 group holiday schemes in just under 65% of the areas responding to the National Old People's Welfare Council questionnaire. Most schemes were in England and Wales. In Scotland about 2,500 elderly people took advantage of group holiday arrangements in 21 areas. Individual holiday arrangements were made either by local authorities or by voluntary organizations in about a third of the areas replying to the questionnaire. Most of the individual arrangements were again in England and Wales. In Scotland it appears that 39 people, from 8 areas, went on holiday under individual arrangements.[2]

(k) *Employment Workshops*

Employment workshops for the elderly existed in about 40 areas according to the national survey, though a more recent (1966) report[3] states that the number of workshops exceeds 60.

---

[1] See *Survey of Services for the Elderly, op. cit.*, pp. 12–13, 15.

[2] This appears to be much less than in 1962, when it was stated that 33 areas ran individual holiday schemes. See Scottish Old People's Welfare Committee, *Results of National Questionnaire in Scotland, November 1962* (duplicated), Scottish Council of Social Service, undated.

[3] National Old People's Welfare Council, *Annual Report for the year ending 31st March, 1966*, p. 20.

SUMMARY

A variety of domiciliary services were available to support elderly people living in their own homes, but information on the extent of provision was variable in quality.

For the established services, health visiting, home nursing and home help, data for England and Wales suggest that there were considerable differences between local authorities and that, with the exception of home nursing, provision in the majority of local authorities was below the standard suggested by the Ministry of Health.

Comparable data for Scotland were not published, and there were no suggested standards for adequate provision, but data made available for this study indicated that the home help service may have been rather better staffed in Scotland than in England and Wales. There were, however, wide variations between individual local authorities.

Comparisons between north and south of the border, and between local authorities, should not be pressed too far. For nursing services the lack of a sound basis for allocating combined duty nursing staff among the different services means that some apparent differences between authorities may have been artifacts.

Higher staff ratios for home nursing and home help often occurred in sparsely populated counties, especially in Scotland and Wales. This probably reflected both the sparsity of population, meaning that more staff were needed to provide the same level of service as in a more densely populated area and the relatively high proportions of old people in the population compared with many other areas. The data on expenditure support this conclusion.

For all three services, health visiting, home nursing and home help, elderly people formed a higher proportion of cases in England and Wales than in Scotland. In neither country was health visiting making a major contribution to care of the elderly. There again appeared to be considerable variation between local authorities.

Social workers working with the elderly were few in number but increasing in England and Wales. No information was available for Scotland.

Comparison between England and Wales, and Scotland, of the proportion of net expenditure on local health services spent on individual services revealed a marginally higher proportion spent on domiciliary services providing care for the elderly in Scotland. The main differences were that Scotland spent a much higher proportion on care of mothers and children, and a much lower proportion on mental health services than England and Wales.

Net expenditure per thousand population on domiciliary services appeared higher in Scotland, but again there were wide variations between local authorities.

Data on other domiciliary services were either lacking altogether or of poor quality. The Ministry of Health was starting to collect data on a wider range of services, including chiropody, and meals-on-wheels. Occasional statistics and National Old People's Welfare Council surveys of services provided by voluntary organizations for the elderly indicated a varying quality in the provision of voluntary services.

PART II

PROBLEMS OF DEVELOPMENT— THE ASSESSMENT OF NEEDS

D*

CHAPTER 5

RESIDENTIAL ACCOMMODATION— PLANNING FOR REPLACEMENT

In England and Wales, the replacement of that part of Part III accommodation, which is in former public assistance institutions by smaller homes has been an unambiguous feature of Ministry of Health policy. The Scottish Home and Health Department has taken a less definite line on this issue, although it too has urged local authorities to replace or improve old establishments. The implications of implementing this central department policy were discussed with welfare officials in the case study authorities. They also raised the question of whether adapted premises should be replaced. These discussions provided the material for this chapter.

THE REPLACEMENT OF FORMER PUBLIC ASSISTANCE INSTITUTIONS

Of the 24 local authorities studied, 4 English counties and 4 Scottish authorities firmly expected to be still using accommodation in former public assistance institutions in 1972. This belief was supported by such comments as:

'The Ministry dogma is stupid because some larger homes are better than some smaller ones. They have got a label put on them but there are hidden virtues in size. We have got wonderful staff in the large homes with great tolerance and understanding . . . Many of the big institutions lend themselves to adaptation so that they are better than small homes. You can have claustrophobia in smaller homes. Where the staff is intelligent and good and the committee are prepared to up-grade accommodation intelligently, then there is no worry.'

'Nobody in these institutions who is capable of appreciating the amenities of newer homes has been denied the opportunity of going to places where they are available.'

'I do not think the old institution would be scrapped now after so much money has been spent on it, at least not for a long time. To replace it would be an enormous undertaking. It would take 9 homes to replace it . . . It is a matter of weighing up and seeing where the money is going to come from. The ratepayers are at the end of their tether, so it would have to be some other source.'

Some officers believed that the Ministry was blinkered by the date, façade and overall size of the building, and argued that larger places meant better staffing provision, more opportunity for residents to meet people of their own kind in 'accommodation of different descriptions suited to different descriptions of the people who require it'.[1] Segregation can be undertaken on various criteria, such as educational background, class, or medical grounds.

There was even some resistance to closing up-graded former public assistance institutions on wich large sums of money had been spent from local authorities whose ten-year plans or a subsequent revision of the plans provided for replacement of these premises. Townsend reported that 'most local authorities came to the conclusion that former workhouses were needed for some considerable time at least. Some of them refrained from spending money on the old buildings because they supposed that sooner or later these would be pulled down. Others which reluctantly began to make improvements found it harder later on to envisage demolition, simply because large sums of public money had been spent.'[2]

A number of premises were shared with hospital authorities, and it was argued that hospitals would have considerably increased expenditure if they were not sharing common services. Running down a former institution means fewer residents so that the *per capita* running costs increase, perhaps dramatically. Financial control was said to be highly centralized in the hospital service, and therefore planning at the level of the hospital itself could be only on a short-term basis.[3]

It was also stated that the hospital authorities, particularly those concerned with psychiatric cases, were concerned at the closure of large establishments to which they were expecting to discharge some of their patients under the policy of 'community care'. 'Geriatric physicians may be anxious lest the reduction of mental hospital beds will add to the pressure on geriatric beds, and may therefore resist admitting the mentally confused to the beds in their unit. The loss of the large institutions may also add many mentally confused persons to the residents of the smaller homes which replace them. All these

[1] National Assistance Act 1948, Part III, s. 21(2).
[2] P. Townsend, *The Last Refuge*, Routledge and Kegan Paul, 1962, p. 415.
[3] See Chapters 7 and 20 for a further examination of relationships between hospital and local authorities in the planning context.

factors further complicate the formulation of future policy.'[1] In one rural county—a retirement area with a higher than average elderly population—the medical officer of health urged the welfare department to retain the former public assistance institutions, because otherwise psychiatric hospitals would have to support patients 'simply because there was nowhere else for them to go'. He claimed that the hospital authorities were caring for people 'at social breakdown point', by which he meant people with psychiatric symptoms but not in need of hospital care, or at least not for long. 'Also we started boarding-out old people from mental hospitals in private homes registered under the National Assistance Act. What we are doing here is providing welfare accommodation under the Mental Health Act. Probably it is the welfare officer's true job but he has not got the powers and it doesn't matter as long as the job is done.' In a large northern county, the medical officer of health had asked his deputy to do some research to try and decide the likely need for homes specially for the elderly mentally infirm. In the past they had believed that they could accommodate people in their existing homes. 'Now as we have a full policy of closing the old type of former institution, we will have a number of elderly mentally infirm who will not fit into the present accommodation and yet who are not really hospital cases either.'

One county official said that there was no determined replacement policy in his authority—although the ten-year plan provided for evacuation—because the institutions were vested in the regional hospital board rather than the local authority, and if the premises were suitable for the sane sick, then there was no real need to remove the mentally unfit anti-social residents. This official thought that institutions were an anachronism, but believed that central department policy was hypocritical, because of the intended or actual use of the same premises for the chronic sick.

In England and Wales, 5 of the 9 county boroughs and all 7 of the counties visited still had former public assistance institutions at that time. One of the 7 counties said there had been Ministry pressure to accelerate the closure of former public assistance institutions. In 2 of the 5 county boroughs the Ministry had refused to give loan sanction for other projects unless clear guarantees were given that the policy of replacing the former public assistance institution would be implemented. In the three others there were strong local pressures for prompt replacement. One of these three had recently

1 National Corporation for the Care of Old People, *Accommodation for the Mentally Infirm Aged*, 1963, p. 18.

inherited the institution as a result of boundary changes. Thus the policy of replacing former institutions was being taken rather more seriously in the county boroughs with institutions than in the counties.

In Scotland, only one of the 8 welfare authorities visited was seriously considering replacing the former workhouse, and plans for this were being discussed with the central department at the time of our visit. In this authority it was said that the old institution had become hopelessly uneconomic after the regional hospital board had vacated its part of the premises. The chief welfare officer claimed that his authority was 'one of the first authorities to get rid of its institution. Others are keeping their institutions for the misfits'. Little evidence was found to contradict this point, though one large burgh was trying to provide new premises for its residents accommodated at that time in a joint-user institution run by the hospital authorities, but had apparently been held up for two years for lack of a report by the district valuer.

One Scottish welfare authority described its old home as purpose-built 'with big rooms and a nice dormitory effect', and not necessarily an old persons' home at all, but for 'awkward cases' like 'the cripples, the mental defectives, the social misfits'—'this home could be drifting into a sort of specialist function for mental cases not certifiable'. The chief welfare officer quoted the National Assistance Act as stating that there should be different kinds of homes to suit different purposes and pointed out that such a policy was difficult to apply in a welfare authority with a relatively small population[1] 'and therefore you need to have one home for the odds and ends'.

Officials of 4 of the 8 Scottish authorities took the view that old buildings would remain in use either because they had recently had money spent on them or because they were satisfactory premises. 'The Scottish Home and Health Department say we have to get rid of the old institution . . . We have spent pounds and pounds on it, and it is just as well furnished as our homes—only the construction is different.' The welfare officer of one of these four authorities admitted that his authority had probably made a mistake in taking over an old place from the regional hospital board but pointed out that it was desperate for beds and an extension to this building was the quickest way to provide extra places.

[1] There are 55 welfare authorities in Scotland. Half of them (27) had an estimated population of under 50,000 on June 30, 1965. 4 of our Scottish case studies had less than 50,000 population on that date, and 4 had over 50,000. A list by rank order of population of the 16 case study authorities in England and Wales would be cut in half at about the 200,000 population mark.

REPLACEMENT OF ADAPTED HOMES

Central department policy has been aimed primarily at forcing the replacement of former public assistance institutions, but officials in some of the case study authorities were much more concerned about the replacement of small adapted homes. One county official referred to converted premises as 'the slums of the future', but it was more often in the county boroughs that the unsuitability of converted homes was stressed. This was probably because county boroughs housed a rather higher proportion of their residents in adapted homes than did the counties.[1]

Although the total number of residents in an adapted home was usually small, there were often several beds in one room, so that the residents were overcrowded and lacked privacy. The matron of one adapted home said: 'There is only one single room. Some are double rooms and some have six beds. Wardrobes are shared between two or three people.' The matron of another adapted home commented on the lack of anywhere for a resident to receive visitors.

Officials were particularly concerned that converted premises were unsuited to the needs of the more infirm residents. There were often no ground floor rooms suitable for conversion into bedrooms or bathrooms for residents confined to wheelchairs. The structure of the building often made it difficult to undertake modifications to provide lifts, sluice-rooms, or washbasins in the bedrooms.

Other comments about the shortcomings of adapted homes concerned the lack of privacy and separate accommodation for resident staff, and harder work for both attendants and domestic staff, thus making for possible recruitment difficulties. In one of the homes visited the matron said that some of the single rooms upstairs were unoccupied, and the two ground floor rooms had extra beds crowded into them because this was the only way the night attendant could provide the necessary care for very infirm residents.

It was also claimed that adapted premises could be expensive to heat and to maintain. However, in some of the authorities for which data on the heating costs of individual homes were available the cost per resident-week of heating in adapted premises was apparently less than that in some purpose-built homes, although it was not completely clear that the figures were comparable.

Thus some officials considered that there was a need to replace adapted homes, although councillors did not always readily agree. As one welfare officer said: 'When I first mentioned in open com-

1 See also *The Last Refuge*, *op. cit.*, p. 48.

111

mittee that members ought to look at the possibility of closing the adapted premises, they fell off their seats.' Nevertheless, some authorities had definite intentions of replacing adapted homes, either by razing the adapted premises to the ground and redeveloping the site, or by selling it and providing residential accommodation elsewhere. 'As the site is in a very desirable area, the finance committee said that we should sell it for private development and let the planning committee find a less valuable site for a welfare home.' Other suggestions were for alternative uses of the premises, such as a home for unmarried mothers or for the mentally handicapped, although some of the arguments against the use of adapted premises for elderly people also apply to these other categories of people for whom the welfare authority also has certain responsibilities.

SUMMARY

4 of the English and Welsh counties, and 4 of the Scottish authorities visited expected still to be using their former public assistance institutions in 1972.

It was not always felt that living conditions for the elderly would automatically be improved by replacing the old institution. It was sometimes believed that the broad aims of the central department did not take account of local circumstances, and that government policy should be more flexible.

There was some concern about the pressure to replace old institutions while there was an overall shortage of accommodation, especially for the elderly mentally infirm.

A few expressed the feeling that the Ministry policy was hypocritical, because it did not extend to pressure on the hospital authorities to replace old accommodation for the elderly chronic sick.

It was also suggested that the homely atmosphere often associated with small adapted homes sometimes concealed severe disadvantages inherent in the overall design of the premises, the very small numbers that could be accommodated, or resulting from a lack of privacy in large shared lounges and bedrooms. Thus some authorities, especially among the county boroughs, were considering the replacement of their least satisfactory adapted homes.

CHAPTER 6

RESIDENTIAL ACCOMMODATION—
THE NATURE OF CURRENT NEED

Replacement of unsatisfactory accommodation is only one of the
factors contributing to the numbers requiring places in residential
accommodation. This chapter shows some of the other influences:
the effect on demand of making new provision; the respective roles
of hospital and local authority in providing beds or places; and the
unclear impact of increased and improved domiciliary services and
sheltered housing. It concludes with a commentary on the overall
effect of these various charges on the age and infirmity of residents
and would-be residents.

EFFECT OF PROVIDING NEW ACCOMMODATION

New accommodation is being provided partly to replace obsolete or
unsuitable buildings and partly to cater for the demand from those
not in residential accommodation. The Phillips Committee, appointed in July 1953 to review the economic and financial problems
involved in providing for old age[1] recognized that the provision of
new accommodation tended to stimulate demand. The Younghusband Report said that it was 'common experience for the opening of a new small home to result in an increased demand for
accommodation in the surrounding neighbourhood'.[2] Several officers
—though none from English county boroughs—referred to latent
demand which was expressed on the announcement, completion or
opening of a new small home. This was further described as coming
in the form of clusters of new applications from areas in which small
homes had been opened, or from areas where some elderly people had
moved into a home and their acquaintances had had an opportunity

[1] *Report of the Committee on the Economic and Financial Problems of the
Provision for Old Age, Cmd. 9333*, H.M.S.O., 1954.
[2] Ministry of Health, Department of Health for Scotland, *Report of the Working Party on Social Workers in the Local Authority Health and Welfare Services*
(Younghusband Report), H.M.S.O., 1959, p. 134.

to see it and hear about it. Alternatively, the rapid build-up of the waiting list soon after the provision of additional accommodation was attributed to the expression of previously latent demand.

It may not be the provision of more attractive accommodation, but the very existence of more accommodation that may tempt elderly people, their relatives or their general practitioners to put names forward for a place. 'I showed the committee figures from the waiting list and recommended that they should not stress them, because general practitioners were withholding names where they knew that accommodation was just not there.'

The assessment of how much new accommodation should be provided was influenced in some authorities by the welfare officer's view that residential accommodation was the answer only when all else had failed. No Scottish authority expressed this view, but three English welfare officers claimed that the policy in their authorities was to regard admission as a last resort. As large institutions still existed in all three cases, it was perhaps partly a realization that the authority could not always offer a good standard of accommodation. 'Lots apply where we feel that they should not be in residential accommodation and at the moment we talk them out of it. It is wrong for someone who can cope to get a place.'

'The county only admits a person into Part III in the last resort . . . When they have been admitted, we try not to lose sight of the individual. With many people it is a question of malnutrition and neglect and people may recover to the point of being able to live alone again. Many cases are regarded as temporary . . . The welfare workers keep a close eye on the individual, because if a person stays in residential accommodation too long, he or she loses the incentive and ability to live in the community again. Three months is a good period to stay in residential accommodation, if they are going to return to the community.'

The policy of planning some places in each home specifically for short-stay residents was not widely followed, though it was generally admitted to be a good idea. If such a service was provided, it tended to be in newly opened homes before they were filled up. Once the home was full, short-stay residents were taken only if there happened to be a spare place when a request was made. The fact that a small number of places were not specifically designated for short-stay residents itself tended to lessen the expressed demand for such a service. One of the arguments against this kind of provision by local authorities was that this service should be the hospital's job, but this was not always considered in the discussions on planning between the hospitals and the local authorities.

THE HOSPITAL SERVICE AND THE OVERALL BED SHORTAGE

In most case study areas, it was believed that a shortage in the overall number of hospital and local authority places for the elderly was a real problem, but the general complaint of welfare officers was that hospital authorities had taken it upon themselves to develop plans for future provision of places and meetings were held to impart their conclusions rather than to provide an opportunity for discussion on priorities and long-term planning.[1] 'Joint consultation on overall accommodation needed can be particularly useful. This is an exercise that is being gone through in some areas today in connection with ten-year planning. It is a mistake to think that this is a remote administrative exercise that has nothing in particular to do with the people who are manning the services. This is not so, and practical workers of all kinds should feel some responsibility for drawing attention to any needs about which they are well informed.'[2]

Welfare officers saw the phrase 'community care' seized upon by senior medical officers and administrators of regional hospital boards and brandished before local authorities with the demand that residential and domiciliary services for those in need should be increased. In return, demands were made by local authorities for better communications with hospital authorities.

In a recent circular,[3] the Ministry of Health not only stressed the benefits of greater co-operation for long-term planning of residential services, but also touched on short-term policies and problems, such as the diagnosis and treatment of the elderly and transfer to and from home, hostel and hospital. Relationships with hospitals seemed to be dominated by the problems created by an overall bed shortage. On the one hand, hospitals were complaining to welfare departments that their beds were blocked by people who were receiving care rather than treatment. On the other hand, local authority officials maintained that the elderly discharged from hospital were sometimes in need of more attention than the residents they were trying to send *to* hospital for treatment. This topic has had a long and not very honourable history. As early as 1951 Hampshire County Council found it necessary to distinguish groups of people who needed more medical attention than welfare homes could provide

[1] A discussion on the problems of planning between the hospitals and the local authorities can be found in Chapter 20, where alternative statutory suppliers of services for the elderly are discussed.

[2] K. M. Slack, Ed., *Some Aspects of Residential Care of the Elderly*, National Council of Social Service, 1964, p. 15.

[3] Ministry of Health, *Circular 18/65*.

but who were not sick enough to be admitted to or retained in hospital.[1] The local authority associations set up a working party which reported in 1954 and the Ministry subsequently undertook a survey of the chronic sick and elderly. The results, published in 1957,[2] emphasized the bad distribution of accommodation, and lack of co-ordination between different authorities, but did not show an overall shortage of hospital beds. Lack of places in old people's homes was a bigger problem. A circular[3] sent to local authorities drew attention to the definition of hospital and local authority responsibilities put forward in the Boucher Report.

This background of conflict over responsibilities has not made the welfare officer's job any easier. The system of mutual exchange of patient for resident—'changy-changy' as one welfare officer put it—hampered local authority attempts to tackle their general waiting list for places. In one county borough, it was seen as the problem of who should provide nursing or convalescent homes for the elderly. These were the kind of homes that local authorities were beginning to run, and even recently built homes were not always designed with such residents in mind, though in Scotland there was some emphasis on developing homes for the 'frail ambulant'. Tension between local authority and hospital authorities over these recurrent problems coloured attitudes, and resulted in relatively unsuccessful attempts at joint planning. Each side had strong and perhaps biased views about the quality of the personnel on the other side and the jobs they should be doing.

Routine matters and local problems were settled—or otherwise—with the geriatric consultant at the local hospital. Welfare officers were not pleased to discover that consultants were often not present at co-ordination meetings held at regional hospital board headquarters, especially as they sometimes felt that the local authority's own problems were more likely to be appreciated by the local consultant rather than by regional board officials. Suspicion by local authorities of the flexibility of those planning the numbers of hospital beds in the future, and a suggestion from the hospital side that local welfare authorities were not very sophisticated in undertaking this kind of long-term exercise has meant no real progress in joint planning.

It seems that welfare officers did not always appreciate that a

[1] J. Parker, *Local Health and Welfare Services*, Allen and Unwin, 1965, pp. 114–15.

[2] C. A. Boucher, *Survey of Services Available to the Chronic Sick and Elderly 1954–5*, Reports on Public Health and Medical Subjects No. 98, H.M.S.O., 1957.

[3] Ministry of Health, *Circular 14/57*.

doctor with clinical skills and responsibilities may not be the appropriate person to spend time on planning the hospital service, although, as Slack has pointed out (see footnote on p. 115), they should draw the attention of planners to clients' needs. The hospital management committee is not a planning body; in the formal structure planning is undertaken at regional board level. It is a matter of conjecture whether the major weakness is in the local authority because the system requires planning, technical and routine skills to be merged in the same person, or in the hospital service where these functions have been separated.

There were some exceptions to the general rather gloomy picture. Meetings with representatives of the regional hospital board were sometimes seen as useful rather than a waste of time because the type and range of problems faced by the hospital board were more fully understood by local government officers as a result of these discussions. 'Personally, I got a clearer idea of the thinking behind the hospital board's approach to planning. I now know that they have to take into account anticipated population movements in relation to maternity beds. This was new to me.' In another case, the chief welfare officer believed that most of the recurrent problems arose from the clash of incompatible personalities, and that the formality or otherwise of the machinery for co-operation was secondary. However, this officer was mainly concerned with day-to-day activities rather than long-term planning.

GROWTH OF SPECIAL HOUSING AND DOMICILIARY SERVICES

Just as the overlap of services provided by the hospital and the residential home caused planning and policy problems, so did the development of special and sheltered housing (outlined in Chapter 3 and discussed in Chapter 8) influence the nature and extent of demand for residential accommodation. It should be stressed that the effect of the increased number of such dwellings on the provision of accommodation is not yet clear. It was not emphasized as a contributory factor by welfare officers in English county boroughs, though one Scottish large burgh claimed that demand for residential accommodation was low because its housing was so good. To a visitor, it seemed probable that the low demand was because the quality of the accommodation in welfare homes was so poor.

One English county welfare officer said: 'It takes four years to produce a sheltered housing scheme and a lot of district councils have not got schemes even in their five-year plans. Also the effect of housing schemes will not show for 10 years because they are concerned with people in their seventies, whereas the demand for residential accommodation is from people in their eighties.' At the 1966 National Old People's Welfare Council conference Robin Huws Jones was right to ask for 'careful, systematic observation of grouped special housing to get what evidence we can to guide policy'.[1]

One hard-pressed welfare officer in Scotland commented that: 'The pressure on domestic help is greater when the pressure is greatest for places in old people's homes.' Recent developments of domiciliary supportive services such as domestic help or home nursing must influence the demand for residential accommodation, but again the nature of that influence can only be guessed at at the moment. Very rarely did welfare officers use information available from other local authority departments, or canvass their colleagues' views on the meaningfulness of figures provided for the ten-year plans and subsequent revisions. Each forecast was apparently made independently of the influence of complementary or substitute services.

Boarding-out of old people is limited in both England and Scotland and is usually run by voluntary organizations. It was not generally seen by the case study authorities as a possible alternative to residential accommodation, although elsewhere it has been claimed that 'nearly all of those boarded-out in the early years of the scheme stayed in the same home until they died or had to enter hospital'.[2] In one large county the welfare officers confessed to knowing little about such schemes but felt that it might be harmful to uproot people. In a county borough where a scheme was in operation, the welfare department was not deeply involved in discussions about boarding-out people, though a welfare officer might contact the boarding-out officer about a particular person (and vice-versa), and would pass on suitable addresses for the development of the service.

When the future was considered (sometimes after prompting by the research workers) as much speculation as planning was evident. 'I can foresee the time when the type of home we are now providing in the county will be superfluous. If domiciliary services can support old people, they can stay in their own homes. Wardens cannot do everything and they are not meant to. You might see the very infirm in an annexe to a hospital as you now see them in a psychiatric hospital. If there is a strong desire to cut out the dichotomy of the

[1] National Old People's Welfare Council, *Putting Planning into Practice*, Report of the 13th National Conference on the Care of the Elderly, National Council of Social Service, 1966, p. 39.

[2] National Old People's Welfare Council, *Annual Report for the year ended 31st March, 1965*, p. 18.

services, there may be a streamlining of the services. Perhaps granny's room attached to houses is the answer and this might encourage relations to look after the old folk more. The problem is what to do with the extra room when granny is gone.'

The exceptions to this pattern are of interest and indicate the kinds of practical steps that can be taken. In one county borough the chief welfare officer did request information about potential need for places in homes from the geriatrician, the home help and meals-on-wheels organizers, and the housing department, as well as from his own subordinates doing routine visits to old people. 'They were not used to being asked . . . but when they discovered that the information is acted upon, they realized it was in their interest.' It was claimed this improved the accuracy of the information provided, but it mainly covered short-term demand rather than long-term planning. Overall, this borough was not short of places, although they were perhaps located in unsuitable premises. This officer forecast that residents would be 'more and more chronic than at present. If you go back 10 years you find the type of people in the homes were reasonably fit, and would have stayed at home if the domiciliary services had been adequate. The type in the homes now could not stay at home even with domiciliary services, because they can't move round, or they are mentally unstable, or they are in a condition of advanced senility, or incontinent, or confined to a wheelchair, or anti-social . . . We intend to go in for more domiciliary work. This is being done only on the fringe at the moment.'

One county officer tried to calculate target figures for residential accommodation based partly on likely developments in other services. Even he did not stress discussions with the senior officers of these other services. This is not to suggest that chief officers were uninfluenced by probable changes in other services, but among the case studies, very few seemed to include such possibilities consciously, formally and deliberately in their own plans.

'We have our known demand at the present time and can anticipate a rate of increase unless there is a disproportionate increase in domiciliary services . . . We took into account that if an effort was made on the domiciliary side and on the housing side, then we could curtail the increasing demand for residential accommodation and hold down the rate of growth for places.'

AGE AND INFIRMITY

The general opinion of welfare officers in the 24 case study authorities was that applicants for places and new residents were more infirm, and older, than was the case in the early 1950's. Three main reasons for this view were suggested. First, there was the movement away from institutionalization towards greater care in the community by 'clearing' hospital beds, low hospital geriatric bed provision, and transfer of chronic sick residents from vacated former public assistance institutions. Second, there were improved domiciliary services and increased sheltered housing so that more applicants for residential accommodation had become so frail that they could not live in their own homes even with supportive services.[1] Third as a consequence of the provision of small homes, there was an increase in demand from people who would not have considered living in an old large institution and this meant that the more infirm had to be given priority for the available places. County borough officials were particularly concerned about what they saw as a trend towards greater infirmity among applicants for places, because they used converted premises which they had found to be unsuitable for physically and mentally deteriorating residents.

In most cases, knowledge of the greater age and infirmity of applicants for places was gained by welfare officers doing or supervising the work of visiting applicants and taking or checking personal details. This information was not always collated to provide a trend over time.[2]

The annual statistical return (Form H.4) to the Ministry of Health on residents in homes in England and Wales asked for details about various handicaps for a number of years, but not about age until 1966. It is not clear how useful the national summary is because there is no guarantee that the criteria of assessing handicaps are consistent within any one local authority—matrons vary in the assessment of residents—quite apart from consistency between local authorities.

Although the proportion of residents materially handicapped in English and Welsh local authority homes, or in other homes in which the residents are the responsibility of the local authority, does not appear to have changed markedly in recent years, there was considerable variation between individual case study authorities over

[1] 'Our Old People', *Socialist Commentary*, January 1966. 'The more successful the community services are in helping old people to live in their own homes, the more those entering the residential homes are likely to be mentally or physically frail—who need very considerable help in the task of daily living but not the services of a geriatric hospital.'

[2] A good example of how local authorities, for purposes of planning, might be able to use information they probably already have in their filing systems or case papers is given by Mike Reddin, 'The Varying Needs of the Aged', *British Hospital Journal and Social Service Review*, Vol. 76, October 28, 1966, pp. 2035–8.

the period 1958–65 (see Tables 5 and 6). Rural counties recorded a low proportion of handicapped residents in their homes, and boroughs in retirement areas recorded high proportions.

If replacement policy is carried out, the requirements for intensive care in the new homes which replace old institutions will be greater than what is provided in recently built homes. Townsend shows that in the late 1950's there was a much higher proportion of severely incapacitated new residents in former public assistance institutions compared with other local authority homes (see Table 24). Thus, his survey also indicated that closure of institutions would imply catering for a higher proportion of severely incapacitated residents in adapted or purpose-built homes. This reason for expecting high demand for intensive care from the more infirm appears to be solidly based.

TABLE 24

NEW RESIDENTS: INCAPACITY FOR SELF-CARE BY TYPE OF HOME (SAMPLE OF 530 NEW RESIDENTS), ENGLAND AND WALES

Incapacity for Self-Care	Former Public Assistance Institution	Other Local Authority Homes
Slight	46·2%	60·4%
Moderate	23·8%	22·6%
Severe	30·0%	17·1%

Source: *Peter Townsend, 'The Last Refuge', Routledge and Kegan Paul, 1962, Table 49, p. 262.*

SUMMARY

Local authorities were trying to increase the amount and standard of the accommodation offered—thus generating more demand—and felt that central department officials and planners of alternative services were not sufficiently sympathetic to the problems that development of community care—including residential facilities—caused. Planning other services in consultation with senior colleagues in the same local authority was not always close, and co-operation with officers in other kinds of organization was even more remote. A larger number of applicants, who tended to be more frail and more advanced in years than applicants in the 1950's, meant pressure on local authority residential facilities at a time when providers of alternative services were making changes in the extent of their services.

CHAPTER 7

RESIDENTIAL ACCOMMODATION—
ESTIMATING FUTURE NEED

In the previous chapter, the basic influences on current need were seen to be the changes in hospital policy, and the growth of housing and domiciliary services, both of which led to greater demand for residential accommodation from the very frail and the very old. Because of these changes in policy welfare officials found it difficult to measure current need, and were therefore even more sceptical about attempts to gauge future need.

In this chapter the reliability of data used as a basis for planning, and the methods used to forecast need in England and Wales when compiling ten-year plans, are discussed. The reasons why many authorities thought that planning was a useless exercise are examined. Lastly the planning of residential accommodation in Scottish authorities, which have not been formally required to prepare long-term plans, is considered.

THE RELIABILITY OF BASIC DATA

How did welfare officers in England and Wales use figures extracted from expressed demand? The waiting list was often regarded as unreliable mainly because it was believed that some people put their names down 'just in case', although attempts were sometimes made to control the waiting list by dividing it into an urgent list and a non-priority list, or by not admitting names to the list until checks had been made on the circumstances of the applicant. Although some officers did believe the waiting list was inflated because it contained names of people who would refuse a place if they were offered one at the present time, no formal consideration was given to the common belief that replacement of old large institutions by new small homes might encourage greater expressed demand for places. In other words, in formulating ten-year plans, the waiting list was often treated as an over-estimate because of the existence of applicants not 'in need of care and attention not otherwise available to them', but was not often treated as an under-estimate because of possible increased demand. One English county assumed a waiting list three-quarters of its actual size for the purposes of the plans, and another cut its list in half, but admitted that its action was arbitrary. Townsend commented that 'until uniform methods of compiling and reviewing waiting lists are adopted it will be difficult to decide how large is the unsatisfied demand for accommodation'.[1]

A number of officials referred to the increasing age and mental or physical infirmity of residents compared with the early 1950's, and remarked that, as well as affecting demand, this complicated any analysis of the need for places, because the rate of turnover might be changing. 'I am certain it is, though we have not yet gone through the records to find out. The length of stay in a hostel is a significant factor for planning. I would expect it to be shorter than it used to be, but supposing it had gone up?'[2] Increasing infirmity also meant that the places available might be unsuitable for the most urgent applicants, for example, places in adapted premises with no lifts and few ground floor bedrooms. It should be emphasized again that welfare officers did not always know the extent of change towards greater age and infirmity. They often came to this conclusion over the years as a result of impressions from their day-to-day work. The changes themselves were not always measured, although the more detailed statistics now required annually by the Ministry of Health could help to indicate trends.

Population projections also sometimes caused difficulties, particularly for county officials. In most cases it seemed that the Registrar-General's figures were accepted, but where the age structure was imbalanced because of overspill or new town policy, local calculations were at variance with the official projections. In one county, the official projections were used because no alternative forecasts were available. 'We took the Registrar-General's population projections, although we do not believe them. The programme is to be amended year by year and so it gives us an opportunity to think again if the projections are not working out.'

FORECASTING NEED

The simplest approach by local authorities to measuring future need for ten-year plan purposes was to count the number of existing places

1 Peter Townsend, *The Last Refuge*, Routledge and Kegan Paul, 1962, p. 239
2 See Mike Reddin's article, 'The Varying Needs of the Aged', *British Hospital and Social Service Review*, Vol. 76, October 28, 1966, for a description of how records could be used.

in homes, add the numbers from the waiting list and then, using population projections, work out what provision should be made over a decade. If this programme was felt to be politically unrealistic, or unlikely to be attained for technical reasons, either a shortfall was admitted in the programme, or it was argued that the local authority area was inappropriate for the calculation that had been undertaken, because of factors such as population structure or migration. Alternatively, the original figures were changed, such as the number on the waiting list on the grounds that this was an unreliable measure.

One welfare officer stated that the original plan in one authority had been compiled by averaging available statistics for all local authorities. Another said that they worked on the figure of 3% of old people in the population needing residential accommodation 'because this is the figure most local authorities work on'. It seems not to have been widely realized that careful attempts at forecasting are potentially helpful precisely because apparently simpler methods have been found wanting.

In a number of cases subsequent revisions of the ten-year plans were based on a simple application of the Ministry's own averaging of the original submission, viz. 18–22 places per thousand population aged sixty-five or over, which is in any case regarded as 'appropriate provision' only where 'domiciliary services are well developed' and 'hospital services are adequate'.[1] Thus, forecasting need had been transformed into a routine return. However, it was pointed out by one welfare officer that such an exercise did have the short-term advantage of 'bringing the laggardly to the average'. This could be described as a minimal achievement.

In other cases the central department figures were used, but were criticized as unhelpful. One borough chief welfare officer commented: 'You need a float of about 10 places. The beds are worked out on the Ministry's norms and population basis and then the 10 is the float . . . The number of places is not very finely calculated in relation to population estimates because you can't do it . . . I work on the basis of hunches which can be just as right or wrong as the Ministry norms.'

Two English authorities, of the 16 studied, had made serious attempts to forecast need. The first, and more naïve, operation used the census projection of population figures and a formula of 20 places per thousand people aged sixty-five or over. Different parts of the county produced different demands because of the number of

[1] Ministry of Health, *The Development of Community Care, Cmnd. 1973*, H.M.S.O., 1963, p. 21.

voluntary homes in different areas. The existence of private homes was ignored except where the county was 'making a contribution like paying maintenance charges'. Finally, the waiting list number was cut by a quarter on the argument that no waiting list is realistic. The particular interest of this county's forecast was a determination to attempt to keep pace with the plan (although considerable reservation was expressed as to its feasibility) allowing for revisions due to circumstances such as national economic policy, which were beyond the welfare authority's control. This attitude contrasted with that of viewing the forecast as a central department return, to be ignored until another return was due and then revised in the light of events rather than as a result of deliberate decisions.

The second case was another county in which the senior welfare officer was concerned about the effect of an apparently changing population structure, and especially the effect of a new town. The age structure of the population in different parts of the county was analysed. The biggest contrast was between the young population of the new town and the larger proportion of very old people in the unchanged rural areas of the county. It was disconcerting to discover that the extent of expressed demand for residential accommodation from different parts of the county did not appear to correspond with the age structure of the relevant populations. Also the population projection figures calculated by the welfare officer did not tally with those made by the General Register Office. 'I contested their figures. The Registrar-General was doing his projections on anticipating an influx of old people into the county in the same proportion as they exist in the community generally. I said there was not sufficient evidence that this was so and that a larger percentage of older people were going into the southern counties . . . I had to rethink my figures for planning and so I struck a figure which was a compromise between the two.' The number of existing places and the level of expressed demand (total waiting list) for places in both local authority and voluntary homes was then standardized by use of the estimated population figures. The result—for the revisions of the ten-year plans—was compared with the Ministry's original guide-line, which was found to be unhelpful (too low) for the county. The figures of places eventually projected were ones 'we think would be needed at a given date'. Turnover rate was mentioned, but not explicitly included in the projections. 'With the increasingly infirm residents we have in homes, we may need fewer places . . . First priority is given to old people living alone who cannot cope on account of their infirmity, and second priority is to assist in clearing hospital beds. This means that those admitted are more infirm now than would be true of five years ago.' However, this officer considered that: 'Short of a complete study of the county we could only make our provision on the basis of the trend we saw. We have not given up the idea of a complete study if we could get someone to do it.' He was also emphatic that 'in future, social work departments should have a built-in research department; we are planning with completely inadequate knowledge'. However, funds were lacking, and the officer said: 'I allocate higher priority to the social workers than to having clerks in an office writing reports. I put my money on staff in the field. I know I am an odd bird. It would be nice to have statistics, although they are only useful as a guide if they can be properly interpreted.'

ATTITUDES TO PLANNING

In discussing the formulation of ten-year plans, welfare officers listed other complicating factors that they either tried to incorporate into the plans, or confessed they were conscious of but left on one side. Planning for the future was regarded as bound to fail by some senior officials in 6 English authorities. Their view was that capital projects were either achieved or not achieved on time, and modifications in the light of subsequent developments were seen as undermining the original plan rather than as influencing a continuous planning process. In other words, the publication of the ten-year plans was seen as producing a political, prestigious, public relations document rather than a working brief.

The complicating factors—besides a dubious waiting list, unreliable population projections and the changing characteristics of elderly applicants for places in homes—were, in the main, the same factors that affected present demand for places.[1]

Increases in domiciliary supportive services could lead either to an increase in need for places from the very frail who had continued to manage in their own homes with this support, or to a decrease because places in old people's homes were not required as other services had replaced the need for them. One example is the service that gives close support to the frail elderly during the day so that they can continue to live in their own homes overnight—either alone or with the support of relatives relieved of a non-stop 24-hour burden of care. 'I have said publicly that day centres will have a marked effect on demand for residential accommodation; it is too early to project

[1] For more direct influences on the building programme for old people's homes, see Chapters 18 and 19.

the figures; when three or four are functioning at their maximum, I will be able to assess their benefit overall.' Even though welfare officers speculated or made estimates on the basis of the ten-year plans for domiciliary services, they did not ask those responsible for planning domiciliary health and special housing services what assumptions they had made about the future level of provision of places in residential accommodation.

The sudden expression of latent demand with the replacement of an old institution by a new small home was thought to imply that planning for the future was a profitless activity. The very rate of replacement might be influenced by external factors such as forceful Ministry policy, and if this rate was accelerated, it might mean that the provision of extra accommodation could be delayed, so that the available number of places was not so high as originally expected. In considering future developments the distinction was not always clearly drawn between the need for places in homes and the need for homes themselves.

In addition, efforts were made to take account of voluntary and private provision but it was easier to calculate the number of beds at present than to forecast the future level of provision from these sources. This was a particularly relevant problem for local authorities in retirement areas, and one county welfare officer said that they did try to estimate what was likely to happen 'but it is not possible to anticipate everything. You can't tell over 10 years. They may be providing for people we are not attracting. I think the finance is getting a bit of a problem for them.' The deputy county welfare officer added that the amount of help from the voluntary homes was not in direct relation to the number of beds 'because the voluntary people are more selective and some even put an age limit on their entrants. It is the local authority which is the last resort. The voluntary organizations are still fighting to keep their costs down.'

One senior officer believed that forward planning was bound to fail, not because of any difficulties in principle, but because basic information was not available and there was no time to obtain and use it. Townsend's yardstick of incapacity for self-care was one of the few analytical tools available and there were naturally difficulties of application. Such measurement takes time and Townsend pointed out that the measure was only provisional.[1] The same welfare officer commented that a ward analysis of census figures helped to locate clusters of old people, and this information could be used to provide

[1] Townsend, *op. cit.*, p. 464. In his subsequent national survey a simpler measure is used. See Peter Townsend and Dorothy Wedderburn, *The Aged in the Welfare State*, G. Bell and Sons Ltd., 1965, pp. 24–5.

a geographical basis for the development of social services for the elderly in general.[1]

Finally, in one other borough, the chief welfare officer believed that developments in community care made planning for future needs just a speculative operation. He kept a large up-to-date register of old people, but it was not clear how much the information gained from this was used for long-term planning as opposed to immediate administrative work.

In contrast to the senior officials of 6 English welfare authorities who felt the exercise was doomed to failure, there were spokesmen from 8 other English authorities who regard the forecasting of future need as a completely irrelevant activity in their special circumstances.

In 2 boroughs the political decision on the rate of provision of residential accommodation was believed to be relatively uninfluenced by officials' forecasts of need, and development of the service was seen to depend on the political power of the committee chairman. In one case, it was admitted that if a survey were undertaken, and the results were clear-cut and unambiguous, a programme could probably be forced through. Another borough was in the throes of substantial reorganization and lacked much of the basic information for planning.

A fourth borough claimed to have enough places but in unsuitable premises. The applicants were usually infirm and the homes were converted houses. 'It depends how long it takes you to get an urgent case in. Here there is no delay. Whether this is a fair judgement, I am not sure . . . It would be difficult to prove that I would want more places if we concentrated on those needing care and attention.' The emphasis in this authority was very much on the development of preventive work in the field. In contrast, Ruck commented that in London in 1960 local authority welfare departments mainly confined themselves to the provision of residential accommodation in terms of services to the elderly.[2]

One small rural county also had spare capacity and was considering replacing its former poor law institution by a purpose-built home with fewer places than the existing building.

3 counties were providing so few places in residential accommoda-

[1] See also National Old People's Welfare Council, *Annual Report for the year ended 31st March, 1966*, p. 3. 'The Sunderland Committee's current report quotes the last census figure of 5,000 old people known to be living alone in the borough, as an estimate on which to base planning for the future.'

[2] S. K. Ruck, *London Government and the Welfare Services*, Routledge and Kegan Paul, 1963, p. 25. This was before the creation of the new London boroughs with welfare responsibilities. Croydon was the exception to Ruck's generalization.

tion compared with the expressed demand that any calculation of need was regarded as quite academic. One official described the ten-year plans as the 'bull's eye and if we hit the dartboard we will be doing all right'.

Some authorities used the word 'planning' very differently from others. In some, planning was taken to relate only to the location of buildings and/or the design of residential accommodation. In other authorities, planning was seen as providing in the future for specific individuals rather than for groups of people with certain probable characteristics. 'If we work things out seriously and sensibly, we can forecast reliably who will need residential accommodation when, and then we can begin to prepare their minds as well as those of their relatives.' An independent observer has pointed out that: 'Those . . . who are especially concerned with plannine know that it is their business to identify the needs of old people ang classify them; it is only by grouping needs that society can plan td meet them early and effectively. On the other hand, those . . . who aro more concerned with practice know that it is their job to help the individual old man or woman.'[1] In some contexts planning seemed to be seen as something that happened at national rather than local level. 'Government departments are planning organizations; it is their job to try to plan centrally the policy on which their Ministers decide. The role of a government department is not executive. The execution of the main plan, making the thing work, falls within the social services run by the local authorities and local people.'[2]

PLANNING IN SCOTLAND

Scottish local authorities have not figured in the foregoing analysis of the planning function and the measurement of need. As with replacement policy (see Chapter 5) it is again necessary to distinguish between the countries, because the background factors are different, markedly so in at least two ways. First, there was no formal requirement to submit regular forecasts of development of the welfare services except for purposes of grant negotiations. Secondly, many Scottish authorities are very small in terms of population, if not in

[1] Robin Huws Jones in *Putting Planning into Practice*, Report of Conferenc of the National Old Peoeple's Welfare Council, National Council of Socia Service, 1966, p. 35.

[2] Dame Enid Russell-Smith, *Ageing—Its Changes and Its Promise*, Report of the 10th Conference of the National Old People's Welfare Council, National Council of Social Service, 1960, pp. 44-5.

area, with the result that the function of measuring need was often seen as a personal activity by a chief or a district officer undertaking a one-man survey.

In three Scottish case study authorities there appeared to be little attempt to measure need at all. Two were burghs which claimed to have more than enough places. The third was desperate for residential accommodation to replace what was the least appealing of all the places visited during the study. In these cases the measurement of need was thought to be irrelevant.

Other authorities did not consider that there was any unmet need: 'It's wonderful how you find out about folks needing help . . . Others don't want help—a number who are up in years manage, and prefer to be independent. There are too many theorists telling people what they should do.' It may well be that in Scottish authorities with a small population unexpressed demand and unmet need are comparatively unlikely. However, those who supplied the services held definite views on what did or did not constitute legitimate need, and these views may have been at variance with other people's judgements. In a small authority the senior officer was less likely to mix daily with other senior colleagues with equivalent skills and experience of this kind, and was thus less likely to have to defend or justify his decisions.

In addition, the population of an authority was in some cases so small that there were not enough people needing places to warrant providing a home that would be economical to run. Therefore, the official running the service may have tended to suppress the expression of need by the few who did require the service. In these circumstances, there was a tendency to continue to use facilities that had been available for a long time, and the quality of service therefore suffered.

There was also spare capacity in one rural county with a scattered population. This meant that despite unfilled places in a new home in one area there were local shortages in another area. In past discussions on the provision of new accommodation for the population of this authority, both the central government advice of providing for $2 \cdot 5\%$ of the population aged sixty-five or over[1] and the results of an old local survey were considered. A home for 26 residents was built, the decision on size being based on the central department's criterion. 'If you refer to the $2 \cdot 5\%$ measure there would be a need for a total of 44 places for the area, and if there were to be two

[1] First published as a minimum objective in the 1963 annual report of the Scottish Home and Health Department, though it had been suggested as a desirable level of provision previously.

homes, this made the size of home somewhere around 22 places. It was with this kind of background that the figure for the northern part of the area of 26 places was arrived at.' Ten weeks after opening, there were 8 residents and 'there is no sign of a rush of applicants'. It appeared that the figure reached by the local survey, which was not used, had indicated the current population's immediate requirements much more closely. Perhaps in the long term there will be demand for all the places available, but there was no sign of this kind of long-term consideration among the officials.

Another county had undertaken a local survey soon after the National Assistance Act came into operation, and the chief welfare officer said: 'I was asked to assess how many would accept and how many would need this type of accommodation. At the time I said there would be many who needed it but it was another matter how many would accept. I got together information from the district officers and the domestic help supervisor as to who might be interested.' In recent years the welfare officer had noticed—but not apparently measured—that people were less willing to go into residential accommodation and that a high percentage of applications were from hospitals. 'Some who have an old person's house will not come into a home until there has been a disaster and then they come via hospital, whereas they would have been better coming in a bit earlier. But if they don't want to, you can't make them.' The implications of these changed attitudes, and the resulting increased infirmity of applicants was leading the welfare officer to reconsider the staff ratio. In addition, new homes were being planned to cater for the more frail and to assist in vacating the former public assistance institution. The number of places to be supplied seemed to be a function of sites available, and of the desire to limit the total number of places in each home, so that it would not resemble an institution.

The medical officer of health of this authority also said that he could not see the need for the number of beds indicated by the central department's advice. However, he admitted he was biassed by the short length of the waiting list, and agreed that this in itself could be a function of the likelihood of obtaining a place. He also said that there was no seeking out of need: 'Our people are not keen on old people's homes. This could be perhaps because we have not provided the service but, as far as I know, I think general practitioners are not putting forward cases because they think they are better at home. General practitioners may also be holding back cases because they know that sometimes there are no beds available or we say that the person is too ill.' If residents were to be taken from chronic sick hospitals, then the need for such accommodation

131

would be proved, but the medical officer of health did not seriously consider this possibility. The welfare officer said that the elected members were 'on the watch about our not doing the hospital's job. We can't afford to slip any further than frail ambulant in terms of provision of care and attention'.

One other county had also noted the central department's advice, and believed that the recommended figure was 'tied up with the hospital plan ideas'. One large burgh accepted the projections of the Scottish Home and Health Department's report on old people.[1] 'We do not believe all the government statistics, although they are something to go on and so we take them into account.' Future need for places was calculated on the basis of 'the ageing population in the future', and the present need, from which the projection is made, is based on 'how many are in care, how many are on the waiting list and how many are in hospital who should not be. There are not many others excluded in this because all the doctors know and also I have been very keen to tell old people to tell us any time they need help . . . There are always some who will slip through the net but I do not think there are many. Neighbours are pretty good at telling us, for whatever motive they do it. Doctors, postmen, milkmen, paper men also tell us.' This belief about good coverage had not been checked by a survey; in fact publicity of a discussion in committee about having such a survey 'was followed by a rush of thugs posing as a survey team'.

Finally, the welfare officer of the eighth Scottish case study authority—another rural county—pointed out that doctors 'choke off requests for places because they know very well that there are none available', but added that the waiting list was kept constantly under review and up-to-date 'by noting when we hear of a death or if a general practitioner comes in and gives information about a name on the list'.

SUMMARY

Doubts about the reliability of the data available on waiting lists, or in population projections, created problems for planning. The greater age and infirmity of residents in recent years led officials to think that turnover might be changing, but they had not measured this.

[1] Presumably a reference to the 1963 annual report of the Scottish Home and Health Department, though the comment could refer to the earlier work of a committee of the Scottish Health Services Council.

Forecasting need consisted of straight projections proportional to population growth in some authorities, and had been reduced to a standard, routine operation by using nationally derived formulae in others. Two authorities had made more sophisticated attempts to estimate future needs.

Most authorities believed that planning was doomed to failure because of lack of skill, time, information or inclination; or believed that it was irrelevant because of other over-riding circumstances, such as desperate shortage of places, or political decisions uninfluenced by technical advice.

In Scotland, there was also little evidence of careful planning for the required number of places in residential accommodation for elderly people in the future. A variety of reasons were given: spare capacity at present; desperate shortage at present; intimate local knowledge of individuals replacing calculations in terms of groups; and the inappropriate application in a particular area of a central department norm.

When England and Scotland were compared, it appeared that attitudes to planning were not very different, despite the fact that English local authorities were required to make forecasts over a 10-year period and the Scottish authorities were not. In a number of case study authorities the pronouncements of central departments were taken as guidelines for planning purposes even when the statements were received with strong reservations. The main impression is that those concerned with running and providing residential services either did not have the time, or did not have the requisite skills to separate out and measure expressed demand, and need, for places in homes.

CHAPTER 8

SHELTERED HOUSING

There were a small number of sheltered housing schemes in operation in the early fifties, but most schemes were still less than 10 years old in 1965 and, as stated in Chapter 3, not all housing authorities had them. For many authorities, therefore, sheltered housing was still an experiment. In this chapter a consideration of the factors which influenced the decisions of those case study housing authorities with schemes to embark on the experiment is followed by a discussion of how plans to develop the service were formulated. Some of the case study authorities were not planning to develop the service, and their reasons for this are examined.

THE ORIGINS OF WARDEN-SCHEMES

Slightly over half of the 41 case study housing authorities had warden-schemes in operation, and 5 or 6 more had their first schemes in the pipeline. Not all of these authorities could say how their first scheme originated, especially if it started some time ago, as some of the officials interviewed were not working for the same authority at the time. Such evidence as was available showed that several factors came into it, and that the relative importance of different factors varied from area to area.

One of the earliest schemes in Britain was built in the mid-fifties by a rural district council in one of the counties visited. The county welfare officer said that the initiative was taken by the rural district council (which was not a case study housing authority) and that it had learned of the idea from a housing authority in a neighbouring county. The county supported the idea by making a grant of £30 per dwelling, and also wrote to all district councils in its area 'saying that it was a good idea and that the county was prepared to help'.

Several housing authorities said that they had learned of the idea from other authorities, and that officials and councillors had visited schemes in other areas. Often the first scheme was built on the strength of sheltered housing being 'a good idea' which was worth trying. One district council official said: 'The question of building the scheme went through without debate. There was no argument about whether they were needed or anything like that.' In another area, councillors had actively opposed the idea on the grounds that grouped dwellings were not suitable for a rural area. The policy seemed to be about to change because: 'One vociferous member of the council in the past objected to warden-schemes, but recently he visited another local authority's scheme and was very taken with the idea, so now he thinks we ought to do something.' In a municipal borough which started to develop sheltered housing about 1959, and had several schemes by 1965, much of the impetus seemed to have come from a strong and enthusiastic housing committee chairman.

In England most of the counties visited had taken some initiative in getting district councils to consider sheltered housing, and there was much activity of this kind in the late fifties, perhaps because the passing of the 1958 Local Government Act drew attention to the counties' powers to contribute towards the cost of sheltered housing, and because after 1958 these powers could be used without Ministerial approval. In the county mentioned earlier the response to the letter sent to district councils in the mid-fifties was limited, and so in about 1958 or 1959 the district councils were invited to a conference to discuss progress and the financial problems of providing sheltered housing. In another county the welfare officer had visited district councils to discuss sheltered housing and said that he knew that two conferences had been held on the subject before he took up his post 7 years previously. In a third county the health and welfare committee chairman had met representatives from housing authorities and encouraged them to think about sheltered housing, and in a fourth county the county clerk had called a meeting. In other cases the welfare officer had tried to encourage development by making personal contact with district council officials.

A few housing authorities mentioned the central departments' policies of encouraging the development of sheltered housing as a factor which had led them to consider the idea. This factor was stressed rather more in Wales than in England, and some of the Scottish authorities had started to think about sheltered housing as a result of a meeting arranged by the (then) Department of Health for Scotland. The available evidence is slight, but suggests that the Welsh Office and the Scottish Office perhaps play a role which is more often assumed by the county councils in England. However, Welsh and (since the 1964 Housing Act) Scottish county councils have the same powers as English counties to contribute to the cost of sheltered housing, and for this reason they probably had some influence on development of the service (see also Chapter 17).

The case studies provided a number of examples of first warden-schemes originating as the result of a chance conversation between a county official and a district council official. A scheme under construction in a Scottish small burgh was said to have originated 'quite by accident. The county medical officer (head of a joint health and welfare department) came to the burgh to discuss sites for a welfare home for the frail elderly, and during his visit we got talking about old people who were not so bad as to need residential accommodation, and the idea grew from there.' In some English counties the suggestion of building a scheme linked with a welfare home had originally been made by the architect, who was interested in making the best possible use of the land available on a particular site. The opportunity for such a suggestion occurred in the course of co-operation between county architects, welfare officers and district councils over finding sites for welfare homes. Sometimes a county borough architect had also suggested a scheme linked with a welfare home to colleagues in the welfare and housing departments.

One county borough acquired a warden-scheme as a result of a boundary change and was considering the provision of more. Whether or not the acquisition of one scheme was the cause of the policy change is difficult to judge, because there had been changes in local authority personnel at the same time.

There was little evidence in English and Welsh case study authorities that requests for plans for sheltered housing when the ten-year plans were revised had much influence on decisions to introduce sheltered housing for the first time. In one authority where it appeared as though 10-year planning did have a direct influence, the story turned out to be much more complex. There had been a proposal for sheltered housing linked with a welfare home (a former public assistance institution) at least 10 years previously. Some bungalows were in fact built but were let by the housing committee, and liaison with the welfare home never developed for reasons which no one clearly remembered. There was still land available, and a second proposal was made, this time for a block of flatlets linked with the welfare home. The first plans for this scheme foundered on disagreements over the need for a lift in a two storey building, and a second set of plans on a problem over the site layout. A third set of plans were said to have been 'a nice design', but the Ministry of Housing and Local Government had said that there would be too many people in the building, and so the architect had to start again. Meantime the dispute about the need for a lift continued, with the welfare officer holding firm to his view that a lift was necessary. As well as opposition from the welfare committee, the Ministry of Housing and Local

Government were opposed to the lift and said that the welfare officer was thinking of the wrong type of resident. Eventually it was decided to have a joint meeting of representatives of the local authority, the Ministry of Housing and Local Government and the Ministry of Health to try to resolve these problems. When the request came for proposals for sheltered housing for the revision of the ten-year plans, the welfare officer included figures for flatlets, but the question of sheltered housing then became entangled with the question of whether or not the former public assistance institution was to be replaced, and at one point the Ministry was threatening to withhold loan sanction for sheltered housing in order to exert pressure on the local authority to replace the institution. Thus the story of sheltered housing in this area began long before the ten-year plans, and at one stage it looked as though the ten-year plans might actually delay the provision of sheltered housing still further, rather than expedite it.

Thus the origins of sheltered housing varied considerably between authorities and were rarely, if at all, associated with any measurement of need for the service. The ten-year plans did not appear, in the case study authorities, to have inspired decisions to provide this service for the first time.

PLANS FOR DEVELOPMENT OF SHELTERED HOUSING

About a quarter of the case study housing authorities definitely intended to expand the provision of sheltered housing, and these were nearly all authorities which already had higher levels of provision.

The way these authorities formulated their plans varied. Some planned to provide so many units of sheltered housing a year as part of their general housing programme, as, for example, a county borough in which the number of units of sheltered housing represented 10% of the total number of houses to be provided each year. Other authorities conceived their plans in terms of providing a sheltered housing scheme for each part of their area. The housing manager of a municipal borough with three schemes in operation and a fourth under construction said: 'A fifth scheme for the south of the borough is in the pipeline, and there is talk of a sixth scheme for the north-west area of the town. The borough is planning ahead.' In a rural district, officials explained how they planned on a parish basis. 'We look at the size of the parish and allow that sometimes we will have to group parishes. We (housing manager and town clerk) do joint reports on ways of grouping the parishes into larger units. We try to work it so that we will build a minimum of 8 dwellings, but we like to get 12 dwellings to a scheme if we can.'

A few authorities referred to attempts to estimate the extent of need for sheltered housing. The welfare officer of an English county said that one municipal borough (not a case study) in his area had, in response to his request for information on proposals for sheltered housing for inclusion in the ten-year plan, asked if he would do a survey to see if there was need for sheltered housing in that area. The county welfare officer did not think a survey was really necessary to establish that there was need, as it was well known that old people lived in poor housing. Nevertheless, he co-operated with the borough in contacting district nurses, general practitioners, social workers and voluntary organizations to ask if they knew of old people living in housing conditions which were unsatisfactory in relation to their age and ability to cope. In this way 77 names were collected, some of which were already on the housing list. The welfare officer of a county borough which was just about to embark on the provision of warden-schemes was studying the reasons for admission to residential accommodation over a period of one year to see how far housing conditions were a precipitating factor, hoping that this would help to indicate the level of need for sheltered housing.

The public health inspector of a rural district council explained that in his area every parish council had been asked to consider whether there was a need for a warden-scheme in their parish, and if so, to submit names to the district council. Some parishes did this, others did not. Eventually the rural district council decided that 4 of the schemes submitted were reasonable, and these went ahead. The public health inspector thought that other villages might have equal need, but their parish councils had been slow and not submitted a scheme. He added that the numbers on the housing waiting list were well below those on the parish council lists, because many people did not put their name down until something was going to be built in their village.

When asked to submit figures to the county welfare department for the ten-year plans required by the Ministry of Health, this rural district council offered what the public health inspector described as 'an intelligent guess'. He took the parish council lists and checked them with the housing waiting list, allowing for the number of older households known to be underoccupying council houses. Next he tried to allow for what might happen in the next 10 years. One factor was that the proportion of old people in the population was increasing faster in the rural areas because of depopulation, but then two projected new industrial developments would swing the trend the other way. Another factor which he thought relevant to population trends, but difficult to measure, was that private development of housing was beginning to pick up 'as the status value attached to living in the country is beginning to show an effect'.

A few other district councils said they had tried to forecast what sheltered housing they would be providing in response to the county council request for figures to submit to the Ministry. Other authorities said that the only figures which went to the county council were the figures supplied with the application for the welfare grant. These figures had the merit of being realistic, in the sense that the schemes would certainly be built, but the figures were not an estimate of total need for the service. A few district council and municipal borough officials said they did not recall being asked by the county for figures for the ten-year plans, although this might have been because the request for figures was dealt with by an official who was not interviewed in the course of this study.

Some housing officials made the point that their housing programmes were submitted to the Ministry of Housing and Local Government, and it was not clear to them why the Ministry of Health was also asking for housing figures. A rural district council suggested that it would have been better if the two central departments had worked something out together.

There had been little discussion between housing authorities and county welfare or health officials on how to estimate the need for sheltered housing. A county official said that estimating housing needs was the housing authorities' job, since they knew how many people they had to rehouse. A welfare official in another county thought the housing authorities might have a formula from the Ministry of Housing and Local Government to help them in planning, because otherwise they would not know what to build. Another county welfare official expressed regret that there had been no talks in connection with the ten-year plans. He said that the welfare department had gone to a lot of trouble to try to estimate needs for its own services, and yet they just accepted whatever figures the housing authorities sent in.

A rural district council official also expressed regret that there had been no discussion about the basis for the figures for the ten-year plan. He said that the county had merely asked for figures, and could not possibly know whether the figures were right in relation to needs, or whether the county welfare department's estimate of need for residential accommodation was right in relation to the figures for sheltered housing, unless there was discussion about what assumptions were being made when assessing needs.

139

It seems that while welfare officers had taken some of the initiative in trying to encourage housing authorities to experiment with warden-schemes they were less sure that they should be involved in the details of policy formulation.

In some county boroughs there had been discussions between housing and welfare officials, welfare officer and architect, welfare officer and medical officer of health, but in others there had been no contact. One welfare officer said: 'Sheltered housing is so serious a problem that we all ought to have got together, but none of us have been asked to do anything. The initiative is surely the town clerk's.' Thus, even where health, welfare and housing services were all the responsibility of one authority, the discussion of issues involving more than one department took place only if someone took the initiative to organize it.

As well as the case study authorities with definite plans for expansion of sheltered housing there were about a dozen others who said in general terms that they expected to provide sheltered housing in the future. Some of these had only recently opened, and some were still designing or building their first scheme. As described in the first part of this chapter, estimates of the extent of need for sheltered housing were not normally a factor influencing the decision to experiment with this service, and this helps to explain why authorities just embarking on the experiment were not yet planning beyond the first scheme.

A few other authorities with no definite plans at the time of the case study visits were small housing authorities with no continuing general housing programme. Some of these already had well established warden-schemes and said that they would probably provide more next time they built some houses. One small authority said, for example, that the timing of the next scheme, and the number of dwellings, depended on when a suitable site could be found.

RESERVATIONS ABOUT SHELTERED HOUSING

Three or four authorities which had provided one or more schemes were not proposing to build any more. In addition, about a quarter of the housing authorities visited had not provided sheltered housing and had no definite plans for doing so. The reasons given varied.

A few authorities were not convinced of the need for this service. For example, the engineer of a Scottish small burgh explained: 'Suggestions for sheltered housing are made every so often. Invariably some interested citizens suggest there is a need and approach the councillors, but so far the council have not thought the need to be great enough.'

The council of another small burgh which had built 28 special houses for old people (30·7 per thousand elderly population) did not think it necessary to employ a warden because all the tenants were able-bodied. It was realized that this situation might change, and that at some future date the council might have to consider appointing a warden and installing an intercommunication system. This particular scheme, the plans for which originally included a community centre which was abandoned because of the cost, was planned before the 1964 Housing (Scotland) Act which gave Scottish welfare authorities the power to contribute towards the cost of welfare facilities in housing schemes for old people, and this might have affected the situation.

Another reason given by the surveyor and housing manager of an English rural district was that the people in their villages were not keen on the idea of warden-schemes. 'In about 1959 the council went into the question. The district was canvassed, and people on the housing list were asked about it. They thought it would be too much like the old poor law institution, and wanted their own home to be free from interference. The council could not get them to see that the idea of supervision was so that someone would know if something went wrong. The people also did not like the idea of a common room, and said they preferred to talk in their own houses.' This authority had been building specially designed houses for old people since the early 1950's and had about 60 of these (32·0 per thousand elderly population).

Most large urban authorities put forward the view that it was better to build small dwellings for the elderly in amongst other housing than to create large colonies of old people. This belief seemed to arise partly from a feeling that it was depressing for old people to be herded together, and partly from the idea that old people in colonies would be more dependent on social services than if they lived amongst younger families.

A county borough with two schemes said that in future they planned to integrate old people into the housing estates. By infilling existing estates with small dwellings they would be able to rehouse older people wanting to move from larger houses without disturbing their social contacts. In allocating dwellings they tried to house people near elderly relatives.

A few other authorities referred to attempts to rehouse old people near younger relatives whenever possible, although many found difficulties in achieving this aim because they had to work within

141

the framework of an allocation system geared to meet a different set of priorities.

According to some case study authorities the Ministry of Housing and Local Government did not approve of colonies of old people.[1] In one area the welfare officer had suggested building bungalows near a welfare home in the early fifties, but the Ministry had not been in favour. The scheme was abandoned, and no alternative kind of warden-scheme was suggested for many years.

In a few cases, doubts about colonies were based on first-hand experience. One county borough described its experience with an estate of over 200 dwellings built for old people several years ago. So many problems arose, some of them because people could not collect their pensions, that eventually it was decided that the welfare department should provide a warden-service. A married couple were employed as 'resident welfare attendants', together with 4 part-time assistants. Although all 200 dwellings were counted as sheltered housing, the welfare officer said that only about 70 of the residents were under warden surveillance at any one time.

However, whether or not it is the size of the colony which leads to social problems is open to question. The first warden-scheme in a municipal borough also originated because problems arose in a group of only 18 old people's dwellings. The housing manager said: 'The old people were reasonably active when they moved in. The danger is that we assume they stay that way and forget that they are growing older. There were one or two tragedies, for example one lady who fell and broke her leg and lay for a long time before she was found, and a man who set fire to his pyjamas, so eventually we let a vacant bungalow to the county council at a peppercorn rent for a warden whom they pay. A bell system was put in later.'

To some extent the arguments against grouping old people's dwellings were bound up with views about the number of dwellings needed before the cost of employing a warden is justified. Most urban authorities were thinking in terms of groups of 30 dwellings, although some talked of groups of 60. In some rural areas the problem was to find enough old people for a grouped scheme. One rural district council did have a warden-scheme with only 2 dwellings and a Scottish county had schemes with 6 units, but most thought that at least 12 were needed to justify the employment of a warden, and some referred to pressure from county welfare departments to increase the

---

[1] The Ministry's view in 1968 was that it wholeheartedly approved of grouped schemes and its only reservations related to size—over 30 dwellings—or to linking schemes with large residential homes.

size of schemes where the county was contributing towards the cost of welfare services.

Some authorities resolved the dilemma of how to justify the cost of a warden without creating a colony by appointing as warden one of the younger old people resident in the scheme. One county borough, for example, had 8 blocks of 8 flats, and one resident in each was paid as a warden. Some rural authorities had also adopted this solution for schemes of about 8 units.

Several rural authorities said that it was undesirable to uproot people from their own villages to go to a grouped scheme, since although they gained the advantages of a warden-service, they lost some of the support and friendship of neighbours and perhaps relatives. Smaller groups of specially designed houses could more easily be provided in people's own villages.

A few authorities attached less weight to the argument that it is better to provide for old people in their own villages. Officers in a rural district council and in a Scottish county landward area said old people were only too glad to move if there was the chance of modern housing, but this seemed to be more a matter of willingness to move from an isolated cottage into a village, to both better housing and better facilities for shopping. The considerations here might well be different from those of the villager moving to another village. Certainly, during a visit to one sheltered housing scheme, a lady asked the public health inspector whether a scheme was going to be built in the village to which she belonged, because although she liked her flat she would like to be in her own village 5 miles away. On the other hand, when an elderly lady in another rural area made much the same comment, it was clear from the rest of the conversation that two of the old friends she said she missed had either died or moved away, and her son had recently married and moved further away, so that her social relationships would have changed anyway.

Some authorities based their reservations about warden-schemes on the difficulties experienced with schemes already provided. A housing manager said: 'There are no more schemes in the pipeline, and there shouldn't be, considering the difficulty I have had in finding clients. I could make one replacement but if two came empty I'd be scraping the barrel. In addition to the 23 we got, we had 40 refusals of offers. This was despite the fact that a lot of these people were living in places with primitive sanitation facilities.' He had not advertised in order to try to let the flatlets, but he had looked through the housing list, asked the medical officer of health, district nurses and local general practitioners to see if they knew of anyone. In the end 3 of the 4 upstairs flatlets in the scheme had been let to young schoolteachers.

Letting difficulties were not uncommon, even in authorities which were planning to provide more sheltered housing. It had taken the housing manager of a municipal borough 60 visits to get 30 applications for the first flatlet scheme because people had got the wrong idea about it. In a county borough, housing department staff had discussions with 120 people before they could let the 24 flatlets in their first scheme. This was partly because the housing department was looking for appropriate people as tenants, appropriate being defined as people who 'had a housing need, were of the right temperament, and with a reasonable standard'. A county welfare officer said that one district council had more warden-schemes than they had old people to put in them, and criticized them for overproviding. Yet he admitted that there were old people who fulfilled the county's requirements (for payment of welfare grant) of being over seventy or being physically infirm or handicapped, but whom the district council would not take because they had not been on the waiting list for two years, or because they lived just over the district council boundary. Thus some letting difficulties were due to the fact that authorities continued to operate a system of eligibility which was originally designed for quite different purposes.

Other letting difficulties arose because of design features in some schemes. Some old people preferred a self-contained flat, and fears that shared bathrooms and w.c.s would not be kept spotlessly clean were cited by one housing manager as reasons why nobody was clamouring for the flatlets, even though tenants liked them once they were there. Attempts to publicize the flatlets through a show in the local press of photographs of the flatlets with the residents 'looking happy' did not appear to have reduced their unpopularity.

Another difficulty which had deterred a few from planning more schemes but had not deterred others, was that of recruiting wardens. One rural district had been discouraged by the experience of its first scheme. The first warden had found herself shouldering the burden of nursing an elderly resident who had been taken ill. Eventually the warden herself became ill and resigned, and it had not been possible to replace her. The surveyor (there was no separate housing manager) had told the warden it was not her job to nurse the old lady but he had at the time no answer to the warden's question: 'What happens when I am left with her?' When the warden left the problem was taken up with the county welfare officer in an attempt to work out a solution before another appointment was made. The solution seemed to be going to take the lines of defining the warden's duties more clearly and increasing the pay, which would not really solve the original problem. The home nursing or night-sitting services provided by the joint health and welfare authority were not mentioned.

Another housing manager described the great strain on a warden of having a bed-ridden resident to care for, even though the medical officer of health had supplied domiciliary services, and this was one of the few areas where some services were available at weekends. This housing manager thought that warden-schemes might work better when they had been going longer, because there would be a better spread of ages and the younger old people would be less dependent. This raises questions about allocation criteria for sheltered housing schemes. The point was made by another housing manager that if you allocated all the houses to the over-eighties you were asking for problems with wardens.

The matron of an old people's home who acted as warden for 18 bungalows nearby pointed out that taking meals out to any of the bungalow tenants who were ill took up a considerable amount of staff time, and that pressures were greatest in winter when the residents of the home also needed more attention. This problem had been solved by taking on two part-time bungalow attendants, to work on alternate days for an hour in the morning, an hour at lunch-time and half an hour in the evening. They reported to the matron if a doctor or medicines were needed, telephoned relatives of the tenants, and carried lunches over to the bungalows. The health department provided home nurses or home helps to those tenants who needed them.

Another problem mentioned was that tragedies could still happen even when old people were living in a scheme with a trained nurse as warden and a call-bell or inter-communication system. Three such incidents described by case study authorities demonstrated all too clearly that one cannot insure old people against every risk, whatever facilities are provided. Such incidents can be very damaging to the morale of the wardens. However, while tragedies made people stop to think, they did not necessarily turn them against warden-schemes.

Other problems over wardens were perhaps of a more transitional nature. Some old people made unreasonable demands on the warden at first through not understanding what her duties were, but this type of problem was usually solved by a tactful explanation.

One authority had only one application for the first warden's post, but thought that this was because it was a new thing. A rural district had little difficulty in filling the first post, but was unable to fill the second. In spite of this, there were plans for two further warden-schemes. This optimism seemed justified in the light of the experience of a housing manager who said that although he had a very poor response to advertisements for wardens at one time, he was now getting a good response. That this housing manager was no longer having difficulty in recruiting wardens may have been partly because, with three or four schemes in operation in a relatively densely populated urban area, it was possible to employ a relief warden who relieved in each scheme one day a week, and partly because a good deal of thought had been given by this authority to training wardens, and giving them support in their work. There is a further discussion of factors affecting the recruitment of wardens in Chapters 13 and 14.

A further reason why some authorities were not planning to develop sheltered housing was that some had other arrangements fulfilling a similar purpose.

Several of the urban authorities with blocks of multi-storey flats employed resident caretakers, who were not usually counted as wardens because they had no specified duties relating to old people. Nevertheless one housing manager used the terms 'warden' and 'caretaker' interchangeably, and another commented that in his previous local authority there was an alarm-bell system connecting old people's flats with the caretaker, who had a pass key. Such an arrangement was suggested by a councillor in one case study authority, although no action had been taken. One housing manager commented that his caretakers in multi-storey blocks kept an eye open for signs of anything going wrong if they had old people among the residents in their block. Another housing manager explained: 'If I have doubts about the ability of an old person I am rehousing to manage independently I would ask the welfare officer to look at them. If he said rehouse, I would rehouse them in a flat because there are caretakers in the blocks who can keep an eye on them. The caretaker keeps a card with the address of the relatives, and he would collect pensions. We do not *tell* old people that we will do all this for them, because they so easily grow dependent on you, but our caretakers and collectors are prepared to do it. They live on the site and know the people.' By housing some old people in a block of flats and regarding the caretaker as a warden some authorities considered that they were making adequate arrangements.

Two Scottish small burghs had schemes similar to warden-schemes. In one there was a row of old people's bungalows opposite a park-keeper's house. The bungalows were equipped with a flashing light warning system, and the park-keeper had been instructed to keep a look-out and call help when needed. In the other there was a voluntary street-warden-scheme covering about three-fifths of the town. This service was organized by the county welfare department, and was not confined to council house tenants. A number of old people in this town also had flashing lights installed in their houses under a scheme organized by a voluntary organization.

One county borough ran a home-warden service as part of the home help service. At the end of 1965 it employed 25 senior home helps as home-wardens, and they were visiting 748 cases. 680 of these cases were also receiving home help, but the home-wardens called daily and provided some help with cooking, shopping and personal care. This service was provided in various types of housing, private and local authority, old and new, but was not included as part of the provision of sheltered housing in the ten-year plan return. If it had been, the figure for persons covered by warden-services per thousand elderly population for that authority would have been approximately 16 instead of 4.

It could be argued that the home-warden scheme just described should not rank as sheltered housing because some old people receiving the service were living in old inadequate housing. However, in one county with a very high rate of provision of sheltered housing, some of the dwellings covered were not specially built for old people. Since 1964 this county and its constituent housing authorities have returned very high figures for sheltered housing, as the county obtained powers under a Local Act to contribute towards the cost of wardens appointed by housing authorities to cover old people living in private housing. Already in early 1966, one of the district councils in this county had received approval for 4 schemes of approximately 25 units each, and this raised its figure of 59·2 units per thousand elderly population to 175·4. These examples of other ways of organizing a service underline one of the fundamental questions about sheltered housing. Is it the small specially designed modern housing or the provision of a warden-service which is the important feature? Not all old people need both.

SUMMARY

Factors which influenced housing authorities to embark on their first sheltered housing scheme included contact with other housing authorities, encouragement by county councils and central government departments, and chance conversations between officials who had met to discuss other matters. The first scheme was usually thought of as an experiment with what seemed to be 'a good idea', and the decision to give it a trial was not related to estimates of the extent of need for the service.

Authorities with definite plans for expansion of sheltered housing tended to be those with higher levels of provision already. Only a few authorities had seriously attempted to estimate the extent of need for the service, and to project the estimates.

This had sometimes been done in response to the Ministry of Health's request for plans, but some housing authorities were not clear why the Ministry of Health and the Ministry of Housing and Local Government were both asking for plans for old people's housing.

There had been little discussion between housing and welfare officers in counties of the basis on which need for sheltered housing should be estimated, and on the relationship between plans for sheltered housing and residential accommodation. Discussions between some of the officials concerned had taken place in about half of the county boroughs. Most authorities embarking on the experiment for the first time had not reached the stage of thinking beyond the first scheme.

Of the authorities who were not planning to have warden-schemes, some were not convinced of the need, or that old people would like them. The strong conviction that it was undesirable socially to create colonies of old people in urban areas, or to uproot people from their own villages in rural areas, also militated against development of sheltered housing in some areas. These convictions were sometimes the result of direct experience or a local survey.

Some authorities with schemes had been deterred from further expansion because of letting difficulties or difficulty in recruiting wardens.

The relationship between letting difficulties, criteria of eligibility for council housing, lack of public knowledge of sheltered housing, and poor design, and the relationship between recruitment problems, selection of tenants, and the use of other domiciliary services were not always perceived. Other authorities had experienced similar difficulties, but had devised solutions and had not been deterred from planning to develop the service.

Finally, some authorities had other arrangements which served a similar purpose to sheltered housing. Some arrangements did not involve the provision of new housing, which highlights the question of whether it is the housing or the warden-service that is the important feature of sheltered housing.

CHAPTER 9

LOCAL AUTHORITY HOUSING
PROGRAMMES AND PLANS FOR
THE ELDERLY

All the authorities visited provided some housing for old people, whether or not they provided sheltered housing. In recent years provision for the elderly had increased in many areas, and the case studies provided illustrations of how and why the policy changed. Following this the ways in which local authorities estimated total housing needs from their knowledge of waiting lists, slum clearance areas, under-occupation of large council houses, and housing surveys are discussed. Plans for future provision for old people were formulated as part of a total housing programme, and it is only by examining the way in which total housing needs were estimated that it can be seen whether or not the housing needs of the elderly were adequately taken into account.

LOCAL POLICIES ON THE PROPORTION OF SMALL HOUSES

Although not all one bedroom dwellings were allocated to old people, and some larger dwellings were, the change in the proportion of one bedroom dwellings built by local authorities throughout Britain between the late fifties and the mid sixties was in part a reflection of their recognition of the housing needs of the elderly.

Many case study authorities said there had been a definite change of policy. A county borough housing manager said: 'For 10 years I begged the Corporation to stop building family houses because I could see from the waiting lists that we were going to be grossly overstocked with larger houses. About 5 years ago they took heed. They stopped building altogether for 6 months and took stock. Then they went on to small dwellings and stuck to this.'

It was a similar story in many other areas, although the date of change varied. A Scottish large burgh started building specially for old people in 1952, but mostly the changes in policy took place in the late fifties or early sixties.

149

Some authorities commented that it was central government policy to concentrate on family houses until about 1954. The redefinition of categories of housing need had sometimes been precipitated by changes in central government policy, and led to increases in the proportion of small houses built. In addition, one rural district said that for a time in the late fifties it had built only for old people because it could only get a subsidy for that and for slum clearance.

Occasionally the timing of the change was influenced by a chance conversation. A housing manager said: 'One day the architect telephoned and said if he put 60 one bedroom flats on a site he was to build on could I let them? I said I could let them three times over. The architect says he has often thought about this since, because at first he didn't believe me, and yet I was right.'

Although by the time this study was undertaken it was customary in most areas for the architect to take advice from the housing department about the proportions of different sizes of dwelling required, one or two housing managers remarked that this had not always been so. 'The architect would come up with a scheme which the council would accept. The proportions of dwellings of different sizes was known only to the architect and you tended to get estates developed that were not balanced. Some were solidly three bedroom houses. Perhaps it was alright then because housing needs were different . . . Now the architect's department appreciates that the housing manager has an essential part to play in advising on the type of property . . . Now there is early consultation with both the architect and the planning department.' That there were still weaknesses in communication between departments was illustrated by a county borough architect who said he imagined (wrongly, as it turned out) that it was the welfare committee which advised the housing committee about the proportion of small dwellings needed for old people.

The scale of the change in policy also varied. Some authorities changed from building about 5% one bedroom to 25–30%, but one had only changed to 10%.

The housing manager of a Scottish large burgh was recommending that 'a reasonable balance' between the various sizes of house should be established throughout the burgh. 'It would appear that, to meet the increasing need for small houses suitable for the aged, 35% of all houses in the burgh need to be of one or two apartments.' In another large burgh the housing manager said that the welfare officer thought that 15% small houses would be the desirable overall average, this having been the figure discussed at a welfare conference.

Other authorities, especially some of the smaller ones, had not had such a definite change in policy. They decided the proportion for each scheme as it came along, but said that in general they were providing some dwellings for the elderly in each scheme.

Thus the housing needs of the elderly were undoubtedly taken into account more in the mid sixties then they had been in the early post-war years, but how adequately depended on how well the needs of the elderly showed up in the information on which local authorities based their estimates of need.

WAITING LISTS AS A BASIS FOR PLANS

Almost all the authorities visited said that the waiting list of applicants for local authority housing was an important source of information, although its relative importance varied from area to area. At one extreme were the small district council which 'plans to deal with the waiting list', and a small municipal borough which claimed that 'the waiting list is the register of need in the area'. Two district councils and a county borough said that the waiting list was the main factor on which policy was based, but that other things, such as slum clearance, were relevant. Only three of the authorities visited said that the waiting list of applicants was not a major influence on policy. One of these was a county borough with a heavy slum clearance programme, and its housing policy was confined to dealing with this. The second was a sparsely populated Scottish county which did not keep a waiting list except for one small part of its area. The third was a small district council which doubted whether the waiting list was a guide to what it should build because it wanted to increase the town's population and rateable value.

Most of the authorities commented that the waiting list quickly became out of date as a register of unsatisfied demand, and consequently they reviewed the list at regular intervals. The frequency of review varied. One urban district council carried out a review every six months, whereas at the other extreme another urban district council and a Scottish large burgh reviewed their lists only every five years. Annual or biennial reviews were the most common. Reviews were carried out by post, and anyone not returning the card was struck off the list. A county borough housing manager remarked that up to 40% of applicants might disappear at a review, but a few weeks later a lot of them wanted to be put back on the waiting list. Some authorities tried to cut down the size of the non-response factor by sending reminders before striking names off the list. Others put non-responders into a 'dead' file but reinstated them in their former position on the list when they re-applied.

None of the authorities commented on the type of applicant who did not return the card at a review, so it was not known whether old people formed an important proportion of the group. One county borough had divided its waiting list into various categories of priority, and replaced the system of postal reviews by the practice of visiting people in the higher priority groups to bring the information up-to-date, hoping that this would reduce the non-response factor.

More than half of the case study authorities kept a separate waiting list for old people, or marked applications so that those from old people were easily distinguished. It had not always been the practice to do this, and there were still a few housing authorities which did not know how many of the applicants on the list were old people. A rural district council offered a guess that the proportion would be about a fifth, and an urban district council thought it would be about a tenth. Most authorities could have found out by going through the application forms, but at least two authorities did not have the date of birth of the applicant on the application form unless the application was for a bungalow. While bungalows in these areas were mainly for old people, both authorities already had other small dwellings for old people, and for planning purposes it cannot be assumed that all old people applying would ask to go on to the bungalow lists.

Even if the waiting list is kept up-to-date, and applications from old people are identifiable, there are still serious limitations to the waiting list as a measure of housing need.

One major limitation is that some housing authorities restrict eligibility for council housing, and do not always review these restrictions to take account of changed circumstances. About half of the housing authorities visited did not accept people on to the list unless they lived or worked in the area. As most elderly people are retired, for them this means living within the area. In areas where the period of residence required is short, an elderly person wanting to live in an area because they have previous connections with it, or because they have relatives living there, can qualify for the waiting list by going to live with friends or relatives for a short time. If the waiting time for a house is also short, this solution may be satisfactory. However, in several areas residence for anything from 1–30 years was necessary to qualify for the list, and the time between going on to the list and being rehoused might also be several years. In general, the longest periods of residence requirements were in areas which considered they had a serious housing problem, and as their housing situation improved the length of the qualifying period was reduced. One Scottish large burgh was considering reducing it from 10 to 7 years, and a Scottish small burgh had reduced it from 5 to 2 years. However, a county borough, which would have been regarded as having a serious housing problem whatever the measure used, had a qualifying period of only one year, although the time waited before being rehoused was several years for most people.

Two seaside towns, one a county borough and one an urban district, pointed out that they needed their three years' residence qualification as a rationing system because people tended to retire there. If they accepted people on to the list too easily it might lead to pressure to increase the total size of the housing programme which could mean less being done for other services. A more serious objection raised by these two authorities was that if housing policy were such that it facilitated retirement to their area, their population structure would become even more weighted by the older age groups than it was already, (17·6% and 18·1% in 1961, compared with 12% for England and Wales) and this had economic and social implications.

A municipal borough admitted that they should accept applications from people in other areas, and the housing manager of a small county borough said that he would like to take old people wanting to come back to a place they had associations with but that there were too many other demands for housing from within the town. The housing manager of a large municipal borough said she felt very sorry for old people who left her area to go to live with relatives and then wanted to come back because it did not work out. By moving away they upset their chances of qualifying for a council house.

A few of the county boroughs with a residence bar made exceptions in the case of former residents or people born in the area, and a municipal borough took former residents on to the list provided they had left the town within the last 10 years.

About a sixth of the housing authorities visited accepted non-residents on to the waiting list but did not rehouse them. This group of authorities included a county borough, a municipal borough, a large burgh, a rural district, and some small burghs. Two small burghs were prepared to rehouse non-residents after a qualifying period on the list, 3 years in one case, and in the other, 5 years for ordinary applicants and 10 years for old people's bungalows. In the other areas rehousing of non-residents was not being considered, although exceptions were made in individual cases. The usefulness of accepting on to the list people who were not to be rehoused was that it gave information which could be useful for planning.

About a fifth of the housing authorities both accepted non-residents on to the list and did consider them for rehousing. This group of authorities included a county borough, a small burgh, an

153

urban district, three or four rural districts, and a Scottish county. The distinction between this group and the previous group is a fine one, since about half of this group said that they only actually rehoused a very small number of non-residents. The small burgh would rehouse only a former resident wanting to come back to the area to retire, and the urban district said it did not receive many applications from outside. Two of the district councils with no restrictions were situated in a county in which the county council had made it a condition for receipt of the welfare grant for sheltered housing that no residence qualification was imposed for this type of housing. The Scottish county and three of the rural districts did house people from other areas, and the county borough housed outsiders and had recently abolished its residence qualification simply in order to let the houses it had built. One rural district housed non-residents leaving a tied cottage on retirement, or a former resident 'though not if they have been away for 30 years,' but only housed others from what it called 'the deferred list' if there were no suitable local applicants. The other two rural districts said that a substantial proportion of applications came from outside the area, about 25% in one case, and a total very much higher in the other, although the applications from old people tended to be fairly local in origin. Both these authorities explained that if they had an application from an old person not resident in the area but wanting to move there to be near a married daughter the policy was to try to rehouse the old person near the daughter.

Two county boroughs, a rural district and a small burgh, some Conservative and some Labour controlled, operated an income bar as a restriction either at the stage of application or at the stage of allocation. Details of schemes varied, but income bars tended to disqualify families with an income of over £20 to £25 per week. In one area where family size was allowed for, the bar disqualified a family of four with an income of over £20 per week, or a single person with an income of over £8 per week. One of the smaller authorities operated the bar by consulting the building societies and taking as the limit the lowest income which the building societies would accept as a basis for a loan. Another county borough abandoned an income bar at the allocation stage because of difficulties in administering it fairly, and because as income rose, more applicants were affected by it. One housing manager said that the income bar did not affect old people, since their incomes tended to be low. The people most affected were young married couples, especially if both were working and both incomes were counted. Without more factual information it is difficult to judge whether income bars operated to the detriment of old people in need of rehousing.

In many local authorities owner-occupiers were not eligible to apply for council housing, but there were some exceptions. Two municipal boroughs made an exception in the case of sheltered housing. The housing manager of one of them commented that, personally, he thought some people who had been allocated a house in a warden-scheme could have made their own arrangements, but 'this is an unfashionable attitude now.' A Scottish small burgh would rehouse elderly owner-occupiers experiencing physical or financial difficulties in keeping up a large house, but such cases were decided individually by the housing committee. The housing manager of a small municipal borough said that they took applications from elderly owner-occupiers whose houses were too expensive or too big, or who were harassed about property repairs. In the past, such people had not been allocated old people's bungalows, 'but the time is coming when the council will have to consider a policy change. The fact that there are a number of documented applications on the list means that there is a record of demand from this section of the population to help in discussing the policy change, and later, if the policy change is agreed, in settling the house-building programme.'

Overcrowding was still the most important element in the definition of housing needs in many areas. A small burgh said that normally applications were refused if they were from people who were adequately housed, and an elderly person living alone in a six room house was adequately housed by statutory standards. Another authority said: 'There are 147 on the old people's list, of which 26 are "housing needs" cases and 121 are technically not. Most of these others are elderly people underoccupying private accommodation.'

Housing authorities differed in what they classified as poor standard housing and this sometimes acted as a restriction on eligibility. In one of the large county boroughs it was only since 1965 that private tenants living in accommodation lacking the five basic amenities had been eligible to apply for a house. The clerk of a rural district council thought that their waiting list over-emphasized the need for housing because they had applications from tenants of private property who had applied simply because they had not got modern conveniences. This attitude differed from that of the housing manager of a large burgh, who agreed that those whose only claim to consideration for council housing was the desire for a house with a bath, or a kitchenette, had every right to feel frustrated. He argued that, while they must wait until higher priorities were met, the housing authority should make every effort to try to meet these needs.

One or two other restrictions on eligibility were mentioned. One rural authority would not rehouse caravan dwellers. Some local authorities did not accept single people on to the list, although this seemed to be changing. One county borough accepted single women, and a councillor had recently suggested that they should also accept single men. A large burgh was just starting to make provision for single people. The housing manager of a municipal borough explained how she had persuaded the council to agree that middle-aged spinsters and widows should be eligible for rehousing. Hitherto the council had always said that there were plenty of rooms in the town for these people. A few years ago, when the housing manager was new, she argued that such people often did a great deal for the town and it was unfair that they should never have the chance of a place of their own. She added that the middle-aged of today are the old people of tomorrow, and thought that this was also a good reason for providing suitable small housing for them.

Restrictions on eligibility limit the value of the waiting list as a basis for planning and not all local authorities were sufficiently aware of the extent to which the restrictions were inappropriate if the waiting list was to indicate the housing needs of old people.

The waiting list may also be unsatisfactory as a planning tool because, as one housing manager put it, 'people are only eligible if they apply'. Many housing authorities thought it unnecessary to publicize the housing service. A county borough housing manager stated: 'Everybody knows that all local authorities except parishes and counties are housing authorities. Housing gets such wide publicity in the press that everybody must know where to apply if they feel they need a house.' Another county borough housing manager said: 'I don't tout for applications. I assume it is known. If anyone is in straitened circumstances over housing they will have an application in. There has been a service since 1919.' A rural district council official said: 'If they do not apply I assume they are not all that badly off.'

An official in a Scottish small burgh commented that young people would always ask for better living conditions but he was not sure that old people would, because they were very independent. A number of other local authorities thought there would be some hidden needs for housing among the elderly. One or two authorities mentioned particular reasons why some old people would not apply. A county borough housing manager said that the 'distressed gentlefolk' type of elderly person would not apply for a dwelling on a housing estate, but that some of them needed more suitable housing and would apply for a flat in a converted terrace house or mansion in a socially

156

superior residential area of the town. Two county boroughs had converted property of this kind. Another official said he knew from experience in slum clearance areas that there must be a lot of old people living in unsatisfactory conditions, but that old people were prepared to live in these hovels at a rent of 3s.6d. a week, rather than apply for a local authority dwelling at 30s. a week.

Some authorities with large waiting lists already, thought there was no point in encouraging anyone else to apply. However, an example from one of the larger county boroughs illustrated how some people who were eligible did not always apply. In 1965, because the waiting period for certain types of dwelling had been substantially reduced, policy was changed so that private tenants with one or more children whose homes lacked modern amenities, or who were overcrowded, could register on a supplementary waiting list. The publicity associated with setting up the supplementary waiting list led many people who were eligible to register on the ordinary waiting list to do so, and there were more new registrations on the ordinary list in one month than there had been in the whole of the previous year.

Five or six housing authorities commented that supply created demand. In a municipal borough, despite the conviction that news spread adequately by the informal network because it was a small town, the housing manager said that he had been besieged by enquiries after building a scheme of old people's bungalows just off the main road, whereas he had had very few enquiries after another scheme was built because it was situated in a quiet part of the town and was therefore less in the public eye. A small burgh had received a lot of applications for old people's bungalows after two schemes were opened, and this was thought to be 'because the houses are attractive and do not look like local authority houses'. A rural district council with a large scheme under construction had hoped that this scheme would be the end of the council's need to build, but the waiting list had not gone down as parts of the scheme were completed and the houses let. Clearly there was a tendency for demands not to be expressed by the public unless there was some hope of their being met.

Two authorities commented that the fact that some people did not apply until they could see something being built affected the value of the waiting list as a planning tool, but one authority still claimed that the waiting list was a reasonable indicator of need, even though their list tended to stay at the same level, and went up when they started to build.

THE EFFECT OF SLUM CLEARANCE PROGRAMMES

Experience gained from carrying out slum clearance programmes led to an increased awareness of the housing needs of old people in most authorities. A municipal borough housing manager said: 'We learn by our mistakes. About 50% of those to be rehoused from slum clearance areas are old people needing ground floor flats. We found ourselves very short of this kind of accommodation at the time when the first credit squeeze brought municipal housing to its knees and there was a three year slow down.' Another municipal borough found that 20% of its slum clearance list were old people, and estimates of the proportion in the county boroughs ranged from 16–70%. The figures quoted must be treated with caution, since some of them were little more than guesses, although others were based on knowledge gained from surveys of clearance areas.

All types of authority commented that a number of old people had been rehoused because of slum clearance. The housing manager of a municipal borough stressed that, although there were a lot of old people in slum clearance areas, not all of them needed bungalows or sheltered housing. Some just needed small houses, and some had other relatives who wished to live with them.

However, the extent to which old people benefited from the national policy of giving priority to slum clearance varied from area to area. Some authorities had very little planned in the way of slum clearance or redevelopment. This may have been partly because they had few unfit houses, but another point of view was put by the clerk of a Scottish small burgh who said: 'The council has been reluctant to have old people moved out of unfit houses, and so old people are allowed to stay for life.' Authorities responsible for housing in sparsely populated areas faced particular problems in connection with unfit houses lived in by elderly people in isolated farming communities.[1]

Moreover, many local authorities had large numbers of unfit houses to replace, and while some tried to include all their unfit houses in estimates submitted to central departments, others only included what they thought they had reasonable hope of replacing within the next few years.[2] The housing manager of a county borough remarked: 'The health department is dissatisfied with our pro-

[1] Scottish Development Department, *Scotland's Older Houses*, Report by a Sub-committee of the Scottish Housing Advisory Committee, H.M.S.O., 1967, pp. 23–4.
[2] *cf.* Discussion in *Scotland's Older Houses*, *op. cit.*, Chapter 2, pp. 21–6.

gramme, but what is the use of condemning if you cannot rehouse the people?' In another large urban area a local authority official said that just after the war the chief public health inspector did a comprehensive survey, but it was out of date before anything could be done about it. He thought that one could only work so far ahead. In these authorities it would be some time before the housing needs of old people in unfit houses were fully taken into account in planning housing policy.

Other authorities did not investigate the structure of households in clearance areas until shortly before rehousing them, since the information was seen as an adjunct to allocation of dwellings rather than as an aid to planning. Knowledge of the population structure of a clearance area was said by one official to be unimportant in an authority with a reasonable number of houses, and with reasonable proportions of dwellings of different sizes. Thus, there was a tendency to confuse the short-term aim of rehousing people about to be displaced with what should have been the long-term aim of ensuring that the stock of houses did have reasonable proportions of different sizes.

UNDEROCCUPATION OF COUNCIL HOUSES

One local authority started building old people's bungalows because it realized that by rehousing old people from unfit houses in family size houses it was creating underoccupation. Many other authorities had gradually realized that their larger houses were underoccupied by older people whose families had grown up and formed separate households. 14 case study authorities stressed that underoccupation was a major problem in their area, and 9 had carried out surveys to measure its extent. One county borough estimated that well over a quarter of its council houses were underoccupied.

However, knowing the extent of underoccupation did not necessarily lead to policies to reduce it. In only 4 case study authorities was it council policy to require old people underoccupying council houses to move to smaller accommodation. In 3 of these the housing manager said that powers of compulsion were rarely used because there were always more old people wanting to move than there was smaller accommodation available. Other authorities said there was no need for the council to have powers of compulsion. 'There is a long list of people wanting to move from larger houses—both council and private—to smaller houses, and it will be a long time before the council need to think about whether or not to use compulsion.' Two housing managers thought the day might come when compulsory powers would be needed, and one of them qualified his statement that there were enough wanting to move voluntarily by adding: 'Mind you, we did not sit back. The staff of the housing department were briefed, and we opened one block of flats to the public one weekend to let them see what the accommodation was like. We also had notices to publicize the small dwellings.'

A number of authorities did ask or persuade people to move, although there was no compulsion. One official said old people were only too happy to move if you offered good accommodation in the right district at the right rent. Another said old people would move because the rents were lower, but in other areas where small flats were being built in central redevelopment areas the rents were often higher than those for older three bedroom houses in peripheral housing estates. Other housing managers persuaded old people to move by pointing out that there would be less cleaning, or that they could move closer to relatives. In one or two county boroughs the housing department offered help with the cost of removal if people agreed to move to a smaller dwelling.

The distinction between persuasion and compulsion is a fine one. The one authority, a rural district council, which both had compulsory powers and used them, had adopted the following practice. A check on underoccupation was carried out every three years, and people who were approaching pensionable age were warned that in a few years' time they would be expected to move. The housing manager visited, and explained why the council thought it wrong that family size houses should be underoccupied. He told people that special houses were being built for older people, and explained about the warden. Visits to see existing schemes were arranged for those who wanted this. When the time for removal came local authority staff assisted. They helped with packing beforehand, and in the new house they put up the beds and made them, hung curtains and laid carpets. When compulsion was introduced there was some resistance and the housing manager had to be firm, but eventually the policy was accepted, and for the next scheme there were enough volunteers.

More than half of the case study authorities did not use compulsion, persuasion, or inducement of any kind. Several Scottish authorities commented that when people wanted to move, the housing department helped with advice about arranging an exchange, and one large burgh gave high priority to old people underoccupying council houses when allocating new dwellings. Many councils, large and small, rural and urban, Labour and Conservative, had discussed the matter, but decided not to do anything about it because it was thought to be inhuman to ask someone to move. One county borough council even insisted that the housing manager should stop his survey of the extent of underoccupation. Another county borough housing manager said he did not want larger houses freed because he did not have enough small dwellings to put the smaller households in, and even if he had, he could not let the family size houses because there was little demand for them.

Thus, although there was in many areas a known unsatisfied demand for smaller houses from older people who wanted to move, and while some authorities had taken account of this and planned to build higher proportions of small dwellings, a few, including some of the larger county boroughs, seemed to be adjusting only slowly.

SURVEYS OF HOUSING NEED

When asked whether they had carried out any surveys of housing need in their area, many officials responded in terms which indicated that, to them, a survey meant an analysis of the waiting list, or of the population of a slum clearance area, or a study of the extent of under-occupation in council houses. Some referred to surveys carried out by the public health inspector, which were surveys of dwellings rather than of households. A county borough housing manager said that, apart from the survey of underoccupation, he was not aware that there was any other information which would be useful to have. Another large urban authority said that there was neither time nor need for surveys because the waiting list was kept fairly up-to-date. In contrast, the housing manager of a Scottish large burgh recognized that because they relied on the waiting list: 'We get a fortuitous selection of people who *want* houses, not of people who *need* houses.' He had recommended that there should be a housing survey to establish facts on which future policy could be based, but his council rejected the recommendation on the grounds of cost. Other authorities, including a large county borough and a Scottish county, said they had neither the staff nor the time to carry out proper surveys.

A few authorities had made some attempt to find out about latent demand, or to project the future demand for old people's dwellings.

In one Scottish county, in which the council took a policy decision in the late fifties to provide houses for old people, the architect advised the council about the total number of houses to be built, and the medical officer and the public health inspector advised about the proportions of different sizes required in each area. The medical officer of health said he did a population projection, taking into

F   161

account the birth and death rates, and the proportion of old people in the population, in order to arrive at a recommendation about the proportion of small houses which should be built. He added that the results were not completely satisfactory, and that the whole problem was complicated by the lack of a clear policy on the underoccupation issue, but that the approach was a reasonably successful one.

In one county borough the welfare officer referred to an analysis of census data for the area done by an outside research worker. This showed that, in 1961, higher proportions of old people lived in the parts of the town which had fewest local authority dwellings, and that old people living alone were often living in poor quality privately rented accommodation. Other authorities referred to census data in a general way, and one or two commented that the delay before the information was available made it less useful for planning purposes.

SUMMARY

Most case study housing authorities were taking the needs of the elderly into account more than they had done in the early fifties. How adequately they did this varied, depending partly on whether or not there was a good flow of information between the different departments concerned with housing within the local authority, and partly on the quality of the information on which the local authorities based their estimates of need.

The main sources of information about housing needs were the waiting list, knowledge of slum clearance areas, and knowledge of underoccupation in council housing. Much of the information available from waiting lists or lists of people to be rehoused from slum clearance areas was collected as an aid to allocation of houses, not as an aid to planning. Some officials were well aware of the shortcomings of the waiting list as a basis for planning, and some had devised ways of minimising them, for example by distinguishing between eligibility to apply and eligibility to be rehoused. Others had not critically examined waiting lists with both the short-term and the long-term uses of them in mind.

Different local authorities had different policies on what groups in the population they accepted as their responsibility for rehousing, and on priorities for rehousing. These policies were not always sufficiently related to present-day housing needs, especially those of the elderly.

Some local authorities seemed insufficiently aware of the extent to which members of the public denied themselves the chance of getting a council house because they did not know how the system of priorities operated, or because they rated their chances of being rehoused as low. Too much reliance was placed on expressed needs, partly because local authorities did not see the point in seeking out unexpressed needs when there were already more expressed needs than they had resources to provide for.

The very real sympathy for the elderly on the part of both officials and councillors had sometimes delayed the development of policies to help them. The view that it was inhuman to ask an elderly person to move from a large or poor standard house because it had been their home for many years sometimes meant that too little weight was given to building old people's dwellings for those old people who would like to move, if only there were suitable and attractive houses available. A few authorities had more positive policies and had devised solutions to the problems involved.

Many housing managers said they had neither the time nor the staff to do surveys, and some had never had the opportunity to learn the necessary techniques. Some did not see how a survey would help, and others did not see the distinction between surveys of property and surveys of households. Some authorities used census data and had tried to project demand for old people's dwellings.

CHAPTER 10

DOMICILIARY SERVICES—PLANNING TO IMPROVE QUALITY

One factor affecting the need for development of domiciliary services is the adequacy of existing services to meet the needs of those old people already receiving them. The comments made by officials in the case study authorities on shortcomings in the quality of services related to the frequency or amount of service available, the availability of services at special times, such as nights, weekends and holiday times, and to the scope of the service.

FREQUENCY AND AMOUNT OF SERVICES

There appeared to be some variation between case study authorities in the frequency of provision of the home help service, although it was not possible to compare patterns of provision exactly since some home help organizers were not able to produce figures to show the number of cases receiving help on different numbers of days per week. Often such variations as did exist reflected the different needs of old people, some of whom need more help than others. In one area, for example, flexible administration of the service enabled some old people to have help for a half-day twice a week, and others, such as those recently home from hospital, to have help for one hour every day, plus a half-day once a week for cleaning.

However, a few authorities said that they had to restrict the amount of help to a maximum number of hours per person per day. These authorities were in the lower part of the range of net expenditure on home help per thousand population among the case studies. One authority, which was finding it difficult to recruit enough home helps to meet the expressed demand for the service, allowed up to two hours per day. Another authority had originally introduced a restriction in the fifties because of concern over the financial implications of the rapid growth of the service, and the maximum allowed was four hours per day. The limited amount of help met the needs of some old people, but as one home help organizer said: 'The limit of three hours a day is inadequate where the case is totally chairbound or housebound.'

In a few authorities the problem was not so much that the service had to be restricted because of pressure of demand, but that, to quote a medical officer of health: 'The service is adequate in size but inflexibly and unimaginatively administered.' An example was provided by an authority in which a half-day three times a week was the *minimum* which old people could have, although sometimes two old people living near each other received half a morning's help if a whole morning was not needed. The organizer said that she was concerned about the three days a week rule, because there was a demand for the service on only two days a week, and perhaps even once a week for some people who only needed help with shopping and heavy cleaning.

In some areas the frequency and amount of home help was related to the frequency with which the meals-on-wheels service operated. Home helps were provided on weekdays when there was no meals service, or the number of hours was increased on these days to enable the home help to prepare a meal as well as doing other jobs. However, in one county borough where the meals service only operated one day a week this service was not given to people receiving home help.

In discussing the frequency of the meals-on-wheels service a distinction must be made between the number of days in the week when the service operates and the number of days in the week on which an individual obtains a meal. Officials in the case study authorities tended to talk in terms of the former, and often there was little collated information available about the number of days a week on which individuals received meals.

The number of days in the week on which the service operated was highest in two county boroughs in retirement areas where the frequency was four and five times a week. Not surprisingly, these two areas also supplied the highest number of meals per thousand population in the second quarter of 1964. In other case study authorities, the frequency of provision varied between nil in some areas of counties to three times a week. The deputy welfare officer of a large county stressed that one meal per week was not sufficient and thought that 'at least three should be provided, and probably four or five'. One county borough welfare officer said he would 'not be satisfied until it is a seven day service'. However, some welfare officers thought: 'The service must provide coverage, even if it is not terribly effective. Two days everywhere is preferable to five days in one area and none in another. The priority is wide coverage; we can step up from there.'

Frequency of provision often depended on the availability of

165

volunteers, since all meals services started before local authorities' powers were extended in 1962 were perforce voluntary services. Harris found, in 1958, that nearly half the schemes had difficulties in maintaining their level of service because of transport problems or shortage of volunteers. [1] Only one case study authority operated a direct service, and although steps had been taken by six or seven authorities to help solve the problems of cooking meals and transporting them, distribution was still almost entirely dependent on volunteers, who were in short supply in some areas. In one county borough the problem of finding enough voluntary workers to take the meals out was such that the welfare officer often had to send clerks from his office to take the vans round. Manpower shortages in the voluntary services are discussed in Chapter 21.

An alternative form of provision of meals for those who are not housebound, or who can be transported, is the lunch club. Harris pointed out that the delivery of meals was costly in terms of manpower and transport, that the meal itself was not as hot, and that clubs had the additional advantage of providing social contact.[2]

9 case study authorities, including 4 rural counties in Scotland and Wales, had no lunch clubs in their area. Frequency of provision in the 15 authorities which had clubs varied from once or twice a week in some county areas to a daily service in a central area club in one authority where meals were prepared in the civic restaurant.

The frequency and availability of chiropody treatment also varied. Although chiropody was provided in almost all the old people's homes visited, matrons often said it was insufficient. It is again necessary to distinguish between the frequency with which the service is available, and the frequency with which any one individual receives the service. The frequency of the chiropodist's visits to the home tended to be greater, as might be expected, for larger homes than for smaller ones, but the frequency of treatment of an individual could be the same. The figures which some matrons supplied showed variations between authorities on both measures. Thus in one authority, a home with 50 places had three chiropody sessions a month, whereas in another, a similar sized home had one session per three weeks. Individual residents in a home in one area received treatment once in 5 weeks, whereas those in a home in another area received treatment once in 8 weeks, although in both these homes some bad cases received more frequent treatment.

[1] A. I. Harris, *Meals-on-Wheels for Old People*, National Corporation for the Care of Old People, 1960, Tables 86, 87, pp. 80, 81.
[2] *Ibid.*, p. 24.

There was little direct comment from most case study officials on whether chiropody treatment for old people living at home was available at sufficiently frequent intervals. However, waiting lists for chiropody were mentioned by several, and a few explained that it was the practice to spread the service by increasing the intervals between treatments at times when the service was under pressure. This was necessary as a short-run measure while problems of increasing the supply of the service were overcome. At times practical difficulties such as shortage of staff, limited finance, or lack of suitable premises could not be overcome except in the long-run, and in such cases the quality of service inevitably suffered meantime.

Occasionally lags in communication within the local authority contributed to the fall-off in the quality of service. For example, a county borough medical officer said: 'We can do laundry within the day and this is important because old people's stocks of clothes are often so low.' A nursing officer in the same authority said: 'The laundry service is terribly busy now – we could do with more facilities. There is no turning down of requests, just a slower turnover.' Delay in communicating this kind of change to those responsible for recommending action to rectify the situation slows down the development of the service.

The importance of good communications was illustrated by the example of one authority (and this was not altogether untypical), in which the home help organizer regarded it as a challenge to her efficiency to manage to run the service on the budget allocation for the year. She succeeded in staying within the limits by paring down the quality of the service, while not refusing help to anyone needing it. To ask the medical officer of health for a supplementary estimate seemed to her to be an admission of failure. This had made for slow development of the service until the medical officer of health realized what was happening and took steps to overcome the problem.

On the other hand, in one of the larger counties a divisional medical officer of health had recommended to the county medical officer that the home help service should be increased because: 'We would like to put the cases in the 3–5 hours group into the 6–10 hours group. At the moment one good clean through a week is all that is possible and it does not meet the need.' This county had organized regular channels for the flow of information about needs from the divisions to the centre.

Decisions about the amount and frequency of service to be given to particular cases may be taken by a number of different people. Most case study authorities employed home help organizers, some of whom had had no training but who decided the amount of help to be given; even then, in all but the smallest authorities, more than one person was involved. A few counties did not employ an organizer, and decisions about the amount of help needed were taken by home nurses or, more often, health visitors, which accounted for some of the variation between local authorities (see Chapter 4) in the proportion of elderly cases seen by health visitors. In some Scottish authorities the amount of help to be given was decided by welfare officers, although in one area the medical officer said that the health department had taken over the service from welfare in order 'to increase its usefulness in both quality and quantity'. Where several people are responsible for taking decisions about the amount of service needed it can happen that different criteria are used by different people. Only a few case study authorities had attempted to codify criteria for the guidance of those taking individual decisions.[1] Even when most decisions are taken by one person there is a case for a check list of criteria as an aid to consistency.

The people responsible for assessing an individual's need for meals-on-wheels varied between authorities, though it was suspected that sometimes chief welfare officers overemphasized the role of their own staff. Usually the assessors were welfare officers, nurses, general practitioners, the Women's Royal Voluntary Service, and occasionally the National Assistance Board (as it then was). Often more than one of these groups was involved. There was no clear pattern between local authorities or different types of area, except that welfare officers did rather less assessment in the counties than their colleagues in towns. In one area it was said that: 'The W R V S accept recommendations from voluntary organizations, general practitioners and the National Assistance Board without question because we have tried to impress that no recommendations be made unless there is need. If there are any doubts, then the matter would be referred to the welfare officers for decision.' In the 1958 survey Harris also found that a substantial proportion of recommendations for the service were not checked for the extent of need by organizers of the service.[2] 12 of the 24 case study authorities spoke of categories of need drawn up to guide assessors,[3] but guidance was less com-

[1] One example of a scheme drawn up for the guidance of assistant home help organizers is reproduced in Appendix 2.

[2] Harris, *op. cit.*, p. 19.

[3] The most frequently mentioned category was those with a physical or mental condition, whether permanent or temporary, which precluded self-help, and no one available to prepare meals. This category included those who were bedfast or chairfast. A wider category included the housebound who could not do shopping, and one county borough took into account the distance from the applicant's house to the shops, and provided meals for applicants who were not completely

monly given in the counties, which accounted for only 3 of the 12.

As well as trying to ensure reasonable consistency of initial assessment of need between different individuals it is also important to have effective communication about changes in need. In the authorities with home help organizers it was usual for the organizer to visit periodically the people who were receiving the service to see whether the amount of help was appropriate. Reassessment visits every three months were the most common practice, although some organizers visited certain cases more often than others, and in one authority the aim was to visit all cases once a month. However, as the number of cases usually increased in advance of the appointment of additional organizers, and as some authorities did not provide a car allowance for home help organizers, the intervals between reassessment visits tended to lengthen, at least for a time. Between visits organizers were dependent on home helps to tell them when the needs of individual old people changed. Home helps in most urban areas collected their pay from the office once a week and this provided an opportunity to tell the organizer of any problems about their cases. In very large urban areas, and in county areas, contact between home helps and the organizers was not always so straightforward, although the establishment of area offices helped. One English county had volunteers acting as organizers in remote areas, and in other sparsely populated areas the home nurse or health visitor dealt with individual problems arising in connection with home help cases to save the organizer a journey.

There was often no regular arrangement for reassessment of need for meals-on-wheels. One or two authorities said they occasionally 'had a blitz on it' to see if some old people were still receiving the service when no longer in need of it, or if some needed more, or less, frequent meals. In many areas the question of providing more or less of the service according to changes in need just did not apply because of the limited frequency of availability of service, so that reassessment was only necessary for cases thought to be no longer in need of the service. Sometimes the motive for a review was because of pressure of demand from new cases, and sometimes it was because volunteers delivering the meals complained that 'some people are never in—they are down at the bowling green or at the pictures, and we have to leave the food at the door'. One county borough had

housebound, but for whom regular shopping was impractical. Three authorities mentioned criteria of age and isolation, two referred to malnutrition or apathy, and there were single references to old people with inadequate cooking facilities, to 'the preventive element', and to lack of skills, especially among single or widowered elderly men not used to fending for themselves.

started to build up a system of revision once it had a team of welfare officers to operate it.

In areas where there was a regular visiting service for the elderly changes in need could be reported by the visitor, so that frequency of visiting became an important consideration. Visiting services are discussed more fully in Chapter 11, but it may be noted here that reporting of needs was seen as a major function of a visitor, especially in the Scottish authorities. In sheltered housing schemes the warden could report changes in need. One problem which arose in the case of wardens or voluntary visitors reporting on changes in need was that of ensuring that the information got to the right place. An example was given in Chapter 8 of how a warden reported needs to the housing authority, but the information was apparently not passed on to the county health and welfare department which was responsible for providing the services required in that particular case.

Some changes in need can be met with an existing service, but often collated information about increased needs would form the basis for a request for an increase in the service. Thus, once information about deficiencies in a service reached the section head there was further need for communication between section heads and the chief officer in the department before plans to deal with deficiencies could be considered. A few chief officers commented specifically on this, and said they were aware of the inadequacy of the system they operated. One medical officer, for example, said: 'If you delegate a function you must have an inbuilt check of what you have delegated. If I were in business, I would have such a check. In practice, I suppose I don't. I have good staff who are probably doing the job properly.' Nevertheless, this officer had available information which had been built up over the years in the form of quarterly reports. Another medical officer of health mentioned 'the need to have sufficient staff in the field to be aware of the problems, and having collected information to be able to collate and use it instead of producing meaningless statistics'. He thought a computer might help in analysis of information, and was aware that records held in his department contained much information relevant to knowledge of the adequacy of services for those already receiving them, but which was never used. Other chief officers, especially welfare officers, stressed that it was wrong to have staff spending time on writing reports and collecting statistics when field-staff for the services were so thin on the ground. This attitude is understandable, but its implications for the flow of information about the adequacy of a service, and the criteria which section heads use for deciding how much service to give, need to be recognized.

AVAILABILITY OF SERVICES AT SPECIAL TIMES

Many authorities said that a major drawback of domiciliary care was that services were not available at certain times.

Lack of services at weekends was said to be a major problem. Very few authorities provided home helps at weekends. One county borough used to provide a service on Saturdays, but so many home helps 'went off sick' that the organizer decided that policy must be changed. Many home helps were married women with children, and had other calls on their time and attention at weekends. However, some areas did have a limited service available. One organizer explained: 'We do not have many working at weekends, but we do have some, especially if they are neighbours', and another said: 'Home helps do Sunday morning work, but only for selected cases who are absolutely helpless. Normally it is a Monday to Saturday service.'

The medical officer of a county borough with a high proportion of old people described how he instituted a special weekend service, which was a mixture of home nursing, home help and a meals service. 'The weekend is the problem. Domiciliary services are not designed for 24 hour care but this is what is being demanded of them. We cannot get people into welfare homes and are giving them support meantime, but they tend to deteriorate and become hospital cases. The geriatrician then does a domiciliary visit but he has no beds. In the 3 or 4 weeks they have to wait until they get a bed, they need not just a domestic help in the morning, but meals morning and evening, nursing care and some supervision because they may be wandering. During the week the domestic helps go in and the service can be daily, but it stops at the weekend. Therefore the weekend service was started.' This service was staffed by three people, of whom one was a retired midwife, one used to be a nursing orderly in a geriatric unit, and one was a member of the Red Cross. The geriatric health visitor made out the list of cases needing hot food taken to them at the weekend. She said that most of them were in their seventies and eighties, and several were bedridden or confused. Mostly they were people with no relatives in the town, and they had nobody to get food for them. Some had refused admission to welfare homes, but a lot were waiting for places.

Home nursing was more often available at weekends for those in need of it, but even with home nursing problems arose over duty rosters because many of the staff were married women with children. Counties, especially sparsely populated ones, faced particular

171

problems because of the amount of travelling involved when nurses had to work a double district while others had time off. The nursing officer of one rural county said that for a time they had an establishment level based on the recommendation of an O and M report, but found they could not manage over off-duty time and holidays. Eventually additional part-time reliefs were recruited, together with a few floating reliefs who had only a light regular district. 'We find the new system excellent. Our visits are up, although our cases are down a bit. This shows that old people are getting the visits even when the nurse is on holiday, and it means that we get a seven day service also, whereas before some were left out on Sundays.' This authority had a high ratio of home nurses per thousand population compared with most other case study authorities.

Another county with a less scattered population had reorganized its nursing services. As older combined duty nurses retired, separate staff were recruited for home nursing, midwifery, and health visiting, and teams of staff based on the larger centres of population served wider areas than the old combined duty districts. The nursing officer explained that 'this has made a difference to the care of old people. Before, if a combined duty nurse had two midwifery cases she couldn't reach an elderly person to undertake nursing functions before eleven o'clock in the morning. Now we are able to give a better service.' Other advantages of the change to nursing teams based in the towns were that it had facilitated recruitment of home nurses, and made it easier to provide a five day week for staff but a seven day service for the patients. These advantages seemed, in a county such as this, to outweigh the disadvantage of the extra travelling involved. This would not hold for very sparsely populated counties.

The same authority had found a solution to the problem which arose in one part of the county because of the demands made on the home nursing service in the early morning to get patients ready to go to the day hospital. 'We called in the Red Cross and got 7 or 8 helpers to help with washing and dressing.' The home help organizer in this area also mentioned the demands on the home help service because of the need to have people ready to go to day hospitals. She said that it was hard to find home helps to work before nine o'clock because they wanted to get their children off to school first. Home helps were also needed to do shopping for people away at the day centre, and at the end of the afternoon to put on a fire so that the house was warm when the old people came home.

In a few authorities this kind of service, involving short periods of time at particular times of day, was provided by a paid good neighbour service—and doubtless in many more areas neighbours provided such a service unrewarded. Although paid good neighbour services were rare, some home help services were in effect very similar. This was particularly true in some counties, where the pattern of settlement was such that home helps were almost inevitably neighbours as well.

It was also true of at least one industrial town with a lot of old houses and a large slum clearance programme. Here home helps were paid for the hours worked during the day, and gave their services voluntarily to the same old people in the evenings if help was needed at bed-time. A few authorities had paid home helps providing an evening service, and in others, home nurses settled people for the night. In some urban areas, however, home helps were recruited mainly from the post-war peripheral housing estates whereas most old people receiving the service lived in the older central areas, so that home helps did not live near the people they were assisting.

Some authorities disliked the idea of paying neighbours. One home help organizer, referring to a circular on domestic help recommending good neighbour schemes, said: 'This is a horrible idea—people should not be paid for goodness.' Others argued that it was only one step from paying neighbours to paying relatives and a line must be drawn somewhere. Indeed, Townsend found that, in Bethnal Green, some of the neighbours and friends with whom old people had contact turned out to be relatives.[1]

Thus although some services were available in the evening, provision was often patchy and domiciliary care was not always available at night. As one county medical officer said: 'If relatives and neighbours can manage on their own at night, society will manage during the day.' Nevertheless, caring for a sick person every night can impose an intolerable strain on relatives. It is also likely that the success of sheltered housing schemes may partly depend on the availability of services at night, since if there are not, the burden of care falls on the warden. An example from one of the case studies where the warden resigned as a result of the strain imposed on her for want of supporting services was described in Chapter 8.

A night-sitter service was provided by about a third of the case study authorities, mostly in urban areas. However, many officials said that the service was little used, and in one or two instances it had lapsed. Valuable though the service could be for someone awaiting admission to hospital, or to relieve the burden on relatives, the sporadic nature of demand for the service contributed to difficulties in staffing it. One authority was wondering whether it would help if

[1] P. Townsend, *The Family Life of Old People*, Pelican edition, 1963, p. 139.

staff were to be paid a retaining fee. How far low use of this service was due to charging policy is considered in Chapter 11.

Several authorities referred to the service available under the Marie Curie scheme, although it seemed that this too was little used in some areas. Carstairs found, in a study of home nursing in Scotland,[1] that desire to conceal the nature of the patient's illness from him had inhibited the full development of this service, but pointed out that in Aberdeen, where the local authority also provided a service at night, this problem did not arise because the staff of both services wore similar white overalls and the patient did not need to know the source of the nurse.

Holidays are another time when domiciliary care may fall short of meeting the needs of the elderly living at home. In areas where local factories all closed for a week or a fortnight at the same time it was often impossible to maintain the level of the home help service because staff wanted holidays at the same time as their husbands. In authorities where there was no regular arrangement about holiday entitlement for home helps (who are mainly part-time workers) some staff just left the service when holiday time came round. In addition home helps and other staff with children at school had family commitments when the schools were on holiday.

The closing of factory canteens and school meals kitchens at holiday times caused special problems for meals services. Over half of the 24 case study authorities were using or had recently used the school meals service as their source of supply. 6 authorities stressed the school holiday problem and 5 of them mentioned other sources of supply during these periods. 2 of the 6 were trying to arrange to keep the kitchens working during the holidays. 'We are now discussing whether we could use the kitchen staff in holiday times at $1\frac{1}{2}$ times normal pay. They are paid a standby rate of half-time during the holiday period.' No authority stated that it was moving away from dependence on the education authority because of this problem, although two authorities in retirement areas said they had never used the schools meals service because of the gap in supply at holiday times.

However, the general impression gained was that the quality of domiciliary care suffered during holiday periods, sometimes to the extent of the service stopping altogether for a week or a fortnight.

One other aspect of domiciliary care connected with the holiday issue is the need for services for people who may normally be cared for solely by relatives, so that relatives can go on holiday. This

---

[1] V. Carstairs, *Home Nursing in Scotland*, Scottish Home and Health Department, 1966, p. 68.

issue was more often raised in connection with facilities for short-stay residents in residential homes or hospitals (see Chapter 6). However, one case study authority had a small number of resident home helps. They worked mostly with maternity cases, but occasionally looked after an elderly person while relatives or companion-helps had a holiday. The disadvantages of this were staffing problems and the cost. This authority paid its resident home helps between £10–11 a week, which was similar to the cost of residential accommodation, although lower than that of a hospital bed. For the most part, support by domiciliary services for relatives while they had a holiday was limited to the normal scope of the services, although a few authorities did try to increase the number of hours of home help.

SCOPE OF THE SERVICES

The third aspect of quality of domiciliary care concerns the kind of service provided by home helps, home nurses, meals services, and laundry services, and this varied between authorities.

While about half of the case study authorities saw flexibility as the keynote of the home help service and did not lay down hard and fast rules, in some areas there were restrictions on the kind of work home helps were allowed to do. Authorities which stressed flexibility tended to have higher ratios of home helps per thousand population than those which limited the scope of the service. Some authorities did not allow window cleaning, or other jobs which involved using step-ladders, because of the risk of injury and the question of insurance. Others did not allow home helps to do spring cleaning or blanket washing.

In contrast one authority allowed long-term cases an additional 10 hours a year for spring cleaning, and a few other authorities were prepared to make extra allowance for individual cases. Policy on whether unoccupied rooms should be cleaned or not also varied. Most authorities allowed the preparation of meals, but while some stressed this as an essential part of the service a few only allowed meals in special cases. Shopping and collecting pensions was part of the service in most areas, although some authorities were concerned at the amount of time this absorbed and in one case there was a stipulation that shopping must be done at local shops. Laundry was also often part of the service. The question of whether home helps did washing or provided meals partly depended on whether there was a separate laundry or meals-on-wheels service. In some cases it was argued that these other services had not been developed because the home helps did this work. On the other hand there was at least one example where a separate laundry service had been started to relieve the home help service (see Chapter 14). In another area home helps took laundry to the launderette provided by the council under the public health scheme. Many of the laundry services catered for bed-linen only, and some for incontinent patients only, although the problem of laundry for the incontinent had considerably diminished with increased use of disposable pads. Most authorities used these, although some mentioned problems of disposal in modern dwellings with no open fires. Few laundry services catered for personal clothing, and so this was often washed by the home help.

Policies varied on whether home helpers were allowed to give personal care to elderly people needing help with washing and dressing. One organizer said: 'We do not mind if home helps do things like washing the patient's hair. We tell the home help to use her discretion.' In another area two of the older home helps were employed to work together on helping elderly people with bathing, hair-washing and care of the feet, and they helped 7 or 8 elderly people in the course of a morning.

In other areas, however, personal care was regarded quite definitely as work for a home nurse. One such area, with a high proportion of elderly in the population, had a staff ratio not much above the national average for home helps, but a very high ratio for home nurses. Another such area had a staff ratio near to the national average for home nursing, and a still lower one for home helps, but had a much smaller proportion of old people in its population.

In another area a combination of fairly high staff ratios for home help and health visitors partly accounted for what seemed a low ratio for home nursing, since a foot hygiene service for the elderly was part of the health visiting service. The extent to which foot hygiene and nail-cutting was carried out by home helps, home nurses or assistant health visitors sometimes reflected the difficulty in staffing chiropody services, but sometimes it was simply a continu-ation of arrangements made before Ministry policy allowed the development of chiropody. A few medical officers simply considered that foot hygiene was a nurse's job. Arrangements such as these were not always popular with chiropodists, who considered that foot hygiene was their job.

Occasionally home helps assisted with bed-bathing, although some areas employed state enrolled nurses to do this work with the home nurses. One authority which found it hard to recruit home helps or state enrolled nurses had 12 Red Cross volunteers who sometimes helped the home nurses. In other areas with less support from other sources bed-bathing took up more of the home nurses' time, or was done less frequently.

The scope of the home nursing service varied in other ways too, depending partly on training, and especially on opportunities for refresher courses and contact with new developments in hospitals. A nursing officer said: 'One factor which might affect the work-load is that we are preparing the nurses in the refresher courses to do stroke rehabilitation on people in their own homes.' Another nursing officer referred to 'the lucky ones' who were admitted to hospital when they had a stroke and were given physiotherapy. She added that her nurses did their best 'but they are no physiotherapists'. She had not spoken of the potential value of a mobile physiotherapy unit to the medical officer 'because the money wouldn't be available, and physiotherapists are in such short supply that the hospitals just wouldn't agree'. In another area arrangements for home nurses to go to the geriatric unit periodically had been discussed. However enthusiasm had waned when the nursing officer found that the physiotherapy department was a poor one, and began to suspect that the geriatrician really wanted the arrangement to help ease the hospital's staff problems.

The quality of meals services sometimes left much to be desired. Two authorities found the school meals food generally unsuitable and were providing their own equipment for preparing meals better adapted to the needs of the elderly. The retirement area county borough which had not used the school meals service had rejected the idea partly on the grounds of unsuitable food. 'The schools provide cold meals for the children on 2 or 3 days per week. Even the schoolchildren complain that they get too many salads. It would not do for us, because it is a hot meal that we want to provide.' It is perhaps worth asking whether the organization of school kitchens must be such that they provide meals unsuitable for the elderly.[1]

The welfare officer of the authority running a direct service regretted that they still could not provide special diets for those needing them, and few other authorities mentioned that diets could be provided. However, one county borough, where the local authority and the Council of Social Service had co-operated to start a pilot scheme in part of the town, diabetic diets, fat-free diets, low residue

[1] In 1958 about a third of the school meals services supplying meals for elderly people were prepared to listen to suggestions from organizers about altering the menu (Harris, *op. cit.*, Table 35, p. 30). 'There is less opportunity for suggesting alterations to the menu where the meal is supplied by the school meals service than any other outside source.'

diets and gastric diets all came within the scope of the service, although it was only available on two days a week.

The quality of meals provided also affected lunch clubs, although White argued that the main value of lunch clubs was social rather than nutritional.[1] Some case study authorities also stressed the value of the lunch club in combating loneliness. The advantage of a lunch club or a club with facilities for handicrafts over a purely social club may well be that the meal or the handicraft facilities provide an excuse to go to people who do not like appearing to need social contacts.[2]

The premises in which clubs were held were sometimes poor and there were problems about heating places such as church halls.

Accessibility of club premises to the population served was also mentioned as an important factor by some authorities. One Scottish large burgh had decided to decentralize lunch clubs because the central area of the town—including the site of the main lunch club—was to be redeveloped, and this provided an opportunity to create lunch clubs in local community halls, thus reducing travel costs. Some urban authorities had travel concession schemes for the elderly, but this was only possible in areas where bus services were operated by the local authority. In one or two case study areas some bus services were council operated and others not, so that only old people in certain parts of the town benefited from the concessions scheme. In rural areas, where more travelling would be involved, more bus services were run by private companies, and the frequency of service was often very limited. An alternative form of transport is the provision of a minibus by the local welfare authority, or the use of a voluntary car service. A few urban authorities were providing vehicles for transporting the physically handicapped to social and occupation centres, but on the whole the question of transport for the elderly to help them to go to clubs seemed to have received little consideration. This was also the conclusion reached by the study carried out by the National Labour Women's Advisory Committee,[3] which found that four-fifths of the clubs surveyed did not have transport. Where transport was unavailable, or its cost to elderly users high, the scope of lunch clubs and social clubs tended to be restricted.

[1] E. E. White, *Clubs for the Elderly*, National Council of Social Service, no date, pp. 60–1.

[2] See J. Raven and K. J. Haynes, 'Social Contact, Loneliness and Clubgoing among Old People', *Journal of the Town Planning Institute*, March 1966, Vol. 52, No. 3, March 1966, pp. 94–5.

[3] National Labour Women's Advisory Committee, *Care of the Elderly*, Second Interim and Final Report, August 1964, p. 33.

SUMMARY

Comments on the frequency and amount of service available, on the limited services provided at special times of day, or at weekends and holiday times, and on the restricted scope of services in some areas all indicated ways in which the present services were failing to meet all the needs of elderly people already receiving domiciliary services. Officials in most authorities were aware of the shortcomings in general terms, but few had tried to quantify the extent to which development to improve quality was necessary in their particular area, as a basis for planning to develop the services.

Some chief officers commented that a great deal of information was available in their records which could have been used to provide estimates of the inadequacy of present provision to those already receiving services, but this information was not used. Shortages of staff, and lack of knowledge of the appropriate techniques for collating and analysing data were mentioned as reasons for not using the information.

Another reason was that some officers were not concerned to try to expand the present services, because they considered that too much was being asked of the domiciliary services. This applied especially in the case of the need for services at night and weekends.

Delays or failures in communication, and occasional misunderstandings between field-workers and section heads, section heads and departmental heads, and between divisional officers (in counties with a divisional structure) and county officers, sometimes meant that the need for expansion of a service passed unnoticed by the chief officers, at least for a time, because inadequacies were concealed by reducing the amount or frequency of service. A few authorities had established regular channels for communication of information, and a few had effective informal channels.

A few authorities mentioned inflexible administration of services rather than inadequate level of provision as an important factor affecting quality. Only a minority of authorities tried to ensure reasonable consistency of criteria for deciding how much help was necessary for individual cases, and, with the possible exception of the home help service, to arrange for regular review of the needs of individuals so that services could be increased or decreased accordingly. Decisions relating to one service were commonly taken without reference to complementary services, although in some areas there was a link between the home help and meals-on-wheels services.

There appeared to be considerable variation between authorities

179

in the kind of care provided by each service although this was partly explained by differences in division of functions between home helps, home nurses and health visitors, and partly related to availability or otherwise of other services such as laundry, meals-on-wheels, and chiropody. Some section heads had ideas for increasing the scope of their service, but had not always communicated them to the chief officer because they thought that resources would not be available for these ideas to be implemented.

Some welfare officers had plans for increasing the scope of the meals-on-wheels service, or for setting up clubs in areas easily and cheaply accessible to the population served, but sometimes plans were thwarted by factors which were partly outside the direct control of the welfare department.

CHAPTER 11

DOMICILIARY SERVICES—PLANNING FOR UNMET NEEDS

The last chapter discussed the adequacy of services for those already receiving them. However, some local authority officials were more concerned about the needs of old people not known to the local authority. This chapter considers the extent to which local health and welfare departments were aware of unmet needs, the ways in which some authorities were trying to find old people in need of services, and how awareness of unmet needs affected plans for the services. Much of the discussion relates to the more firmly established services such as home nursing, home help, chiropody and meals-on-wheels. However, except for home nursing, even these are not always available, [1] especially in the more isolated rural areas. Thus an awareness of the need for extension of services to areas not yet covered, and for new kinds of services is also important.

AWARENESS OF UNMET NEEDS

Some authorities referred to pressure on existing facilities as evidence of needs which were not being met. A county borough welfare officer said that the social centre for the elderly was grossly overcrowded, which indicated the need for larger or additional premises to satisfy the high level of expressed demand. In a few departments there was a waiting list for the home help service, although it was usually considered that this service must be provided straightaway. Several commented that they sometimes had to withdraw help temporarily from old people in order to meet urgent demands from maternity cases or cases of sudden illness, and one medical officer said he would prefer to have one home help always ready to go out, without having to take one off a job. However, this policy could be difficult to follow in areas with recruitment difficulties. Moreover, as home helps were

[1] *All* local health authorities in Britain *provided* a home help service (see Chapter 1), but some sparsely populated areas of certain counties were not covered by the service.

paid by the hour in most places, they did not like being a standby. Some 'robbing Peter to pay Paul' may be inevitable, but as a medical officer pointed out, it was important for the organizer to take the trouble to explain the difficulty to the old person concerned.

Some authorities had waiting lists for chiropody, but on the whole domiciliary services, unlike residential accommodation and housing, did not have waiting lists as a measure of expressed demands which were not being met.

This, perhaps, partly explains why some authorities claimed there was little or no unmet need in their area. Sometimes indications of possible unmet need were noticed but not acted upon by those in charge of a service. One home help organizer, for example, described how she had noticed that a new case in a street in which there had not previously been cases often led to several other new applications.

Many authorities thought there was little unmet need for services, especially home nursing and home help, because they were dealing mainly with cases referred by professional workers rather than with direct applications from the public, and all referrals were accepted. In most authorities practically all home nursing cases were referred by general practitioners or hospitals, and in some areas this was also true for the home help service. Only a few case study authorities insisted on a medical certificate from general practitioners for all home help cases, including two Scottish authorities where the service was run by the welfare department. Most accepted referrals from home nurses, health visitors, welfare officers and hospitals without a general practitioner's note, but only a few also accepted referrals from other sources, such as the Ministry of Social Security officers, voluntary organizations, local authority councillors, ministers, the police, relatives or old people themselves, without bringing in the general practitioner as well. Those with the most liberal policy on this matter did not find it created difficulties, and said they turned down very few requests because most of them came from competent people. As long as requests could be met more or less straightaway the level of service was considered by some to be adequate.

However, some authorities were aware that cases known to general practitioners or other professional workers were not always referred. The chief nursing officer of a large county had noticed that the figure for home nursing visits had dropped compared with the previous year, and said: 'Perhaps the nurses are letting the general practitioners think that they are very busy and so the general practitioners are not giving them work.' In another area it was said that a few years ago the home nursing service had been under heavy pressure and so the general practitioners had started to withhold cases. Then the introduction of oral antibiotics, disposable syringes, and incontinence pads, had eased the pressure considerably, but general practitioners did not seem to realize that the home nurses could now take more cases. There were occasional comments that general practitioners did not understand the kind of work which a home nurse could do, and under-rated her skills.

It was felt that general practitioners did not always know what services were available, especially older general practitioners who had lost touch with recent developments. Medical officers and nursing officers frequently referred to the failure of general practitioners to realize the contribution which health visitors could make to care of the elderly and the mentally ill. Moreover, some home help organizers thought that general practitioners could contact them more often. One county medical officer distinguished between general practitioners in the town and those in the country: 'The doctors in the town almost automatically send in a home help when they send in a home nurse. The country doctors do not ask for home help, either because they have been disappointed in the past when they asked and did not get it, or because they assume or know that the neighbours will do it.'

Two chief welfare officers said general practitioners were reluctant to recommend people for meals-on-wheels because it involved form filling. It is also possible that eligible people may fail to receive services because of the lack of a central referral point, to which busy professional workers could pass on requests.

A few commented that general practitioners did not refer cases because they did not know about the needs themselves. One medical officer of health spoke of a survey carried out in Scotland which showed that general practitioners did not know the needs of all old people in their practice, as only one-tenth of the old people saw their doctors regularly, and over three-fifths had not seen their doctor for six months.[1] A study in England and Wales in 1955–6 also found that, although care of the elderly formed an important part of the general practitioner's work, between a quarter and a third of all old people had not seen their doctor for over a year,[2] and the findings reported by Townsend for 1962 were very similar.[3] While some old

[1] A. F. McCoubrey and I. A. G. MacQueen, 'A Survey of Old People in a Rural Community', *Health Bulletin* (*issued by the Chief Medical Officer of the Department of Health for Scotland*), Vol. X, No. 3, 1952, p. 47.

[2] General Register Office, *Morbidity Statistics from General Practice, Vol. 1* (by W. P. D. Logan and A. A. Cushion), Studies on Medical and Population Subjects No. 14, H.M.S.O., 1958, pp. 27, 58.

[3] P. Townsend and D. Wedderburn, *The Aged in the Welfare State*, G. Bell and Sons, 1965, p. 60.

people are not in need of either medical care or social services, research studies such as those by Williamson[1] and Richardson,[2] have shown that not all medical needs are reported to general practitioners far less all social ones. Cartwright[3] showed that, if anything, elderly people living alone saw less of their general practitioner than other old people, and the ones who saw him most were those living with younger people. This was partly because those living with relatives were older and frailer than those living alone, but this finding raises important questions about the adequacy of arrangements for the early detection of remediable needs. Knowledge of some of these studies led some medical officers to argue that the time was not yet ripe for the setting up of health advisory clinics (see also Chapter 20) for old people because the referral system was through the general practitioners who did not know all their elderly patients.

However, some medical officers continued to place a great deal of faith in general practitioners. One medical officer was surprised that the night-sitter service had never been much used, because he said: 'I told all the general practitioners, and they should know who needs it.' Another medical officer criticized the findings of a local survey of unmet need, and said that when the local authority told general practitioners just to ask for home help the need turned out to be not very great.

Other medical officers commented on research studies showing unmet needs for services, but were doubtful whether findings in other areas were applicable to their own. For example, one claimed: 'The only decent survey done was Sheldon's and that was twenty years ago in an industrial city in the Midlands.' Another commented: 'Townsend is pretty useless for us here.' The consensus of opinion was that research studies were either too specific to one area, or too general for one to know how one's own area fitted into the picture. For all the doubts about research findings, some still thought that only where university teams had done a specialized study was the extent of the problem known.

Unmet needs for services such as meals-on-wheels and chiropody were mentioned more often than unmet needs for home nursing and home help. Some spoke of 'not knowing how great the need for chiropody really is', or of 'the potential demand for chiropody being infinite'. Referring to meals-on-wheels, officials from over half of the

[1] J. Williamson et al., 'Old People at Home: Their Unreported Needs', *Lancet*, 1964, 1, 1117.

[2] I. M. Richardson, *Age and Need*, Livingstone, 1964, pp. 21-2.

[3] A. Cartwright, *Patients and Their Doctors*, Routledge and Kegan Paul, 1967, pp. 196 *et seq.*

case study authorities spoke of 'only scratching the surface'; of expecting 'a flood of applications' when a new area was covered, or of the service being a 'fleabite'. In the second quarter of 1964 the provision of meals in 21 of the 24 case study areas[1] ranged from 7·1 per thousand population (mid-1964 estimate) to 119·4. Only in Scotland was the present level of service considered adequate, yet 4 of the 7 Scottish authorities for which figures were available were among the 6 lowest providers. Welfare officers in 2 counties and 2 large burghs stated that there was little demand for the service.

It was firmly believed in some counties and small towns that neighbourliness and family care still counted for a great deal. This was suggested as a reason why there was little demand for a service by a Scottish medical officer who said: 'It is amazing how these . . . villages provide for their old people through neighbours and families. Sons and daughters have tended to stay there because it is a mining community.' However, in another area where a similar statement about family care was made by a welfare officer in relation to mining communities in northern England, the local authority still intended to enlarge its own meals-on-wheels scheme.

Health and welfare officials in small authorities, many of which were in Scotland, tended also to think that there was not much unmet need for the established services in their areas. As one Scottish medical officer of health put it: 'There must be cases in the county where the odd old person needs home help—but there is no proof of this. I have spoken to people about this, and I doubt if a drive to find people needing and not getting the service would produce any. You might find some in big cities where people get lost more easily.'

Even where there was a general feeling that some needs were not being met, local authority officials were doubtful about 'the point at which we ought to interfere'. The pride and independence of old people were said to account for low demand for services. In some areas it was thought that the meals-on-wheels service had not developed because: 'Some old people feel that if the van is seen at their door it is labelling them as accepting charity.' One home help organizer was bothered because 50% of referred cases never materialized. 'Some of this is because we say we have cases in greater need once we know the full circumstances, but a lot of it is because people will not accept home help and say they can manage.'

Evidence from research studies also shows that old people in need, as judged by others, will not *all* accept services. It was reported in

[1] Information was not available from the WRVS for two of the case studies, and the figures for a third were incorporated in a total for an area larger than the health and welfare authority.

1958, for example, that about a quarter of 'needy older folk' were likely to refuse the meals-on-wheels service.[1] Nevertheless, this is not to say that no old people who need the service, and are not getting it, would refuse it if it were offered.

Some case study authorities paid little attention to the possibility that some refusals, especially refusals of home help, might have been because of charging policy. The extent to which charges acted as a deterrent is difficult to judge, as it would vary from authority to authority. Two English case study authorities had recently made the home help service free for people over sixty-five, and several others provided it free of charge to those receiving supplementary pensions, while a few provided it free to anyone whose only income was a state old age pension. The practice of charging old people with supplementary pensions as a way of recouping money from the National Assistance Board (now the Supplementary Benefits Commission in the Department of Health and Social Security) was much more common in Scotland than in England and Wales, which presumably was the main reason why Scottish authorities recovered a much higher proportion of the cost of this service from charges than did English and Welsh ones. In 1963–4 only 1 of the 16 English case study authorities recovered more than 18% of the cost, compared with 7 out of the 8 in Scotland. Some authorities assessed old people for charges if they had capital (usually taking NAB practice as a guide), and thought that this might bear rather unfairly on the elderly. Three English authorities reduced charges after the first few weeks, and said that this tended to favour the elderly, who constituted most of the long-term cases. On the other hand one or two authorities increased charges after a month on the grounds that the local authority service was an emergency service, and that there should be a positive incentive to people requiring a long-term service to make their own arrangements. Medical officers of health were much more concerned at the way in which charges for the home help service deterred maternity cases, especially in view of the increase in 48 hour discharges from maternity hospitals in some areas, than they were about charges deterring the elderly.

It was argued that most old people paid nothing or little for home help. One English county home help organizer provided an analysis of charges, showing that $28 \cdot 5\%$ of the cases were paying no charge, $56 \cdot 8\%$ were paying the 5s minimum weekly charge, $7 \cdot 5\%$ were assessed cases paying only 5s, and $7 \cdot 2\%$ were assessed cases paying more than 5s. Similar evidence was provided elsewhere, and it there-

[1] A. I. Harris, *Meals-on-Wheels for Old People*, National Corporation for the Care of Old People, 1960, p. 78.

fore seemed unlikely that the level of charges acted as a major deterrent to use of the service, except perhaps in Scotland. What some authorities failed to realize was that it was the way in which charging policy was explained to old people which might act as the deterrent. In one Scottish authority, for example, the nursing officer said: 'I decide how many hours help are needed, and tell people the charge is 4s per hour. If they have a supplementary pension the case is referred to the welfare officer for assessment on the cheap rate, otherwise they just pay the full rate unless I suspect there is hardship and that they are just keen to exercise their independence.' To announce the charge first and then explain that you do not pay it if you have not enough money puts an elderly person with limited means in a position in which he might find it difficult to give the true facts without loss of self-respect.

In areas with a night-sitter service there were frequent comments that the service was little used, and some officers were surprised at this. It seemed likely that the level of charges might well act as a deterrent to use of this service. In one area, for example, the charge was 3s an hour, and the sitter would be there for 10–12 hours in a single night.

Charges for meals-on-wheels, lunch clubs, laundry and chiropody varied from place to place, although there was always an element of subsidy from the local authority or voluntary organization providing the service. Officials commented on the way charges for these services stayed the same for years, and rarely seemed to think that charges would act as a deterrent.

It was sometimes said that there was no unmet need for meals or laundry because the service was provided by home helps. Another reason given for why there was no need for a laundry service was that the home nurses would know if there was a need, and as they had not said anything, therefore. . . .

Thus awareness of the existence of unmet needs, and for the need for new services varied. At least one, and often more, of the officers interviewed in each of the case studies was prepared to talk of the possibility of unmet needs, but awareness was usually couched in general terms, and one official added: 'Supposing there is unmet need, how do we find it?'

FINDING UNMET NEEDS

Although many authorities said they did not see how they could be sure that all elderly people in need of services were receiving them, various ways of finding needs had been discussed or tried out.

PLANNING LOCAL AUTHORITY SERVICES FOR THE ELDERLY

(a) *Increasing Public Awareness of Services*

A home help organizer, who thought that 'You have to go out and look for need', supplied the medical officer of health with figures for the service for different areas in the county. They noticed that one area with no local area organizer had an unusually low number of cases compared with other areas. So an additional area office was created, bringing the service nearer to the public in that area, and the service soon began to develop.

There was little interest in the idea of general publicity for the services in order to try to increase public knowledge of them. This was partly because it was thought wrong to invite the expression of demands which could not be met, and partly because: 'It is difficult to get across to the ordinary man in the street what services are available.' One county borough said there had been publicity for the home help service in the local press, and that the service was mentioned in the welfare department's handbook. Information about the home help service was included in the tenant's handbook issued by one Scottish case study authority to all its council tenants. One or two welfare officers were trying to get slips with information about local authority services put in pension books, although in some cases there had been difficulties with the Ministry of Pensions and National Insurance (now the Department of Health and Social Security) about this. In a large authority where this had been done once, about 2,000 pre-paid cards were returned to the welfare department, and followed up with visits by a welfare officer or a health visitor. In one or two areas services such as chiropody had been advertised in places such as clinics and churches.

Many authorities thought that it was not the general public which needed information about local authority services, but the general practitioners. They had concentrated on publicity in the form of handbooks or news bulletins for general practitioners, but some medical officers had found this a futile exercise: 'I've given up trying to educate the general practitioners about local authority nursing work after countless bulletins and sherry parties. They are little use. The ones who respond are the ones who are already converted.' Some local authority officers suggested that general practitioners were reluctant to refer cases 'because it involves form filling'.

It was not only general practitioners who were criticized for ignorance of the services and failure to refer people, but also hospital staff. A county official said: 'District councils are awfully ignorant although they can act as links between the public and the services', but he praised certain individual district council housing managers.

There were also failures in communication within the health and welfare authority, both between health and welfare departments, and even between sections within the same department. One welfare officer, for example, said: 'We wanted to know who was having domestic help because we thought these were people who might well need meals . . . The domestic help organizer wouldn't give information . . . and would not even give it to the superintendent health visitor.' Sometimes these communication barriers were erected as a result of respect for the confidentiality of information about individuals being carried to the extreme, but sometimes they resulted from staff with years of experience of inadequate services losing heart and ceasing to make requests.

(b) *Liaison with Hospitals*

In some areas liaison arrangements between the local health department and hospitals had been developed to improve the system of referring cases to both the home nursing and the home help service. Some hospitals automatically notified the local authority when any patient of pensionable age was discharged, so that even if a service was not specifically requested, a health visitor could visit and decide whether help was needed. This system is similar to that for notifying all births so that a health visitor can visit. Occasionally, hospital medical social workers notified the local health authority of impending discharge of elderly patients so that a home help could prepare the house beforehand, although other local authorities raised difficulties about this, saying that it was unwise to have a home help in the house when the owner was not there. The quality of liaison varied considerably. Sometimes the arrangement only worked with the geriatric hospital (or wards), but in other areas general hospitals and mental hospitals also co-operated.

One case study authority described the work of a health visitor who acted as liaison officer between the other health visitors and the local geriatrician: 'At first she made home visits and talked to general practitioners, and so helped the geriatrician to determine priorities for admission to his beds. This is not necessary now because the geriatrician does not have a waiting list any longer, and therefore the question of priorities does not arise. The system still works very much over discharges from hospital, where the liaison helps to make sure that the home is ready and that the services are laid on.'[1] Arrange-

1 For a description of a similar system where a geriatric social worker is employed by the local authority see R. B. McMillan, 'Assistance from Local Authorities and Others in the Home Care of the Aged', in Supplement No. 1, *Journal of the College of General Practitioners*, Vol. VI, February 1963, p. 41.

PLANNING LOCAL AUTHORITY SERVICES FOR THE ELDERLY

ments such as this accounted for some of the variation in the proportion of health visitor visits to the elderly (see Chapter 4).

(c) *Attachment of Local Authority Staff to General Practice*

In 7 or 8 of the 24 case study authorities the attachment of health visitors or home nurses to general practice was making inroads on the problem of finding unmet need. A county medical officer said: 'Some general practitioners have told the health visitors to pick out old people from their record cards and visit them. This has led to the health visitor finding old people she did not know of before, and also to her bringing to the general practitioner's notice some medical problems which he did not know about because he had not been called in.' In another county the medical officer had studied a year of health visitors' work before and after attachment in one area of the county, and found a striking change in the number of visits to old people. Fry also reported that 12% of all visits made by the health visitor attached to his practice in one year were to old people. This is nearly twice the national (average) figure, and this was before the start of the system of visiting all those in the practice who were over seventy and had not been seen by their doctor for a year.[1] Attachment of health visitors to general practices was also said to have helped to overcome some of the problems of co-ordination between different services. Sometimes comment related to co-ordination between general practitioner and health visitor, where both had found that they were visiting the same old person, and the sorting out of the frequency of visits together had resulted in saving of time for both of them. The health visitor could also co-ordinate different local authority services. This advantage of attachment was also stressed by Fry.[2]

In a few areas home nurses, or in counties combined duty nurses, were also attached to general practice. A nursing officer described how 'the nurses went round the old people in the practice, and to their horror collected two blanket baths in the first ten patients'. It was also said that attachment had resulted in more home confinements, and in increases in other aspects of a nurse's work, through better contact with general practitioners, and a better realization on the part of the latter of the work a nurse could do. An experiment which showed the range of work a nurse can undertake in general practice was well described by Weston Smith and Mottram.[3]

[1] J. Fry *et al.*, 'The Evolution of a Health Team; A Successful General Practitioner Health Visitor Association', *British Medical Journal*, 1965, 1, 181.
[2] *Ibid.*
[3] J. Weston Smith and E. Mottram, 'Extended Use of Nursing Services in General Practice', *British Medical Journal*, 1967, 2, 672.

190

Attachment had developed furthest in some of the English counties, although one or two county boroughs had attachment in parts of the town.[1] One Scottish urban authority also had experimental schemes, but in other Scottish areas studied attachment was not often mentioned. In most areas attachment seemed to have originated at the request of a group of general practitioners. Most officials in the local authorities had welcomed the approach, and were keen for more schemes. However, it was felt that both health visitors and general practitioners must want attachment before the system would work, and the counties concerned had taken a great deal of trouble to discuss the organization of schemes beforehand, and smooth out possible misunderstandings. Few local authority officials were willing to try to impose attachment schemes, but they were discussing the idea with general practitioners in the hope that gradually all would come round to wanting it.

Problems occasionally arose because local government boundaries do not coincide with the boundaries of general practice populations. 'We have only got the committee round to the idea of agreeing to cross-boundary working as an experiment. We were helped in this because one of the neighbouring authorities was a pioneer of attachment, but the treasurers hit the wretched financial problem. One wants a knock-for-knock arrangement and one a repayment system, and they are still fighting it out. It is difficult because a lot of doctors in their area have patients in ours, but doctors in our area do not have many patients in theirs.'

A few authorities thought that attachment was a desirable development but that you could only do it if you had enough staff.[2] As was said in one county borough: 'I can't divide 26 health visitors among 40 practices.' Not all these authorities had particularly low health visitor staff ratios compared with the national average, but then some areas had a much higher proportion of small practices than others, and it had proved easier to introduce attachment in areas where general practitioners had already formed group practices or partnerships of at least three or four doctors. Another factor which was more often stressed by the authorities with low staff ratios was that general practitioners' patients were scattered all over the area, and that

[1] For a survey of the position in 1963 see C. D. Baker, 'The Extent in England of Health Visitor Attachment to General Practices', *Journal of the College of General Practitioners*, Vol. 8, No. 46, September 1964, pp. 171–88. This survey also indicated that attachment was more extensive in counties than in county boroughs.

[2] Baker, *op. cit.* reported that 19 out of 47 county boroughs with no attachment schemes gave staff shortages as the reason, compared with 2 out of 22 counties.

attached health visitors would waste a lot of time travelling. A study carried out in Leeds certainly showed that in some areas the problems of introducing attachment might well prove insuperable, since health visitors reported that in 50 consecutive families visited in each of the 66 geographical districts the total number of general practitioners involved ranged from 5 to 56, although in nearly two-thirds of the districts only 15 to 24 doctors were involved. It was also found that about a quarter of the families were visited by more than one group of doctors, so that attachment would have involved some duplicating of health visiting.[1] However, many of the case studies which emphasized this problem had not collected the relevant information for their own area, and when attachment was tried out, their reservations proved to be unjustified. One, for example found that: 'There was not so much extra work as was thought because the doctors' practice populations were often concentrated in particular health visitor areas.'

Fears about the extra travelling involved were also expressed in some areas where it was not the policy for health visitors to use cars (see Chapter 14), or where there was difficulty in persuading committees to be more generous with mileage allowances. These fears were not usually based on calculated estimates about what would happen if attachment were introduced, and experience in some areas had proved such fears to be unjustified. The report of a study in Keighley stated that, although cars were essential, the increase in travelling was not as much as had been expected.[2] A report on an attachment scheme in Aberdeen stated that by zoning the practice, and visiting each part of the practice at regular times, the health visitor was able to organize her work so that little extra travelling was involved.[3]

It was sometimes argued that attachment was a less relevant issue for rural areas because there the home nursing and health visiting functions were often performed by one person, and contact with general practitioners was easier, at least in theory, because general practitioners valued home nursing skills and because, often, only one nurse and a small number of general practitioners were involved.[4]

[1] J. M. Akester and A. N. MacPhail, 'Health Visiting and General Practice' *Lancet*, 1964, 2, 405–7.

[2] J. Butterworth and V. P. MacDonagh, 'General Practitioner and Health Visitor', *Lancet*, 1964, 1, 549.

[3] F. A. Forbes, 'A Health Visitor Attached to General Practice', *Health Bulletin (issued by the Chief Medical Officer, Scottish Home and Health Department)*, Vol. XXII, No. 1, 1964, p. 20.

[4] Baker, *op. cit.* reported that 9 out of 22 counties with no attachment schemes gave 'already close co-operation' as the reason.

(d) *Registers of Elderly People*

In areas with no attachment of health visitors to general practice one of the problems of finding unmet needs among the elderly was the lack of a reasonably complete list of old people. 10 of the 24 case study authorities kept a register of the elderly[1] and 2 others thought it would be a good idea to set one up. On the other hand, 3 of those with registers had doubts about them, and 3 of those with no registers said they did not intend to create a register because it was impossible to complete it satisfactorily (especially in a rural area) and keep it up-to-date without spending large amounts of staff time. One authority had obtained names and addresses of people of pensionable age, and whether or not those people were living alone, as a result of a household survey carried out in the area some years previously. 'Unfortunately the welfare department has never kept it up and now we only strike off the names of people who have died. We find these in the local paper which the clerk looks at every day. Not keeping the survey up was a bit unfortunate, but we did not have the staff.'

One welfare officer referred to the freedom of the individual and his entitlement *not* to be registered. Two English counties mentioned this too, and quoted the (then) Ministry of Pensions and National Insurance as being unwilling to divulge information, though pre-paid postcards could be inserted in pension books. On this same issue the committee of the Royal College of Physicians (Edinburgh) were advised that governmental approval or support for a registration scheme operated through pension or executive council records 'would be unlikely to be forthcoming on the grounds that the stamp of official approbation could not be given to a scheme which many old people might regard as an intrusion on their privacy'.[2]

Welfare officers who valued their registers said they helped to find undetected needs (perhaps at an early stage, thus avoiding the need for a place in residential accommodation), created public awareness, were useful for quick reference in an emergency, and as a check list for the distribution of gifts. These officers considered that the staff time involved was a worthwhile investment, and had tried to keep the registers up-to-date. In one case the register was checked against applications for travel concession passes on municipal transport, and in another the help of the Gas Board was enlisted, because they 'have a system for inspecting appliances in the homes of old people to see that they are safe . . . although the development of non-lethal gas

---

[1] Excluding registers compiled by health visitors or other nurses.
[2] Royal College of Physicians (Edinburgh), *The Care of the Elderly in Scotland*, 1963, p. 47.

may eventually make a difference'. However, in two authorities where the chief welfare officers had a register, the chief nursing officers appeared not to know of its existence.

(e) *Warden Services*

A Scottish rural county was compiling a register for its urban areas with the help of street-wardens. If cases were reported to the welfare office other than by the street-wardens it was taken as indication of the need to check on the warden. The main function of a street-warden system, apart from being an attempt to create an early warning system, was to create a sense of identification with the neighbourhood on the part of elderly people and to induce a sense of neighbourliness among those who might be able to help. In all, 5 case study authorities had street-warden schemes in part of their areas, and even they had faced difficult problems, such as the fading of early enthusiasm, the desire for privacy by the people who might be helped, shortage of volunteers in the places where they were most needed, and the low need for any services on first reaching pensionable age.

The growing practice of housing authorities appointing and paying wardens to see that old people living in a defined area were managing, and for reporting new needs to those who supplied services was basically similar to the voluntary street-warden system. Paid wardens were usually associated with sheltered housing schemes, but as described in Chapter 8, some authorities had appointed wardens to keep an eye on old people who were not living in grouped dwellings. In the case of the authority with powers under a Local Act, and of the one with a home-warden service as part of the home help service, the old people were not necessarily council tenants. Some of those where the welfare officer kept a register were authorities with no sheltered housing schemes or paid wardens.

(f) *Visiting Services*

The idea of registers or street-warden systems was often closely linked to that of a regular visiting service. All the case study authorities had some kind of visiting service, described variously as social visiting, voluntary visiting, routine visiting or friendly visiting. The common characteristic was that they were not undertaken by nursing personnel nor was the visit undertaken specifically for curative or preventive health purposes, except in a few areas where health visitors did more visiting of old people than usual.

Half of the case study authorities saw the reporting of needs as a major function of the visitor. A welfare officer said: 'Visitors can see whether the house needs tidying, whether a home help is needed, or meals-on-wheels. A good visitor can find out other needs by regular visitation, whether pensions and sickness benefit are being collected. There is also a fund to help rent arrears or to get someone a new suit. They can get the doctor if necessary. Perhaps an old body doesn't want the doctor, but a sensible visitor can try to arrange this.'

Two other services provided by visiting were companionship and practical help. Officers from a third of the case study authorities referred to alleviating loneliness, companionship and conversation. A quarter referred to shopping, reading, fetching coal, writing letters, getting library books, preparing people to move into residential accommodation or helping them to stay in their own home by giving practical help. Variations in the emphasis put on different aspects of visiting were considerable, but were not associated with type, size or location of authority, except that Scottish local authorities seemed to put more emphasis on the reporting of needs than on companionship or provision of practical help.

One authority stressed that the meals-on-wheels service was in part a visiting service, and others emphasized the value of the home help as someone who could report needs, and also provide a sympathetic ear for the elderly people in her care. In some areas the home nurse was also seen as a visitor. A nursing officer commented: 'It is hard to tell when a nurse has finished a case because often they just go on popping in.' She suggested that when the nurse no longer needed to visit she ought to give the name and address of the case to a health visitor, so that the health visitor could take over.

For old people living in council houses in areas with door-to-door rent collection, the regular visiting of the rent collector was said to be of value in detecting that an old person might need help. There was virtually unanimous agreement among case study authorities that old people were prompt and regular rent-payers, and that if problems did arise the Ministry of Social Security were always helpful. Rent collectors sometimes also passed information on to health and welfare workers, or to the housing department about need for decorating in areas where some decoration for elderly tenants was undertaken by the housing authority. However, in some areas there was an increasing tendency to collect rents in offices, or by post, rather than at the door (this has always been the more usual pattern of collection in Scotland), and for the frequency of collection to be reduced in order to cut the costs of collection. With larger numbers of council houses in many areas it was pointed out that a collector no longer knew his tenants as he used to.

Seven of the county boroughs and all the Scottish urban authorities employed housing visitors in the housing department, although the ratio of housing visitors to the number of council houses varied. One county borough had 7 for 9,000 houses, another had 5 for 25,000 houses, and a third had 3 for 40,000 houses. However, it was difficult to evaluate these variations without more information about the nature of the work done by housing visitors, since the duties varied. Sometimes housing visitors were concerned with lettings as well as welfare functions.[1] Often they were dealing mainly with people who were about to be allocated a house, or who had just moved into one. A few authorities said that housing visitors did pay occasional visits to elderly tenants to see that they were managing. However, few of the smaller housing authorities had welfare visitors on the staff, although officials in many areas said that the welfare component in housing work was increasing, and a few smaller authorities were thinking of appointing a welfare visitor.

Contact between the housing department and the welfare department over elderly tenants needing help tended to be much easier in the county boroughs than in the counties, where some district council housing officials said they had little contact with the county welfare staff.[2] This was so, despite the fact that the selection of housing authorities for case study was biassed (for reasons outlined in the Introduction) towards authorities located near the county town or with a local area welfare office. However, the finding is less surprising when one considers that area welfare officers in counties were sometimes responsible for very large areas. For example, one welfare division visited had a staff of 6 welfare officers (and 7 clerks) to cover a total population of 232,000 in an area of 260 square miles. A divisional medical officer said there had been little contact with welfare officers, but that now there would be a welfare officer based in the same town he hoped there would be more contact. Thus in some counties the problem was not that contact was bad, but that there was no welfare officer accessible enough to have contact with.

Over half of the case study welfare authorities used welfare officers as visitors, but the visits were mainly routine checks to see whether

---

[1] For a discussion of social welfare work by housing authorities in Buckinghamshire see M. Jefferys, *An Anatomy of Social Welfare Services*, Michael Joseph, 1965, Ch. XIV.

[2] *cf.* Jefferys, *op. cit.*, p. 203: 'With the exception of the LCC welfare workers, direct contact between housing officers and personnel of other branches of the social welfare service was relatively uncommon.'

circumstances had changed or not. As Arkley also found in Reading: 'The welfare officer was regarded as someone with whom one discussed a specific problem.'[1]

One case study authority was trying to run a comprehensive local authority visiting service as well as encouraging voluntary action. A survey had been undertaken in order to establish a register of the elderly, and information was kept up-to-date by means that the authority was not prepared to divulge. A particularly interesting feature of this scheme was the attempt to establish criteria for deciding who should be visited more frequently than others. The division of the elderly population into those 'at risk', and others, reflected what had already been done in the health visiting service in relation to children. In the welfare scheme old people not living alone and not in need of services were visited every six months, whereas those defined as 'at risk', namely those living alone and the over-eighties, were visited every six weeks. This welfare officer did not have a particularly large staff, although he was building it up, but he used clerical staff to help out with visiting the low risk groups. In addition, a large co-ordinating voluntary body organized many services for the elderly including visiting for companionship.

The notion of concentrating visiting on 'at risk' groups among the elderly was also mentioned by some other case studies, where more of the visiting was done by health visitors, or by voluntary visitors. In one or two areas it was the practice to visit the recently bereaved. It is known that these constitute an 'at risk' group. White, for example, reported: 'A significant number of members stopped attending the club at the time of bereavement and never felt equal to the effort of taking up membership again, though they felt they would like to do so.'[2] Other studies have reported excess mortality among the recently bereaved.[3, 4] It was also suggested in the course of this study that an old person living with just one other old person was 'at risk', since if one was taken ill, the burden on the other might very quickly become intolerable.

Some case study authorities referred to social workers (as distinct from welfare officers) in health and welfare departments, as general routine visitors, but others saw them as people who would arrange

[1] Joyce Arkley, *The Over Sixties*, National Council of Social Service, 1964, p. 45.
[2] E. E. White, *Clubs for the Elderly*, National Council of Social Service, no date, p. 73.
[3] M. Young and B. Benjamin, 'The Mortality of Widowers', *Lancet*, 1963, 2, 454.
[4] W. D. Rees and S. J. Lutkins, 'Mortality of Bereavement', *British Medical Journal*, 1967, 2, 13.

for practical help, such as clothing, or convalescence. Often social workers were working primarily with the elderly blind or deaf, or with the elderly mentally ill. A county medical officer of health explained that the health department had built up a staff of 28 mental health officers, half of them trained, mainly as a result of the 1959 Mental Health Act, whereas 'the welfare officer has not had a strong social work set-up though he is beginning to catch up now'. As a result health department staff did a lot of work with old people where mental problems were involved. Another county had inherited from pre-1948 a joint staff for work with the mentally ill, mentally subnormal and old people, with the health and welfare department each paying half of the salaries. This was seen as the nucleus for a social work service under a senior social worker, and with social work offices throughout the county. These authorities saw social workers as specialists providing support for those old people with particularly difficult problems referred to them by regular visitors. It might be noted here that in the few authorities which had them, it was usual for geriatric health visitors to operate as specialists, taking on the more difficult cases seen by non-specialist health visitors. In one authority with a high proportion of elderly in the population it was the ordinary health visitors who saw 'only referred cases where there is some special problem', because it had been easier for the welfare officer to recruit welfare officers to do such regular visiting as was done than for the medical officer of health to recruit health visitors.

There were, therefore, many different arrangements for visiting the elderly. Some visiting was aimed primarily at detecting needs, some at providing practical help, some (especially voluntary visiting) at preventing loneliness, while some visiting was incidental to the performance of other duties. However, with a few exceptions the visiting was far from comprehensive, and there was probably a considerable amount of overlapping. This does not matter in so far as visiting is purely sociable, but duplication of visiting for the purpose of finding needs for services may involve an inefficient use of visitors' time, and the lack of co-ordination may mean that some old people who need regular visiting are not visited at all. Very few officers had any clear idea about frequency of the voluntary visiting services. Local authority welfare departments usually said they had too few staff to operate a comprehensive service, and in the absence of powers under the National Assistance Act to provide domiciliary welfare services it was not easy to develop, even when the need to do so was clearly accepted.[1] Health, welfare and housing departments

[1] Under the Health Services and Public Health Act 1968, the way is officially open for the development of domiciliary welfare services.

within the local authority, and in counties separate housing authorities, were all involved, and the quality of liaison between them varied considerably. In the circumstances the findings of unmet needs was still partly a matter of chance.

MEASUREMENT OF UNMET NEEDS

Attempts to measure the extent of unmet need uncovered by some of these developments aimed at finding individual unmet needs were rarely made. The increase in demand for home help, meals, chiropody, laundry or other services which resulted from the introduction of health visitor attachment schemes, welfare or voluntary visiting schemes, could sometimes have been assessed from information available in the various departments, but the information was not often used.

In one or two areas it was thought unwise to try to evaluate the effect of health visitor attachment on the health visitor's work-load when the scheme was still experimental. It was claimed that, when some of the personnel involved were still not completely convinced that the system would work, attempts to evaluate the effects of the change might jeopardise the whole experiment.

In the few cases where the effects of the change had been studied it was not suggested that the results had been used to *estimate* the likely effect for the local authority area as a whole if all health visitors were to be attached.

A few authorities talked about local surveys to find out the total extent of unmet need. If a laundry service, or a night-sitter service was suggested, it was almost the standard technique to ask round general practitioners and home nurses to see if they could provide sufficient names to convince the medical officer of health and the committee that there was a need. For meals-on-wheels, clubs, or visiting services, welfare officers often also asked local old people's organizations, churches, the (then) National Assistance Board, and district councils, for names of people who might benefit from the service. The comprehensiveness of these surveys depended on how well the nurses, doctors or voluntary workers knew their area, and the number of old people living in it. Further difficulties could arise if services were made available on the basis of survey estimates, because when it came to allocating services to individuals, some people had adapted to managing without the services and did not see themselves as needing them.

One or two authorities commented that old people could be missed

199

in the kind of survey just described and advocated wider surveys. An English county had carried out a survey of old people in their own homes in the early 1950's. 'The health department did not know then, and does not know now, all the old people who might benefit from services. The department had a feeling that the voluntary organizations were dealing with those whom they knew and liked . . . others were being left. The survey was an attempt to sort out needs.' The survey was carried out in four parts of the county, two urban and two rural, by health visitors and social workers.

Health visitors had carried out a survey in one Scottish authority, and a second was discussing the possibility of a survey 'to find out who are the old people in the town, what they are doing in life and what life is doing to them; to detect conditions such as malnutrition; and to find out both whether the old people are using the services which the town has got, and whether they want or need services that the town does not have'. In part this officer's ideas stemmed from his reading about surveys carried out elsewhere, and in part from a meeting called a few years previously by the Scottish Home and Health Department at which the need for surveys was discussed.

The majority did not consider that they could do surveys, saying they had neither time, staff nor money to do this type of work. This was understandable in small authorities, where the medical officer of health himself could be involved in regular clinic work, but lack of time and staff were also mentioned by larger authorities. The medical officer of an authority with a population of nearly half a million said: 'I am so busy just keeping day to day things running that it is hard to find time to sit back and think radically ahead—yet a department of average size is not big enough to justify its own research unit.' A similar comment was made in an authority with a population of about a million.

It was not only the problem of finding time and staff, and freeing people from routine work, that hindered survey work. In one large English county the medical officer said: 'There ought to be two kinds of doctors in a local health department, clinical doctors doing specialized preventive medicine and medical administrators whose tools should include statistics, epidemiology, operational research, etc., and you need either a statistician who has worked in the medical field or a doctor who knows about statistics.' A Scottish county medical officer said he had never asked for staff for research, partly because of the economics of it and the cost in relation to the value of the outcome, and partly because of the size of the department. 'This department (serving about 100,000 people) might *just* be big enough to justify a statistician.' An English county with four times that population still thought it was too small for research purposes. 'We sadly lack something like an operational research group within the health department. My hope lies in the Royal Commission on Local Government. One could have a region supplying this operational research service, although there would still be a need for smaller authorities of a quarter to half a million population working in local areas. The trouble with O. and M. as it exists at the moment is that one cannot expect them to have a fundamental understanding of all the authority's services. The regional set-up could have a section specializing on health and welfare.'

Many authorities were emphatic that, even if they did have time and the skills to do a local survey, they would not do one. 'To do a survey at the moment would be completely wrong. A survey produces findings and the problems are such that we could not hope to cope with them. It is wrong to do a survey if you cannot follow up and do something about the problems you find.'

This attitude was partly related to the difficulties some local authorities had in staffing services. As a medical officer said: 'Even if there is unmet need—where am I supposed to get the home helps from?' Officers' attitudes to surveys could also be influenced by expectations about the views of elected members.

Some officials said it was easier to convince a committee to experiment with providing a new service if you did not tell them how vast the potential demand was likely to be. A medical officer of health, for example, described how the chiropody service in his area was developed by periodically reporting that there was a waiting list to committee and 'letting the service grow'. Others referred to the value of a waiting list for home help, or for a lunch club, as proof for the committee that there was need for expansion of the service. The public's expression of demands which could not be met was thought to carry more weight with elected members than estimates of probable total need, the implications of which might even impede the introduction of a new service altogether.

One of the risks with a new service was that it might not succeed, and some officials were wary of possible failures because they thought it might prejudice the committee against other new developments in the future. It was not always realized that this is one of the strongest arguments for trying to assess the extent of need for a service beforehand.

Some officials were themselves concerned at the prospect of 'opening the flood-gates' of demand for services. In one area the Council of Social Service had carried out a survey, and suggested the need for a laundry service. The medical officer asked home nurses about the number of cases they had who would require this, and on the basis of what they told him decided 'there was nothing doing, because if you open this door you will run into trouble'. Then he began to doubt himself, so he put it to committee, who said they would leave it to the medical officer of health, and so nothing was done.

The same medical officer later gave a clue to why some officials shy away from planning the development of services. He said: 'Perhaps there should be some means of a *selective* laundry service for old people, but you do not know where to start.' The lack of attempts in many areas to establish selection criteria to help decide the amount of service needed by individual cases has already been referred to in Chapter 10. Evasion of this same problem was also a factor underlying some of the comments made about charging policy for the services. Some thought charges necessary as a rationing system, and that services such as home help or laundry would be 'wide open to abuse' if there were no charges. This opinion was maintained in spite of the fact that a high proportion of old people receiving the service were not paying charges. However, the two English case study authorities which had made the home help service free to all cases over sixty-five said that the change in policy had not led to an unmanageable increase in the service, because they only gave it to those who were genuinely in need of it. Certain officials in other authorities also appreciated that criteria by which to decide priorities among needs should be the objective. As a health visitor superintendent expressed it: 'The need is enormous, and it is a matter of getting those with the priority needs.'

SUMMARY

Awareness of unmet needs for services, and of needs for new services varied, although at least one official in every case study authority thought there were people in need of services but not receiving them.

Some lack of awareness was due to failure to realize that general practitioners and other professional workers did not always refer people in need, and may not themselves have known of those in need.

Findings of research studies were not always believed, and some authorities found it difficult to relate findings in one area to their own because they thought local circumstances were different.

In small towns and rural areas it was thought that neighbours and family still provided more care than in large industrial cities. The pride and independence of old people was said to account for some unmet needs, but some authorities were insufficiently aware that charges might act as a deterrent, depending less on the level of charge than on the way charges were explained to old people.

Much awareness of unmet needs was couched in general terms, in the absence of facts to serve as proof.

Various ways of finding individuals with unmet needs were described by different authorities. These included general publicity, educating the general practitioner and other professional and voluntary workers to use the services, hospital liaison schemes, attachment of health visitors and home nurses to general practice, registers of old people and visiting services based on them, and warden services. Ways of solving the problems associated with these policies have been found by some authorities, although the same problems have, at least for the time being, defeated others in different circumstances.

Only in a few cases had attempts been made to measure the amount of unmet need uncovered by the methods described, and the possibility of estimating the likely unmet need in the whole area from the measurement of unmet need found in one part of an area had not been exploited.

Two or three authorities described local surveys (one of them a proposed survey) designed to discover the extent of unmet needs, but many authorities said they had neither time, money, nor staff with the necessary skills, to design and carry out surveys. This point was made by large authorities as well as by small ones.

Some authorities considered it wrong to carry out surveys to find people in need when they knew they could not supply the services. This attitude was partly the result of difficulties in staffing the existing services, and partly because it was said to be easier to convince committees of the need for growth if development was gradual, and based on the expression of demand by the public. Some officials were themselves loth to find out the full extent of needs, often because they failed to appreciate the need to establish criteria for determining priorities for services when demand exceeded supply. A few appreciated the need for setting criteria but did not seem to know how to go about it. Other authorities had devised workable criteria.

It is also possible that the emphasis on the scarcity of supply of resources rather than on the measurement of needs was partly the result of failure to see the purpose of planning, but this is discussed in the next chapter.

CHAPTER 12

DOMICILIARY SERVICES—
THE TEN-YEAR PLANS

The previous two chapters concentrated on the awareness of the local authorities of the need to improve the quality and the quantity of domiciliary services. In 1962, local authorities in England and Wales were asked to submit ten-year plans for health and welfare services to the Ministry of Health, and to revise the plans annually. This chapter considers the bases on which plans for domiciliary services were formulated in the case study authorities, and the extent of consultation with supervisors of different services. A comparison is then made with Scottish authorities, which had no formal plans. Finally, the attitudes of English and Welsh authorities to long-term planning are described.

BASES FOR THE PLANS

The most frequently mentioned factor was the obvious one of population growth. Some health departments were simply planning to increase staff in direct proportion to population growth, but most were also aware of the tendency for the proportion of elderly in the population to increase. One county which was not planning much increase in services because its total population was static seemed not to pay much attention to the ageing of its population, but this was partly because in a rural area with combined duty nurses a decline in domiciliary midwifery can be balanced by an increase in home nursing without any changes of staff.

Some authorities also referred to the social class structure of their population. One or two industrial county boroughs remarked on the higher proportion of social classes IV and V in their population, and the tendency for older working class people to need more from the health and welfare services because of low incomes, poor housing conditions and poor health. In an industrial borough in the Midlands the effect of social class structure was said to be partly off-set by the extent of family care.[1] However in northern towns which were hard hit by the industrial depression in the 1930's, it was said that many of the present generation of old people did not have family in the area, as the younger people had moved away in search of work and had not returned.

Authorities responsible for services in retirement areas, such as spas and seaside resorts, commented that as well as having a high proportion of old people in the population they had higher needs for services because the old people did not have family near enough to help. Thus when one of a couple died, the other was completely alone. This factor was said to be more relevant to some areas than to others, because some retirement areas were populated mainly by wealthy elderly people who employed private domestic help, or by people who would not accept help from a public authority even though they might no longer have the means to pay for help privately.

Family care and neighbourliness were said to mean less need for publicly provided services in rural areas and small towns (see also Chapter 11).

However, although some facts about total population, age structure and social class structure were available for local authority areas, factors such as the extent of family care could only be based on general impressions gained by experience. Even the population projections were regarded as unreliable for some areas, especially counties, and the weight attached to the expected increase in people in the older age groups varied. A few officers seemed fairly confident that old people in the future would be healthier than the present generation of elderly because of improved standards of living and of medical care. This possibility was tentatively suggested by Richardson as a result of his study in North-East Scotland.[2]

Some authorities referred to factors which they thought relevant but unpredictable because they depended on the outcome of other policies. A medical officer in an industrial area said: 'We can do projections of the elderly population, but how can we tell what is going to happen to chronic bronchitis if we do smoke control?'

Some plans for home nursing and health visiting were based on staff ratios recommended by the Queen's Institute of District Nursing, or the Jameson Report on Health Visiting.[3] A few authorities accepted these ratios unreservedly, but one county medical officer, for example, said that he had planned for 1:5,000 population rather

---

[1] cf. P. Townsend, The Family Life of Old People, Pelican edition, 1963.
[2] I. M. Richardson, Age and Need, Livingstone, 1964, pp. 109 and 119–20.
[3] Ministry of Health, Department of Health for Scotland, Ministry of Education, An Inquiry into Health Visiting, H.M.S.O., 1956.

than for the Jameson Report's average figure of 1:4,300 because 'this county is the kind of place that has fewer problems of a social kind than somewhere like Birmingham'.

In a few of the counties, studies of the work-load for the nursing services had been carried out, and one county nursing officer said: 'This study is the basis of our plans for future development on the nursing services side.' The medical officer of this authority added: 'We have not done any assessment of needs for places for the elderly mentally infirm, and we have not done any assessment of appropriate case-loads for mental welfare officers. What we really need is a work study like we did for the nursing services, but then we do not have an equivalent of the county nursing officer with an overall responsibility and interest for this side of the work.'

Another county medical officer said he had tried to allow for the present shortfall in services, but, as already described in Chapters 10 and 11, local authorities rarely attempted to measure this, even though many admitted in general terms that services were inadequate. For the ten-year plans the most usual practice was to extrapolate from past trends. 'Staff for the ambulance service increases by 4–5% per annum and there has been 12 to 14 years of this kind of creep upwards. The same goes for the home help service and nursing. Most projections forward are on the basis of the sort of thing that has taken place in the past with some plusage of what you would like.'

One or two attempts to estimate total need for particular services had been made. A medical officer described the way in which he had formulated plans for training centres: 'I asked for a map showing the distribution of where mentally sub-normal children lived . . . We looked at this in relation to the findings of research studies about what the prevalence should be if everybody were ascertained, and revised our figures accordingly.' No mention was made in any case study authority of a similar exercise being undertaken in connection with services for the elderly, perhaps because of the lack of research studies providing a method of estimating the prevalence of needs in local areas.[1]

Other attempts to estimate need for a particular service included exercises undertaken by the welfare officers of two county boroughs. One, who was developing a day centre for old people, said: 'I did my homework and related the size of the building to the number of the aged within a hundred yards of the building. I also took into consideration the pensioners who were actively engaged in an occupation who would make little demand on the day centre. There will be

[1] B. P. Davies, *Social Needs and Resources in Local Services*, Michael Joseph, 1968, makes an important contribution in this field.

evening patronage from them.' The second welfare officer was concerned about the 'old people who are not able to get out of their homes under their own steam or who would not move out . . . We know a lot of people in their own homes who just do not do anything and get completely apathetic. Their relations have died and they sit back and do nothing and do not bother to eat. The inactive elderly have been identified by setting up an observation register of old people . . . there are now a thousand old people we visit regularly, because they are at risk . . . As a result of the register, we have started our own club.' This was almost the only example met of the use of a register of old people as a basis for estimating need for a service.

However, some authorities found it difficult to believe that there was much shortfall in present services. There were references to having revised the figures upwards as a result of Ministry pressure, but without any conviction that an increase in services was necessary.

In some authorities, revisions of the ten-year plans for staff were based more on the national average or the Ministry norms than on anything else. Comments such as: 'There is no need to spend more money on that service because we're already above the average'; 'We like to be in the middle of the road because it's safe'; or 'The Ministry's averages are useful . . . we're near them', illustrate the possible dangers of indiscriminate use of Ministry standards.

Other authorities were critical of the Ministry standards. One or two said that arguments about being 'below the average' were useful to help convince committees that expansion was needed, but added that as their own figures in the ten-year plans were suspect they did not take figures for other local authorities seriously. One medical officer showed his appreciation of the situation by saying: 'The recommended staff level based on averages cannot be relied on as figures, but if you have big differences then it is a pointer to indicate where one should look.'

CONSULTATION OVER THE PLANS

In some areas, failure to take account of present deficiencies in services may have been partly because some sections heads were not involved in the process of drawing up plans. In one county borough the nursing officer and her deputy said that they had discussed together what they should be planning for the future, how they could do more preventive work, and what would be the effect of developments such as attachment of local authority staff to general practices, but that in relation to the ten-year plans 'the heads of department

207

were not taken into discussion . . . we have had no request to assess our future needs'. The home help organizer in the same authority was concerned about the effect of the ageing population on the demand for her service but, when asked whether she had a say in considering the future of the service, said that 'this had not really come up'. In another county borough, the health visitor superintendent appeared to have been closely involved, but not the home nursing superintendent.

In contrast, other medical officers had called a meeting of all section heads, or had asked them to provide figures and make written suggestions about what needed to be done. In some of the larger authorities, chief nursing officers had themselves prepared the staff estimates.

In counties with an area or divisional structure the officers with the closest knowledge of local needs may be divisional medical or nursing officers, or home help organizers. One county medical officer said he did not discuss the ten-year plans with divisional medical officers because they had no responsibility for mental health services, ambulances or midwifery, which were 'the main services'. This overlooked the fact that the divisional medical officers were concerned with the home help service.

In other counties divisional officers were consulted, and an area nursing officer described how she tried to keep track of what was happening in her area: 'I asked folk in the villages about what building was taking place . . . whether the population was an immigrant one, or whether there was a change of population distribution within the district. If there was no immigration, needs would be no greater, but if there was immigration, there would be increased need for child welfare and school health services, but not a great change in general nursing. I also get ten local papers from my staff . . . it is an easy way of getting the first wind of change.' In this way she was able to keep the county nursing officer informed about what was happening locally.

In some case study authorities health and welfare departments had discussed plans together, and in a few cases the health and welfare services came under the one department. However, the general impression gained was that, as one medical officer of health said: 'There is not really intelligent planning in the way of beds in old people's homes, numbers of flats, and beds in hospitals . . . yet the hospital and the welfare cases are linked with the domiciliary services and the number of old people's flats. It is difficult to know precisely how they are inter-related.' When asked how far the substitutability of related services had influenced the plans for his authority, he added: 'That sounds too logical, and in fact was not how it happened.'

Plans were sometimes, but not always, discussed with other bodies, such as hospitals and voluntary organizations, which also provided services for the elderly (see Chapters 20 and 21), but again the tendency was to plan each service separately, and without allowance for the possibility of substitution of one service, or group of services, for another. The fact that some domiciliary services were supplied mainly by voluntary organizations was sometimes given as a reason why planning was not possible.

PLANNING IN SCOTLAND

There were no ten-year plans for local authorities in Scotland,[1] but much the same picture emerged from discussions with Scottish medical officers of health about future developments. A county officer said that no expansion of services was planned because the population level had remained steady for some time. The ageing of the population had led to an increase in demand for home help, but it was not known whether this would continue, as demand had been steady for a year or two and the apparent annual increase of about 5% was due to increased costs. Two other county officers spoke of population projections, and the proportion of old people in the population, and one criticized the projections. Two authorities referred to the Queen's Institute of District Nursing recommended staff ratios for home nursing, and one was critical of them, saying that no allowance was made in the ratios for the sparsity of population, or for whether the nurses worked on a geographical basis or a general practice basis.

The small size of many Scottish local authority departments tended to mean that consultation between section heads could easily take place, but there was still a strong tendency to consider developments in individual services in isolation. Problems of co-ordination with alternative suppliers of services were also discernible, just as they were in England and Wales.

ATTITUDES TO TEN-YEAR PLANS

Reactions of medical officers of health to being asked to submit plans

[1] The Scottish Home and Health Department informally discussed with at least the larger local health authorities their plans for developments involving buildings, and one medical officer of health referred to this as 'the five-year plan'.

for the next ten years varied. One medical officer of health described the plans as 'a spur to doing something', and another said they made him think more about priorities for development within the local health services: 'It is so easy to be a bit fragmented. One does separate reports on separate subjects and does not put them together and think about priorities.'

In two or three areas the first request for ten-year plans had coincided with a new medical officer of health taking up his post, and provided him with an opportunity to expand the services. In addition, about half of the case study authorities said that the plans were of some use as a tactical weapon in committee, or in competing for resources in the treasurer's or architect's departments.

Three of the larger counties visited claimed that the request for plans had made little difference. In one: 'There is no more planning because of the ten-year plan than there was 15 years ago. All it has required us to do is to put into figures what we would have done anyway.' In the second, the medical officer said: 'The Ministry requests for a plan have led to some change in county council plans and the way they think about the future . . . but there is nothing new in the actual plans themselves.' A third medical officer said: 'With capital works and buildings you have to start years ahead. The ten-year plans created some minor problems on gearing up, especially on the revenue side, but really they were the obvious development, and so were accepted and welcomed.'

In one county borough the ten-year plan was described as 'just another of these damn returns', and in another the medical officer said: 'We put in what we saw was needed for replacement and expansion, but we treated it as an exercise that wasn't very much worth while.'

One medical officer of health said that the ten-year plans were not of great interest because it was the welfare officer who built welfare homes, and that was where forward planning was needed. This emphasis on buildings rather than on staff was partly related to knowledge that sites had sometimes to be earmarked years ahead, especially in heavily built-up urban areas, and partly to the view that it was useless to plan to increase staff when it had always been impossible to recruit enough staff to fill established posts.

Preoccupation with recruitment difficulties had affected the way in which some authorities formulated their plans for staff. Several had submitted 'realistic' figures based on what they expected to be able to recruit, rather than 'idealistic' figures based on what they thought they needed to provide an adequate service. For the second revision of the ten-year plans the Ministry of Health offered guidance on this point, requesting that staff figures for the first three years should be based on expected recruitment, and for later years on expected needs. However some authorities were still claiming in 1966 that their figures were 'realistic'.

It is difficult to judge how far this was due to failure to understand the purposes of long-term planning, and how far to doubts about whether anything would come of the plans at national level. That both elements were involved is well illustrated by a remark made by a medical officer of health who was doubtful about the value of returning idealistic figures: 'The only possible good it could do is to the country because it would show what should be provided in the way of places for training, and it might mean that salaries would be put up in order to make the jobs more attractive.'

An added criticism of the ten-year plans was that they were based on the assumption that numbers of staff must be increased in order to improve the services. Some medical officers of health considered that, especially if there were recruitment difficulties, the most appropriate way to improve the services was to redeploy staff in order to make better use of their time and skills.

SUMMARY

Factors which were thought relevant to the formulation of the ten-year plans were population growth, the increased proportion of old people in the population, social class, and the extent of care by family and neighbours. Officials were often sceptical about the quality or paucity of information available, and there were other factors, such as the effects of changes in the environment on health, which were wholly unmeasurable.

Some authorities were aiming at staff ratios recommended by working parties. Others had studied the work-load of their own nursing services and used the results as a basis for plans.

The need to make good present deficiencies in the services was mentioned by some, but there had been few systematic attempts to estimate the size of the deficiency. In planning to expand services, the most common practice was to project past trends.

Some authorities did not admit to a shortfall in present provision, and there was a tendency in some areas to regard levels of provision corresponding to the Ministry norm or the national average as a safe level.

In some authorities section heads within the health department, and divisional officers in counties, had not been involved in the preparation of plans, but in others their detailed knowledge of local situations had been used.

In most authorities, each service was planned separately from other services which might be complementary to, or a substitute for, it.

The approach to planning in Scotland was similar to that in England and Wales.

Attitudes to the ten-year plans varied. In some areas the plans had acted as a spur or were a useful tactical weapon, but some larger authorities said that they always had planned ahead. In other areas planning was said to be an irrelevant activity for the local health services, which depend on staff rather than buildings. Many authorities either did not see the purpose of estimating demand for staff, or doubted whether anything would be done to increase supply. Some argued that redeployment of existing staff was a more worthwhile activity than planning to have more, when staff were hard to recruit.

Thus, most local health authorities saw the ten-year plans as useful up to a point, but few were enthusiastic, and few claimed that there had been any major change in the way they approached planning. Their whole attitude to planning was tempered by their concern with the practical problems of recruitment, finance, sites and architects' services, and by the existence of alternative suppliers for some services.

PART III

PROBLEMS OF DEVELOPMENT
—THE MOBILIZATION OF RESOURCES

CHAPTER 13

STAFFING—RECRUITMENT DIFFICULTIES

The cool reception afforded by some local authorities to the introduction of ten-year planning was, as described in the last chapter,
partly explained by the difficulties experienced in obtaining staff for
the services. The extent of recruitment difficulties was therefore
discussed in some detail with officials in the case study authorities.
Many reasons for the difficulties were suggested or implied. Those
relating to the general nature of competition for staff and to social
factors affecting the supply of staff are considered in this chapter,
and those associated with the employment policies of the local
authorities themselves in Chapter 14.

EXTENT OF RECRUITMENT DIFFICULTIES

(a) *Home Helps*

A few all-purpose authorities said they had considerable difficulty in
recruiting home helps. One medical officer said: 'There is no difficulty
with committee, who accept the home help service as one of the most
valuable parts of the National Health Service. The difficulty is
getting people.' In another area the medical officer said: 'The major
stumbling-block to the achievement of anything is our inability to
recruit more than half the domestic help we need.' These two
authorities had, in 1965, a low ratio of domestic helps (wholetime
equivalent) to population.

In other all-purpose authorities the situation was quite different.
'We have excellent recruitment' said the home help organizer of a
county borough with a staff ratio close to the average for England
and Wales in 1965. The Scottish large burghs all commented that
recruitment for this service was not really a problem, and the medical
officer of health of the one with the second highest staff ratio of all
the case studies said: 'We always have a big waiting list for jobs.'

Three or four authorities, all with high staff ratios relative to the
national average, said they had just started to experience difficulty.

As one medical officer said: 'There is no problem with the committee over plans for domestic help at the moment because the establishment caters for 100 and at the last count we only had 86 wholetime equivalent. The problem is that we cannot get domestic helps. This is the first time we've met this difficulty and it has lasted 6 months.' Another medical officer said he only started to have recruitment difficulties and high turnover of staff after the service was expanded a year previously.

Almost all the counties in both England and Scotland mentioned some difficulties. Some officers in counties distinguished between different parts of the area, like one who said: 'We do have our difficulties, especially in the rural area . . . The fringe areas of towns are a bit difficult . . . There are not so many problems in urban areas.'

In one of the more sparsely populated counties recruitment was 'not too bad . . . we have a bit of difficulty in two of the small towns and in isolated areas'. Difficulties in isolated areas were mentioned in all the sparsely populated counties studied.

Most of the more populous counties occupied an intermediate position in the table of staff ratios, while the counties with high staff ratios were the sparsely populated ones where a high staff ratio was more an indication of the sparsity of population served than of a high level of service. Of the two counties with very low staff ratios, one had just started a service, and the other did not have many recruitment difficulties, but did operate its service mainly on the principle of allocating only one case to each home help, so that a large number of staff were included in the relatively low figure of wholetime equivalents.[1]

Thus for domestic help, the extent of recruitment difficulties helped to explain the variable development of the service in different areas.

(b) *Health Visitors*

In the case of health visitors, several authorities said there had always been difficulty. The nursing officer of an industrial county borough said the establishment for health visitors had not been altered from the level approved in 1948 because only recently had it been possible to staff all the posts, and there were two posts vacant again at the time of this study. In such circumstances it could be difficult to convince a committee that the establishment should be increased, as the nursing officer of a rural county explained: 'Our health visitors

[1] Domestic helps in this authority worked on average 0·18 of whole-time in 1965, whereas the average for the county case study authorities was 0·39.

are few and far between. They have a load of 12,000 in each area and this is quite twice as much as it should be. When I ask for an increase in establishment I am told that in the past there have been vacancies, and there are still vacancies now, so why do I want more establishment?' However, the reverse could also be true. In a county borough with a strong and vigilant establishment committee the medical officer explained his success in getting agreement to his proposals: 'We knew we would get this establishment through committee because they know that we simply could not recruit that number.'

Almost a third of the case study authorities said they had not had serious difficulty in recruiting health visitors. Only one or two of these were able to say confidently that recruitment was good. Of the others, one was a small county borough which had for the last few years succeeded in achieving a steady increase of one a year with the exception of one year, and two were Scottish authorities which thought there might be greater difficulty in the future than there had been in the past. One or two counties were difficulty to classify, both because the issue was complicated by the practice of combined nursing duties, and because the medical officers of health seemed more optimistic about recruitment than the nursing officers in charge of the service.

In general, those who complained most of recruitment difficulties had, in 1965, the lower ratios of health visitors to population, and vice versa. However, one of those citing difficulty had a ratio equivalent to one which said that recruitment was fairly good, and two others which claimed that recruitment was reasonable had low ratios. Of these, one area had had a bad patch in recruitment a few years previously, and one was a county in which there had been difficulties throughout the fifties. The establishment had been increased on two or three occasions but the medical officer was still, in 1959, writing that health visitors continued to carry heavy case loads because of shortage of staff. In 1962 this authority had achieved its full establishment (which had again just been increased) for the first time in many years, and a further four new posts were filled the following year. Thus the low staff ratio in these two counties was related to past recruitment difficulties even though recruitment was easier by the mid-sixties.

(c) *Home Nurses*

Few authorities had experienced serious difficulties in recruiting home nurses in the 1960's, although in the early 1950's there had been problems in many areas. A few authorities, mainly those with high staff ratios, said confidently that recruitment was good, but the majority said that 'on the whole they managed' to get the staff they needed. Thus the variation in home nursing staff ratios cannot be attributed mainly to recruitment difficulties.

(d) *Chiropodists*

Recruitment difficulties frequently impeded the development of the chiropody service. One medical officer said that his policy was to build it up a little each year, but development 'had got to be played down because of the staffing difficulties', and another said that: 'The need for chiropody is enormous. We are limited by the supply of chiropodists, but we must expand.' One county no longer had a chiropody service as a result of staffing problems, and in another, the medical officer said that a neighbouring county had discontinued its direct service because of staff shortages.

(e) *Welfare Officers*

Many authorities commented on difficulties in recruiting staff for welfare services. The welfare officer of a large industrial county borough said: 'I wanted four welfare officers and got one. Two answered the advertisement, but one was unsuitable.' Another welfare officer said: 'If one welfare officer left now I would be lucky to replace him in a year or eighteen months.'

The chances of obtaining welfare officers with a social work training were poor for all authorities because of the general shortage, and Younghusband training courses were of relatively recent origin. The main hope was to recruit untrained staff as welfare assistants and to train them. Some authorities had not yet introduced schemes for sending people on training courses, and had therefore not found out whether or not there were problems in recruiting welfare assistants. Among those who had tried to recruit welfare assistants, experience varied. In one county, which incidentally had also managed to recruit one or two trained welfare workers from other local authorities, it was said that: 'Recruitment prospects are bright and improving all the time. Originally welfare assistants were not the type we wanted academically. Now they are better. They are the near misses for university places. But we are still getting people whose first choice is not that of being a social worker.' Another county had not fared so well. 'We have had three girls who left to get married. Not many boys are interested, and one we appointed recently went to the treasurer's department instead—he probably gets more money there.'

A county borough welfare officer said: 'I do not get the calibre I want. I get the ones with only one or two O levels, not four or five.' A similar comment was made in one of the Scottish counties: 'For the 3 posts in the office I had 76 applications. Many did not have the right number of O levels for Younghusband training, but they would have made excellent welfare officers.'

Some authorities mentioned recruitment of older people to train as welfare officers. 'We have odd applications from the more mature person but these people are not of the academic standard that we want. These are people who are failures in other fields.' A county welfare officer described his attempt to recruit older trainee welfare assistants: 'This aim was completely unrealistic. Anyone in their mid-twenties who was worth having had already got career prospects elsewhere. There were five posts and we picked some individual characters. It was not an unqualified success. The chap from our own central office didn't make it, and the chap from a housing department didn't stick it. The others did reasonably well, but one got married, one went to University to do specialist social work training, and the one that's left is the bright hope of the welfare officers.'

One or two authorities had fared better. 'The last two welfare assistants we recruited were one who has a diploma in social studies (not a recognized qualification under the new charter for local government officers), and one who had a B.Sc.'

(f) Staff for Residential Accommodation

The staffing of residential homes for the elderly was studied by the Williams Committee appointed by the National Council of Social Service in 1962.[1] Comments made by officers in case study authorities reinforced the findings of this wider survey.

Some difficulties were experienced in finding matrons, such as the rural county 'a long time with no applicants for the post of a matron who was due to retire two years ago'. In another area the welfare officer said they had fared quite well in recruiting matrons, but added: 'We are stumbling from expedient to expedient.'

Many would have agreed with the statement of a county borough welfare officer that 'matrons are hard to get but assistant matrons are harder'. Some authorities had several vacancies for assistants, and in an industrial county borough it was said to be 'fantastic to get any reply at all from an advertisement for an assistant matron'.

[1] The report of this inquiry is published in the National Institute for Social Work Training series, under the title *Caring for People*, Allen and Unwin, 1967.

With other grades of staff in residential homes the situation was generally better, although there could still be difficulties, especially in finding resident or night staff. Some authorities mentioned difficulty in getting cooks, and one county argued against providing meals for the meals-on-wheels service from the kitchens of old people's homes on the grounds that it was hard to get cooks as it was, and so they must not be overloaded. Other authorities said that, although they could manage to get ancillary staff, they had little choice. As one welfare officer said: 'They pick us, we don't pick them.'

Scottish case study authorities did not have serious difficulty over staff for residential accommodation, although several commented that it was hard to get resident staff. One or two mentioned that it was sometimes more difficult to get staff for homes in isolated areas than in towns.

(g) *Wardens*

Some authorities had difficulties in recruiting wardens for sheltered housing schemes. A county welfare officer, who had some say in the appointment of wardens, said: 'With some appointments there is virtually no choice of who to appoint, but in the new town we had better applications.' A rural district official said: 'The selection of wardens is difficult because the number of people available and willing is limited. For one scheme we advertised and chose what we thought was the best of a poor lot. In two other schemes the local councillor recommended a person—both of these worked out well.' An urban district had experienced considerable variation. For their new scheme there had been a short list of five, but for earlier schemes they had only one application in one case, and none at all in the other so that in the end one of the residents in the scheme had been appointed. Two urban authorities had experienced difficulty in the past, but said that the situation had improved.

Altogether, rather more than half of the case study authorities with warden schemes did not have difficulties. It was not uncommon to have 9 or 10 applications for a warden's post, and one urban district had had over 100 applications for one post.

FACTORS AFFECTING RECRUITMENT

Many case study authorities suggested explanations for the presence or absence of recruitment difficulties in terms of competition, either with employers offering different types of work, or with employers offering the same kind of work but perhaps with different conditions of service. Some mentioned other social and economic factors.

(a) *Availability of Alternative Employment*

Light industry such as food processing, boot and shoe, or clothing manufacture was a competitor for people who might staff the home help service in urban areas. Some authorities, including those in mining areas, explained their lack or recruitment difficulties by reference to lack of light industry.

A home help organizer commented: 'A lot of industrial centres have started here in the last five years and there was an increase in the shop population after slum clearance. This has taken our labour force and quite a number of my women have gone', suggesting that industrial development might impede the development of the home help service. However, in another area the organizer had lost several home helps when a new biscuit factory opened, but 'most of them came back again because the job of home help gives them scope for the exercise of initiative'.

In seaside resorts and other holiday areas there were often problems in the summer. Officials in one area said that some people were only willing to work as home helps in winter because they took in tourists for bed and breakfast in the holiday season. A county home help organizer said that in one seaside resort old people who had private home helps in winter came to the local authority for help in summer because the helps went to work at the holiday camp. The local authority often found it difficult to meet this increased demand, because it too was competing with the holiday camp for labour. However, in another holiday resort it was said that: 'There is no comparison between seasonal work in hotels and home help. People who want to do the latter are people with a sense of vocation, they want to do some sort of social work and this is a practical way of expressing that urge.'

A county medical officer said he anticipated few problems over home helps in the towns because the pay was good compared with that for other jobs, and there was an established tradition of women going out to work, but there would continue to be seasonal problems in agricultural areas because 'in this county a lot of women work at the picking and have their traditional round of farms to do'.

Thus the availability of alternative kinds of work affected recruitment of home helps in very different kinds of area. A few similar points about competition from light industry were made by welfare officers in connection with recruitment of domestic and attendant staff for residential accommodation.

221

With qualified grades of staff the question of competition with other kinds of employment more often arose at the stage at which people decided to train for a career. Speaking of recruitment to home nursing and health visiting, the nursing officer of one large county explained: 'There are other openings for girls now, especially teaching, and even with the high birth rate years coming up to school leaving age this still does not help.' The medical officer from a rural county with good recruitment said this was 'because we are an exporting area for nurses because of the social structure . . . nursing is a favoured outlet for the intelligent girl'. However, the county nursing officer thought that 'teaching is still the highest status profession in this part of the county'.

(b) *Availability of Alternative Employers*

To some extent local authorities were competing with other employers for people to do the same kind of job.

Some authorities, especially those with a fairly large middle class element in their population, said it was hard to get home helps because there was plenty of opportunity for private domestic work. One of the attractions of private work was thought to be that it was not such hard work to clean a middle class home with modern equipment as to clean some of the homes which a home help had to tackle. The fact that many local authorities encouraged old people with the means to find their own domestic help may have excluded some domestic helps from the supply of labour for the local authority service.

A similar point was made in relation to the chiropody service. 'Chiropodists are subsidized by the local authorities, who pay on a sessional basis for a contracted number of sessions, and this encourages them to remain in private practice.'

In the case of the nursing services there was little mention of the private employer. Competition for nurses was described by one officer as 'a tug of war between the hospital service, home nursing, midwifery, health visiting and being married'.

Competition with hospitals was more frequently mentioned by large urban authorities than in country areas where opportunities for doing highly skilled nursing work were less. In one city, the nursing officer said: 'We are ringed with large hospitals and those who want to nurse can get jobs in hospitals near their homes. Only those with home commitments or who are unwilling to conform with hospital routines will come to local authorities.' In another town, the nursing officer said that nurses had left the local authority because 'they said they could not see bed-bathing as their job for the rest of their lives—not after being staff nurse on a ward'.

A welfare officer, discussing the problems of staffing residential accommodation, said: 'The problem is that if we take hospital-type patients we need nursing staff—but then the hospitals need qualified nursing staff and we would be competing with them.' However, another welfare officer said: 'I do not think I am robbing the National Health Service by taking nurses, because those who come to us are ones who would not go on working in hospitals anyway, for example the older ones.'

Other officials said that employing nurses in residential accommodation meant 'taking nurses away from our own local health services which cannot get trained staff'. Competition with other parts of the local health and welfare services was also mentioned in connection with wardens for sheltered housing schemes. An urban district council official, describing the applicants for a warden's post, said: 'There were eleven applicants, of which one was a male nurse, one worked at an old people's home, one at the old public assistance institution, and one at a children's hospital. The rest were housewives.' Elsewhere, a county official said: 'We get applications from some wardens to go and work in residential accommodation.'

(c) *Other Factors*

In a few areas recruitment of home helps was said to be difficult because of the social structure of the area. A welfare officer explained: 'There is a higher proportion of middle class residents in this area because it is a high cost of living area. There are a lot of executives who commute, and so there are not the women who would want to do the domestic help type of job. The women here have had professional training and are secretaries, etc.'

In other areas it was hinted that the availability of home helps depended partly on affluence or lack of it. An official in a rural area said: 'We have probably managed to recruit domestic helps all right because there is a low per capita income so that every little helps.' The medical officer of an industrial town said: 'Recruitment is variable because if there is short-time working in industry people want extra cash and become part-time home helps. If there is plenty of money about they don't want the work.'

Many health and welfare staff were married women, and one nursing officer explained: 'We get health visitors when their husbands come with a job, and lose them when their husbands go. The trouble is that there is not a lot of work for men here apart from fishing.

Quite a few have left because their husbands could not get a job.' On the other hand, an authority in an area with large industrial firms based on modern technology, had plenty of enquiries for home nursing posts from people whose husbands were coming to work in the area. In one rural area it was said: 'We have a reputation for being a pleasant area, and many girls come back and marry local farmers.'

Several counties commented that many girls who left rural areas to train as nurses returned later to look after elderly parents. The nursing officer of a Scottish county said that approximately half her staff, including the younger ones, were from the region, many from within the county itself.

Some authorities commented on demographic and social changes and their likely effect on staffing of health and welfare services in the future. A county medical officer, for example, said: 'Our stability may be changing now. We used to have spinsters who came in in the 1930's and these are now retiring. Now more of our recruits are married or have relatives they want to live with. Our incomers are more mobile. We do have a bit of difficulty now in recruiting to fill vacancies.' Jefferys also commented on the past dependence on single women to staff social welfare services, and how the trend towards earlier marriages, and a higher proportion of all women marrying could mean that it might not be possible to depend on lifelong spinsters for staff in the future.[1] Some case study authorities provided figures showing the age structure of their nursing staff. In one area, for example, 19 out of 40 health visitors were over fifty, 15 of them single women. In another, 7 out of 28 health visitors were over fifty-five, including 2 over sixty who were continuing to work on a year to year basis. Few authorities had analysed information on the age structure of the staff in order to think ahead to the problems that were undoubtedly approaching them.

SUMMARY

It was more difficult to recruit home helps in some urban areas and in isolated rural areas than in other areas. Most authorities had difficulties in recruiting health visitors. Some were finding it easier by the mid-sixties, and few had serious difficulty in recruiting home nurses. In many areas, shortage of chiropodists was a brake on development of this service. It was hard to get trained welfare

[1] M. Jefferys, *An Anatomy of Social Welfare Services*, Michael Joseph, 1965, pp. 301-2.

officers, and many candidates for welfare assistants' posts did not have the educational requirements for Younghusband training courses. Attempts to recruit older people to train as welfare officers had only limited success. Many authorities had difficulty in finding supervisory staff for residential accommodation, especially assistant matrons. It was easier to get some kinds of ancillary staff, especially in Scotland, but not resident staff, night staff, and cooks. A few authorities had difficulties in recruiting wardens for sheltered housing schemes, but others had received many applications for such posts. On the whole recruitment problems were associated with the type of staff rather than with the type or size of local authority, and some authorities had difficulties with some grades of staff but not with others.

Some authorities explained their recruitment difficulties by reference to competition from light industry or the holiday industry for home helps, and from teaching for nurses.

There were opportunities for home helps and for chiropodists to work privately, and this could diminish the supply of staff for the local authority services.

There was competition between the hospital service, local health services and local welfare services for nurses, and also for staff in the nursing auxiliary/home help/welfare home attendant grade. Wardens in sheltered housing schemes had sometimes also been nurses or worked in residential accommodation.

Other ways of explaining the ease or difficulty of recruitment included reference to the social structure of areas, the level of affluence, the availability of employment for the husbands of married staff, and the tendency for nurses to return to country areas to look after elderly parents. Some authorities referred to the long service of unmarried nurses now approaching retirement age, and thought there might be difficulties in the future because new staff would be more mobile.

Most authorities commented in general terms on local characteristics affecting recruitment, but none said they had attempted to analyse data available in census volumes or Ministry of Labour publications, and few had examined the age structure of their own staff, staff turnover and reasons for staff leaving, or the previous careers of people applying for vacancies, in an attempt to estimate the probable future supply of staff for local health and welfare services.

CHAPTER 14

STAFFING—EMPLOYMENT POLICIES

Some authorities contributed to their own recruitment difficulties by failing to adapt employment policies, and it is to these policies that the discussion now turns. Local authorities differed in how they recruited staff, and in policies on the employment of married women, part-time workers, older workers, and partly skilled staff. There were also differences in the attitudes of local authorities towards trying to solve recruitment problems by sponsoring training, or by offering improved terms and conditions of service.

RECRUITMENT TECHNIQUES

There were interesting differences in the ways in which local authorities tried to recruit staff. A few authorities relied to a surprising extent on people approaching them to ask for a job, and some had successfully managed to staff their health and welfare services on this basis.

One authority said that the last time there was a vacancy was the first time it had ever had to advertise for a health visitor, and one county had a waiting list of applications for nurses' posts from people working for other local authorities, or from married women doing other work but wanting to return to nursing.

On the other hand, some authorities did not always have people ready to step into vacancies. Most authorities did advertise for nursing staff, but there was a tendency to rely on other methods. Some said that about half of their nursing posts were filled by people who had been personally recommended, and advertising was seen as a last resort. It was not always appreciated that this practice of relying mainly on local and personal knowledge might mean that potential recruits were missed.

Often the district nurse, welfare officer, or health visitor was expected to find home helps. This may be the most effective method in sparsely populated areas, but is more difficult to justify elsewhere. One or two larger authorities relied on health visitors to recruit home helps, arguing that: 'If a health visitor does not know of a suitable person, nobody else will.' Yet one such authority had eventually appointed a person to recruit home helps in areas in which there seemed to be serious difficulties, and recruitment had subsequently improved.

In many authorities it was not the usual practice to advertise for home helps. A county official said: 'In certain areas there are difficulties in recruitment. We have been told we can advertise but that we must satisfy ourselves that the applicants are suitable.' This suggests a lack of understanding of the purpose of advertising, and of techniques for selecting staff.

Reluctance to advertise may have been due to the dislike some local authority officials seemed to have of refusing a job to an unsuitable applicant. A domestic help organizer said: 'We try to stall unsuitable applicants at the preliminary interview. We get people who are really wanting to do only a little light work, and we stress that domestic help can be hard physical work. If we cannot put our finger on why they seem to be unsuitable, we note this on our list and don't offer them a case—hoping that they'll go off and get another job somewhere else.'

Some authorities were reluctant to try to recruit domestic helps through the labour exchange, arguing that, 'the ones they have sent from time to time are not suitable people'.

In contrast, a county organizer said that when she was first dealing with a seaside area where recruitment was difficult she 'badgered the daylight out of the employment exchange. They got so sick of me they sent people regularly to me every week.' This organizer had also contacted housing managers to ask about suitable people, put notices in post offices in the rural district, and in local papers. She added: 'If you want somebody in a village you usually see the policeman.'

However, many authorities who did advertise, and did use the labour exchange still had difficulties. In one county borough, for example, the medical officer said: 'I moved away from the traditional style of advertisement. The idea was to emphasize the social service aspect of home help rather than the money. It did produce applicants, but not all we wanted.' Other authorities mentioned instances when advertising and other efforts to find recruits had been unsuccessful, especially when the vacancy was for a trained health visitor or welfare officer. The welfare officer of a large county said: 'We advertised a vacancy for a qualified welfare officer, and sent a notice to every university with an applied social studies course plus to every college with a full training course just before the final examination time, but in spite of these efforts we had no applications at all.'

227

When recruiting nursing staff, some authorities took a very short-term view. A nursing officer said: 'I do not try to recruit through the schools or Youth Employment Service. From the point of view of long-term policy this would be O.K. but it does not help immediate needs.' Some argued that hospitals were 'not interested in a recruitment policy for nursing as a whole', in spite of the fact that local authority nurses have to undergo hospital training first. However, some authorities thought hospitals did consider, in a general way, the needs of local authorities for nursing staff, and some nursing officers addressed groups of hospital nurses about the work local authorities do. Some areas had exchange schemes, such that hospital nurses spent a short time working with local authority nurses, and local authority nurses attended study days in hospitals to learn about new techniques.

EMPLOYMENT OF MARRIED WOMEN

Just as a few authorities added to their own difficulties by not publicizing vacancies effectively, so a few authorities reduced the number of potential recruits by not employing married or part-time staff as nurses, and occasionally as matrons or assistant matrons for residential accommodation. This made it hard to evaluate statements about recruitment difficulties, unless they were qualified by information about employment policies. Two examples from the case studies illustrate this.

'We have had no real trouble in recruiting home nurses but we are dependent a lot on married women and if we are asked to expand the service there might be a problem.'

'We are fortunate over staffing because although scraping the barrel we have so far always managed to scrape it successfully and keep up to strength with only short gaps. I have never been in a position to have to consider employing part-time nursing staff or partially trained staff. The nursing superintendent and I have considered the problem and feel that one day we may be forced into it. There are married women in the area who would do at a pinch, but I would be reluctant to employ them because of the difficulties.'

Another authority had an official policy of not employing married staff, but admitted that about a fifth of its staff were married, because they were the only ones available.

With certain exceptions, authorities in Scotland employed relatively fewer married staff, and authorities in the north of England relatively more. In the south of England the situation varied, but most authorities were willing to employ married staff, the general attitude being typified by what one nursing officer said: 'There is no reason why we should not employ them, if they can prove that any children are properly looked after. We do not like taking ones with very young children.'

Some authorities had changed their policy but were still missing some potential staff. A nursing officer said: 'Apparently there used to be a policy of not taking married staff. I hit on it because I found a trained health visitor applying for a job as an area home help organizer and I phoned her and asked her why. She said it was because the council did not employ married nurses. We were increasing our establishment of health visitors at the time, so I took her on here.'

Authorities which employed a high proportion of married staff did not encounter insuperable problems. Several commented that local authority hours were suitable for staff with children, and that this gave the local authority an advantage in competing with the hospital. There were some problems in trying to provide a service at weekends if staff had children, and some difficulties arose in school holidays, but problems were more often mentioned in connection with home helps than with nursing staff.

Although turnover could increase, because of husbands changing jobs or staff leaving to have children, some authorities thought that, on balance, turnover was less with married staff because they tended to stay in the area. The nursing officer of one rural Scottish county said it was better to have married nurses in isolated areas, because otherwise you would never get a nurse to stay there.

COMPULSORY RETIREMENT OF STAFF

Some authorities insisted more rigidly than others on staff retiring on reaching retirement age. A home help organizer said: 'One home help was seventy-four and we had to retire her because the medical officer of health found out and said she would have to go. Now she does it privately.' In other authorities: 'The home helps retire when they are past work. They can draw pension at sixty, but often they just cut down their hours so that they earn less than £5 a week.'

Nursing officers commented on a growing tendency to enforce retirement of nurses at sixty. However, some employed nurses on a year to year basis after retirement, and one nursing officer commented that there were older nurses in some of the small remote communities, because only older ones would work there.

USE OF ANCILLARY STAFF

Attitudes to using staff with less training to do less skilled jobs also varied. This issue was particularly important in relation to home nursing, since much of the care needed by elderly patients was basic nursing rather than highly technical nursing care. The Queen's Institute of District Nursing recommended that local authorities should make more use of the state enrolled nurse (SEN),[1] and local studies of home nursing, carried out at the initiative of nursing or medical officers in a number of case study authorities, had also provided evidence of scope for the use of SEN's.

However, there was still some resistance to change. In one authority, the medical officer admitted that more use should be made of SEN's but said the nurses found the idea hard to accept. In another area it was the medical officer who was unenthusiastic, while the nursing officer thought that auxiliary staff could perfectly well do bed-bathing. The general attitude in many areas seemed to be that expressed by this medical officer of health: 'If necessary I will put up with taking less skilled staff. It might be forced on us, though this will be later here than in some other areas because we are a pleasant town and can get staff.' The Queen's Institute of District Nursing report[2] stressed that the severe shortage of SRN's made it even more desirable that SEN's should be employed, but several case study authorities said it was *not* difficult to recruit SRN's, especially if they were prepared to employ married nurses and part-timers, and to arrange hours of duty such that they could employ nurses whose home commitments militated against their working in hospitals.

One specific objection to employing SEN's was frequently made by county authorities. 'There could be dilution, especially for old people needing only minor nursing, but when you have got to have a trained nurse anyway for some things, dilution is not feasible in a county.' There were several comments about the wider scope of a home nurse's work in a rural area since 'every nurse in the rural area is on her own and has to be able to do everything, from vaccination and immunization to collecting prescriptions'.

[1] L. Hockey, *Feeling the Pulse*, Queen's Institute of District Nursing, 1966, p. 128.
[2] Hockey, *op. cit.*, p. 130.

The Scottish Home and Health Department study[1] confirmed that nurses in remote and rural areas performed a different role from nurses in other areas.

Five county boroughs already employed attendants to help with bed-baths, and one other used the services of 12 Red Cross VAD's. One county had bathing attendants in a few urban areas, and other authorities were thinking of introducing them 'because we are getting larger numbers to help in and out of baths, especially in old people's housing. This is particularly true where there are no daughters, and it is a waste of a trained nurse's time.'

One county borough employed foot hygiene attendants to do simple jobs like cutting old people's toe nails under the general supervision of health visitors, although this arrangement was said to be unpopular with the chiropodists. In another, teams of home helps helped with bathing and foot hygiene.

Some authorities had successfully relieved health visitors of routine clinic duties, and even of routine home visiting. In one county borough, where health visitor case-loads were in practice twice as large as those recommended by the Jameson Committee, 6 assistants had been introduced to help. 'There are no recruiting difficulties for assistants and after a time the health visitors found how useful it was to have lesser qualified people available.'

Two or three authorities said they were considering appointing 'welfare assistants' or SEN's to do routine visiting of old people under the overall supervision of a trained health visitor. There was some confusion over the relationship between the health visitor and social workers employed by either the health or the welfare department. Some authorities thought of the health visitor as the routine visitor with the social worker as the specialist, whereas others saw the health visitor as the one to visit and assess a case, and then pass on to the social worker those with purely material needs, or with no immediate needs. This confusion about the relative roles of health visitor and social worker may have hindered the development of policies designed to make the best use of highly trained and scarce womanpower.

TRAINING

Most authorities had accepted the need to recruit nurses without district training or health visitors' certificates, and sponsor them for

[1] V. Carstairs, *Home Nursing in Scotland*, Scottish Health Service Studies No. 2, Scottish Home and Health Department, 1966.

training. The same applied in the case of welfare officers and Young-husband courses. However, policies on paying salaries to students in training varied. One small county sent nurses to train as health visitors on full pay with a rebate for rent and rates of their house, but several other authorities paid only a proportion of salary—usually 75%, in spite of a Ministry circular suggesting that staff seconded for training should be on full pay.[1]

Some authorities only sponsored students for training when they had difficulties in filling vacancies, and this intermittent intake for training meant that there was no steady flow of trained staff becoming available each year. As the Mallaby Committee pointed out, short-ages of places on training schemes for health visiting was not yet a problem, since not all available places were filled.[2]

Many authorities required sponsored students to contract to stay with the authority for one or two years after training, or to reimburse the authority for training expenses. This policy was thought by the Mallaby Committee[3] to deter potential students, especially married ones, and thus contribute to the national shortage of health visitors.

The fact that an increasing number of staff were married and had families put authorities with no local training facilities at a dis-advantage compared with those who had. A nursing officer said: 'We hope we can give staff district training. Our people have gone away to train, but now many are married and cannot get away, and cannot afford to pay two rents.' In another area: 'Now there is a local training scheme for health visitors we are finding a lot of people whom we could have trained previously if we could have done it locally.' One county did not appoint home nurses unless they stated they were willing to do district training, but in spite of this, some nurses had never done it because the training involved a residential period away from home and the nurses had family commitments. In an attempt to surmount this difficulty the county had started a system of in-service training. 'The students work on their own districts for the whole of the period save three weeks. They have to go to the nearest big town for some lectures, but can come home again. They have tutorial days as well, organized by an area nursing officer with a special responsibility for training.' Nevertheless, the medical officer of health hoped that this would be a once-for-all measure to clear the backlog, because he preferred people to go away for training to get ideas from other places.

[1] Ministry of Health, *Circular 8/65*.
[2] Ministry of Housing and Local Government, *Staffing of Local Government*, H.M.S.O., 1967, p. 44.
[3] *Ibid.*, pp. 45–6.

One county had taken a firm line on training for welfare officers. There were schemes for sending existing officers as well as young newly recruited welfare assistants. The committee had agreed that promotion would be given only to qualified staff. While this aroused some resentment at first, it was accepted because the older ones could go on courses if they wished, although there were difficulties for them both financially, and in terms of family responsibilities.

The age structure of the staff in some departments also made for difficulties. A county nursing officer said: 'The difficulty is that we did not send people away to do health visitor training in the past. About half the staff are unqualified, but half of these are over fifty-five and it is thought that local authorities should not send people over fifty-five to train.'

Counties operating a combined nursing service had difficulties over sending people for training because of the multiple training required by one person. Similar problems arose in welfare departments, where welfare officers sometimes also performed other functions such as registration of births, deaths and marriages. While some of the more urban counties were successfully managing to separate welfare and registration as welfare services developed, it was less easy, and perhaps less desirable, to do this in rural areas. If the functions were not separate, it was difficult to send people to train. As one Scottish county welfare officer said: 'We have no trained welfare officer, and cannot justify having specially trained people. If you send a welfare officer away you may find yourself without your district council clerk and your NAB officer too.' District council clerks in this county also performed housing management functions.

Another problem was that of trying to expand services at the same time as sending staff for training. This was particularly acute in small departments, such as many of the Scottish authorities. The absence of one member in a staff of two or three created greater difficulties than in a staff of twenty or thirty. The same applied even in small health departments. 'With one or two away on some course or other you can, with a staff of ten, easily find you are at half strength because there might be others off sick or on leave.'

Training for social workers was accepted policy in some areas, but there were still many where elected members did not see the need. A county welfare officer commented that the establishment committee was geared to dealing with administrative staff and had no concept of social work, and no advisers except from the clerk's and treasurer's departments. Teachers, and nursing staff in the health department, were not under the control of the establishment committee, but the welfare officer with his requests for social workers was. In a rural county with a small staff the welfare officer said: 'We had a district welfare officer who retired. I wanted to get someone who would go to a Younghusband course but the committee did not think it necessary to replace him. They just do not understand what a social worker could do. Part of the problem was because the O and M study done by an outside firm recommended that the welfare department should not have any social work staff. I asked why and they said it was because of the size of population. But I knew that the same people had done a study of another county and had recommended a social worker for there, and yet that county's population is less than ours. But I found out later that the draft O and M report had been seen by members of establishment committee before it was discussed with chief officers.'

This lack of understanding of the role of social workers was also commented on by several large authorities. It was also said that some committees would agree to extra nurses, but not to health visitors because they did not fully understand what a health visitor did.

Some authorities were not enthusiastic about sending matrons and assistant matrons in residential accommodation on training courses run by the National Old People's Welfare Council on account of the cost, and the need to employ a relief matron meantime. The same arguments were used in connection with training for home helps, home help organizers, and wardens in sheltered housing schemes.

About a quarter of the case study authorities provided some in-service training for home helps, partly in the hope of improving staff morale and helping recruitment, and partly because some thought that training was desirable in the interests of a good service.

'I tell the home helps they are part of a welfare state and that they are as essential as district nurses and health visitors. If you get this sense of duty over, you keep your staff.'

'We run a course for twenty home helps one afternoon a week for four weeks, and pay them to come. We cover things like the role of different sections of the health department, shopping on a budget, cooking quickly, efficiently, and on all sorts of appliances, washing, etc. When we asked what they would like if they were on a repeat course they all said first aid and home nursing. About two hundred wanted this.'

Some officials did not favour training home helps. A medical officer of health had turned down the suggestion on the grounds that he did not want to put off the uneducated ones. One organizer who ran a successful training scheme stressed that training had to be appropriate to the needs of home helps, but that given tactful handling, training was valuable. Another official feared that if home helps had training they would start to develop restrictive attitudes about the kind of work they would or would not do, and so reduce the flexibility of the service.

In another authority the inclusion of basic nursing in a training course had unforeseen consequences. 'We tried training the best ones to do basic nursing care with the idea of relieving the home nurse. But they went off and got jobs as auxiliaries in hospitals and so we decided it was not worth it. So we concentrate on the domestic side.'

Often the general attitude was that home helps and attendants in residential accommodation did not need training, but one authority uttered a word of caution on this in relation to the future. 'So far we have been able to meet the need, but the type of home help is changing. We started with people who came because they were dedicated to the service but the ones we get now just think of it as a job. Standards in homes generally are falling, as people who come to us as home helps now were brought up in homes where both parents were working.'

Qualification requirements impeded the development of the chiropody service in some areas, but here there seemed to be no question of the local authority sponsoring training. One authority said: 'We could not get qualified chiropodists so we provide the service through chiropodists found by the Old People's Welfare Association although the borough took over the full cost. The borough administers it, and authorizes the treatment but the OPWA makes the payment to the chiropodist.' In another area: 'The chiropodist was unqualified but got on the register. He resigned and the service has packed up. We have repeatedly advertised for a chiropodist with no response. We are not allowed to use unregistered chiropodists who are available locally and the nearest registered ones are 20-30 miles away.'

One or two counties argued that it was better to provide the service by contracting with private chiropodists, because otherwise in a rural area a directly employed full-time chiropodist would spend a lot of time travelling.

PAY

National pay scales for grades of health and welfare staff covered by Whitley Council or Joint Industrial Council agreements operated as a mixed blessing. A county medical officer said: 'The national scales for health staff are fortunate for us because they compare well with prevailing wage rates in industry and other employment, whereas in some areas the reverse is true. This plays into our hands and we can get staff.' Several case studies, especially the industrial towns, were in the reverse situation. Although some paid above the national scales, many did not 'because of the socialist members on the council'. Even those which did pay above the scale did not always succeed in solving recruitment problems as a result.

Low pay for a trying and responsible job was cited as one reason for difficulties in recruiting matrons and assistant matrons for residential accommodation. In spite of this, although most authorities paid an extra £60 p.a. to matrons with a nursing qualification, there was not always extra pay for having attended the National Old People's Welfare Council six months training course for matrons.

Several authorities commented that national pay scales meant that fringe benefits were necessary in order to get staff, and they had to try to keep up in the competition. For example, a medical officer described the way in which a policy of paying removal expenses for health visitors was introduced: 'We asked the health visitor superintendent, and went through journals and looked at advertisements. Also we often got enquiries about health visitor posts which were withdrawn when we said we paid no removal expenses. We wrote round all local authorities to ask what they did and found that we were behind on this. This was used as an argument for the case we put to committee. Of 41 local authorities which replied, 37 give removal grants.'

However, several officials opposed fringe benefits on the grounds that it did not really solve the fundamental problem in a situation of overall shortage, 'because if you attract people by paying extras then it only means somebody else does without'. It was also pointed out that: 'You cannot publicize what you are doing too much because eventually you get back to square one.'

HOUSING

It was sometimes thought that local policies on provision of houses for health service staff affected recruitment. A county medical officer in an area which had little difficulty in recruiting nurses said: 'We are already attractive and so make it more so. Our plans for new houses for nurses started before the ten-year plans. Previously we owned a third, rented a third, and a third of the nurses made their own arrangements. A lot of the rented ones were unsatisfactory, and this led to a policy of building so many per annum to replace these.'

One very small authority had also decided on a policy of building individual houses for nurses, but had previously lost a nurse to another county which had already built houses. A few county authorities were beginning to have doubts about building special houses for nurses, since later population changes could mean that the house was badly situated. Alternatively the new occupant of a post might be a married woman who already had a house. These authorities were beginning to think of buying houses as needed, and selling again as needs changed.

Some authorities still had a district nurses' home, which had often been provided originally by a district nursing association. In some cases these had been converted into independent flats; in others, new houses were provided for the nurses and the home converted for use as a mental health centre, welfare clinic, or training centre for home helps. In one or two cases the intention to convert to other uses had been thwarted, at least temporarily, by the Ministry's refusal of loan sanction because of the general economic situation. The old type of communal home was seen by most authorities as a disadvantage in terms of attracting staff to fill vacancies.

Although most authorities provided housing for home nurses and midwives, many did not provide it for health visitors. Some said this had an adverse effect on recruitment, and examples were given of health visitors leaving to go to a local authority which did offer a house. In counties this seemed of less importance, partly because some staff were in combined duty posts and qualified for housing as home nurses, and partly because in some counties the housing authorities co-operated in housing health visitors, and in other areas it was not difficult to qualify for a house as an ordinary applicant. The main reasons given for not housing health visitors were that they did not need to live so near their work as a district nurse or midwife, and that if health visitors were offered council houses, other kinds of social workers and welfare officers would want houses, and a line had to be drawn somewhere.

A few authorities said that housing for nursing staff was becoming a less important issue, since so many were married women who had their own houses, or were 'girls who come home to their parents and want to live at home'.

The development of housing to replace communal homes for nursing staff raised issues over rents. The Whitley Council agreements provided for scales of charges for accommodation, and because the

Whitley scales were based on nurses' homes, they were below the level of council house rents in many areas. This led to problems, particularly in counties, where the housing and the health authority were not the same. In one county, nurses had to pay the council house rent, although it was above the Whitley scale, but in several other areas it was usual to charge the nurse on the Whitley scale and for the health authority to pay the difference. However, in one area, this brought its own complications: 'If the nurse wants to live in her own property we let her. Where the nurse lives in a county property she has a reduced rent. The tax people concluded that they were getting something for nothing and some of them will get a bill from the Inland Revenue for over £100. We are losing staff as a result because they are asking "Why should we be messed about?" Both sides are right. Our legal people have been all round it and there is no way out. Because we say a nurse may live in her own house, she is liable.'

In the past most authorities tried to staff welfare homes on the basis that at least the matron and her assistant would be resident, and attractive accommodation designed to give resident staff privacy in their off-duty time has been seen as one way to obtain and keep staff. Despite Ministry opposition, one case study authority had started to build separate bungalows for matrons. The welfare officer explained that they were short of beds for old people. By converting the matron's accommodation they could get 3–6 more units, and it was cheaper to build bungalows than to add new accommodation for the matron on to existing buildings. It might be added that it was increasingly a matter of providing housing for the matron *plus her family*, since the single matron was already something of a rarity.

However, some case study authorities were beginning to think in terms of having all non-resident staff in the future, which implied that night staff would be needed. The welfare officer of one of the larger authorities said: 'In the homes for infirm residents I am not going to have a resident matron. I am short of five assistants now, so in future I am going to have two matrons per home—not resident, and not both working at the same time, and I will cut out assistants altogether.' If matrons and assistants are to be non-resident, the issue of whether or not the local authority will provide housing for them, the charge to be made for it, and its relation to the salary paid, will arise.

The case of wardens of sheltered housing schemes was rather similar, although there was, at the time of the case studies, no generally agreed pattern of wage levels,[1] and in some cases, a rent

---

[1] One suggestion made is that the rate of pay for female attendants on the aged and infirm (Class 1 of the Ancillary Staffs Council of the Whitley Councils for the

free house was the only payment made. In larger urban authorities it was more common to pay a higher money wage,[1] and charge normal rent for the house or flat. One such authority said the wage had been fixed at £8 per week so that wardens were eligible for the superannuation scheme. However, another authority said that wardens who were paid a much lower wage were eligible for the pension scheme, while adding that: 'They would have to work for 40 years before being entitled to a pension because it is worked out in relation to the number of hours per week worked. The wardens do only 8 hours, and mostly are old age pensioners already.' Another urban authority appointed married couples as joint caretaker and warden for groups of 24 flatlets, and paid the husband a basic wage of £11 11s 0d per week, and the wife £3 16s 2d per week on the assumption that she works 18 hours.

Smaller authorities more often provided a house or bungalow rent and rates free, but paid a wage of about £2 per week for groups of 8 dwellings, and about £3 15s 0d per week for groups of 15 dwellings. The quality of accommodation varied. In some cases central heating was included; in others it was paid for separately, or else heating was by conventional means. In a few cases the wage was of the order just described, but the house was not rent free. One or two of the authorities in this category, and of those who did not pay a money wage at all, had experienced difficulty in obtaining wardens, although the reason given for the difficulty in some cases went beyond matters of pay.

Without knowing more about whether potential wardens operate in a local or a national labour market it is difficult to judge whether comparison of pay conditions between local authorities is a relevant exercise, since if they operate in a local labour market the appropriate comparison would be with other employers competing for the same kind of people. Nevertheless, as sheltered housing grows, the whole issue of wardens' pay and conditions of service will have to be considered if sufficient numbers of staff are to be attracted to the work.

Health Services) is comparable (West Midland Old People's Welfare Committee, *The Warden in Grouped Dwellings Schemes for the Elderly*, Midland Advisory Office of the National Council of Social Service, February 1965). The National Old People's Welfare Council expressed the hope that in the near future wardens' salaries would be arranged by the usual negotiating machinery (National Old People's Welfare Council, *Wardens and Old People's Dwellings*, National Council of Social Service, Ref. No. 712, 1966, p. 12).

[1] Some case study authorities based their payments to wardens on Joint Industrial Council scales.

TRAVEL ALLOWANCES

Another factor thought to affect recruitment was the policy on travel allowances, especially for nurses' cars. Most authorities paid travel expenses for district nurses, midwives and health visitors, for whom travel between cases was inherent in the nature of their work. But while many areas provided either car or mileage allowances—or the choice between the two—for district nurses and midwives, some reimbursed the health visitor only for travel by bus. Since some health visitors in fact used their own cars it was a bone of contention with them that they could not claim a mileage allowance while district nurses could. A particularly anomalous situation arose when a district nurse used to having an allowance trained as a health visitor and so disqualified herself. The main explanation for the policy was that if health visitors were given car allowances, other social workers would want them. Midwives and home nurses were treated differently because they had to carry equipment, and speed of getting to a case could be crucial.

As well as feeling that lack of car allowances for health visitors discouraged applicants for jobs, a few nursing officers suggested other reasons why the policy should be reconsidered. In one of the smaller towns, for example: 'New houses are being built further out and buses do not always go that far, or not very frequently. There is only one bus up and one down from the area in the morning. The health visitors find they have to walk one way.' A second reason was that health visitors attached to general practices were working with practice populations rather than defined geographical areas, and were able to do home visits only if they used a car, since general practitioners had patients scattered round the town.

Counties were more generous over travelling allowances than industrial towns, but this was partly because of the greater prevalence of combined duty nurses, and partly because the greater dispersion of population in rural areas made the use of a car essential.

The attitude often found in industrial areas was explained by the medical officer of a large county borough: 'For many years the corporation resisted giving car allowances. They have gradually accepted, but there is still more resistance than you will find in some authorities. The allowances are pretty tight, but as long as we don't exceed the number of allowances for the service the health department is allowed to allocate them. It is difficult to increase the allocation except at review time every two years. The position is good compared with five years ago. There are two factors behind the change in attitude. First, the realization that it is one of the fringe benefits which determines whether a person comes here or not. Secondly, a lot of time can be lost going hither and thither about the city.'

However, he added that: 'The reason for resistance is now partly the high degree of traffic congestion, and it would mean providing parking space for the staff.' It could be slower to go by car than to walk in congested towns, and some smaller towns which were not congested in winter, could be very congested in summer. These considerations pointed to the need for a flexible policy such as that achieved by those urban authorities which operated a pool for travel expenses.

Several authorities offered loan facilities for car purchase. Here again it was in the older industrial areas that facilities were poorest: 'There is no car purchase system here. I wish there were . . . the council ought to accept the national conditions because this would probably help in recruitment. At least we should not have a disincentive to coming here, and it would prevent staff from comparing us with nearby authorities and deciding to move.'

Travel allowances were becoming an issue with other grades of staff. One or two officials were concerned at the lack of mileage payments for chiropodists doing domiciliary work, although other authorities did pay a mileage allowance. Two English counties paid a mileage allowance to home helps in rural areas. This operated on a small scale only. In one authority the policy originated because there were problems in obtaining staff for cases in particular areas, and there happened to be two home helps with cars who were willing to use them.

In the other authority, the policy was more general, but take-up was limited because not many home helps had cars. Some authorities, including a few county boroughs, paid home helps for travelling between cases. Others, including some counties, did not, nor did they all count time spent travelling between cases as working time, despite the fact that in rural areas cases were not always close together, and rural bus services could be limited or non-existent. This evidence showed that expenses were not necessarily paid where the rationale of doing so was strongest, but it was not clear that this operated as a deterrent to home help recruitment.

A few authorities suggested that the council policy of not paying travel expenses militated against recruitment of staff for residential accommodation, especially for homes in rural areas, on the outskirts of towns, or in parts of towns where the immediate neighbourhood was not a good catchment area for staff. Given low wages compared with their competitors for female labour, travel expenses could be a significant marginal factor.

NATURE OF THE WORK

Finally, local authorities varied in the extent to which they recognized and tried to overcome staffing difficulties due to the nature of the work. A few authorities commented that 'scarcity breeds scarcity', and conversely. In a county which fared reasonably well in recruiting health visitors it was said that: 'Health visitors come back from refresher courses glad that they work here. The case loads are reasonable. Health visitors in some local authorities have twice the case-load.' The contrast is provided by an area with difficulties in recruiting home helps: 'Recruitment is a vicious circle. The ones we have work very hard. They tell their friends this and put them off. One can't break into this.' It could, therefore, be difficult for an area with a low level of service to start to develop.

In the case of domestic help, the hard work, which was mentioned by several authorities as a reason for recruitment difficulties both present and future, was partly because many homes in which helps had to work did not contain modern equipment. Some health departments held a small stock of cleaning equipment, but this was usually intended for helps working with problem families rather than with the elderly. One or two examples were found where the provision of equipment was thought to be someone else's job. One organizer said: 'We explain to old people that they are expected to provide what is needed. If they cannot do so then we tell the geriatric health visitor, who tells the welfare visitor, who tells the National Assistance Board and arranges that they will pay for what is needed. If that fails, I do get a bit on petty cash in the health department for the barest essentials.'

A county borough medical officer was convinced that the home help service had to be made more efficient, given shortage of staff and growing demand. His authority had made financial provision in the estimates for one or two vans which would be equipped with vacuum cleaners, buckets and brushes, and he was trying to find a way of providing hot water from the vans.

He had done a survey of the work done by his home helps (there was a whole-time equivalent of 80–90 staff) the previous winter, and found that they lit a total of 212 coal fires a day, which he described as 'a nonsense'. His findings illustrated that provision of modern housing for the elderly could make a substantial contribution to the solution of problems of staffing the domiciliary services.

The interdependence of services was also illustrated by the story of a county borough home help organizer: 'I found a home help washing incontinent laundry in the bath because there were no other facilities. The patient was an old lady living alone. I thought something ought to be done and put the idea of a laundry service to the medical officer of health. Now we provide linen, which is picked up by our van three times a week and taken to a laundry at the public baths. This is one of our most valuable services.'

However, some authorities claimed that provision of modern housing, or development of other services to deal with heavy work such as laundry still did not remove the original staffing problem. Again it was the low level of services all round which was the key factor. A county home help organizer said, of a seaside retirement area: 'There are some old people's flats—bed-sitting rooms in a building with a lift—with a warden in overall charge. In the rest of the town old people get five meals a week from the WRVS meals-on-wheels service and those in the flatlets get none, because others have greater need. Also the home help service already had a lot of cases in the town—worse cases than these—so few in the flats get help. They are just left on their own. We had a meeting about this. The housing manager said "see how much easier it is when the old people live in flatlets", to which the WRVS organizer's rejoinder was that when you took old people out of substandard flats and rehoused them, all that happened was that another old person moved into the substandard flat. Therefore the domiciliary service still goes to the older places and it is not easier at all.'

In some authorities residents in sheltered housing did receive domiciliary services, but there was always the risk that the presence of the warden lowered the priority of the case, imposed an extra burden on the warden, and contributed to difficulties in recruiting and retaining wardens. An example was described in Chapter 8, and there were indications from other housing authorities that, as sheltered housing grew, this could become an important issue. One district council said that for their first warden-scheme: 'We got exactly the person we wanted. Her husband works on a poultry farm nearby and they have two children. The warden herself is very much a home-bird, and her mother-in-law, who is seventy but very able-bodied, is one of the old people in the scheme and so she is able to stand in for the warden when she and her family go out and away. This is very fortunate and I am not sure that we could repeat this success elsewhere.' For the second scheme there had been a few enquiries for the warden's post, but no takers—'they all seemed to be afraid of being tied to the place'.

The nature of the job could also adversely affect the recruitment and retention of staff in residential accommodation unless there was skilful management. A good matron could do much to create a good working atmosphere for other staff. Even so the strains imposed on the staff of a small home by the absence of even one member of the team through illness, or because of a vacant post, could be considerable. Matrons and assistants also needed support from welfare staff, and from others who understood the strains and stresses of their work.

The social image of the job was also important. In one case study area a young married couple were training as assistant matron and superintendent. They posed the particular problem that it could be difficult for youg members of staff to find friends. They met other matrons sometimes, but were so much younger that they had few interests in common. Relations with other matrons were good but the couple said: 'They are not a source of friends. It is quite a problem, because if you tell your contemporaries that you work in an old people's home they're either morbidly interested, or else they look at you as though you've got some dreadful disease and hive off.' This also illustrated the difficulty of introducing changes—in this case that of trying to encourage young people to make a career in the welfare service—without blows to morale wrecking the policy before it had a chance to become firmly established.

SUMMARY

Some local authorities relied on personal contacts when recruiting staff for health and welfare services, and did not advertise or contact the labour exchange, even when they were short of staff. Others made more positive efforts to find staff, but were not always successful. There was some evidence of lack of knowledge of techniques for recruiting and selecting staff.

Some authorities did not employ married nurses or were not making full use of this source of staff. Others found that married nurses gave good service.

Compulsory retirement on reaching pensionable age was strictly enforced in some areas, but others let staff who wished to do so continue to work on a year to year basis.

There was resistance in some areas to using state enrolled nurses unless forced to by inability to recruit registered nurses. It was not thought feasible to use SEN's in rural areas. County boroughs more often employed bathing and foot hygiene attendants to relieve home nurses than did other types of authority. Some authorities relieved health visitors of routine clinic work, but in terms of developing a visiting service for the elderly there was evidence of confusion about the respective roles of health visitors, social workers, and welfare assistants.

Most health authorities accepted the need to sponsor nurses for district nurse or health visitor training, and some welfare departments were seconding welfare assistants for social work training, but authorities tended to take a short-term view and sponsor students only when they failed to recruit trained staff. Deterrents to potential students, especially to married staff with families, included inadequate pay during training, fixed contracts for a specified period with the sponsoring authority, and lack of local training facilities. Small authorities found it difficult to spare staff, and the multiple nature of duties carried out by nurses and welfare officers in rural areas also created problems. Elected members were often said not to understand the need for social work training. Training for staff in residential accommodation, wardens in sheltered housing, and home helps, was considered not to justify the cost in many areas, but in others, some training was given in an attempt to recruit and retain staff. Lack of trained chiropodists affected the service available in some areas, but local authorities did not sponsor chiropody students.

National pay scales helped authorities to recruit staff in areas where other wage rates were low, and vice versa. Those adversely affected were mostly industrial towns, and socialist councillors often opposed paying above the national scales. Several authorities resorted to providing fringe benefits, but many opposed this policy on principle because it did not solve the basic problem, nor did it ensure that resources were distributed so as to meet the greater needs.

Policies on provision of housing varied. Some authorities were converting former nurses' homes to other uses, and providing new homes and flats in order to attract nursing staff. Others were buying houses, and selling again as needs changed. Some said housing was not an issue now that so many staff were married. Not all authorities housed health visitors, and few housed social workers. To provide attractive accommodation for supervisory staff in welfare homes was considered important, although some authorities were beginning to talk of non-resident matrons. In sheltered housing schemes, rent free housing was often an important element in the remuneration of the warden.

Some authorities had more generous policies on travel allowances

245

and help with car purchase than others. Many did not provide for health visitors to have cars, in spite of poor bus services to outlying estates. This policy may also have impeded the development of attachment to general practice. Industrial towns were least generous, and in some it was argued that traffic congestion and parking problems meant there was no point in staff having cars. Travel allowances for chiropodists were also an issue. Few authorities paid mileage allowances to home helps in rural areas, but policies on travel expenses and payment for time spent travelling varied, and expenses were not always paid where the rationale for doing so seemed strongest. The cost of fares was seen by some as a deterrent to staff for residential accommodation.

Many recruitment problems seemed to stem from the all round low level of the services, and the public image of the services. Hard work for existing staff led some to leave, and also to tell other people that it was hard work. A few authorities were trying to provide equipment, or develop laundry services in order to lighten the work of the home help, but many were not doing so. The provision of small modern housing for old people was still on too small a scale to have much effect on the problem.

CHAPTER 15

FINANCE—CAPITAL PROJECTS

The development of some local authority services for the elderly involves the provision of buildings, the capital cost of which is often met by borrowing, though some smaller developments, such as extensions to existing homes for the elderly may be financed from revenue. A small amount may also come from donations and gifts. This chapter discusses the ways in which decisions are taken on what capital investment is to go forward each year and how it is to be financed. The central government is deeply involved in the control and guidance of capital investment, and so the role of central departments is also discussed.

CAPITAL PROGRAMMES

Half of the treasurers in the case study authorities said that they had a rolling capital programme for at least two years ahead (mainly for 5 years). Some treasurers with larger programmes in effect put a confidence limit at the end of two years. One county borough finance officer discussed with the clerk's department how far the capital programme should look ahead, and both departments asked health department officials what they thought of the ten-year programme. 'They said "Not much", because it was just a hazy prediction of what they might like.'

Although the forward programme for health and welfare was usually made consistent with the programme laid out in the ten-year plans, there was no confidence at all in the figures, or even in the usefulness of announcing a programme for more than five years ahead. After the fieldwork for this study, in 1967, the Ministry of Health asked local health and welfare authorities to submit three-year rolling capital programmes. This suggested that the proposals in the early years of the revised ten-year plans could not be used by the Ministry for indicating provisional loan sanctions for projects. This was in line with the views of many case study authorities on capital programming.

The Royal Institute of Public Administration stated that three or five-year budgets appeared to be most common and reported that an Institute of Municipal Treasurers and Accountants' survey in 1955 'recommended five years as the minimum desirable for effective planning in a period of economic stability, but three years as the most that could be reviewed with any degree of realism in the conditions of frequently changing government policy and economic circumstances then prevailing'.[1] The Maud Report stated that two-thirds of county boroughs, two-fifths of counties, a third of non-county boroughs, a sixth of urban and rural districts and just over two-fifths of the London boroughs had a capital budget covering a period of at least three years. Smaller counties and larger boroughs were more likely to have a capital budget. In the main, the period covered was three or five years, the latter being rather more popular in all types of authority, except counties and London boroughs.[2]

The twelve case study authorities with no programme were mainly English counties or local authorities in Scotland and the commonest reason for not having a programme was the belief that central departments effectively controlled capital programmes.[3]

The total capital investment in one year was limited by the capacity of the architect's and surveyor's department and of the building industry. In one county borough the architect's department advised the capital priorities committee whether the collated capital programme 'is capable of being carried out by the labour force in the area, and within the capabilities of this department'. The treasurer was also concerned with the impact of the capital programme on the rate level, and this put a limit on the size of the programme. 'This year the capital priorities committee considered the financial effects of the capital programme on the rate. The treasurer's staff in conjunction with spending departments estimate future running costs of projects. Often you cannot get firm costs from spending officers. Then it is the finance committee's job to decide if the future running costs can be borne. This year the capital priorities committee has rather usurped the finance committee's function in this respect . . . '

Spending officers of two case study counties admitted that their

[1] Royal Institute of Public Administration, *Budgeting in Public Authorities*, Allen and Unwin, 1959, p. 216. The IMTA survey was published in 1957 under the title *Local Authority Borrowing*.

[2] Ministry of Housing and Local Government, *Management of Local Government, Vol. 5, Local Government Administration in England and Wales*, (by M. Harrison and A. Norton), H.M.S.O., 1967, p. 241, Tables XXXIX on p. 574, XXXIXa on p. 595.

[3] The role of central government is discussed later in this chapter.

capital estimates were unrealistic[1] and were rightly cut down by the finance committee.[2] The RIPA study group publication stated: 'A budget prepared centrally has been found more accurate than the total of the separate committees' estimates, which are frequently over-optimistic in reckoning how much can be accomplished in the year.' It added further that 'allowances must be made for this in the finance budget in order to avoid borrowing more than is necessary'.[3] It recommended retrospective comparison of results with the budget as a deterrent to bad estimating or dilatoriness in the execution of authorized schemes. 'These benefits of budgetary control . . . deserve special emphasis in the local government field because of the widespread tendency to adopt annual capital expenditure estimates which in the aggregate invariably prove much higher than actual expenditure and are consequently incapable of being used as a basis for the finance budget or a yardstick, along with the estimated cost of each scheme, for reviewing the actual results.'[4]

CAPITAL PRIORITIES

The RIPA study group stated that capital expenditure budgets 'assist the council in working out priorities between different kinds of capital work, and so developing criteria against which to examine individual schemes put forward for approval'.[5] They did not show how priorities were worked out nor did they give examples of criteria developed. The Maud Committee research officers believed that long-term budgets had the effect of requiring assessment of priorities and the development of yardsticks, but they also stated that 'the precise method of settling these priorities and the major factors and personalities influencing the final decision obviously vary as between authorities'.[6] Jackson stated that 'it is not possible to judge on evidence the respective merits of putting more money into, say, health services rather than into schools or roads. Nor is that a technical problem that could be solved by a panel of learned and disinterested municipal treasurers. These decisions are the stuff of politics in both the narrow party sense and in the wider sense, and political judgments must prevail.'[7] Griffith suggested there might be

[1] More treasurers would have agreed.

[2] It was also stressed that capital projects were not rejected because high running costs were anticipated, although they would have a marked effect on the rate level.

[3] *Budgeting in Public Authorities*, op. cit., pp. 213, 220.   [4] *Ibid.*, pp. 243–4.

[5] *Ibid.*, p. 214.   [6] *Management of Local Government*, op. cit., p. 242.

[7] R. M. Jackson, *The Machinery of Local Government*, 2nd edition, Macmillan, 1965, p. 151.

an operating principle related to the grant system but the indications were not clear.[1]

'It is not unknown for a local authority, particularly a county borough where all services are in competition, to take the view that the education department has had "a good run" since 1945 and that the claims of highways, for example, should now be attended to more closely. And of course it is no coincidence that this attitude seems to be growing at a time when the central government is making available, in grant money, more financial assistance to the highways department of local authorities. If this is a real trend—and the evidence is not yet clear—then finance committees will become more powerful than they have been during the last 20 years . . .'

Carter also agreed that decisions on priorities were difficult, but believed that certain clues were available to help judge a project.[2]

'Where there is no question of a calculable profit, even one accruing to the public at large, there are still three lines of thought which may be pursued in judging a project. Firstly, we can ascertain the extent of the population for which the service is required . . . Secondly, we can look at the scale of provision in other areas . . . Thirdly, we can look at alternative methods of fulfilling the object of the works.'

In 7 of the 12 case study authorities with rolling programmes, the welfare or medical officer, or both, referred to the programme, and in only one local authority was it strongly felt that welfare took low priority. This was related to the influence of the committee chairman, and other comments on priority were also linked with judgements on the role of the elected members.

In all, 6 of the 24 authorities referred to the need for a good spending committee chairman with political acumen and a way with his colleagues. 5 authorities (including 4 that also referred to the qualities of the chairman) felt that the welfare department did not have a claim to high priority in capital programming. Education was usually cited as the favoured rival,[3] though in one Scottish large

[1] J. A. G. Griffith, *Central Departments and Local Authorities*, Allen and Unwin, 1966, p. 121.

[2] T. E. Carter, 'Capital Investment by Public Authorities: Local Authorities', *Local Government Finance*, Vol. 68, No. 11, November 1964, p. 394.

[3] One Scottish medical officer believed that education got priority in the past because of the higher percentage grant. This was one of very few positive references to the influence of the grant system, which was not in general believed to have a major impact on the rate of development of services.

burgh (large burghs are not education authorities) a welfare officer said of the council: 'They prefer housing construction or roads where they can see things developing.' At least three welfare officers said that some councillors had an old-fashioned image of welfare, and other officers hinted that this was sometimes true. Such an attitude had its effect on priorities and programming of capital projects.

Spokesmen from three authorities claimed that their demands were usefully backed by the ten-year plans, and this was the main reason why they did not have major problems in capital financing. 'The plan helps me to formulate to the committee the various stages. It helps in the allocation of money. Finance committee has never stopped any capital expenditure on homes.' The same welfare officer also pointed out that if he satisfied the committee that new buildings would result in financial saving, then he had no problems in obtaining capital finance.

'I pointed out that the cost of maintenance of people in a hospital board bed was several pounds a week more compared with in a purpose-built home, even allowing for loan charges. Finance committee saw the point, so I quickly established the idea of closing the public assistance institutions . . .'

ROLE OF CENTRAL GOVERNMENT

However, much depended on central government decisions on where capital investment was to be restricted. Until 1958 capital expenditure on local authority health and welfare services was very severely restricted. The Ministry of Health required local health authorities to draw up programmes of building works each year for submission for Ministry approval, i.e. loan sanction, and the authority to obtain controlled materials. In 1953–4 a total of 130 health projects (in England and Wales) involving capital expenditure of £1,135,792 (excluding equipment) were allowed to go ahead, but there was a backlog of projects submitted to the Ministry between 1950 and 1954–5 and involving a proposed capital expenditure of almost £4 million, still waiting for loan sanction.[1] Because of this backlog the Ministry stated[2] that they could accept only the most urgent new proposals from local authorities for 1955–6. On October 26, 1955, the Chancellor of the Exchequer and the Minister of Housing and

[1] Ministry of Health, *Annual Report for 1954, Cmd. 9566*, H.M.S.O., 1955, p. 107.
[2] Ministry of Health, *Circular 26/54.*

251

Local Government asked local authorities to keep capital spending for 1956–7 within the limits of 1954–5 and to undertake only urgent new works. On February 17, 1956, and in Circular 3/56, the Minister of Housing and Local Government stated that it was not possible to recommend loan sanction for capital works except to meet the most urgent needs, such as provision of accommodation for nurses, as lack of this was thought to be a factor in recruitment difficulties in the domiciliary services. Also exempted were occupation centres for mental defectives, presumably because of the very long waiting lists for institutional places for mental defectives. Support for this contention came from a report on progress made during 1955 on the provision of occupation centres by one local authority, which contained the comments: 'Fortunately, occupation centres do not come under the restriction on capital expenditure to the same extent as infant welfare clinics, and it is hoped to continue with a modified building programme . . . The waiting list for admission of defectives to institutional care was 179 compared with 247 at the end of 1954.'[1] In 1956, only 80 health projects (costing £530,342) received loan sanctions.[2] 1957 brought some relaxation of restrictions, and 134 projects costing £1,327,549 were allowed to proceed.[3] Nevertheless, throughout this period developments involving capital expenditure depended on the local authorities' ability to convince the Ministry of 'extreme urgency', or their ability to finance projects other than by loan. Even then it should be remembered that it was not until November 1954 that the last of the controls on building materials was lifted. Furthermore, there was a disincentive to financing capital expenditure on health projects out of revenue, since it was laid down that if such expenditure exceeded certain limits it would not qualify for the 50% grant unless the Minister so decreed.[4]

1958 brought a slight improvement for health projects. In Circular 60/58 issued in November, the Minister of Housing and Local Government announced that the government wished to bring forward some capital expenditure on health and welfare projects. Local authorities were invited to consider projects which could be submitted for loan sanction within three months (later extended to six months) and which could be completed by the end of 1959. This move led to approval of additional capital expenditure amounting to

1 West Riding of Yorkshire, *Report of the County Medical Officer of Health for 1955*, p. 6.

2 Ministry of Health, *Annual Report for 1956*, Cmnd. 293, H.M.S.O., 1957, p. 103.

3 Ministry of Health, *Annual Report for 1957*, Cmnd. 495, H.M.S.O., 1958, p. 110.

4 *Statutory Instrument No. 578*, 1949.

£3·6 million divided roughly equally between health and welfare.[1] The ordinary building programme for 1959 was higher than the previous year by some £600,000.[2] This, together with the programme under Circular 60/58, meant that the total value of health projects approved for 1959 amounted to almost £4 million, which was more than the programme for the three previous years together.

In September 1959, Circular 25/59 asked local authorities to submit a programme of health service projects and another of welfare projects for which they wished to receive loan sanction in 1960-1, together with tentative programmes for 1961-2. The programmes submitted for 1960-1 were receiving Ministry consideration by the end of 1959 so that the local authorities could be informed at an early date which schemes would receive loan sanction. This attempt to give local authorities a better opportunity to organize their resources for their various building projects marked the beginning of forward planning in the local authority health and welfare field. (It might be noted here that the Board of Education first instituted three-year programmes for school building in 1927.) As such, it must be related to other social policy developments and seen as the early stage of the movement towards ten-year plans.[3] What is often forgotten now, is that community care was no new concept in 1959 (see Chapter 1). What seems to have happened about 1958-9 was a decision somewhere at national level that the time was ripe for implementation of post-war legislation. Until 1958, health and welfare had low priority at *national* level in the allocation of limited resources.

After 1959 loan sanction for health and welfare projects was granted at a much higher level than it ever was in the fifties, rising from £9·0 million in 1959-60 to £14·6 million in 1960-1, and then again to £19·3 million (of which about £13 million was for welfare projects) in 1963-4. There was a temporary set-back for some capital projects (but this time *not* for health and welfare projects), due to government restrictions imposed in the summer of 1961. It should be added that in the period of economic retrenchment of the mid-sixties (see Ministry of Housing and Local Government Circulars 62/65 and 42/66) the housing, hospitals and schools programmes were unaffected whereas local health and welfare projects were liable to be postponed or cut back except in development areas or areas of high unemployment.

[1] Ministry of Health, *Annual Report for 1958*, Cmnd. 806, H.M.S.O., 1959, p. 199 *et seq.*

[2] Ministry of Health, *Annual Report for 1959*, Cmnd. 1086, H.M.S.O., 1960, p. 146 *et seq.*   [3] Griffith, *op. cit.*, Table 57, p. 433.

To conclude, capital expenditure on health and welfare services was severely restricted throughout the fifties, only the most urgent projects being given loan sanction. Therefore one would expect the relative increase in revenue account expenditure to be less than, say, for education with the caveat for health services that expansion in domiciliary services was less dependent on capital expenditure and more dependent on availability of womanpower. Furthermore, given the overall low level of investment, one would expect the impact of capital expenditure on revenue expenditure to vary much more between areas, with welfare more vulnerable than health.

The fieldwork for this study was carried out between September 1965 and November 1966—another period of restraint in public expenditure.[1] The national economic climate was naturally reflected in comments made by local authority officers. Nearly three-quarters of them commented that capital programmes had been cut back. Welfare officers (particularly from county boroughs) seemed more concerned because of the delays on residential accommodation than medical officers of health, who found their proposals for hostels for the elderly mentally infirm, nurses' homes, day centres or clinics delayed, but whose domiciliary services were unaffected by restrictions on capital programmes. The medical officer of a Scottish large burgh said *a propos* of the postponement of his new clinic: 'I am not fussy about the chromium-plated stuff, because I think it is staff that count more than the premises.'

Two English county medical officers of health complained that the effect of delay was to lose them their place (often to education) in the queue for the architects' and quantity surveyors' services (see also Chapter 19), and one of them was faced with the additional problem of developing a multi-purpose site during the period of credit squeeze (see Chapter 18).

One of the seven authorities which did not refer to a cutback was in a scheduled development district and was financing its programme of purpose-built residential accommodation out of revenue. (see below). The other 6 authorities (two English counties, one Welsh and three Scottish), had not been affected either because nothing was being put forward—they tended to be rural authorities with scattered populations—or because negotiations were so protracted that 6 months' delay was hardly noticed, or because the problem of resource allocation at local level overshadowed the national policy of restraint.

It has already been noted that the influence of central department

---

[1] See, for example, Ministry of Housing and Local Government, *Circulars* 62/65, 42/66.

policy led some case study authorities to believe that rolling capital programmes were unhelpful. The Royal Institute of Public Administration believed that the activity of central government had been crucial.[1]

'Since World War II government policy as to loan sanctions has generally kept local authorities' capital investment below what they themselves wished and thought they could afford to spend, and below what they could raise the money to finance. They have, therefore, felt no immediate need of capital expenditure budgets to assist in limiting their capital investment or keeping it in line with the supply of money available to finance it.'

Of the ten case study authorities that felt that capital project financing was adequate, all but two referred to cuts in the capital programme because of central department measures.

REVENUE CONTRIBUTIONS TO CAPITAL

One way of avoiding government restrictions on capital projects was to finance them from revenue. Medical or welfare officers from about a third of the case study authorities used revenue contributions, but only two financed large projects, such as a new home for the elderly, in this way.

As already mentioned, there was a limit to financing capital projects in health departments from revenue in the fifties under the percentage grant system. The other main disincentive (and this still applies) is the sudden burden on the rates, so that, in the main, minor capital projects such as extensions, or renovations of former public assistance institutions, were financed from revenue.

Two welfare authorities rejected the idea of financing new residential accommodation from revenue because of the impact on maintenance charges, or because such a move would be unfair to other services. An English county welfare officer believed that more capital expenditure on old people ought to be financed from revenue, but felt that high loan charges were justified with continued inflation, because the real charges could be less over the time of loan repayment than if the revenue account was charged. On the other hand, a welfare officer from a Scottish large burgh was not keen on

---

[1] *Budgeting in Public Authorities, op. cit.,* p. 214.

capitalizing unless large sums were involved. 'If it is a thousand or two, it should go through revenue, even if it added a little to the rates.' Presumably this officer would capitalize expenditure for a new home for elderly people. Another English county which financed residential accommodation from revenue cut its programme voluntarily in response to government policy. Another was prepared to use a revenue contribution on a modest scale during a period of retrenchment, if it seemed necessary: 'There was a house which came on to the market in the middle of the credit squeeze and so we suggested to the treasurer that we should buy it out of revenue so as not to miss it, even if we did not do anything with it until we could get loans again.'

Three chief welfare officers said they were not interested in methods of financing capital projects, though one threw in the reservation 'unless there is some effect on the standard charges for residential accommodation'. Apart from this possibility, the mode of financing could well affect the timing and speed of capital development, and the question remained whether the local authority treasurer would listen to suggestions on methods of financing from his chief officer colleagues.

SUMMARY

Half of the case study authorities had rolling capital programmes—five years being the commonest period. A ten-year period was felt to be too long. The other half of the case study authorities looked no further forward than a year, mainly because they believed that the central department controlled investment programmes.

In general, officers of spending departments felt that services for the elderly did not suffer markedly in comparison with other services, but in some areas it was felt that elected members could play a stronger role to obtain higher priority for the welfare department in capital programming. The ten-year plans were helpful in making demands known, and in supporting the case for high priority, but they were probably more influential in the spending committee than in the finance committee.

More influential than local decisions was central department control over local authority capital developments as a tool of national economic policy. This was stressed by the fact that the fieldwork for this study was carried out in 1965–6 during a period of restraint in public expenditure.

The stratagem of avoiding central department control by financing capital projects from revenue was not used widely, partly because of the burden on the rates, and even those case study authorities which did finance large projects from revenue respected the central government's policy of restraint in 1965-6. In the main, financing from revenue covered minor developments, such as renovations or extensions to buildings.

CHAPTER 16

FINANCE—REVENUE EXPENDITURE

The annual preparation of revenue account estimates is one of the most fundamental of local government functions, and the means by which they are compiled can influence the rate of development of services. This chapter considers the role of the treasurer's department and the finance committee in matters of staff establishment, resource allocation and priority determination.

The bulk of the chapter concentrates on methods of preparing estimates and examines the idea of budget rationing or expenditure control, together with the views of local government officers on the effectiveness of the system.

No case study local authority was short of ideas for developing services for the elderly, if extra finance could be made available in the revenue account estimates. The demand for some services, like home help, was believed to be limitless; and other services, such as developments to aid the mentally disordered or the physically handicapped, were known to be only in their infancy.

ESTABLISHMENT CONTROL

In several authorities, there were complaints about the attitude of the treasurer's department or the finance committee to expenditure directly linked with staffing matters, e.g. training costs, travel expenses. As described in Chapter 14, caution in these matters was believed to deter recruits, especially the potentially mobile, relatively skilled, more senior staff. Moreover, one officer blamed car allowance problems for the fact that six public health inspectors left.

One county borough health department found that recruitment problems led sometimes to over-estimation on expenditure, and in the following year estimates might be pruned just as recruitment prospects improved. The home help service tended to suffer particularly, both because it was a high cost health service (accounting for nearly a fifth of total net expenditure on local health services) and because recruitment tended to be easier just when the general economic climate became more wintry.

The biggest problem for planning services for the elderly occurred when staffing decisions were effectively removed from the spending department's control. In just a few authorities there were examples, or hints, of decisions on priorities not only between but also within services being taken in finance or establishment committees. One example occurred in an English county where the chief welfare officer agreed that the finance committee should control the money, but stressed that the spending committee should determine priorities. 'If I could have my way on priorities . . . I would still go for social workers first . . . Here, if I had asked for general division clerks, I would have got them on the grounds that the population was increasing. If I ask for a principal social worker, it takes me four years to get it, and yet this one is worth several general division clerks. So why do they not give me the money they would be willing to give me for clerks and let me use it as I think best?'

Both the medical officer and the nursing officer from this county further illustrated the welfare officer's point. They had adopted the standard of one health visitor per 4,500 population because:

'It is the figure put out by the working party on health visitors,[1] and we thought that we could not ask to go beyond this in the foreseeable future because of the committee and finance . . . We have a fight about this each estimate time.'

'It makes things easier at estimate time to refer to the ten-year plans. Having approved something in principle we hope that the elected members will not quarrrel with the estimates.'

RESOURCE ALLOCATION

Increasing establishment levels is just one of the problems faced by elected members in allocating resources for the forthcoming financial year, and it is not an easy job to distribute a limited amount of money among competing demands. Nevertheless, nearly half of the welfare departments in the case study authorities said that finance committees (or sub-committees) were reasonable and sympathetic in resource allocation, and just over half of the health departments felt there were no grounds for complaint. Various reasons for this satisfactory state of affairs were given.

[1] Ministry of Health, Department of Health for Scotland, Ministry of Education, *An Inquiry into Health Visiting*, H.M.S.O., 1956.

First, officers of spending departments found that they could show there would be saving on the revenue account if new developments took place. An example of this would be the replacement of joint-user premises run by the hospital service by new or adapted premises run by the local authority.

Second, paradoxical reasons could be put forward to show that resource allocation was fair to services for the elderly. Either requirements were moderate, realistic and thus acceptable to the finance committee, or original estimates were inflated so that subsequent cuts did not really hurt.

Third, support could be given to demands, either by powerful elected members who were publicly or personally committed to developments, or by the use of ten-year plans as evidence of the need for more staff, equipment, etc.

Fourth, it was suggested that amends should be made for past neglect or maladministration of the service (this applied particularly to welfare) by both elected members and officers in other local authority departments.

In a minority of authorities planning problems were said to be caused by a lack of sympathy for health and welfare services, and uncertainty about likely future levels of allocation of finance, although there was practically no suggestion that cuts in the present standards of service were being seriously considered, unless such a policy were to be advocated by the spending department itself. In this minority, the main comment was that health and welfare services for the elderly came low in the rank ordering of priorities at estimate time. One county borough medical officer of health believed that new services were only cautiously adopted because of the financial implications—not because they would necessarily be large, but because they were unknown.

Suggestions for the development of health and welfare services might be dropped because of the lack of influence of the committee chairman or other spokesmen at the party group or even in committee. In an English county the medical officer of health realized that the finance committee might not know how urgent the new development could be. 'I have not really faced the question of the division of the cake between departments. It is the finance committee's job but the departments would have to give them some idea of the urgency of new projects.' Education was still occasionally regarded as running away with resources but feelings were not very strong about this major spender, partly because much education policy was known to be decided centrally. 'If the estimates sub-committee feel they should hold increase in expenditure to $12\frac{1}{2}\%$ and they know that education are going ahead with a statutorily required scheme, then the other expenditure limits must be toughened. Perhaps any gross above $7\frac{1}{2}\%$ is out.'

One chief welfare officer wanted a guarantee that he could have financial backing to develop a service before he started it. 'I am not going to take on a service unless I am going to be allowed to develop it . . . I was asked to do meals-on-wheels. I went into it . . . and I said yes, but only if the council would guarantee that I could develop this service as necessary. It never works if you say that you will start a small service and then be able to prove the need for extending it. If you start a small service, you go on with a small service.'

In contrast, officers in a Scottish authority were concerned that the financial implications of developing a service might frighten the finance committee into rejecting the whole idea. The medical officer of health said: 'If we had done a survey of chiropody needs six years ago, the results would have been so frightening that the council would never have agreed to start it. So it was better to let it grow.'

THE TREASURER'S ROLE IN ESTIMATE PREPARATION

Methods of preparing revenue account estimates[1] were discussed with officers in the case study authorities, because the system used might influence the rate of development of health and welfare services compared with the other services with which they were in competition for resources. The main differences found were basically similar to those summarized in the 1959 report of the Royal Institute of Public Administration.[2]

'Some treasurers prepare a brief for the finance committee listing the items which could be struck out if any deletions are needed, and the finance committee report to the council recommending detailed alterations in the estimates. Elsewhere the finance committee concern themselves mainly with the total level of the estimates for each main service, leaving spending committees to say exactly where the desired cuts can best be made.'

---

[1] Some of the procedural arrangements for preparing a revenue budget are described in A. H. Marshall, *Financial Administration in Local Government*, Allen and Unwin, 1960, Chapter XX.

[2] Royal Institute of Public Administration, *Budgeting in Public Authorities* Allen and Unwin, 1959, p. 116.

The disadvantages of the system of specific cuts were said to be that it tended to mean that reductions had to be made in overall expenditure at a late stage in the estimate preparation process, and that the cuts were suggested by members or officers who were not closely concerned with the service under scrutiny. In contrast, the system of setting a financial limit at a relatively early stage in the estimate preparation process gave more time to the spending committee and its officers to decide where to make reductions in the growth of expenditure, but the limit had to be set by a rule-of-thumb formula which did not take account of the specific needs of the service in question.

Attempts had been made by some authorities to overcome these difficulties by introducing 'budget rationing' or 'expenditure control' systems. The aim of these was to set for each committee a rate of growth of expenditure which was consistent with an acceptable rate of growth of total expenditure for the local authority, and then to leave the detailed control of how to develop services within the limit set to the spending departments and their committees.

The medical officer of health of one authority approved of the idea of giving each spending committee a target to work to. 'I rather like the newer approach . . . although it is early to say yet. There obviously has to be a limit to what you can have, but having said what the limit is, we should be left to determine our priorities and not have to do this in front of finance committee . . . It is the detailed control that I think is wrong, for example, saying that they will let you have this for chiropody but not for mental health.'

The medical officer of health of another authority also approved of the system. 'You make your estimates in accordance with the ceiling. This leads to officers trying to be efficient and trying to go for the sacred cows which you had always thought you just had to do, and tended to go on perpetuating. For the first time, I found myself really going to town on certain items, for example, welfare food distribution was cut by cutting the number of distribution points.'

The main difficulty with this system was in setting the targets. Various ways had been tried. Some finance officers tried to construct objective standards by reference to planning or financial standards external to the local authority, such as the National Plan, or the total relevant expenditure considered for rate support grant purposes. For instance, one treasurer said: 'From the National Plan, information was derived concerning the rates of growth applicable to major local authority services over the five years 1964–5 to 1969–70 . . . The services account for 87% of the county council's rate and grant borne expenditure, so the National Plan growth rates have been adopted as the basis for the county council's plan . . . Where the National Plan does not give a percentage increase, the percentage applicable to a like service, where available, is used. Thus the libraries and museums committee use the same percentage as education, and fire brigade use the same percentage as police. Other committees which are mainly concerned with expenditure on staff, use $3 \cdot 5\%$, which is the rate of increase being recommended for the staff manpower budget.' The main disadvantage of this method was that it involved the assumption that local services should grow at the same rate in all authorities, regardless of the fact that some authorities might have poor services or abnormally high needs, and might need to grow faster than the national average rate of growth for that service. One authority which used the National Plan figures as a guide claimed that it was only justified in doing so because it was an average authority.

Wreford[1] has described how the permitted national rate of increase of expenditure for general grant purposes could be a satisfactory determinant for the rate of increase in services in a local authority, given certain conditions. 'For the average authority, the estimates approved by the Minister of Housing and Local Government for general grant have a certain relevance . . . We knew from our researches that, in Somerset, the total expenditure which did not rank for general grant had, since 1959–60, increased at almost exactly the same rate as had that which did.' However, he admitted that such a system as this could not be applied to non-county boroughs or county districts, and might be unsuitable for less 'average' counties.

Another authority operated a budget rationing system in a different way. 'Before the estimates process starts, the estimates sub-committee considers the overall situation, and comes to a particular feeling about what total expenditure could be. Last year it felt that there should be a rise of not more than 10% and that this should apply to each committee.' This method also had its shortcomings. The welfare officer in this authority said: 'If you start with a low standard it is very difficult to get up to a good standard within a controlled regular rate of growth . . . Welfare would be restricted because it has been underprovided for in the past, and so you would not get development. The system tends to favour services such as education which have previously reached a reasonably high standard.' As Jones[2] stated: 'It is not a natural sequence for each service

1 F. C. Wreford, 'Rationing the Rates', *Local Government Finance*, Vol. 69, No. 11, November 1965, p. 446.
2 G. C. Jones, *The Local Authority Budget*, Joint Committee of Students' Societies of the Institute of Municipal Treasurers and Accountants, 1966, p. 158.

to progress annually at a uniform rate in terms of expenditure.'

In fact, the case study authority just referred to admitted that in practice it had been necessary to vary the 10% for some services to allow for special circumstances, and the treasurer added that 'there were always special circumstances'.

Another problem which made it difficult for a local authority to operate a system, even if it could devise one which was acceptable to spending committees, was that some expenditure was not fully under the local authority's control. Reference was made to the effect of pay awards made by national negotiating bodies, to the quota system for establishment control in education, and to the effect of central department decisions on loan sanctions, which are reflected in revenue account expenditure as loan charges once capital projects are under way. It has been suggested that central policy decisions affected the situation even more directly.

'Changes in policy during the currency of a budget may be brought about by several causes . . . The important factor is the influence of changes in government policy on the policies adopted by other public authorities. This is especially marked in local government where great use is made of Ministry regulations and circulars to prescribe the terms and conditions on which local services may or must be provided.'[1]

Nevertheless, the county treasurer for Somerset is quoted as saying, in relation to his authority's plan for expenditure control, that 'while a large proportion of the annual expenditure increase is caused by national factors, a considerable section remains within a council's ability to determine'.[2] In the case study authorities which were trying to operate expenditure control systems, it seemed that the touchiest point was still that effective control of the development of services would lie in the treasurer's department. Some finance officers thought it was wrong that they should mould policy, while others were more concerned that the system would break down once the spending department or the elected members understood how it really worked.

'We acted like God last year and said, for instance, that welfare deserved 14%. No one realizes in the first year what you are doing. We bluffed—it will not work next year. The method of having targets

[1] *Budgeting in Public Authorities, op. cit.*, pp. 122–3.
[2] *The Times*, February 21, 1966.

is fun but it will founder on who it is that fixes the targets and what they should be.'

LONG-TERM REVENUE FORECASTS

None of the case study authorities put any strong emphasis on the use of five-year programmes to help create a long-term revenue forecast, an instrument which Marshall considered to be of first-rate value.[1] 'A long-term revenue forecast . . . is comprehensive, embracing the effect on future rates of the trends of both capital and revenue expenditure. It thus reflects the cost to rates of new capital items, and also projected developments of services and anticipated additional expenses not connected with capital expenditure. It is the document which gives the local authority the clue to what it can afford and hence to the pace of development of all kinds.'

Wilson[2] also pointed out that there was no machinery for making estimates for more than one year ahead, and if there were, a forward financial plan would allow more rational decisions on the desirability of certain kinds of expenditure before the degree of commitment was too great. He added that the three main inadequacies hindering forward financial planning were (a) lack of clear formulation of goals by the council, so that an estimate of future demand for funds could be made, (b) inefficiencies in planning procedures and (c) a lack of detailed understanding of the components of growth of local authority expenditure, listed as inflation, population served, expansion of level of service and productivity, together with a time profile, as it could not be assumed that costs, say, of a *new* capital project, changed smoothly over time simply varying as a function of the previous four components. In brief, local authorities did not have enough information on which to base good policy decisions.

SUMMARY

In summary, there was concern in some local authorities that the staffing and establishment activity, and incidental staffing costs, were too closely controlled by the treasurer's department, and this had a direct impact on the rate of development of services.

In the main, health and welfare services get reasonable priority

---

1 Marshall, *op. cit.*, pp. 263–4.

2 A. G. Wilson, 'Forward Financial Planning in Local Government', *Local Government Finance*, Vol. 71, No. 11, November 1967, p. 438, *et seq.*

in resource allocation, because actual demands on resources were not seen to be high, because the ten-year plans gave support to demands for more resources and because it was felt that these services might have had a raw deal in the past. Where problems were thought to exist, they were mainly attributed to the unknown financial implications of a policy decision to develop a service or to the lack of drive or interest among elected members.

Revenue account estimates could be reduced by suggested specific cuts or by a decision on financial targets within which the spending department had to work. Financial targets themselves had to be decided by some kind of rule-of-thumb formula. Budget rationing was one possible technique, and attempts were made to use objective criteria to avoid the accusation that the treasurer or the chairman of the finance committee were laying down policy for specific local authority services. Such criteria included the use of external standards derived from the National Plan or from rate support grant calculations.

Opposition to budget rationing existed (particularly in county boroughs) for a number of reasons: the level of resources did not match the level of need; special circumstances undermined external standards; external standards might not be appropriate for a particular area; level of expenditure was really determined elsewhere during wage-level negotiations and through loan saction decisions. In reply, it was suggested that the local authority was to a certain extent a free agent.

Evidence of long-range revenue budget forecasting was not found.

CHAPTER 17

FINANCE—HOUSING FOR THE ELDERLY

The provision of housing specially for old people created particular financial problems. The desirability of siting housing for the elderly in or near town centres rather than in peripheral housing estates increased costs because central sites were more expensive, although the extra cost was partly offset by special 'expensive site' subsidies. Inclusion of special design features, alarm-bell or intercommunication systems, common rooms, laundry facilities, lifts, and provision of special fittings, central heating or cookers all tended to raise costs. There was also the recurrent annual cost of paying a warden, perhaps paying for a gardener or groundsman, and the sporadic cost of paying for interior decoration, where such services were provided. The financial burden of such services was not always known in our case study authorities because large-scale provision of housing specially for the elderly was of recent origin. Old people need many of these facilities and yet, because of low, fixed incomes, they may be unable to pay the higher rents that accompany the provision of convenient, good standard accommodation, except through support from the Ministry of Social Security, which they may not wish to use.

In this chapter the rent policies of local housing authorities are discussed, including rent rebate schemes, rate fund contributions to the housing revenue account, rate relief, policies on providing special fittings and services, and the special grants from welfare authorities to housing authorities in relation to welfare features in sheltered housing. Apart from rate relief, these policy matters illustrate *local* ways of reducing the cost of housing to the elderly, and they should be considered against the national background of subsidies of house building costs by government grant, briefly outlined in Chapter 1.

RENT STRUCTURE

The planning of housing for the elderly can be complicated by local rent policy. In the sixties, there has been a move to link the rent system for municipal housing to gross value of the dwellings, a policy advocated in both central and local government publications.[1] Nearly half of the 27 English and Welsh housing authorities visited were operating such a policy.[2] By using gross value, an 'objectively' derived standard rent was calculated. Even in Scotland, where there was a tradition of low rents and high rate fund contributions to the housing revenue account, a similar trend was observable, although the rent income required to balance the housing revenue account appeared to be calculated after a rate fund element as well as an exchequer subsidy had been subtracted from gross expenditure.[3] Nearly half of the 14 Scottish housing authorities visited (which included the 4 counties responsible for housing in their landward areas) operated on the basis of gross annual value.

Those case study authorities which had not adopted the external criterion of the valuation for rent policy purposes tended to make their own evaluation, as they felt that they had better knowledge of the desirability of certain types and sizes of dwellings, certain estates and different areas of the authority than the valuer.[4] 'The maisonettes will come down in rent . . . simply because they are an unpopular type of building and are hard to let. You have to be governed by supply and demand in the letting job.' Occasionally, the two systems were mixed; gross annual value was used but the percentage of gross value applied to particular dwellings varied according to the characteristics of the dwelling or the area.

Concessionary rents for old people's dwellings also existed (and some confusion arose because they were sometimes referred to as rebate schemes). In the 27 English and Welsh case study housing authorities,[5] 2 county boroughs, 3 municipal boroughs, 4 urban districts and 3 rural districts mentioned some form of rent concession. However, in half of these 12 authorities, this system of support was

[1] See, for instance, Ministry of Housing and Local Government, *Housing in England and Wales*, Cmnd. *1290*, H.M.S.O., 1961, *Circular 46/67* on rent rebate schemes, and R. Wilson, *Housing Finance*, Joint Committee of Students' Societies of the Institute of Municipal Treasurers and Accountants, 1967, p. 29.

[2] Some case study authorities felt unable to introduce new rent structures because of the July 1966 policy for price restraint, which was in turn followed by the announcement in November 1966 of a further period of severe restraint.

[3] According to the Scottish branch of the Institute of Municipal Treasurers and Accountants, all Scottish housing authorities listed in *Rating Review 1965–6*, Part 5 (small burghs with a population of under 9,000 were omitted) made a rate fund contribution to the housing revenue account varying from 5·9% of total income in Bute to 61·2% in Orkney (p. 33).

[4] For a summary of the case against the gross value method of rent fixing, see R. Parker, *The Rents of Council Houses*, G. Bell and Sons Ltd., 1967, pp. 61–2.

[5] Comprising 9 county boroughs, 6 municipal boroughs, 5 urban districts and 7 rural districts.

either gradually dying out or was limited to very few dwellings such as 'pre-war old people's bedsitters', or was actively opposed by officers, although still supported by elected members. The commonest form of concession was not to raise rents of dwellings for the elderly when a general rent increase was adopted, or to raise rents by a less than proportional amount. In one municipal borough a much lower percentage of gross value was applied to these dwellings, and in one rural district rents were pegged in order not to lose the county subsidy on sheltered housing. In one municipal borough, three urban districts and two rural districts, there was no rate fund contribution, so the 'loss' on old people's dwellings was borne by other council tenants.

In Scotland, of the 14 case study housing authorities, 4 (1 county of city, 1 county, 1 large burgh and 1 small burgh) mentioned nominal rents, or excluded dwellings for the elderly from rent increases. 'There is a low rent for special old age pensioners' houses. We just thought of a figure, but it is related to our pre-war improved single-end's rent of about 5s a week.' Rents were in any case low in Scotland, averaging 16s 2d per week in November 1965, and ranging from 7s 8d to 22s 10d,[1] because of the rate fund contribution, and because of rent rebate schemes which operated in 1965–6 in all but 4 of the 24 larger urban areas and in about half of the small burghs and counties and which cost about £750,000.[2]

RENT REBATES

The operation of an objectively derived standard rent system requires the operation of an extensive rent rebate scheme to cater for low-income households,[3] as well as good contact with the Ministry of Social Security.

In the English and Welsh housing authorities visited, 12 had rent rebate schemes and 15 had not.[4] (8 of the 12 housing authorities with

[1] Scottish Development Department, *Rents of Houses Owned by Local Authorities in Scotland 1965*, Cmnd. 2907, H.M.S.O., 1966, Table 1, p. 5, Tables 4 and 5, p. 7.

[2] *Rating Review, op. cit.*, Part 5, Column 11.

[3] The issue of high-income households, surcharge schemes, etc., tended not to apply to elderly households, though this could change if more housing authorities started to cater for elderly owner-occupiers underoccupying dwellings which the elderly found difficult to keep up.

[4] In 1965–6 about 44% of housing authorities in England and Wales operated a rent rebate scheme. Urban districts were less likely to have such a scheme than other kinds of local authority. The comments made in case study authorities

concessionary rents for the elderly had no rebate scheme.) At least 4 authorities without rebate schemes expected to introduce one soon or felt that it would become necessary.

Occasional use was made of rebate schemes, where they existed, to facilitate the transfer of older, smaller households to smaller dwellings. Stopping short of compelling people to move, housing authorities refused rebate altogether to low-income households of elderly people underoccupying family council housing or paid the lower level of rebate appropriate to the cheaper smaller dwelling to which they were trying to persuade the elderly household to move.

This device was not widely used and it was not likely to be very successful, because as 9 of the 12 authorities with rebate schemes stated, it was the job of the National Assistance Board to supplement the income of elderly people with little or no income except the retirement pension to enable them to pay a 'reasonable' rent. The Milner Holland Report commented: 'There seems to be no settled national policy on the question whether local authorities should fully subsidize the housing needed for these people, or whether the National Assistance Board should meet their housing costs.'[1] Parker also commented on the lack of a policy.[2] According to the Allen Report,[3] about half of retired households in council tenancies were receiving a rent allowance from the National Assistance Board, which should 'cover the gross rent set by the local authority. To some extent therefore a local authority is relieved of the need to consider whether high or increased rent levels will fall heavily upon its older tenants.'[4]

One case study authority claimed that rent rebates did not involve the elderly because dwellings for this age group were already cheap.[5]

about the existence or not of a rent rebate scheme did not always tie in with the returns listed in Columns 63 and 64 of IMTA *Housing Statistics 1965–6*. It was suspected that some housing authorities made their returns to the Institute on the basis of having some kind of differential rent scheme, but not necessarily of the rent rebate kind.

[1] Ministry of Housing and Local Government, *Report of the Committee on Housing in Greater London, Cmnd. 2605*, Milner Holland Report, H.M.S.O., 1965, p. 30.

[2] R. Parker, *op. cit.*, p. 75. See also Ministry of Housing and Local Government, *Circular 46/67*, p. 4.

[3] Ministry of Housing and Local Government, *Report of Committee of Inquiry into the Impact of Rates on Households, Cmnd. 2582*, Allen Report, H.M.S.O., 1965, Table 305, p. 120.

[4] R. Parker, *op. cit.*, p. 74.

[5] R. Parker, *op. cit.*, p. 67, stated that what people could afford to pay in rent should be a major concern of councils in setting their rents. 'We have not discovered any authority which based such calculations on the Supplementary Benefit Commission's (formerly the NAB) scale which is presumably supposed to represent the minimum income required after the payment of rent and rates.'

Only one of the 12 authorities with rebate schemes referred to a joint operation. 'We give the pensioners the maximum they are entitled to under the rebate scheme and then the NAB may give the rest. We include old people in the rebate scheme, because we do not think it is fair to put the whole burden on the NAB.' Parker referred to compromise solutions such as less than full rebate, rebates provided to those anticipated to be on short-term benefits, or rebates continued for those in receipt of them before going on to supplementary benefits.[1]

No doubt, many housing authorities would see no reason why local authorities should help the national exchequer in this way. More striking was the distinction between those local authorities who referred to the NAB in a challengingly defensive manner, as though not entirely sure of their ground, and implying that NAB officers were unwilling ever to hand over a penny, and those authorities which were in close, regular contact with the Board and appreciative of its help and co-operation. 'Before fixing the high rents, the council told the National Assistance Board of every likely case and the board told the council which tenants would qualify and offered to get in touch with all of them to see if they needed help.'

In Scotland, 9 of the 14 housing authorities visited had rent rebate schemes (including 3 of the 4 which also had concessionary rents), 3 of the 5 with no rent rebate scheme anticipated having one in the future. At least 4 of the 9 authorities with a rebate scheme excluded the elderly because of the NAB rent allowance.

In brief, rent policies were undergoing review and structural change. There was a trend—encouraged by central government[2]—away from concessionary rents or fixed low-level rents, to a system of standard rent charges (linked to gross annual value or a variant of this) plus a rent rebate scheme and/or income supplementation (including rent allowance) from the Ministry of Social Security. The trend was also observable in Scotland, but at a different level because of the tradition of high rate fund contributions to the housing revenue account.

RATE FUND CONTRIBUTION TO HOUSING REVENUE ACCOUNT

A standard rent scheme with a rebate might imply that rate fund contributions to the housing revenue account need no longer operate.

[1] R. Parker, *op. cit.*, p. 75.

[2] See, for example, Ministry of Housing and Local Government, *Circular 46/67* on rent rebate schemes. A brief review of central government attitude to local rent policies is given in Chapter 1 of R. Parker, *op. cit.*, and for Scotland up to 1964 in R. D. Cramond, *Housing Policy in Scotland 1919–64*, Oliver and Boyd, 1966, pp. 74 *et seq.*

When the statutory requirement to make a rate fund contribution to the housing revenue account was abolished under the Housing and Town Development (Scotland) Act 1957, with the declared object of giving local authorities greater freedom to decide what proportion of their housing expenditure should be borne by tenants and what proportion by ratepayers, the Secretary of State for Scotland said that he hoped local authorities would continue to make a rate contribution.[1] In England and Wales, however, the statutory contribution was abolished under the 1956 Housing Subsidies Act because it was the intention of the Minister 'to encourage local authorities to raise rents and give rebate or subsidy only where this was needed'.[2]

In Scotland, in 1965–6, all major local authorities made contributions.[3] Of the 27 case study authorities in England and Wales, over half made a rate fund contribution in 1965–6,[4] but in only 3 cases was the subsidy over 10% of total housing revenue account income.

However, Parker[5] argued:

'The provision of council houses is of general advantage to the whole community, whether it be in the form of increased rateable hereditaments, the removal of ugly, squalid slums, or the provision of accommodation for workers in local industry. Certainly, where large-scale slum clearance occurs it seems hardly just that the council tenant should bear a large part of the cost whilst the area benefits in general but makes no financial contribution.'

If this is accepted, there is then no reason why 'legitimate' contributions to the housing revenue account should not be regarded as relevant expenditure for rate support grant purposes. Under the 1966 Local Government Act rate fund contributions to the housing revenue account were excluded from relevant expenditure for purposes of calculating the amount of grant.

[1] Cramond, *op. cit.*, p. 40.   [2] R. Parker, *op. cit.*, p. 43.

[3] In 1965–6 the average rates contribution was 37·1% of total housing revenue account income for counties of cities, 35·6% for large burghs, 28·9% for the larger small burghs and 35·1% for the counties. In England and Wales, the percentages were: 7·8 (82 county boroughs); 18·3 (18 London boroughs); 10·7 (Greater London Council); 4·0 (199 non-county boroughs); 4·2 (349 urban districts); and 3·0 (312 rural districts).

[4] Well over a third of the English and Welsh housing authorities listed in IMTA *Housing Statistics 1965–6* made no rate fund contribution in that year (see Column 25). The proportion in our sample was higher because a third of the case study housing authorities in England and Wales were county boroughs, most of whom did make a contribution (67 of 82 listed), whereas they constituted less than 10% of the authorities listed in the IMTA publication.

[5] R. Parker, *op. cit.*, p. 45.

RATE RELIEF

The cost of housing to occupiers, and by implication demand from the elderly for housing, could be affected by means other than rent systems and rate fund contributions, e.g. rate relief. The 1966 Rating Act was passed during the period of visits to case study authorities. The main concern of local authorities was with the extra financial burden placed on the rates by having to bear a quarter of the relief granted, and the administrative costs of running both the relief scheme and an instalment arrangement for payment.[1] Some suspected that this was a 'political' bill and that the administrative implications had been glossed over. The Minister, for example, did not expect detailed checking on income levels by the local authority, but one rural authority expected problems over incomes of casual agricultural labour[2] and a county borough did a 10% check and found such a high proportion of inaccurate information, e.g. net rather than gross income, omission of bonus or overtime earnings from applicants in employment, that they felt they had to do a complete check of this group of applicants (which tended to exclude the elderly).

By later visits, some authorities could see the effects of the legislation. Broadly, just over half of the applications expected (based on Allen Report findings) had been made. Officers felt they had not got through to the inclusive rent-payer despite—in some cases—intensive publicity in the press, in libraries, by informing community leaders such as secretaries of pensioners' associations, by circular letter (often with rate demand notes) and by personal contact with low-income families. One housing manager thought it helpful to tell the treasurer of rent rebate cases on the assumption that they would probably also be eligible for rate relief.[3] A treasurer said:

'We wrote to every private and corporation tenant as well as to direct ratepayers. The criticism that people were missed out should not

[1] For an early statement on administrative aspects, see F. Crowther, *Practical Problems of Administering the Rating Act 1966*, Joint Committee of Students' Societies of the Institute of Municipal Treasurers and Accountants, 1966.

[2] R. Parker pointed out that, whilst wives' earnings were usually taken into account for rent rebate purposes, there were exceptions 'in rural areas where wives' earnings are casual and seasonal and associated with picking and gathering in the fields' (*op. cit.*, p. 68).

[3] In contrast R. Parker reported a council intending to match the percentage reduction in rates under the 1966 legislation by an equivalent reduction in net rent. 'If you qualify for the one, you qualify automatically for the other' (*op. cit.*, p. 67).

273

apply here. There is still a marked difference between applications from direct ratepayers and others, particularly private tenants. My theory is that, first, there are private and corporation tenants who, in spite of the publicity, still feel that they do not pay rates. Secondly, it is a higher proportion of conservative and independent-minded people who pay rates directly, because this includes the owner-occupiers. This group would tend to go for national assistance less than other groups would. There is an element of a split between working-class and semi-middle class. This scheme is not a charity, so middle-class people came forward more readily, especially when they found that we were very courteous and open-minded.'[1]

Elderly people were not always mentioned specifically, partly because supplementary benefits, if applicable, were supposed to cover rates,[2] but in some cases application for rate relief from elderly households revealed circumstances where supplementary benefits would be payable but were not in fact made. Only in two northern county boroughs had the characteristics of applicants and successful applicants for rate relief been analysed. In one, 61% of applications, and 78% of applications granted had come from pensioner households. A finance officer said: 'We have not scooped up all the old people, and I have been surprised at the number of old people who have been existing simply on their old age pensions and are not getting national assistance.' In the other borough nearly 87% of successful applicants were pensioner households.

Under the earlier 1964 Rating (Interim Relief) Act, a householder in England and Wales could receive relief if his rates increased by over 25% or £5 (whichever was greater) between 1962–3 and 1964–5. The relief was limited to a maximum of the amount by which the rate increase exceeded the £5 or the 25% and the local authority had discretion in deciding whether hardship was caused. The local authorities' conditions for eligibility were such that few applicants qualified for relief.

'Interim relief was an opportunity to invent a scheme and it was perhaps rather like the present one. We fixed the income limits

[1] Another officer thought that the scheme might have been successful because rate relief was seen as a kind of tax-dodging, which was a respectable middle-class habit, whereas accepting charity (national assistance) was not.

[2] The Allen Report stated: 'Over 98% of households receiving assistance have their rent (including rates) met in full . . . What is certain is that rates cannot be the cause of hardship to a household receiving national assistance except in a very small number of cases, because the National Assistance Board normally pay them in full.' (*Cmnd. 2582, op. cit.*, pp. 99, 104.)

lower than the present Act does and not one person qualified. Therefore, we did not pay anything.'

'I think we were rather mean and I felt a bit guilty about the scheme because I think I was not generous enough. We got very few applications and most of those who did apply did not qualify . . . We stuck to the PAC[1] levels plus mortgage payments and rent, and I think I was a bit mean.'

Prior to the 1964 Act, local authorities had power to waive payments on grounds of poverty (under the 1925 Rating and Valuation Act, England and Wales, and section 244 of the 1947 Local Government (Scotland) Act) and it was said that any such application was considered on its merits. More usually, it was said that it was the National Assistance Board's concern to ensure adequate income levels and therefore there was no need for rate relief. This was the policy of some of the 14 Scottish authorities visited, but a majority of the Scottish case study authorities did offer rate relief up to a maximum of £15 a year, beyond which any further relief would have reduced the allowance from the National Assistance Board. (Scottish authorities were visited before the 1966 Rating Act came into effect.)[2]

The effect of the 1966 Rating Act, which was more generous than the supplementary benefits scheme because the income levels at which eligibility for partial relief operated were higher than the Ministry of Social Security levels for supplementary benefits, may have been to increase the potential house mobility of the elderly, because certain financial constraints preventing a move to property of a higher rateable value (e.g. a modern purpose-built flat) were removed. Alternatively, it could be argued that the rate burden of an underoccupied house was lessened, so that the Act might reduce the need to move because of financial pressures. Mobility of the elderly is a factor relevant to planning housing for them, and this is an area where further research is required to isolate the reasons why retirement pensioners move or do not move.

COST OF 'EXTRAS'

Rent levels of housing for the elderly can also be kept down by

1 Presumably a reference to public assistance.
2 Less common reasons for giving rate relief included something wrong with the demand notice, or a special element in the demand notice, such as scavenging, which might not be a service available, especially in some remoter areas.

cutting out, or not including, certain services or features in the accommodation, or by trying to shift the cost of 'extras' on to the Ministry of Social Security. In the case studies there was considerable variation in the provision of 'extras'.

Interior decoration and re-decoration were sometimes cut down or cut out because of the cost or because of labour shortages. A selective approach was sometimes adopted, such as providing materials to certain households after considering applications on their merits. Alternatively, decoration ceased to be provided automatically, but was retained for the elderly, or for those elderly who were infirm, or had only a small income, or had no relations nearby. In other cases, it was anticipated that re-decoration costs would increase, and that the service would have to be stopped.

'We do one room every seven years. This is not much. It is normally the staircase which is the most difficult and the most expensive. In bungalows we do either the bathroom and w.c., or the kitchen, or the livingrooms. This service is reflected in the rent. If we did more, rents would go up. I can see it going by the board. Tenants will be asked to do the rest now.'

One county borough cut its decoration service, because 'the only other way is to cut repairs and maintenance, which is not a good idea, or to increase the repairs fund, which means increasing rents'.

Where money was spent on re-decoration, either the cost was met from the housing revenue account, or the recipient of the service was charged through a rent increment. In the former case, the effect on the rent of an individual elderly household was minimal, because the cost of a service provided for selected tenants only, was pooled. In the latter case, there was a definite effect on rent levels if the service was provided by the housing authority, but a few authorities hoped that the tenants could get re-decoration done, and have the cost offset by a contribution from the Ministry of Social Security.

'There are no facilities for redecoration. We bully the National Assistance Board or call up Toc H. The council have gone into this and calculated it would cost £70 per house to do them up at the end of a tenancy and the housing revenue account can't stand it.'

A similar pattern of limited or selective provision of gardening services was found, especially for old people. Again, there was concern about the way the service could expand and become very expensive. Was it reasonable to confine the service to council tenants, when the reason for it was the infirmity of the occupier rather than the dwelling tenure? One Scottish housing officer summarized the problem as follows: 'People's families are too busy to do gardens for old people and the NAB won't pay. Parks Department charge Housing for doing the work. Old people can't ever pay the bill and the problem goes round and round.'

In another authority, there was a large problem of neglected gardens. 'We cut down nettles and brambles and send the bill to the tenant. If the bill is not paid, it would probably be written off, but, in fact it has always been paid. The NAB are very helpful. The reason for sending the bill is to forestall demands from other tenants.' A housing manager referred to previous experience in a new town, where rents were increased by 6s a week to cover the costs of the parks department. He added that in his present authority, he was pressing relatives to do gardening.

Another way of keeping rents down was to cut out the provision of fittings. At least 6 housing authorities had stopped providing cookers either for financial reasons or because people were found to prefer their own. In a reference to housing standards and cost yardsticks, Wilson[1] pointed out that 'as a corollary to the introduction of additional facilities, local authorities should, of course, consider whether any existing items (e.g. wash boilers installed by the council in an age when (it is estimated) one family in three has a washing machine and launderettes are often within easy reach) are superfluous in the light of contemporary social conditions'. However, without clear evidence that elderly households share in 'contemporary social conditions', local authorities need to consider having a selective policy in order not to create hardship for this group of tenants.

In at least 2 of the 6 authorities which had stopped providing cookers, it was as much the maintenance as the capital and installation costs that were prohibitive, so in effect they gave the existing fittings to the tenants. 'It was either that or put the rents up. We let them do the maintenance. I guess a number have got new cookers by trading in the ones we gave them.' In another authority, the cooker was withdrawn when the house came empty, so that there was a store of second-hand cookers 'which we overhaul if they are worth it and the NAB will help old people to pay the installation costs of one of these. I have let some of these cookers go to old people in non-council houses also.' In general, the NAB were seen as helpful in supporting the costs of consumer durables, as well as in helping the elderly to meet heating costs, particularly when moving from an older open coal fire dwelling to a modern dwelling with probably

1 Wilson, op. cit., p. 20.

an unfamiliar form of heating. In one Scottish burgh, funds from voluntary activities and donations had been pooled to provide night storage heaters. At the time of this study, it had not been decided how to pay the running costs. 'We have not got the National Assistance Board to agree to help with the running costs, although they do say that they consider applications for help on their merits.'

The financing or subsidizing of these fittings or services could, like other housing costs mentioned above, have had some influence on the potential mobility of elderly households.

GRANTS FOR WELFARE FACILITIES

Another technique for reducing housing costs to the elderly related to the dwelling rather than to the occupier. Whereas expenditure on rent and rates tended to be modified according to the income of the household, provision of grants from welfare authorities to housing authorities to cover the cost of special features in sheltered housing was, like the government housing subsidy system, linked to the dwelling.

All seven English and Welsh case study county welfare authorities were using their powers under section 56 of the 1958 Local Government Act to pay contributions to housing authorities within their boundaries for sheltered housing schemes. The earliest had started these payments in the mid-fifties (under section 126 of the 1948 Local Government Act) and the most recent of the seven started in 1963–4. Net expenditure per thousand population on this item ranged from under £10 to over £100 in 1965–6 (the national range was from £2 2s 0d by Northumberland to £141 13s 0d by Rutland).[1] In the case study authorities, the highest level of net expenditure was borne by the county which started earliest, and the lowest by the county which started in 1963–4. The level of grant tended to increase over time because of increasing costs, and until the 1958 Local Government Act the maximum grant that the Minister would approve was £30 per dwelling. In 1965 and 1966 in the case study authorities the following types of arrangements were to be found: a maximum of £40 plus a possible contribution to a percentage of both the installation and running costs of the heating system; a choice of £30

[1] All except 2 of the 56 English and Welsh counties (the exceptions were Breconshire and Radnorshire) whose financial statistics were published in the Institute of Municipal Treasurers and Accountants' *Welfare Services Statistics 1965–6* made contributions to housing authorities (see Column 13b).

for 60 years or £35 for 30 years; the possibility of creating two or three levels of grant up to a maximum of £30; and higher unit grants for the first 20 dwellings in any scheme than for any number over 20.

In addition, one authority had introduced a second grant which reduced the interest rate on borrowing by the housing authorities down to 4%; another had analysed grants made by county welfare authorities and, as a result, had increased its unit contribution by £10 per annum from £30 to £40; a third contributed a sum equivalent to half the loss on the housing revenue account created by special housing for the elderly.

What were the implications of these varying contributions to housing authorities on planning services for the elderly? First of all, the arrangement was open-ended from the county's point of view, because the housing authorities were responsible for the timing of their house building programme and for its location and distribution. This made it difficult for the county to plan welfare services for the elderly, unless it felt that its grant had a decisive influence on provision (if not location) of sheltered housing. However, it was not clear that there was such an effect on the county's planning of welfare services. In the county with the interest reducing grant as well as the unit grant, the five years following the introduction of the former saw twice as many housing authorities begin sheltered housing schemes as had had them before, and about three-quarters of all the dwellings completed by the end of 1963–4 attracted the interest reducing grant. An urban district in the north of England referred to the announcement of the county grant for sheltered housing as a 'God-sent opportunity', and a rural district in East Anglia said: 'We would not have had the special scheme without financial support from the county, because we have got to think about balancing the housing revenue account.'

In contrast, two municipal boroughs—both eligible for grants—claimed that they did not go out of their way to get them.

'We heard last week from the county that they are prepared to make a grant . . . subject to our complying with the rules they lay down. Some local authorities get that end buttoned up before they choose tenants, whereas we choose our tenants and hope that most of them will comply with the qualifications . . .'

'We are not fussed about the grant, though the claim is put in in the interests of the housing revenue account. The county council can technically approve the tenants, but they never query the borough's selection. If they did, we would tell them to keep their grant.'

279

One housing authority in a case study county refused to ask for grant, because it feared it would lose control of tenancies. 'Knowing the attitude of some county officials, they would expect to have a full say, and I would see them in blazes first.'

Second, such an open-ended system made for problems in allocating financial resources, so that other county welfare services had to be pegged because of the drain on resources caused by an increase in sheltered housing. A sudden drain on financial resources might not give the county any real choice in whether or not to switch resources from homes for elderly people to intensive care of the elderly in their own homes. This had implications for local health services, general medical services, the Ministry of Social Security and voluntary organizations, as well as other county welfare services. In the county with the interest reducing grant, an elected member was reported as saying that the county would have a better chance of fulfilling its capital programme on welfare if they were not paying the grant (or perhaps not paying it from the welfare committee's rate fund account).[1] Although the county claimed it was intended to be only a temporary pump-priming operation, it was nevertheless thought to be politically difficult to stop financial support of this kind, and an outcry was expected from the housing authorities when the decision to stop the grant was announced. There was such a reaction, but the intensity of feeling was lessened because the 1964–6 Labour administration introduced its Housing Subsidies Bill, whose provisions were intended to create an interest reducing grant as the basis of the national housing subsidy system.

One county treasurer doubted that unit grants really affected the development of other welfare services, for two reasons. First, like a long-standing tax, an old subsidy was no subsidy. Second, the schemes were not economic for the housing authorities and although there might be over-provision of sheltered housing, this would be caused by political and social factors, not by economic ones. These reasons do not altogether hold because housing authorities will continue to provide sheltered housing, thus increasing annual grant payments (most of the grants are paid over a 60 year period, and the running costs of warden's salary, etc., will continue indefinitely),

[1] In one county the warden's salary was paid from the home help account, but the unit grant for the sheltered housing was paid from the finance committee account. 'There is logic in it, because in understanding the financial relationships between the county and the district councils, it must be realized that this covers a wide range of activities and therefore it is better to leave it in one committee's account. . . . With one account, we are more likely to secure uniformity of policy.' The county was in fact considering transferring grant payments to the health and welfare committee.

and if housing schemes are going to be provided for political and social reasons, this does not preclude accepting financial aid.

Three housing authorities emphasized the inadequacy of the grants, though in no case did this imply that the low level of grant would discourage provision of special housing. The clerk of a northern municipal borough said:

'The county council pays a sum equivalent to the extra cost of providing special features, but nothing which represents the saving to them for not having to provide Part III accommodation.'[1]

Third, the county welfare departments might find it difficult to estimate the extent to which need for residential accommodation would be affected by encouraging sheltered housing through such financial contributions, because, as the county welfare departments stressed, it was not their role to select tenants, though sometimes they were prepared to put names forward for consideration. As they did not control the selection of tenants but merely approved or disapproved the housing authorities' choice as constituting eligibility for the grant, it could be difficult to decide how many dwellings were tenanted by people 'otherwise . . . suitable for admission to accommodation provided under Part III of the National Assistance Act 1948' (to quote one county's conditions of financial aid to district councils).

In general, the conditions for grant aid required not only the existence of a warden, a warden's dwelling, a warden's telephone, a communication system between tenants and warden (ranging from a simple bell system to a sophisticated two-way intercom), perhaps central heating and a common room or guest room, but also that the tenant should fulfil the housing authority's usual requirements on length of residence in the area, be of pensionable age or, if younger, handicapped or infirm.

Counties made a number of other criticisms of this kind of financial aid for sheltered housing. First, there was the danger that an attractive grant might persuade housing authorities to ignore other categories of housing need. Second, there was the accusation that encouragement by central departments of this county-to-district subsidy system was an evasion of government responsibility. Third, the accounting point was made that if all housing authorities within an administrative county provided sheltered housing so that grants were spread evenly, there was no real benefit. 'A county council

---

[1] The number of Part III places provided by the county in question was very much below the average for England and Wales.

giving a grant to a district council borders on the ridiculous. It is the same ratepayers. You spread the burden over the county instead of just the district, but if all district councils provide equally, you would be back where you started.'

The arrangements in the 4 Scottish case study counties varied, and contrasted with the situation south of the border. One county had had no discussion with the small burgh housing authorities. Another had provided a sheltered housing scheme in its landward area (where the county is the housing authority) and was paying the warden from the welfare account. Other schemes without a warden were let by the welfare department rather than by the county housing factor, who simply advertised the dwellings. These schemes were seen 'as a sort of alternative to Part III accommodation'. A third county stressed the delicacy of the problem of being both a welfare and a housing authority in the landward area, but a welfare authority only in the small burghs, though its policy was to provide a grant without pressing it on the small burghs. The fourth county was at a similarly early stage[1] but its offer to make a contribution to one small burgh had been refused because of the fear of losing control of letting rights.

For local authorities responsible for both housing and welfare services, there was less apparent advantage in transferring contributions from one account to another.[2] The 4 Scottish urban case study authorities had not considered the matter at all, either because there were no such housing schemes, or because the amounts involved were such that they could be easily accommodated in the housing revenue account, or because concessionary rents for housing for old people were already at a very low level and needed no further support. In England, 2 county boroughs did not refer to the matter, 4 made no grant to the housing revenue account, and 3 did.

Of the 4 making no grant, one housing manager said that overlapping functions caused problems. One treasurer said that there were no sheltered housing schemes in his authority and if there were, such a transfer would merely be an unnecessary piece of book-keeping. Another treasurer said that if the amounts involved became large, they would consider a contribution from the welfare account. Another housing manager said that he would welcome the grant, although

[1] The power to make contributions of this kind became unambiguously clear only with the 1964 Housing Act (s. 101).

[2] Flatlet accommodation plus communal facilities for old people can also be provided under s. 21 of the National Assistance Act 1948 if the authority's approved scheme allows for this, but provisions by these means is relatively unusual.

it would come out of the same local pockets, because the housing department could use the money thus released for other purposes.

In 3 case study county boroughs, money was transferred to the housing revenue account. In one case, the grant was paid by the welfare department to cover general running expenses of a bungalow scheme (and the warden was a home help paid by the health department). In a second authority it was argued that there should be a contribution from the rate fund (not the welfare account) because the ratepayers as a whole benefited from the welfare work undertaken by caretakers in housing schemes. There was also a welfare account contribution towards the upkeep for some rent-free memorial homes. In the third authority, the housing committee were disturbed at the cost of dwellings for old people, so the difference between the actual cost of the dwellings and the cost of a similar ordinary, standard dwelling was computed, and the welfare department paid a unit grant of £30 per dwelling per annum to cover the difference. Running costs, e.g. warden's salary, were also charged to welfare. The welfare department accepted that this was a good idea, especially as this service for the elderly was expected to develop. In this authority, the welfare department had taken over the job of appointing wardens and alloating tenancies.

Contributions to housing authorities or housing revenue accounts do not constitute part of relevant expenditure for rate support grant negotiations and calculation, though most other expenditure on the welfare services rate fund account is regarded as 'relevant'. This issue was not raised by financial or other officers in the case study areas.

SUMMARY

About half of the case study housing authorities had adopted a rent structure based on gross annual value, and concessionary rent systems were becoming less popular. Most housing authorities were certain that it was the role of the Ministry of Social Security to supplement the income of elderly households, and not the function of housing authorities to subsidize the housing of the elderly through a rent rebate scheme. The trend towards comprehensive differential rent schemes might affect the overall demand for small dwellings for the elderly. If the elderly were underoccupying family dwellings and were eligible for rebate, withholding full rebate could affect their attidude towards moving. A rebate scheme also meant that the elderly might feel they could afford to move from low standard, low rent dwellings to higher standard, higher cost dwellings, particularly moving from the private rented sector to the public housing sector.

Demand for housing by the elderly might be modified by the operation of across-the-board subsidies like rate fund contributions which were not based on income levels of individual households. Rate relief schemes might also affect housing demand, but this kind of subsidy was linked to the incomes of individual households. Taken together, these new or recent administrative procedures could have a marked impact on planning and forecasting the number of small dwellings required for the elderly in future.

Housing costs to the individual occupier were also affected by the provision of fittings or certain services, like decoration. Some had ceased to provide such facilities in order to cut costs and thus keep rent levels down.

Grants to cover welfare facilities in sheltered housing could influence housing authority policy on the provision of small dwellings specially for the elderly or handicapped, but the welfare authority might not be able to control the extent and distribution of the provision. Such a development could affect the planning of residential and domiciliary services for the elderly by the health and welfare authority. The open-ended nature of the grant could drain the financial resources of the grant-giving authority, leaving them little flexibility in resource allocation for welfare services, unless the grant was paid from an account other than the welfare rate fund account. These problems were faced mainly by counties in England and Wales. Their expenditure on these welfare facilities did not constitute part of 'relevant' expenditure for rate support grant purposes.

CHAPTER 18

SITES

In some case study authorities officials said that the problems of finding sites were almost as great as those of obtaining capital finance for developments involving building projects. Thus, the availability of sites could be a major factor influencing the order in which buildings were planned, and one of the main reasons for revising plans which were originally formulated on the basis of decisions about social priorities. The discussions held with health, welfare and housing officers, and with local authority architects, threw some light on the nature of difficulties over sites, and on how some authorities were evolving ways of overcoming the problems.

THE PROBLEM OF FINDING SITES

In some urban areas the problem was that the only prospect of a site was in a redevelopment area, and health and welfare departments sometimes had difficulties in establishing their claims in competition with the housing committee. As one welfare officer said: 'Now we have only slum clearance and redevelopment areas and it is not always feasible to fit an old people's home in. It is the planning department's job to find sites for homes. Welfare department say what district they want a home in and the planners try to find somewhere. Usually they are housing committee sites which the housing committee do not want and so they can be allocated to other uses.' Another welfare officer claimed that his situation was better than it used to be because progress on overspill schemes had eased the position on housing.

Architects and planners were sometimes insufficiently aware of the needs of departments such as health and welfare. An architect-planner, describing the process of planning a redevelopment area, said: 'It starts in the office here with planning. Really it is the housing that counts because if you look at any town map the largest percentage is zoned for housing. You must plan for other facilities in the early stages—it is hopeless to try fitting them in afterwards.

The demands for sites in the development areas are made known through the estates surveyor. We also have some ideas of our own through applying planning principles—for example, we know schools will be necessary.' It seemed that the application of planning principles did not always include consideration of the need for health clinics or old people's homes. Thus unless the health and welfare officials were aware of redevelopment plans at an early stage, and took the initiative in pressing their needs for sites, they could find themselves left out.

There were some examples of health and welfare departments missing opportunities for sites through not being clear about what they wanted. This had happened more than once with health projects, because of uncertainties about whether the building should be a health centre, a group practice surgery for general practitioners or a local authority clinic. An architect-planner described what had happened in his area: 'A general practitioner approached the estates surveyor about a site in the new development area. Then the executive council got involved and was talking about group practices, and then the local health department butted in and said it wanted clinics, and as soon as they did that the negotiations with the general practitioners fell flat. So we do not know what they want there—health clinics, group practices or what, and the site we were thinking of we have put to housing now anyway.'

Even when the claim to a site for a health or welfare project was established, the dependence on redevelopment for sites could affect the timing of projects. 'You are guided by the timing of the whole development. The site might be available in three or four years' time after slum clearance, and even if the project is urgent you might still put it three or four years ahead if the promised site is a good one.'

In rural areas, and on the fringes of urban areas, the problem was more that of obtaining land from farmers. An official from one of the highland counties explained that: 'If there are not problems with big landowners then there are problems with crofters. We get the bog or a heap of stones.'

A few authorities said that site availability was not a particular problem as the council owned a lot of land already. However, when land had to be bought, many local authorities disliked resorting to compulsory purchase. This attitude was found in urban areas as well as rural, but was very strongly held by some county councils and rural district councils with a number of farmers among the councillors. In addition to a general dislike of using powers of compulsory purchase, several authorities stressed that they had to have a strong case for doing so. A county architect explained: 'We can only use a compulsory purchase order if we have compelling arguments that there is no alternative site, and this would be very difficult for us to do.' This implied that arguments that the site was particularly suitable for accommodation for old people would not be thought of as 'compelling'.

Purchase of privately owned land by negotiation was at times protracted and difficult, and the problems were exacerbated if there was also disagreement in a local authority committee about the relative merits of sites. 'There is not really practical difficulty over sites but there is great difficulty in getting one agreed. It is no good approaching landowners until the committee have said which one they would like (the welfare committee had been discussing which would be the best site for a new welfare home for several months), and yet the landowners may be laughing up their sleeves at all the publicity about which sites are being considered because they have absolutely no intention of selling.'

The larger authorities tended to have had rather less difficulty than smaller ones in finding sites. The welfare officer of a large county, for example, said that they had enough sites to keep them going, and that if there was a problem in one area, they would build in another. Thus the wider area and larger population served provided a flexibility not so easily available to smaller authorities.

In general, counties had more flexibility of this kind than county boroughs, although it was a county borough medical officer who said: 'Site availability is easy if you can put what you want anywhere in the city, but if it has to be in a specific area it may be more difficult.'

Some authorities phased their development programme on the basis of where sites were most easily available, which sometimes meant that new old people's homes and health clinics were not built in the areas with the greatest need. An official from a large county said: 'At first when we got sites we just put homes on them. The homes were not related to the catchment area and this was because of the problems of finding sites.' It followed from this policy that old people needing a place in a home quite often had to go to a home in a different part of the county from that in which they had previously lived.

THE PROBLEMS OF FINDING SUITABLE SITES

The problem of finding sites was partly that of finding sites *suitable* for old people's housing, homes, or clinics. Most authorities stressed

287

the importance of old people's homes and housing being located 'in the community', near to facilities such as shops, post office, bus stop, church and pub, and on flat sites wherever possible.

Some authorities, unable to find suitable sites, were not building for the elderly meantime. 'It is no good putting old people's housing on the outskirts away from the shops', was the reason a district council gave for not building any more until they had found a central site. This kind of consideration was particularly relevant in small towns which did not have a local bus service.

Other authorities, faced with the same problem, had decided to accept that new housing for the elderly would be unsuitably located: 'There is no room in the town centre for new houses. They will be on the perimeter, so old people will be in new places away from the shops.'

Sometimes planners did not attach much weight to the special needs of the elderly. A district council wanted to build old people's bungalows on a central clearance site, but said that: 'The town and country planners rejected this because the site was zoned for industry. Then they changed their mind and said it should be residential, and then they changed their mind again and said the land should go for shopping development.'

In one of the county boroughs where a welfare home was being replaced, the finance committee wanted to sell the site because it was in a desirable area, and asked the planning committee to find a less valuable site for the new welfare home.

Some authorities had tried to pursue a policy of building for the elderly on gap sites in order to provide dwellings near to shopping facilities, and near to other types of housing. This policy could be difficult to achieve because contractors were not interested in this type of small job. In one or two larger authorities infilling was ruled out because the Ministry were more willing to give approval for schemes using industrialized building methods.

In rural areas other considerations affected the suitability of sites. A public health inspector, discussing the siting of sheltered housing schemes in a rural district, said that some of the need for sheltered housing was in areas where there was no sewerage scheme, and where other development was not envisaged. Several rural authorities had, on the advice of the central department, bought up land quite cheaply just after the war but later found themselves faced with the dilemma of whether to build on the land they owned in areas which still had no sewerage, electricity or piped water supply, and where facilities such as shops and buses were poor, or to build elsewhere on land which they would have to buy at five times the price. Other rural authorities had almost used up the land they bought in the 1940s, and said that they could only develop in the future if they acquired land at today's price.

DEVELOPMENT OF PROCEDURES FOR FINDING SITES

Evidence from some of the case study authorities suggested that problems over sites were being tackled more effectively by the mid-sixties than they were in the early stages of capital development in the services for the elderly.

An architect commented on the way planning for health and welfare was improving in his authority: 'We know the general programme for things like welfare homes—that it is the policy to do two a year, but we do not know *where*. We do know this more now than we used to. The welfare officer has said he wants them included in redevelopment areas and the same applies to health centres, but it is important to know what departments want *early* if we are to get the plan right.'

In some counties, the lessening of difficulties in obtaining sites for welfare homes was mainly due to the co-operation of the district councils. One county council, for example, had sent out a circular in which the desirable site features for welfare homes were detailed, and the district councils had responded well to the request for help in finding such sites. As a result, the county had changed its priorities for projects: 'Now the object is to provide homes more on a catch-ment area basis rather than just where there are sites. We still have difficulty, and this will always be so, but the probability of getting sites is now higher.'

Not all the counties were as helpful in return to district councils seeking sites for old people's housing when, for example, buildings such as old public assistance institutions were being demolished.

In one county an improvement in the situation with regard to sites for health department projects had followed the development of administrative procedures. The medical officer of health said: 'Within this past year relations with the planning department have clicked. This is partly because of the appointment of an adminis-trative officer in the health department who has time to devote to this. It is also partly because the deputy county clerk is willing to take the initiative in calling a meeting of officials who have interests in sites in particular areas.' He also referred to the practice adopted by another county in which 'the county clerk instituted quarterly meetings over the building programme. The clerk, architect, planning

K   289

officer, and land agent would sit all the way through, and other chief officers would come in for their bit. Anybody could get kicked for not getting on with their contribution to the capital development programme.' The situation in one of the county boroughs was also said to have improved as the result of better communication with the planning department, and the setting up of a forum for the discussion of developments involving several departments. 'A chief officers' conference is held weekly consisting of the town clerk, treasurer, estates surveyor, architect, town planner, public health inspector, medical officer of health, the housing manager, and others as required. If necessary a special sub-committee is formed to deal with something. The kind of matters they deal with are slum clearance and acquisition problems, the allocation of land in a given area as between education and parks etc.'

IMPACT OF CENTRAL DEPARTMENT POLICIES

Some case study authorities, however, pointed out that even if site planning was more effectively co-ordinated at local level problems could arise because of the central departments' control over loan sanction. Periodic government restrictions on capital expenditure on health and welfare projects created serious difficulties for authorities where the claim to a site for a health and welfare project in a redevelopment area had been established, yet at the time the redevelopment was taking place the authority could not get loan sanction. A welfare officer, who had succeeded in getting sites in redevelopment areas, said: 'We are very disappointed with the Ministry because we have made great efforts on sites. We had got three sites—and now we have three homes on the stocks and we cannot get loan sanction. We are being fobbed off with trifling queries about plans—this is stalling.'

Another aspect of the problems created by national decisions on priorities related to schemes involving more than one local authority department. 'Co-ordination is done on an *ad hoc* basis when several departments have interests in a site on one place. However, if you link up with other departments you get problems because you need a bigger site, and also because priorities differ in different departments, and Ministries differ in what they will allow to go forward.'

Other criticisms of the central departments related to cost limits. Trying to meet the criteria for suitability of sites for accommodation for old people, or having to build on a difficult site because this was all that was obtainable, sometimes made for high site preparation costs. An official from one of the highland counties said with feeling: 'We had to excavate twelve feet of peat for the site of one of our old people's homes', and an architect in an industrial county borough referred to the high cost of site preparation because 'the stone is never very far down and the slopes are quite violent'. Although central departments made some allowances when setting cost limits for the high cost of preparing difficult sites, some authorities felt that the central department did not appreciate the full extent of the problem.

SUMMARY

It had sometimes been difficult to establish claims for sites for welfare projects for the elderly and for other health projects against the more insistent demands of other departments, especially the housing department. Planners were not always aware of the needs of health and welfare departments. Sometimes opportunities were missed because health or welfare departments were not sure what they wanted.

In some urban areas health and welfare projects had to wait for redevelopment schemes, since no other land was available. In rural areas the problem was more often that of obtaining land from farmers, and dislike of using compulsory purchase powers often meant that site purchase was a slow process.

The capital programmes of larger authorities, especially counties, were less often delayed by difficulties in finding sites, but the practice of building where sites were available often meant that the greatest social needs were not met first.

Some problems arose because the requirements of health, welfare and housing departments for sites for buildings for old people, although modest in size, involved special features.

Where communications between client departments and planners, architects, or estate surveyors, and between county councils and district councils had been improved, and systems of co-ordination of capital programmes had been developed, some of the problems had diminished.

Even where co-ordination was good at local authority level, difficulties still arose because of the way in which control over capital expenditure was exercised by central departments.

The consequence of these problems over sites was that developments did not always take place in an order of priority related to needs.

CHAPTER 19

ARCHITECTURAL SERVICES
AND BUILDING RESOURCES

About a quarter of the health and welfare departments in case study authorities referred to queues and bottlenecks in the architect's department being responsible for delaying projects. The main reasons for this were shortages of skilled staff, the effect of central departments' policies, and problems of communication between client departments and technical departments. In addition, difficulties sometimes arose over contracts for buildings for old people.

SHORTAGES OF ARCHITECTS AND QUANTITY SURVEYORS

Most case study authorities considered that delays in the architect's department were not due to discrimination against health and welfare projects. As a medical officer said: 'Our department gets a fair crack of the whip compared with other departments. There was some difficulty a few years ago when the architect was short of staff. A lot of projects fell behind schedule, though I don't know whether health projects more so than anything else.'

Interviews with architects confirmed that some authorities had difficulty in recruiting and retaining skilled staff. The Mallaby Report stated that there was a national shortage of architects in 1966, and that the shortage in local government was particularly marked. Of the posts in their sample, 17·4% had been vacant for 6 months or more, and 13·3% were filled by persons possessing less than the desirable qualifications.[1] Some of the case study authorities which were short of architects were small ones, but large authorities also had problems. One large county had been as much as 25% short of its establishment figure at times during the previous few years. Another authority had a sixth of its posts in the architect's department unfilled, the vacancies being mainly for architects. This

[1] Ministry of Housing and Local Government , *Staffing of Local Government*, H.M.S.O. 1967, p. 30

authority had just lost five assistant architects to the Regional Hospital Board which was offering higher salaries to attract people to work on a new district general hospital. Another case study authority had lost five quantity surveyors, mainly to private practice, in the previous year, and had managed to recruit only one replacement.

Many other case study authorities said their staffing position was 'not too bad', although some commented on the high mobility of staff. Mobility of younger staff was approved of on the grounds that it widened their experience to work in different places. However, mobility was said to create its own problems in a situation of overall shortage by tending to force up salary levels.

CAPITAL PROGRAMMES

Some local authorities, especially the larger ones, had capital programmes, and architects agreed that this made it easier to plan a smooth flow of work. 'The introduction of the three-year capital programme by the council a few years ago made it much easier for us because we could see what was coming well ahead. When you only do one year at a time you end up with a lot of things going out to tender all round about Christmas because you have to do it within the financial year—so you are going out at a time when contractors are not interested and you get bad prices.'

Some authorities planned capital programmes on the assumption that architectural services would be available, but a few had devised ways of formulating capital programmes which took account of the availability of these resources. In one case study the architect explained: 'Very often a project is tied up with other developments— and we have got to get roads in first—so we try to get two or three committees all to move ahead at the same pace. Phasing is effected by the capital priorities committee, which is the king-pin of the system, because it determines what money shall be spent on what. Each committee draws up a programme and these are collated. Then I advise the capital priorities committee whether that programme is capable of being carried out by the labour force in the area and whether it is within the capabilities of this department.'

In authorities with a three-year or five-year capital programme it tended to be this programme, rather than the ten-year plans for health and welfare, which mattered, but one or two English health and welfare officers thought the ten-year plans were useful as a tactical weapon in relation to both the treasurer and the architect, and some architects said it was useful to have a general idea of what might be coming along in the way of health and welfare projects.

IMPACT OF CENTRAL DEPARTMENTS' POLICIES

However, local authority capital programmes were difficult to formulate since some central government departments gave little notice of what would be allowed to go forward and, as one architect said: 'Things are not adequately integrated at government level. The Ministry of Transport may have so much available for loan sanctions and yet we need this plus some for the Ministry of Housing and Local Government scheme we had approved. We need the roads and the housing scheme together, and yet the Ministries do not have money for this.'

A number of case study authorities commented that health and welfare projects were sometimes at a disadvantage in the competition for the resources of the architect's department because of the way in which central government departments operated. A medical officer of health said: 'The Department of Education and Science has a more realistic policy about the allocation of capital resources, and this leads to our education department booking architects' time ahead. By the time we get Ministry of Health sanction for a project we are too late to get our share of architects' time. For example, we heard about two weeks ago (i.e. mid-May) what we should go ahead with in the current financial year.' This, together with shortages of staff, may explain why one or two welfare officials felt that the welfare department's work was accorded low priority by the architects, and why a county nursing officer was moved to say: 'Education takes nine months of the year, then police, and then the rest. This is what one feels. The architects have an awful lot of work and a great thrust of education building.'

Even in a county with a large enough architect's department to have a separate section working for the health, welfare and children's committees, central department policy was said by the section head to create problems for the smooth working of the section. 'The Ministry of Health and the Home Office do not tell us far enough in advance what will be allowed to go forward. We cannot plan if we know which items will be included in the Ministry's programme only in the current financial year. Only once since 1961 have we heard *before* the current financial year and then only in March. This is useless because the pre-contract period of work is twelve months. Therefore either we anticipate what will be included and run the risk of semi-abortive work, at least in terms of starting dates, or we scrabble like mad and just squeeze in at the end of the financial year. It leads to problems within the department—and especially in that it gives the quantity surveyors a bad spread of work. We need to know at least two years in advance. Education have a three-year programme but I am not sure how well it works.'[1]

Moreover, the whole exercise could be upset by government decisions on priorities for capital expenditure every time selective restrictions were imposed, since national decisions on priorities sometimes conflicted with the local decisions which formed the basis of the capital programme. This uncertainty surrounding local capital programmes had made some architects wary of planning the work of their department to fit in with the programme. 'We have sometimes had a scheme left in mid-air because of Government policy although not recently. We try to anticipate this by easing off work on schemes which we think are not going to come off.' Furthermore, when a deferment of health and welfare projects was imposed by the government, local authority architects were transferred on to other projects. Thus, when restrictions were lifted there were no architects available, and health and welfare projects had again to wait their turn, or go to outside architects. This had happened in several case study authorities, architects transferring to education and housing projects because of the government cutting back on libraries and old people's homes.

Central government departments were criticized for being unrealistic about the effect of deferring projects. A medical officer of health said: 'The Ministry say you must prepare plans ahead and have things all pigeon-holed ready. This is not amenable to the architect's department when they are so short-staffed. They will not work on something the Ministry may not allow to go ahead for six years.' Architects made the same point about staff shortages, and also said that it was not practical to do drawings for projects which were not likely to be built for some time, because ideas on design changed, which might mean redrawing the plans later.

Departments not badly affected by staff shortages often did work on deferred projects, in order to keep staff employed. It then became a game of guessing which projects would be demanded first when restrictions were lifted. According to one architect: 'As soon as a ban comes off all departments will be screaming for buildings. We gently coast along those for which the client will be screaming

<hr />

[1] In 1967, the Ministry of Health asked local health and welfare authorities to submit three-year rolling capital programmes, so that provisional loan sanction could be indicated well ahead.

loudest. Knowing which department this will be is a matter of experience.'

One way to overcome problems due to shortages of architects, and to the uneven flow of work because of central government policy, was to put work out to private architects. The disadvantages of doing so were summarized by one of the architects: 'Cost is one disadvantage of outsiders. It surely must be dearer, although I have no figures, because they have their own overheads and profits to make. A second disadvantage is that they may not fully appreciate what the client really wants. This is a two-edged criticism because often a client does not really know either. A third disadvantage is that an outside architect has no subsequent responsibility for outside maintenance. We haven't in one sense, but other bits of the council have and we hear about it and have to live with it if we slip up. Outsiders do not have the same drive to see there are no subsequent problems. The fourth disadvantage is the impact on our staff—on recruitment and retention of staff and on whether we get good calibre people.'

Other case studies provided evidence to support these views. A health department which had to go to private quantity surveyors for two mental health projects as a result of staff shortages and the local authority resources being transferred to education buildings during a period of capital restrictions said that, as a result, the cost of each project went up. There was some feeling that, although it was all right to go out to private architects for housing, and many smaller housing authorities worked entirely with outside architects, projects such as an old people's home were specialized in nature, and better done by architects experienced in this kind of work. The same was said of health projects.

On the other hand some authorities had had very satisfactory service from private architects on health and welfare projects. A few local authority architects said that using private firms added to the burden on senior staff in the local authority department, 'saying what is wanted, liaising, keeping tabs on what is going on'. In some authorities client departments dealt direct with the private architect, and the council architect was hardly involved at all, but in others the client department relied heavily on the council architect to act as spokesman, which could mean that council architects spent a lot of time doing liaison work of a not very rewarding nature. On the staff issue also, some felt they were caught in a vicious circle 'because the more we put work out to private offices because we haven't got the staff, the less our chances of getting staff because they will go to private offices'.

USE OF STANDARD PLANS

Another solution to the problems of providing architectural services was the use of standard plans. Several authorities were attracted by the principle of rationalization which preparation of standard plans implies. 'Standard plans are a good thing although they are dull for the architect and may mean you lose staff. There is a lot of technical time wasted, and a clinic which is good enough for one town is surely good enough for another. In housing you get all these local authorities with their own architects and all the firms with their own architects as well. There is a big waste—although in a sense industrialized building is solving this problem for us.'

The practical advantages of using standard plans to deal with uneven work-flow because of central department policy on capital expenditure were illustrated by the experience of a large county, where the architect explained: 'The design of old people's homes was standardized round about 1960, and this standard was super-seded by a new one in 1962. Then we put forward a yearly programme of building a given number of homes. The only work in the office was to provide foundations to suit the sites. The turn-over in the depart-ment was 6 weeks because they were standard dwellings. At the end of each year the Ministry of Health gave us one or two homes that we were allowed to build from someone else's allocation because that somebody else had not got as far forward as they thought.'

However, while 3 or 4 of the larger counties had made good use of the possibilities afforded by standard planning, others had tried and failed, and some argued that standard planning was inappropriate to their circumstances. The successful counties had been building mainly on flat sites. Elsewhere the architect claimed that it was impossible to use standard plans for welfare homes because of the great variety in shapes and levels of sites. Another architect said: 'We did once use the same plans twice, but had to make so many alterations that it wouldn't have taken any longer to design a new home from the start.' Other authorities said they were too small to use standard plans. Old people's homes were not built frequently enough for a standard plan to be a real benefit since ideas on design changed fairly rapidly, and local authorities did not want to repeat mistakes. A further argument was that in a small urban authority 'standardized plans would have been a menace because we don't want the buildings looking the same'. Even in counties, using a standard plan can create a stigma. Old people like the building to be as unobtrusive as possible and to fit in with the scene. Moreover, some counties considered it important to have homes of different sizes to meet the needs of different sizes of population cluster.

COMMUNICATION BETWEEN CLIENT DEPARTMENTS AND ARCHITECTS

Some problems and delays in the past were due to lack of experience in building old people's homes and health clinics on the part of the architects, and lack of experience of briefing, and of commenting on sketch plans, by client departments. Health and welfare departments were sometimes at a disadvantage compared with education and housing departments which not only had larger programmes, but also fewer set-backs from restrictions on capital expenditure. 'With briefing, the education department know what they want, probably because they have had so many projects. Health and welfare departments are less clear, but it is an ever-changing world and they have to try to keep up-to-date.'

Occasionally architects lost patience with clients who did not seem to know what they wanted. 'We asked for a brief for a clinic from the medical officer of health, but after 6 months we got a few words saying it should be capable of serving a population of 10,000 to 15,000. I put it in the pending tray.' On the other hand welfare officers in three English counties emphasized the problems caused by the turnover of architects. One of them said: 'When I had clarified my thoughts, I found myself confronted by a new architect.'

As well as difficulties in communication over the initial briefing, there were often problems at later stages because of the inability of client departments and committees to read plans. Some architects did not see it as their responsibility to explain plans, arguing that it was too time-consuming, and that to use models was too expensive. However, some did accept responsibility for explaining plans to clients, and one architect described how his department used a set of modulex as an aid to explaining plans.

Experience clearly helped to overcome these problems.

'The welfare department is high on the list of departments for good briefing. They have done this kind of job before and have become experienced in briefing the architects.'

'Nowadays welfare give use very little briefing. The size of home is pretty well settled policy and apart from any new ideas coming up, we *know* our brief.'

A few client departments had tried to overcome communication problems by making one person responsible for liaison with the architects, so that he could build up experience over time and be known as the expert on this. This had been done in a joint health and welfare department, and also in a housing department in one of the housing authorities.

Elsewhere, architects were working towards standard briefs, and even standard sections of buildings, for although there were reservations about using standard plans, several authorities were interested in the possibilities of some degree of rationalization of the process of creating plans. A county architect commented: 'We use the standard form,[1] worked out in conjunction with the deputy welfare officer. I envisage that we will still get briefs for future homes but we will also have our research notes on particular parts of homes collated. We have done research projects on laundries and kitchens but not yet on the rooms in which old people live, and on the environment generally.' In another case study a start on collation of information had been made by the welfare officer, who explained: 'The department get detailed criticisms from the matrons which are incorporated into comments to the architect so that he can use them for the next building. I would like to go a stage further but I can't do it yet. I would like to provide a complete brief, which can be amended regularly. At the moment there is an area of common agreement, which is not recorded, and changes are discussed.'

Thus the initiative to record and classify past experience came sometimes from the client, sometimes from the architect. In another authority the housing manager criticised the architects for 'doing silly things and they don't learn. They still offer drawers with no handles, but a ridge underneath which someone with arthritis could not open, and there are other things like hand grips to baths, handrails to outside steps etc.' Yet he had only started to keep a list of points to check with the architect when instructed to do so by the chairman of the housing committee.

In some authorities housing design and fittings were apparently little discussed by architect and client department, as the following two examples show.

'The amount of information available to the housing department

[1] See Appendix 3.

from experience is not used as it might have been. House designs are more or less static. It might be a waste of time if everybody sat down to discuss design. I do not know if in the long run we could do much. Everybody has been anxious to get on.'

'There is some consultation with the architect although it could be better. We see plans when they go up to committee but plans at this stage do not necessarily include all the fittings. If the architect is bringing in something new he might have a word with us before-hand, but often we do not know until the building is handed over.'

By contrast there was close consultation between housing manager and architect in some case study authorities. In a municipal borough: 'The housing and architect's departments try to get together. The architect asks for information on types of families and special features like old people. He asks if anything should be incorporated, whether the types of windows are all right, whether there should be any changes of fittings.' This architect was said to have 'his heart and soul in his job'. In one county borough the housing manager took the initiative in keeping the architect informed of developments in design. 'These things should come from the housing department because the manager there should know the need and be up-to-date in appliances.' Another housing manager described his authority as 'enlightened' because architects and housing manager co-operated over plans, and added that in the larger county borough he had previously worked in 'the place was too large to have liaison'.

Some authorities had carried out surveys or experiments with design features. In one district the housing manager described how 'I even used my mother-in-law as a guinea pig—how far she could stand on a chair without wobbling so that we could get an idea of how big the kitchen should be and what height we should make some of the shelves and furniture.' In another, the housing manager had carried out surveys to try to establish what was important, and design was discussed in great detail with the architect, who was said to be 'interested in old people, and he tries out improvements and suggestions every time'.

Not all case study authorities were convinced of the value of consulting the users of buildings in order to learn from past mistakes. One architect said: 'We did once consult matrons of old people's homes about design but it was hopeless. Each one has his own ideas and none of them tally.' Another authority incorporated suggestions made by the matron of one new home into the next one, only to find that some of the extra facilities were not used. This had led to the view that: 'Above all we have to guard against individual idiosyncrasies. It is all right to ask for views, but you have got to *sift* them. This is the architect's job.' Other authorities had concluded that sifting views was the welfare officer's or housing manager's job, and again, in some areas, no sifting was done.

Some officers who had tried to conduct user surveys had difficulty in interpreting the results. One architect, speaking of welfare homes, said: 'Some say you should talk to old people themselves. When I have done this they say what they think I want them to say.' A housing manager who was keen that there should be systematic evaluation of housing said: 'In future we hope to carry out a systematic survey 3–6 months after occupation. We did one survey and everybody said they were delighted, but I decided I had asked the wrong questions. Then we tried another one which we have not finished analysing yet. The idea is to give a report to the architect so that it can be referred to. It is too much a matter of hit or miss just now.'

Most authorities said that the Ministry of Health's building notes on design of residential accommodation[1] were helpful. Some used them as a starting point from which to build up their own system by compiling 'more detailed notes for ourselves. We have found ways in which the Ministry's building notes are at fault—the amount of space in the kitchen is extravagant.'

Other authorities perhaps relied too heavily on the building notes. 'The Ministry have introduced a larger number of changes than welfare department have in terms of design. A lot of our brief comes from the Ministry building notes and other publications. The trouble with these is that they get out of date very rapidly. This is especially true of health projects but it also applies to others. We submit plans based on Ministry recommendations and the Ministry architect says they are out of date.'

As well as this criticism of the building notes, some architects were concerned that the purpose of welfare homes was not at all clear. One, discussing how a new home which he had designed was functioning in practice, said: 'The whole system of old people's homes has gone astray because they thought of the fit young old and not the frail infirm old, which is what they are getting.' Another architect was concerned at the lack of guidance on what sort of environment it was desirable to create for the elderly in homes, and he also questioned whether they should be building homes at all, or 'ought we to be building flats and bungalows, and providing

[1] Ministry of Health, *Local Authority Building Note 2—Residential Accommodation for Elderly People*, H.M.S.O., 1962.

a place for the elderly to go for a short period when they are off colour?'

Architects who had designed residential accommodation for the elderly could have given useful advice to colleagues designing houses for the elderly, especially sheltered housing. However, in some areas it seemed that not a great deal of consultation took place.

In one new sheltered housing scheme visited the fixed overhead shower was disliked by the residents, and the housing manager did not know that flexible shower fittings were available, yet a new welfare home not very far away had them.

In the county boroughs housing and welfare work were quite often done by separate sections in the architect's department, and the extent to which ideas were shared depended on the extent of informal contact with colleagues. In others, some of the work went out to private architects.

In the counties an additional problem was created because there were separate housing authorities. Where county councils were paying grants towards the cost of welfare features there was some opportunity for county architects to see plans. However, housing authorities often did not know whether county architects saw the plans when the question of the grant was being decided. County architects said that mostly they did, but that it was a 'token gesture', and one added that even if he did notice something he thought might be better done differently it would be impolitic for him to say so—'you have to mind how you tread'. In another county the architect used to be involved, but asked to be excused from it because he saw no point in the exercise. 'I used to look at the plans submitted and suggest various things—for example separate fuel stores—but these things were rarely taken up. The question of Ministry of Housing and Local Government approval was always quoted at me as a reason for the district councils doing what they wanted and not what I suggested. Also the plans came in after tenders and loan sanction had been received and therefore it was too late for any effective alterations to be done.'

Some county welfare departments exercised a watching brief over the design of sheltered housing, either by laying down criteria for qualification for the county council grant, or by informal contact between the welfare officers and the district council. One county had a special sub-committee of the welfare committee to see plans and meet representatives of the district councils and their architects, but the county architect was not involved except over planning permission for the site. The county welfare officer described the work of the sub-committee as 'to watch things like the position of light switches, meters etc., although a lot of the district councils have their work done by the same architect, who tends to know about these things. The sub-committee also suggested that some bungalows should be suitable for wheelchairs with ramps, wide doors, and storage space for the wheelchair, on the grounds that it is cheaper to provide these facilities at the start then to have to adapt later.'

The Ministry of Housing and Local Government's series of book-lets on design of old people's housing[1] were mentioned by several housing authorities. Some were critical about sizes, and about shared bathroom facilities, but on the whole the notes were considered useful.

Some authorities regarded Ministry guidance as a useful beginning, to be supplemented by their own experience. 'While the book is handy, we have already gone into it thoroughly, and learned by experience that what would suit one person would not suit another.'

However, many authorities put most of their housing work out to private firms, and not all of them were sure of the extent to which private architects were aware of the special needs of the elderly. A rural district council used to send Ministry circulars and other Ministry advice to the private firm which did most of its work, because 'they should know what is expected of them'. Other councils put work out to several firms, and although they often tried to find firms with previous experience of designing for the elderly, did not always see it as the council's responsibility to ensure that designs catered for the special needs of old people. Comments from case study authorities illustrated this attitude.

'The private architect was given a free hand to design accommodation according to requirements for aged persons. From past experience the architects managed to incorporate the facilities the old people needed.'

'There are phases about whether common rooms in sheltered housing are used or not, and you get a bit of falling out. Therefore in one scheme there are two rooms. The architect just did it. I suppose he got the idea from somewhere else.'

Sometimes it was said that the conditions for the county council grant, together with the need for Ministry approval to schemes, served as a check on design.

1 Ministry of Housing and Local Government, *Flatlets for Old People* (1958), *More Flatlets for Old People* (1960), *Some Aspects of Designing for Old People* (1962), *Grouped Flatlets for Old People* (1962), *Old People's Flatlets at Stevenage* (1966), H.M.S.O.

However, not all authorities approved of the extent of Ministry involvement in design, and a county borough architect complained that: 'Ministry staff are too inclined to dabble in technical things which our own staff could do.'

A further factor which inhibited local authority interest in special design features in housing for the elderly was that: 'For housing we do a package deal with a particular builder and this limits our decisions about whether to incorporate various design features or not. If we had our own architect it would be different.' Another official thought 'the package deal contractors would watch things themselves'.

PROBLEMS OVER BUILDING CONTRACTS

The special nature of accommodation for old people sometimes made for difficulties in finding contractors. 'An old persons' home is not a terribly attractive job to the contractor, because contractors want repetitive work like housing, and labour also wants it. With a one-off job you have to keep referring to the plans, and the contractor includes increased wages in the tender to pay over the line in order to keep his workers.' Even with old people's houses the preference of contractors for large-scale jobs, and the development of industrialized building methods had created some difficulties over contracts. As an architect in an authority which had decided that it only needed to build one bedroom accommodation said: 'There are very few industrialized building firms who provide one bedroom houses apart from bungalows, and these are a waste of land.' The Ministry was pressing this authority to undertake some industrialized building of two or three bedroom houses (which it did not need), whereas the local authority was more concerned with whether the industrial building firm would change to producing one bedroom accommodation.

Pressure of general demand on the building industry affected the attitude of potential contractors. Some case studies commented that the cut-back in general employment opportunities in the mid-sixties, and in contracts for building firms, had eased labour problems and made contractors more competitive and more interested in the otherwise unpopular one-off jobs. At the same time, local authorities were being restrained by central departments from going out to tender, so that they were unable to take advantage of this situation.

Case study authorities with a scattered population tended to face repeated difficulties in getting contractors. One authority said that although they advertised in the national press only small local firms were interested in tendering. In some remote areas there were no local building firms, and the fact that skilled labour and materials had to be brought considerable distances added appreciably to the costs. One county architect said: 'We're lucky if we get one response at a price acceptable to the central department. We have had an awful tussle over tenders for the proposed new nurse's house in an outlying part of the county. Central department keeps refusing to accept tenders on the grounds that they are too high. This has gone on for 3 or 4 years now, and while the first tenders were around the £4,000 mark, the one that's in now is nearer £8,000 for exactly the same specifications. The central department would have been far better to let us get on and build it in the beginning—but no, they said "readvertise" and every time we readvertise the tenders come in higher than before.'

Another area had a similar experience with a housing development including some houses for old people. Architects were appointed in 1959, and tenders first invited in late 1960. It took three attempts before a contractor tendered at a price acceptable to both the council and the central department, and work eventually started on the scheme in 1964.

These difficulties put the more remote areas with scattered populations at a considerable disadvantage compared with authorities which could benefit from the economies of large-scale activity.

SUMMARY

About a quarter of the health and welfare departments studied referred to delays in the architect's department.

Some authorities, both large and small, were short of architects and quantity surveyors, and had a high turnover of staff.

Authorities with three or five-year capital programmes found it easier to ensure a smooth flow of work through the architect's department, especially when the capacity of the architect's department and of the local building industry were taken into account in formulating the programme.

Local capital programmes could be upset by inability to get loan sanction from central government departments at the right time. This was partly because different central departments had different procedures for allocating capital resources, and partly because of the effect of selective restrictions on capital expenditure, which often operated to the detriment of health and welfare projects.

Several authorities tried to solve problems caused by staff shortages and uneven flow of work by putting work out to private architects, or using standard plans, but both these solutions brought further problems.

Some difficulties were due to failures in communication between client departments and architects. As experience of designing for the elderly grew, failures in communication tended to diminish. Development of standard briefs, and advice on design published by central departments helped. A few authorities had experimented, not always successfully, with surveys of design features. However, experience and expertise in designing for the elderly were often still not used to the best advantage.

Package-deal contracts and the development of industrialized building tended to militate against inclusion of special design features for the elderly.

Some difficulties were experienced in getting contractors for one-off jobs, especially when the local building industry was overloaded. Central government policy usually made it impossible for local authorities to take advantage of times when the local building industry was slack.

Sparsely populated local authorities tended to have severe difficulties in getting contractors at all.

CHAPTER 20

ALTERNATIVE SUPPLIERS—
OTHER STATUTORY BODIES

Local authority health, welfare and housing departments have no monopoly of provision of services for the elderly. Services are also provided by other public bodies, voluntary organizations, and private enterprise. The existence of alternative suppliers made the process of planning more complex, and it was difficult for a local authority to decide how much of a service, or what aspect of a service, it should aim to provide itself. The problems of planning in conjunction with voluntary organizations and private enterprise are considered in later chapters. This chapter concentrates on the ways in which local authority health, welfare and housing departments regarded the role of other bodies which derive their powers to provide services from parliamentary statutes, the main ones being Regional Hospital Boards, National Health Service Executive Councils, the Ministry of Social Security, and local authority departments other than health, welfare and housing.

REGIONAL HOSPITAL BOARDS

Hospital authorities differ from other alternative suppliers of services for the elderly in that regional hospital boards are specifically charged with planning functions, and in that, like English and Welsh local authorities, they have been required to prepare ten-year plans. The Ministry of Health from the start recommended consultation over plans between regional hospital boards and local authorities[1] In 1965 the Ministry again suggested that greater co-operation would be beneficial in planning residential services for the elderly. It was stressed that an attempt should be made to estimate future demands for medical, nursing and social care services for large areas, so that priorities for development could be agreed, and suggested that regional hospital boards should call meetings of relevant local authority officials and general practitioners.[2]

[1] Ministry of Health, *Circular 2/62*.   [2] Ministry of Health, *Circular 18/65*.

Meetings had been held, but had not often resulted in better co-operation over plans (see also Chapter 6). Some welfare officers saw no point in meetings unless both sides were willing to amend their plans as a result of discussions. One said that in his area: 'Theoretically, we have had discussions in that we have had meetings and sent them copies of our schemes. They had no observations. They did not show us theirs until it was in print and could not be altered.' Another official remarked cynically: 'If we started trying to liaise plans between the local authority and the hospital, it would just slow things down even more.'

In a few cases the unsatisfactory outcome of consultation over plans for residential care was thought to be due to clashes of personality, but the most common reason suggested was finance. One of the welfare officers just quoted added that hospital authorities 'said they had no money anyway. The local authority is just supposed to have the money from rates to do things. So practically there has been no liaison with hospitals over ten-year plans.' Another welfare officer described the views of his committee about the policy of expanding residential accommodation rather than hospital bed provision for the elderly: 'The welfare committee protested because they feel that in 1948 a certain role—with certain funds to do it— was allocated to the welfare committee, and if the role has changed —which it has—there should be a reallocation of finances as between hospitals and local authorities. . . . We have rather nebulous exchanges with the RHB at the moment, because they formulated their policies without consulting us. We told them about our plans, but they do not amend theirs at all.' Complaints from local welfare authorities about inadequate hospital provision and unjust burdens on the ratepayer, who was subsidizing a service whose charges should have been met by the Exchequer, were made as early as 1951[1] and became much more serious in the sixties with the growing emphasis on community care. The local authority associations observed that sources of finance available to local authorities were far more limited than those available to the government, and warned that if they were not able to meet the extra expenditure needed to expand their services, the Minister's hospital plan would be imperilled. 'The Minister was unmoved. . . . The local authority case was a strong one, but the government refused to acknowledge it. No specific grants were made for the local authority health and welfare services.'[2]

Some local authority officials were also concerned about the

[1] See J. Parker, *Local Health and Welfare Services*, Allen and Unwin, 1965, pp. 114–18.
[2] J. Parker, *op. cit.*, p. 175.

appropriate staffing of residential accommodation to provide for old people needing nursing care and night attention (see also Chapter 13). Yet there seemed to have been little discussion between hospital and welfare authorities about the deployment of nursing staff.

Medical officers of health were involved in similar issues about the division of responsibility for care of the elderly mentally infirm. Whether to provide special hostels or not was a genuine problem. Was it really the hospital's job to look after the elderly mentally infirm? Spokesmen from a third of the case study authorities said that it was, but some of these had mixed views. 'We told the hospital board we were prepared to think about hostels.' The majority accepted the responsibility for looking after this special group (as recommended by the Royal Commission on the Law relating to Mental Illness and Mental Deficiency), though most were not sure that separate hostels were required, even if they were already providing them.

Only 6 medical officers of health, including 2 in Scotland, had asked for data from hospital authorities, or general practitioners, on the number of elderly patients in mental hospitals suitable for discharge to hostel accommodation. Both the Scottish ones said that they had not received very helpful information. One said: 'They have not done much to provide us with figures—I suppose it is because it is difficult to see whether a given patient would be dischargeable, if facilities were there.' His authority was prepared to consider providing hostels if there were clear indications of need for them.

There was little evidence that the relationship between demand for home nursing and the availability of cottage hospitals had been discussed between local authorities and hospital boards, although in one case study the county nursing officer stated that demand for home nursing was less in areas served by a cottage hospital.

It was sometimes argued that incontinent elderly patients should be in hospital, and that therefore the local authority should not start a laundry service for old people being nursed at home. If hospital beds were not available, then the hospital should provide the laundry service.

Chiropody was another service which some local authorities thought should be provided by the hospital. The medical officer of a retirement area county borough said that his policy was 'bedevilled by a pig-headed general practitioner on the health committee who argues that this service ought to be done by the hospital'. In another large town, also a retirement area, hospital authorities were accused of failing to provide chiropody. In this instance, some chiropody services had formerly been provided in a foot hospital, which was taken over by the hospital board in 1948. This local authority saw the later policy of encouraging development of local authority chiropody services as an attempt by the government to push the burden of responsibility back on to the local authority, having failed to develop the service in the hospital.

There was also a problem over development of physiotherapy. Hardly any case study authorities were able to provide a domiciliary physiotherapy service. One medical officer stated that the mobile physiotherapy service in his area had ended because it was very expensive and it was 'Ministry policy that this should be a hospital service'. A nursing officer in a retirement area believed that a mobile unit would be worthwhile and 'could work on the rehabilitation of strokes and help the bad arthritics'. It could continue the useful treatment started in hospital, because not all patients could go to hospital for outpatient sessions. Shortage of physiotherapists was seen as the major problem. There was again little evidence that hospital boards and local authorities were attempting to plan together for development of this service, or for other rehabilitation services.

Two case study authorities referred to the possibility of preparing meals in hospital premises for delivery to people in their own homes. Such an arrangement would have advantages, especially in relation to provision of special diets. However, in one case the idea was abandoned in favour of other arrangements, and in the second case the scheme was abandoned because of cost.

Part of the explanation for lack of progress in planning for local authority services in conjunction with plans for hospitals was the large number of different authorities involved. Each regional hospital board had to liaise with several local authorities,[1] and some local authorities had to liaise with two regional hospital boards, and in England perhaps with the board of governors of a teaching hospital group as well. Moreover, some local authority personnel thought that consultation with the geriatrician at the local hospital was more likely to lead to better co-operation than consultation with the planners at the regional board (see Chapter 6).

However, it seemed that the more significant bar to co-operation was the division of responsibility without a clear-cut division of function. Too often this led to failure to develop a service, because each side could argue that the other side should do it. In this study,

[1] The largest number of local health and welfare authorities in one hospital region was 27 in Western Scotland. Wales had 17, and Birmingham, Leeds and Manchester each had 16. Wessex and the Northern Scotland Regions had the lowest number of local health and welfare authorities (6).

only the views of local authorities were sought. One of the research workers had previous experience of similar attitudes on the hospital side, for example, a geriatrician's proposal that the regional hospital board should be asked to accept as a minor capital scheme a plan for converting a disused building into a small flat, to be used for the rehabilitation of elderly people before discharge home, was turned down on the grounds that rehabilitation was 'the local authority's job'. New ideas were particularly likely to fall foul of this problem of divided responsibility.

In a few areas new services were being developed by both the local authority and the hospital. An official in a retirement area studied explained how the health department was planning a day centre for the elderly, including the elderly mentally infirm: 'We anticipate providing for 30 a day initially. We fixed on this because we don't know what the total need is and so we want to see how it goes. Also, it goes arm in arm with hospital provision, as they have about 15 a day going to their day centre now.' As Farndale has pointed out, the difference between day hospitals and day centres is often in administration rather than in function.[1]

In the case study areas day centres, where they existed, had more often been provided by hospital authorities than local authorities. Some local authority officers approved of day centres being closely associated with the hospital because it meant that patients could go through the out-patients' clinic to the day hospital, because physiotherapy and occupational therapy were primarily jobs for the hospital, which had the staff and equipment, and because transport costs were low.[2] Other officers thought that day hospitals were not appropriate in rural areas because of the transport needed, and one county welfare officer had doubts about bringing patients to hospital doctors rather than doctors doing domiciliary visits. He concluded that the popularity of the system in hospital circles stemmed from staff shortages, rather than from its proven value for patients.

In a few areas day centres were provided by the local authority, or by a voluntary organization. One county welfare officer had planned for extra space in welfare homes so that some old people could be cared for there during the day but return home at night, but in another area it was thought that such a system would be resented by the other residents. A Scottish welfare officer described his 'day nursery for old age', which was run by a voluntary organization supported by local authority money. Both this officer and the one

[1] J. Farndale, *The Day Hospital Movement in Great Britain*, Pergamon Press, 1961, p. 79.

[2] *cf.* Farndale, *op. cit.*, p. 77.

who provided day care in welfare homes were surprised at the low level of demand for the service. This was also the case in a day centre run for the housebound by a voluntary organization in an English retirement borough. The chief nursing officer reported: 'The people who go are the housebound and these are probably the only ones that we can get there. . . .We usually have one or two vacancies even though the centre is well used.'

Thus, day centres were being developed in a few areas, but often on an *ad hoc* basis and without full discussion between local authorities and hospitals about whether co-operative effort would produce a better service.

Only one of the 24 case study areas had a special clinic for old people already functioning. In addition, a Scottish authority had a social club for which undergoing a medical examination used to be a condition of membership. The club still existed, but medical examinations had been discontinued. Many of the local authority medical and nursing officers interviewed mentioned the clinics operating in Bristol, Rotherham, Rutherglen, Salford and Twickenham, and in about half of the case study authorities such clinics were thought to be a good idea. Three authorities had fairly definite proposals for providing clinics. In other areas it was argued that the hospital, which already had the necessary diagnostic equipment, was a more appropriate location for the service. All the main suggestions that the hospital was the most appropriate location for the preventive service came from officials in compact urban areas. Some authorities said they were not planning clinics because 'we have not yet reached that stage of development', and raised the question of relationships with general practitioners.

NATIONAL HEALTH SERVICE EXECUTIVE COUNCILS

The general medical services are provided by general practitioners who work under contract with local executive councils. Executive councils have only limited planning powers, but their local medical committees can to some extent serve as the forum for discussion of policies in which the general practitioners have an interest. Many medical officers of health had links with general practitioners through the local medical committee, or through the local branch of the British Medical Association, but planning in conjunction with them still created many difficulties.

Six case study authorities thought that clinics for the elderly could not be provided yet because of the unwillingness, sensitivity or opposition of the family doctors. 'If the general practitioners had the time, training, inclination and vision, they should really be doing it, but they won't for many years to come.' Three other authorities looked forward to involving general practitioners, hoping that general practitioner opposition would lessen as health visitor attachment developed. The chief medical officer of a retirement borough believed that clinics were a good idea but said that, before formulating a positive policy: 'One needs better visiting by general practitioners. They should routinely visit old people once a month. Health visitor attachment could help this but at present there are problems in suggesting it, because it may not be practicable. If such routine visiting showed up the need for a screening clinic, then I would consider it.'

Attempts to involve general practitioners in discussion of the ten-year plans had not always succeeded. One county medical officer invited all general practitioners in the area to a meeting. Of the 57 invited, 30 replied, 18 accepted the invitation, and 3 actually attended the meeting.

One of the larger counties had successfully co-operated with general practitioners over joint clinic and surgery premises, but in other areas the local health department had missed sites for clinics because of lack of agreement with executive councils about what should be built (see Chapter 18).

The question of bringing the other services (dental, ophthalmic, and pharmaceutical) which come under the aegis of executive councils, into the same premises had not apparently been given much consideration, although it must be remembered that only local authority officers were interviewed. The lack of effective planning machinery for these services was a major problem for those local authorities who wanted to conduct planning activities on a co-operative basis.

MINISTRY OF SOCIAL SECURITY

In theory the function of the Ministry of Social Security and its Supplementary Benefits Commission (which were still the Ministry of Pensions and National Insurance and the National Assistance Board at the time of the study) was quite separate from that of local authorities and other bodies providing services in kind. However, local authorities have powers to charge for some services, and this led some to argue that the Ministry of Social Security should supplement the retirement income of old people who cannot afford to pay for what they need. The services most affected are home help, housing and laundry, and the issues which have arisen are discussed in Chapters 1, 17 and 22 respectively, and so need not be repeated. In general, lack of information about the present, and probable future, income distribution among old people in local areas, and lack of a clear policy about how far local authorities should aim to provide free or cheap services for the elderly because of their limited income, created problems for the planning of local authority services. Relationships with local officers of the Ministry of Social Security were often good, but these officers were not responsible for major policy decisions.

OTHER LOCAL AUTHORITY DEPARTMENTS

Plans for developing services for the elderly may also have to take account of developments in services which are the concern of other departments in the local authority. The other departments most involved with services for the elderly in case study authorities were education, parks and baths.

Education departments provided premises for old people's clubs in some areas[1], and this could be a key factor in making the development possible. As one welfare officer said: 'The finance committee say there can be as many clubs as we like providing that we use existing premises and do not ask for new ones. We use the education committee's youth clubs during the day and they are used by the kids themselves in the evening. A youth centre costs £30,000, and you can't afford to spend that amount of money and use it only between 6 and 8 p.m. Education has been most helpful and they are asking only a very small rent. They provide caretaking, heating and light. It is all out of the same pocket in the end.'

Community centres were also often the responsibility of education committees. In 6 case study authorities they were seen as suitable places for the elderly to meet and have a meal, though in 2 of the 6 such a scheme had not yet started. A welfare officer outlined his idea as follows: 'My idea is to go out into areas and to work from there, with a community centre as base for everything. There could be an old people's club, a base for meals-on-wheels, lunch clubs and one could have the NAB in as well. I think this in prefabricated buildings would be better than doing it in church halls.'

The education department was also frequently involved in supply

1 *cf.* E. E. White, *Clubs for the Elderly*, National Old People's Welfare Council, no date, p. 44.

of meals for the elderly. The problems of obtaining suitable meals, and of keeping the service for the elderly running when the schools were on holiday, were mentioned in Chapter 10. In 3 case studies lack of kitchen capacity was a problem. In one, the welfare officer had been offered meals from a school kitchen 'but the education department plans went slightly awry' and the proposed arrangement was cancelled. In another area the school meals service was being decentralized and 'the welfare department was asked to make other arrangements because in 2 or 3 years the kitchens could not provide the meals'. In this case the education department was thinking ahead, and as a result the welfare officer had reasonable notice that he would have to find an alternative supplier for meals.

Local authority parks departments, apart from bringing much pleasure to many old people through the provision of public parks and facilities for bowls, were often involved in the maintenance of gardens and drying greens in housing schemes. Gardens were normally the tenants' responsibility, the activities of the parks department being confined to cutting down weeds and nettles in extreme cases of neglect which had led to complaints from neighbours. In some authorities common grassed areas or the gardens in sheltered housing schemes were maintained by the parks department. Most housing authorities studied said that there were problems over gardens—more often with young tenants than with older ones but most said some old people were unable to manage. As a result 1 municipal borough stopped providing old people's houses with gardens, but this had the disadvantage of denying some old people an interesting and absorbing hobby. A few authorities had voluntary bodies helping with gardens, but there were complaints that voluntary enthusiasm did not last long. Schemes organized by schools worked better, but school holidays were a problem. Therefore a number of authorities were gradually beginning to see that the local authority might have to do more to help the elderly with gardens in future. In a Scottish large burgh the housing manager said: 'A few years ago we tried a scheme with the parks department and were flooded out with applications. Parks department could not cope because they do not have the staff.' It was a similar story in 3 or 4 other authorities.

In urban areas the department responsible for baths and wash-houses was sometimes also involved in the provision of services, especially laundry for the elderly. In 1 Scottish urban authority the provision of a laundry service for bedridden elderly patients being nursed at home had been approved by the council, but 'so far it has not got under way because the starting date hinges on progress on reconstruction of the local baths'. When capital development restrictions were imposed by central government the baths department was often one of those treated as low priority for capital development, so that occasionally provision of laundry services suffered as a result.

In a study of public baths and washhouses in London it was found that not only was the service valued by elderly people who did not have a bath in their own homes, but by elderly people who needed help in getting in and out of a bath, or who appreciated the availability of the baths attendant to help if necessary.[1] This study revealed how the service provided in public bathhouses had unofficially adapted to meet social needs, and the findings had important implications for policies on the future of public bathhouses.

Thus the planning of other local authority services may have implications for the planning of health, welfare and housing services for the elderly.

SUMMARY

Planning in conjunction with regional hospital boards was not always a productive exercise, although in some areas local authorities and hospitals had each acquired a better understanding of the problems faced by the other.

Some local authorities said hospital boards were not prepared to amend plans after discussions. The main factor underlying the lack of progress seemed to be finance. Hospital authorities were said to lack money for development of services for the elderly, and some local authorities thought that the development of community care was a way of pushing responsibility back on to local authorities without augmenting their financial resources to enable them to meet it. The same feelings applied in relation to mental health services.

Discussions with hospital boards were dominated by the question of beds, and places in residential accommodation. Policies on co-operation over staff matters, the relationship between home nursing and cottage hospital services in rural areas, chiropody, physiotherapy and other rehabilitation services, and the possible use of hospital laundry and kitchen (especially diet kitchen) facilities for services to old people living at home, had only rarely been discussed.

Some of the difficulty was due to the large number of different authorities involved, and overlapping of administrative boundaries, but the main issue seemed to be that of the unclear division of function—with the financial factor never far away.

New services tended to fall foul of the problem of divided responsi-

[1] H. Rose, 'Public Baths Revisited', *Lancet*, 1966, 2, 1302.

bility, a good example being that of day centres or day hospitals. Sometimes no service developed; elsewhere 2 similar services developed side by side. Special clinics for old people were another development impeded by doubts about whose job it was to provide them. In this case the general medical services were also involved.

Problems for local authority planning were created by lack of effective planning machinery for the general medical services, and by the apparent lack of interest in joint efforts by general practitioners in many areas, although good co-operation existed in others. Local authorities often felt that approaches by the local authority would be resented by general practitioners, because of their longstanding suspicion of the local authority. Progress was more likely if good relationships could be built up gradually.

In a few areas local authorities were concerned not to develop or subsidize certain services such as laundry, home help, or rent rebates for the elderly because it was thought that the Ministry of Social Security should be supplementing retirement incomes so that the elderly could pay the normal price for the service. Local authority planning was complicated by the fact that planning on the pensions side was done at national, not local level.

Other services for old people were provided by the education, parks, or baths department of the local authority. Problems of co-ordination of planning could arise because of central departments' policies on capital developments and because, in the counties, local authorities could be involved in the provision of these services.

In general, the role of other statutory bodies complicated the planning process. Some bodies were theoretically providing complementary services and were not, officially, alternative suppliers of services for which the local authority was responsible. In practice such a distinction was hard to maintain.

CHAPTER 21

ALTERNATIVE SUPPLIERS—
VOLUNTARY ORGANIZATIONS

Voluntary organizations have been making a small, but increasing, contribution to the housing of the elderly in recent years, and they also provide old people's homes, especially in Scotland. Moreover, the development of certain domiciliary services for old people has been mainly due to voluntary action, since local authorities did not have the necessary powers. The existence of voluntary bodies as alternative suppliers added another dimension to the planning process, and in this chapter the ways in which local authorities took account of the voluntary contribution are considered.

HOUSING

Housing associations and voluntary organisations were already contributing to the housing provision for old people in some of the areas studied, as described in Chapter 3. In most cases the contribution was small, but one county borough welfare officer went so far as to say that the extent of voluntary provision was such that he was not critical of the limited local authority provision, granted that his area had had a severe housing problem to face, and had concentrated its efforts more on family housing.

A few housing authorities were keen to encourage housing associations.[1] A county borough housing manager said: 'Provision by housing associations is the third arm of housing for the future. The day of the private landlord is gone. Nobody is buying property for letting on an investment basis. We have tried to encourage the development of a housing association.' The housing committee of a Scottish small burgh had taken the initiative in approaching the Abbeyfield Society, although the negotiations were unsuccessful

[1] National Old People's Welfare Council, *Report for the year ended 31st March, 1966*, p. 8, stated that two counties had appointed voluntary housing officers to encourage the idea of forming housing associations to meet the needs of some of the elderly.

318

because it had proved impossible to find a suitable property for sale at a suitable price.

An English county borough was actively encouraging the setting up of a housing association to built 18 flats by 1967–8 for old people who were owner-occupiers, but wanted to sell their houses and live in smaller accommodation. The flats were being designed by the borough architect and the housing department was to let them. This local authority was sure of a demand for this type of accommodation as in the previous 3 years more than 100 old people had registered as wanting to sell their property in order to live in smaller accommodation.

Other authorities did not agree that housing associations had a useful contribution to make. One county borough turned away a voluntary organization wanting to convert an old house into flatlets to let to old people at unsubsidized rents, on the grounds that the contribution it could make would be small in relation to what the council was doing. It was suggested that the voluntary organization would do better to approach an urban or rural district council where they could supplement a small local authority programme. The housing manager of a Scottish large burgh said: 'In this area there is not much interest in housing associations because in the council's view "we are the people", and council housing together with private development is enough.' Another view was that, because of the high rents charged, such provision would not help to reduce the local authority's waiting list. In a few areas the local authority had some say in the allocation of tenancies in schemes provided by housing associations or voluntary organizations, but it was still argued that this did not help the local authority, again because of the high rents charged.

On the question of financial help the general attitude was that requests for loans from housing associations would be considered on their merits. Some authorities confused housing associations with housing societies, like the treasurer of a Scottish county who thought that the Housing Corporation was the appropriate body for a housing association to approach for a loan. An urban district council official in England said he thought housing associations would borrow direct from the Public Works Loan Board. In England especially, where the county councils were welfare but not housing authorities, there was considerable confusion about the local authorities' powers to lend to housing associations. Two county councils were not sure whether they had such powers, but another county said that it had sometimes lent money, and a fourth had turned down an application for a loan because it thought the scheme was a poor financial risk and doubted whether old people would be able to afford the high rents, not because it thought it did not have power to lend.

At least 1 municipal borough and 2 rural district councils had made 100% loans to housing associations building for old people, but one of the larger authorities would only make a 90% loan because it was thought to be desirable that a housing association should have a financial stake in the scheme, and that it should be able to raise 10% from legacies or donations. One or 2 treasurers remarked that at times when capital finance was difficult for local authorities there was less willingness to consider requests for help from other bodies so that the success of a request partly depended on opportune timing.

Some authorities said there was no problem about help with finance, but that they could not help with land, as any available sites were wanted by the local authority. This view was held by some local authorities with large slum clearance problems, but the problem of sites was also singled out as the main stumbling block for housing associations in the future by other housing authorities. A few had helped over acquisition of sites, but 1 rural district council which was firmly in favour of housing associations, and had tried to help a self-build association by getting land for it from the county small-holdings committee, had then met a further difficulty 'because the Regional Study Group then said that the land should be held mean-time'. Two years later they were still waiting for the planning decisions to be taken.

For the first revision of the ten-year plans, local health and welfare authorities in England and Wales were asked by the Ministry of Health to submit figures for sheltered housing provided by housing societies, which would now be called housing associations,[1] and for provision planned by them for the next 5 years. It was not altogether clear what information the Ministry wanted, and case study authorities differed in whether or not they included figures for actual provision made by those voluntary organizations and charitable trusts which were not registered as housing associations. Difficulties also arose over the distinction between sheltered housing and a residential home or hostel. As one welfare officer said: 'There is a voluntary home for gentlewomen registered as an old people's home under section 37. This has 7 places in bed sittingrooms, and to me is

[1] The Ministry of Health used the term 'housing society' on forms sent to local authorities as an appendix to Circular 21/63. The 1964 Housing Act gave the term 'housing society' a special meaning, and it now relates only to non-profit-making organizations which cover their costs entirely by rent income—that is without the aid of exchequer subsidy. The appropriate term for the Ministry of Health to use in later revisions of the plans is 'housing association'.

sheltered housing with a warden.' Moreover, local authorities did not always know the extent of voluntary provision in their area, since they knew only of those organizations which had applied for help from the local authority.

The ten-year plan figures for future provision by housing associations also excluded possible provision by other voluntary bodies. In most cases the proposed provision was likely to be achieved, because the figures related only to schemes under construction or in an advanced stage of planning. The general opinion on the local authority side was that one could not forecast for 5 years ahead because housing associations did not have a five-year plan. Of the 16 English case study authorities, only 1 county had obtained information about plans for the next 5 years, and then from only 1 of the larger national organizations. Thus, judging by the number of new housing associations set up in the mid-sixties (see Chapter 3) to build for the elderly, it was probable that actual provision in the subsequent 5 years would exceed the ten-year plan figures, perhaps substantially. This view was also expressed by Sir Keith Joseph: 'I note that some local authorities do not seem to have reached in their inquiries all the housing societies (associations) in their areas, because some housing societies do not plan 5 years ahead and there will be many more housing societies (associations) being set up now which do not exist at the moment and whose contribution cannot, therefore, have been taken into account.'[1]

In Scotland, the Scottish Development Department approached the larger voluntary organizations and housing associations directly for information about existing provision, and also asked local authorities to tell them about any voluntary organization making provision for old people in their area. However, it was not easy to judge how complete a picture the Department had of the extent of present provision, not was it clear how much the Department knew about plans for future provision.

This lack of knowledge about the extent to which voluntary organizations would be contributing to the need for special and sheltered housing for the elderly in the future made it impossible for local authorities to take it into account when formulating their own plans.

RESIDENTIAL ACCOMMODATION

The extent of voluntary, and private, provision of old people's homes

[1] National Old People's Welfare Council, *Planning for Ageing*, Report of the 12th National Conference on the Care of the Elderly, National Council of Social Service, 1964, p. 33.

appeared to be associated with the extent of local authority provision (see Chapter 2). What was difficult to establish was whether voluntary provision was high because local authority provision was low, or whether local authority provision was low because voluntary provision was high.

In general, local authorities were sympathetic towards applications for places in voluntary homes, especially if there were special circumstances such as an application from an elderly blind person to enter a voluntary home for the blind, or an application from a person who needed more nursing care than a small local authority home could reasonably offer, and who could be accommodated in a home run by a religious order providing this type of care. Such homes were not necessarily within the boundaries of the local authority, which could raise problems about negotiating what payment the local authority would make. The usual practice in England was for all local authorities to accept whatever financial arrangement was agreed between the voluntary body and the local authority in whose area the home was situated.

However, some reservations were expressed about the use of voluntary homes. A Scottish county, finding that the number of supplementation payments was increasing, became more reluctant to make the payments if the home was outside the local authority boundary. It felt that it lacked control of admission, and therefore lacked control of expenditure on residents in voluntary homes.

Some local authorities voiced concern about standards in some voluntary homes, or about whether voluntary organizations would be able to continue to meet the cost of running homes in the future. Some authorities commented that voluntary organizations could choose their residents, and as a result the local authority found itself with more of the very infirm and the anti-social.

Only one local authority knew of plans for further voluntary provision of new homes for the elderly, though others knew of extensions planned for existing homes. The new venture was in a retirement area, but even there it was believed that voluntary organizations were turning their attention to the provision of housing for old people rather than welfare homes. This belief was expressed in 4 other authorities and the trend was applauded, one suggested reason being that the running costs, especially staff costs, of housing schemes would be more within the reach of voluntary organizations than the running costs of welfare homes.

Existing provision of voluntary accommodation certainly influenced the demand for local authority places, but, apart from assuming that existing voluntary homes would continue to function, local

322

authorities appeared to have made little attempt to plan in conjunction with voluntary organizations.

DOMICILIARY SERVICES

Voluntary organizations played an invaluable role in the development of certain domiciliary services for the elderly after 1948, making progress possible on services for which statutory powers were lacking, such as visiting services,[1] and meals-on-wheels until 1962, or where central department policy prevented the use of statutory powers, as was true for the chiropody service in England and Wales until 1959. It has always been the policy of the Ministry of Health and of the Scottish Home and Health Department to encourage co-operation between local authorities and voluntary organizations, and English health and welfare authorities were asked to consult with voluntary organizations when formulating ten-year plans for developing services.[2]

Two medical officers of health mentioned consultation with voluntary bodies over the preparation of plans—'in the revisions we tried to take account of their comments'. A third authority was trying to include them (along with county welfare and nursing officers) in a planning committee of the local medical advisory committee which was concerned about services for the elderly.

In other areas welfare officers, nursing officers, or elected members of health and welfare committees were also members of the local Old People's Welfare Committee, so that formal consultation of the kind described by Morris[3] was perhaps a less relevant activity. This association of local authority personnel, particularly welfare officers, with voluntary organizations was also found in Scotland. Indeed, in one Scottish authority the chief welfare officer was so closely involved with the Old People's Welfare Committee, on which several voluntary organizations in the area were represented, that it was meaningless to talk about plans for developing local authority services apart from plans for developing voluntary services.

Nevertheless, the general impression given in many areas was that

[1] The Health Services and Public Health Act 1968 made possible the direct provision of a welfare visiting service.
[2] Ministry of Health, *Circular 7/62.*
[3] M. Morris, in *A Study of Halifax*, National Council of Social Service, 1965 reported that the medical officer of health sent a questionnaire to the main voluntary bodies 'asking them what they could do and how many volunteers they could supply'.

local authorities did not attach much weight to planning for long-term development in conjunction with voluntary organizations. A medical officer who had not consulted voluntary organizations over the ten-year plans gave as his reason that: 'We cannot discuss everything with everyone', implying that voluntary organizations were low on the list. This is not to say that the present contribution made by voluntary organizations was thought to be unimportant. With the exception of a few authorities in which no voluntary organizations were known of, or where there was a past history of hostility between local authority and voluntary bodies, all the case study authorities were appreciative of existing voluntary services. However some of the reservations voiced about voluntary organizations helped to explain the lack of long-term planning.

One factor mentioned was lack of co-ordination between voluntary bodies, and the fact that 'not all voluntary bodies want to be co-ordinated'. In two retirement areas it was said to be difficult to have an efficient voluntary visiting service because individual voluntary bodies regarded their visiting lists as confidential. In another area, changes in local government boundaries had exacerbated the problem: 'The voluntary organizations . . . want to keep their identity, and we can't do much about co-ordination or amalgamation at the moment. It has got to come from them.' In some areas welfare officers were trying to encourage co-ordination, and there were examples of its being achieved through the local Council of Social Service, or, in one case, through a committee chaired by the local mayor. 'The only way to get the voluntary organizations together is to bring them in on something which is not a voluntary organization. . . . The mayor has the standing as a non-biased person, and so he can make it work.' Where voluntary organizations saw each other as rivals and were not prepared to co-operate it was more difficult for the local authority to involve them in the planning process.

Several local authority officials doubted that voluntary organizations could cope with provision of services on a large scale. In the opinion of a welfare officer: 'A voluntary body will never run a good meals-on-wheels service. It could not give 5 meals a week or deliver meals to a larger number of people.'

A major reason in some areas was that voluntary organizations suffered from the same problems of labour shortages as the local authority services themselves. Half of the case study authorities referred to lack of voluntary manpower for the meals-on-wheels service, and a quarter to shortage of manpower for voluntary visiting, 3 of them exphasizing that the need for visitors far outstripped supply. Shortages of volunteers were thought to be due to various local circumstances. A medical officer in a retirement area said: 'Volunteers are in short supply because of the social structure of the place and because it is not a settled community.' Other areas which mentioned particular difficulties were those with a scattered population, or industrial areas with full employment. Jefferys, in her study of Buckinghamshire, commented on the counter-attraction of television, the heavy commitments of men who travelled to work in London and only returned home late in the evening, and competition from other welfare organizations, as factors limiting the supply of volunteers.[1]

However, some areas were not short of volunteers, and some of those which were, thought it was because the voluntary organizations were unco-ordinated, or because the local authority did nothing to organize potential volunteers. 'The problem is to get suitable people. . . . You see the same batch of citizens every time. There is a tremendous untapped source. People are waiting to be asked but will not put their names forward.' In this authority, and others like it, the major planning problem was thought to be that of estimating the size of the potentially available voluntary labour force.

A second major problem was that voluntary organizations did not always have the financial resources to operate on a large scale, or to operate services needing skilled staff, such as chiropodists or social workers.

Knowing these problems existed led some authorities to talk of taking over services. There were 8 examples of a service having been taken over in the 24 case study authorities, and 10 other forecasts that this was likely to happen in the future. Taking over the service was most often mentioned in connection with chiropody, but there were a few references to meals-on-wheels, and to 'an explosion in the development of social work . . . this might be where voluntary organizations have less part to play in future'. At times officials hinted that elected members were reluctant to take over services. A medical officer of health said: 'On chiropody we are sadly lacking because in a county council like this there is great sympathy for voluntary effort. That is all right up to a point but you cannot expect them to provide on a wide scale. I think chiropody now ought to be part of an organized service. However, a direct service would cost a lot and the council are evading this.'

An alternative to taking over services was to strengthen local authority backing for them. This could be done in various ways, of which the most obvious was for the local authority to give financial

[1] M. Jefferys, *An Anatomy of Social Welfare Services*, Michael Joseph, 1965, pp. 274–5, 276.

support.[1] However, many authorities were wary of increasing financial support for services over which they had no control. Indeed, in an authority in which the meals-on-wheels service had been taken over, the reason given was that the voluntary organization 'got names from any old place and kept asking for more and more money'. In another area the medical officer said: 'At the moment, we have no control over the extent of the chiropody service—how could there be?' There was a common tendency 'to feel you should not criticize what voluntary organizations are doing', yet local authority officials sometimes considered that a service was inefficiently run, or were concerned that they did not even know how the service operated. Most local authorities gave some financial help to voluntary organizations, and they seemed particularly willing to support administrative costs (where they were not providing the administration itself), but the lack of any system of checking on voluntary services paid for out of local authority grants clearly inhibited development of this kind of help.

In one authority the need for some kind of control was well illustrated by the crisis which arose over financing a home help service run by a voluntary organization. The arrangement by which this local authority provided an emergency service to cover short-term needs, and a voluntary organization provided a long-term service for the elderly, originated before 1948. A proportion of the cost to recipients was reimbursed from exchequer funds, and the cost of administration of the service was a charge on the accounts of the voluntary organization. When the voluntary organization introduced conditions of service for the home helps parallel to those agreed nationally for local authority home helps costs increased, but there was no likelihood that the proportion of cost met from exchequer funds would increase. After discussions with the voluntary body and examination of the accounts, the local authority agreed to underwrite the cost of providing the service. However, the voluntary organization then found that higher wages attracted more recruits, and the service expanded. The voluntary organization had to ask the local authority to increase its financial contribution and, as the request came after the local authority's estimates had been prepared, a supplementary estimate was required. This was granted, but the local authority decided that it must know by what criteria the voluntary organization was deciding how much help people needed, and that a financial limit should be set to the rate of expansion.

[1] Central departments have encouraged local authorities to use their powers to do this, e.g. Ministry of Health, *Circular 18/64*; Ministry of Housing and Local Government, *Circular 43/64*.

Another reason for doubts about giving financial help to voluntary bodies was associated with the view that voluntary activity was characterized by passing waves of enthusiasm. Speaking of the development of old people's clubs one official said: 'The county council does not give money, but it will provide chairs, covers, cups and saucers. This means that if the club folds up, they can collect the equipment. If we gave away money, we could not get it back.'

About a third of the case study authorities commented on the waxing and waning of enthusiasm for voluntary work, and argued from this that long-term work could not be safely left with voluntary bodies. Some also said that voluntary workers were too unreliable to be providing essential services, and that too much work tended to fall on the shoulders of the few who were reliable. The difficulty was that there were no sanctions against volunteers who failed to carry out what they had undertaken to do.[1] Some of these authorities thought that voluntary organizations could play a useful role in other ways, in what a county borough medical officer described as 'non-essential but desirable work, such as social visiting of well old people'. Similarly, a Scottish county medical officer thought voluntary organizations could well provide services 'not involving emergencies and not involving unpleasant jobs, nor jobs which must be done'.

In contrast to the view that voluntary organizations could not be relied on to provide essential services, some officials said that reliable work was done by volunteers 'if you harness them to do a specific job'. Moreover, a county borough medical officer who criticized volunteers because 'when we wanted them they wouldn't be coming in', added that 'the meals-on-wheels service proves me wrong because there is strong discipline there'. Identifying the need for a specific job and for good organization as factors essential to a successful voluntary service had led some officials to consider the appointment of paid organizers.

One case study authority, an industrial northern town, had appointed to the staff of the welfare department a person responsible for stimulating and guiding voluntary activity in the area. A start had been made on the implementation of a plan for having a voluntary lunch club in each sector of the town. Once a club was established, its day-to-day management was carried out by local voluntary organizers, but the advantage of having a paid organizer in the background was that, if local voluntary leadership failed because

---

[1] cf. Jefferys, op. cit., p. 268. Salaried workers said one difficulty of working for a voluntary organization was that: 'Voluntary workers are often unreliable and undependable and no pressure can be brought to bear because they *are* voluntary.'

someone left the area or had to resign, there was someone to act as a temporary substitute and also, if necessary, to take the initiative in finding a new organizer.

The problem of shortage of good voluntary organizers, rather than of volunteers themselves, was one factor which influenced the views of certain nursing officers who believed that a system of voluntary visiting would work best under the general control of the area or geriatric health visitor, thus using volunteers but bypassing voluntary organizations. Some welfare officers shared this view that voluntary visitors needed skilled supervision and guidance. One said: 'We want to bring in the voluntary organizations to do more frequent visits than our staff can. They do well, but they do not always see what is needed.' The idea of training volunteers to recognize needs, to recognize their own capabilities and attitudes, and to know how to bring in relevant services was applauded by a number of officials, especially in the county boroughs.[1] However, it was also said that: 'Training would only be satisfactory with a paid organizer, who was preferably a social worker—a person to whom the voluntary visitor could refer problems, and who had the ability to continue the training process and deal with any problems arising.'

A few authorities did provide training for voluntary visitors, including 2 county boroughs in which welfare officers mentioned regular meetings of voluntary visitors to discuss problems. Others feared that attempts to provide training or to organize voluntary effort might frighten volunteers away. As the welfare officer of a Scottish large burgh said: 'You have to be very careful with voluntary workers, because if you try to regiment them, you lose them.' There were several other comments to the effect that voluntary organizations preferred to be independent and do things their own way.

Thus, some authorities wanted to encourage voluntary activity in connection with essential services and saw the appointment of paid organizers or the development of training for volunteers as ways of ensuring a good and reliable service. A few were not sure how to implement these ideas without alienating the volunteers.

At times the reluctance of voluntary workers to receive advice from local authority personnel seemed to be imaginary rather than real (and it must be remembered that only the local authority side of the question was studied). Even where there did seem to be a communication barrier some local authorities had found a way round it. In one county, for example, an area nursing officer said: 'We were

---

[1] Suggested training programmes were published in Appendix III of the *Manual of Voluntary Visiting* prepared by the National Old People's Welfare Council.

getting complaints from the nurses that the loans depot run by a voluntary organization never had things. I told the county nursing officer, yet when she told the voluntary organization they could have an increased grant from the council they said they did not need it because they had plenty of stuff. So I asked her to come with me to see the depot. They had little in stock and did not know what was out on loan. The organizer promised us a list of everything they have and then we shall say what we think they should hold in order to provide an adequate service. There is no problem about money for them if it is needed.' There was no suggestion that these measures taken by local authority officers to improve the quality of a service alienated the volunteers.

Several case study authorities expressed other ideas about the role of voluntary organizations. A Scottish medical officer said: 'There will always be something that the local authority either cannot or is not allowed to do, but voluntary organizations do not have to wait for amending legislation before they can act.' Pioneering has often been described as one of the key activities of voluntary bodies,[1] although Slack pointed out that voluntary bodies cannot claim the pioneering role as theirs exclusively.[2] However, a few case study authorities believed that voluntary organizations were well suited to try out new ideas 'because they can make a mess and get away with it, whereas there would be an awful row if a local authority failed with the ratepayers' money', but one welfare officer added that: 'Local authorities have got to prod . . . they have got to produce the ideas.'

Six case study authorities also saw one of the key roles of voluntary bodies as pressure group activity. They should 'keep the council on its toes', 'prod the local authority along', and act 'as a body critical of the exercise of statutory functions'.

The distinction between pioneering new services and pressure group activities is perhaps a fine one, since the development of a new service may lead to pressure on the local authority to give more financial backing, or to take over the service. In the past, pressure at national level has also been of importance. The National Corporation for the Care of Old People, for example, believed that the total achievement of voluntary bodies in providing chiropody services was 'very considerable and the fact that local authority chiropody services may now take over the responsibility is in no small degree due

---

[1] See, for example, Ministry of Health, Department of Health for Scotland, *Report of the Working Party on Social Workers in the Local Authority Health and Welfare Services*, Younghusband Report, H.M.S.O., 1959, p. 300.

[2] K. Slack, *Councils, Committees and Concern for the Old*, Codicote Press, 1960, pp. 126–7.

to voluntary committees having shown the need and the way to meet it'.[1] Much the same could be said of the meals-on-wheels service. However, as described earlier in this chapter, the presence of a voluntary service could sometimes delay the development of a public service in an individual local authority.

SUMMARY

A few housing authorities actively encouraged the development of housing associations. Others did not, partly because it was thought that housing associations did not help to solve the local authority's housing problem, and partly because some local authorities were unsure of their powers to help financially, or wanted to reserve any available sites for local authority use.

Local authorities did not always know the full extent of housing provision for the elderly made by voluntary organizations in their area, and argued that they could not take account of possible future voluntary provision because voluntary bodies did not have long-term plans.

For the ten-year plans most English and Welsh authorities only took account of provisions in housing association schemes which were in an advanced state of preparation. The exception was a county which had consulted one of the larger national voluntary organizations about its plans for the next 5 years. There was general confusion over whether the Ministry of Health wanted to know about provision by voluntary organizations not registered as housing associations, by charitable trusts, and almshouses. There was also confusion about whether some types of voluntary provision were 'housing' or 'old people's homes'.

Existing provision of voluntary homes was normally taken into account in the local authorities' plans, although the catchment area of a voluntary home did not necessarily correspond with the area of the local authority in which it was situated. Only a few authorities knew of plans for future voluntary provision. Some thought that voluntary bodies were turning their attention more to housing, and this trend was applauded by welfare officers.

Despite the vital role voluntary organizations have played in developing domiciliary welfare services, there appeared to have been little formal consultation with them about plans for domiciliary services. In some areas this was because local authority personnel,

[1] National Corporation for the Care of Old People, *Chiropody for the Elderly*, 1960, p. 3.

especially welfare officers, were so closely linked with voluntary organizations that formal consultation was hardly necessary. In a few areas there was no known voluntary activity.

In general, not much weight was attached to long-term planning in conjunction with voluntary organizations. Problems arose in some areas, especially in counties, because voluntary bodies were unco-ordinated. Elsewhere the local Old People's Welfare Committee, or the local Council of Social Service acted as a co-ordinating body, and this made consultation over planning easier.

Many authorities doubted whether voluntary organizations could cope with large-scale or long-term developments, because they lacked manpower or financial resources, or both. In some cases the solution was thought to be for the local authority to take over the service, but elected members sometimes opposed this. Alternatively, the local authority could support the voluntary organization, but this raised problems of control.

There were criticisms in some areas of the unreliability of voluntare services, and some officials concluded that essential services must by publicly run. In other areas officials had tried to overcome the problems of ensuring a good and reliable voluntary service by the appointment of paid organizers and by training volunteers. Some authorities thought that voluntary workers would regard advice from the local authority as interference.

The pioneering role and pressure group activity were seen as important functions of voluntary organizations by a substantial minority of the case study authorities.

The general impression was that voluntary provision, if the quality of service was good, was welcomed, but local authorities tended to think that they could not bank on an extension of voluntary activity.

CHAPTER 22

ALTERNATIVE SUPPLIERS—
THE PRIVATE SECTOR

Estimating the extent to which the needs of the elderly were likely to be met by the private sector was another problem faced by local authorities when planning to develop services. The private sector makes a contribution to the housing of the elderly, and private old people's homes can reduce the demand for local authority places. Domestic help and chiropody are both available privately to those with the means to pay the market price, and so are commercial laundries, and restaurants. To some extent, private firms co-operate with local authorities to provide laundry, meals and employment facilities for the elderly. This chapter considers how local authorities took account of the contribution made by the private sector.

HOUSING

Of all dwellings built in the case study areas between January 1945 and December 1965, the proportion built by private developers ranged from 6% to 90%. Private housing developments were rather more important in the English and Welsh case study authorities than in the Scottish ones, as Table 25 shows.

Areas with a low proportion of private development were mainly those with declining population, low prosperity, and poor employment prospects. In some the attitude of the local council was also an important factor. In one area it was council policy to own as much housing as possible so as to 'control the people coming into the area and let property at fair rents'. Another council also believed that it should own as much as possible, but did not actively discourage private development. In a third area, a housing official commented that the town was rapidly becoming one vast council estate, which he thought was undesirable from a long-term point of view.

Whilst the objection to private development was mainly a reflection of political beliefs, it was also associated with problems of obtaining sites for housing in heavily built-up areas with a high level of need for new housing. As sites were few and far between the local authority wanted first call on those that were available.

At the other extreme was an area where the council gave low priority to housing in planning its capital programmes because the main demand in the area was for owner-occupation. Four other case study authorities thought that the demand for owner-occupation had recently increased in their areas, partly because high council house

TABLE 25

DWELLINGS BUILT BY PRIVATE DEVELOPERS AS A
PERCENTAGE OF ALL DWELLINGS BUILT BETWEEN
JANUARY 1, 1945 AND DECEMBER 31, 1965 IN
41 CASE STUDY HOUSING AUTHORITIES

Case Study Housing Authorities in	No. of Authorities with Private Dwellings as a Percentage of Total 1945–65 Dwellings between:				Total No. of Authorities
	0–19%	20–39%	40–59%	60% and over	
England and Wales	4	10	10	3	27
Scotland	6	6	1	1	14

Source: *Derived from Ministry of Housing and Local Government, Housing Return for England and Wales, 31st December, 1965, Cmnd. 2886, Appendix,* H.M.S.O., *1966; Scottish Development Department, Housing Return for Scotland, 31st December, 1965, Cmnd. 2885,* H.M.S.O., *1966.*

rents encouraged more young people to buy houses, and partly because of changes in the social structure of the area. In areas such as these, there may be a need for the local authority to provide for the elderly, or to ensure that the private developer does so. One authority stated specifically that it was building a high proportion of small dwellings because the private developer catered for the need for larger dwellings.

A few authorities said 'quite a lot' of old people who retired to their areas bought their own houses. The clerk of a rural district council said: 'Private developers are building 1 bedroom bungalows. This is surprising but this is a retiring area. We do not have a measure of housing demand in the district, because most of the people retiring here are outsiders, and as far as housing goes they are not our concern.' Another housing manager, in an area which would

333

probably not be thought of as a 'retirement area', said private developers had built a lot of 2 bedroom bungalows which the better-off old people bought. These authorities were well aware of private housing developments, but took the line that private developers were providing for a different group of people from the local authority, and saw no particular need to co-ordinate plans.

A Scottish small burgh said it was desirable but difficult for a local authority to plan in step with private developers, because what private developers wanted to build depended on their assessment of the market. Thus there was no point in the local authority trying to plan more than about three years ahead, because they could not estimate what the private developers' contribution would be beyond that.

A county borough housing manager said: 'I do not know what control there is over size of dwellings because my department does not have much to do with site disposal. I imagine the decision on house sizes is left to the private developers.' This implied that co-ordination was the responsibility of the planning officer, who was probably more concerned with land-use planning and control of densities than with house sizes.

Planning departments presumably did have information on house sizes in private developments, but probably did not have information on the extent of owner-occupancy among the elderly, nor on the extent to which elderly owner-occupiers wanted to sell and buy a smaller house. The census does not give housing tenure groups by age-groups for local authority areas, but it has been estimated that in England in 1962, 43% of households where the housewife was over sixty owned or were buying their homes,[1] and the comparable figure for Scotland in 1965 was about 28%.[2] Even if the extent of owner-occupancy among the elderly were known, there would still be a need for information about the size and quality of dwellings which they occupy, and about their desire to sell the larger house and buy a smaller one. No local authority department studied had this information, although housing, welfare and health department staff sometimes knew of individual cases. Brockington and Lempert[3] give some information for Stockport on elderly owner-occupiers and the size of dwellings but did not ask about willingness to move.

[1] J. B. Cullingworth, *English Housing Trends*, G. Bell and Sons Ltd., 1965, p. 34.
[2] J. B. Cullingworth, *Scottish Housing in 1965*, Government Social Survey, 1967. Derived from unpublished Table IV-87.
[3] C. F. Brockington and S. M. Lempert, *The Social Needs of the Over 80's*, Manchester University Press, 1966, p. 40.

ALTERNATIVE SUPPLIERS—THE PRIVATE SECTOR

Arkley provided similar information for Reading.[1] Richardson,[2] in
his survey in the North-East of Scotland, did ask old people whether
they preferred to stay in their present house or to move. He did not
give tenure-group, although it is relevant to the present discussion
that fewer people in social classes I and II wanted to move than in
social classes III, IV and V. Preference for staying put increased with
age, and there were some differences between town and country, but
even so a substantial minority of those aged seventy and over were
dissatisfied with their present house. Shenfield reported that in
Birmingham three-quarters of the respondents in her 1948 survey of
people over seventy lived in non-council houses and just over 10%
in council houses. She also reported that 18% of them 'urgently
wanted to move from their existing housing and this percentage was
as high as 28% among old people living in the inner rings of the city'.
A quarter of those wanting to move did so because the house was
too large, and 7% because of overcrowding.[3] Studies such as these
indicated that the problem was there, and several of those interviewed
in the case study areas were aware of it in general terms, but without
much fuller information for each local area it would be difficult to
argue that planning departments could or should have attempted to
influence what the private developer was building.

One local authority was co-operating with a private builder to
provide housing for old people, and the background to this was of
some interest. After the opening of a local authority scheme in 1963
many applications had come in from old people 'who could well
afford to buy'. The private builder was not willing to build speculatively for them, presumably because of doubts about the market, but
was willing to build for the local authority. Therefore the local
authority advertised in the press about a proposed scheme for houses
built for the local authority but to be let at an economic rent, and
soon had a list of applicants.

RESIDENTIAL ACCOMMODATION

Officially, the extent of private provision of residential accommodation for old people is known to local welfare authorities because
private homes are supposed to register with the local authority.

[1] J. Arkley, *The Over Sixties*, National Council of Social Service, 1964, Table
19, p. 32.
[2] I. M. Richardson, *Age and Need*, Livingstone, 1964, pp. 47-8.
[3] B. Shenfield, *Social Policies for Old Age*, Routledge and Kegan Paul, 1957,
Appendix III, p. 220 and pp. 139.

However, two English 'retirement' counties spoke of the difficulty of enforcing this legislation. One of their welfare officers said: 'There are 23 or 24 private homes in this county and there are probably as many more not known to us.'

Urban authorities placed less stress on the problem of unknown homes, perhaps partly because of their readiness to accept the proprietor's definition of a home. In one area, for example: 'We take the line that if they call it an old people's home, they have got to register. If they have a sign saying "guest house" and it is full of old people, that is not our concern—although the legislation is delightfully vague.'

The whole problem of the line of demarcation between old people's homes, hotels, guest houses and boarding houses[1] created difficulties for authorities who tried to enforce the legislation. 'We had trouble with one licensed home because the proprietor is trying to get students through the education department, and therefore claims that her house is not for old people in the main. We got the police, the town clerk and the public health inspector to help, but we may be licked.'

Some case study authorities commented that the standard of accommodation in private homes was not always good, but as one official said: 'Because we are in a plight in the county, we have got to learn to live with the private homes. If the county was inclined to wield the big stick, there would probably be an outcry of public opinion, and it would be difficult to find legislation to use in court. If we were successful in closing a home, we have then got to accommodate 10 or 20 people.'

Discussing the future role of private homes, one welfare officer said that nobody thought of opening one under 10–20 guineas a week,[2] and another was opposed to private homes on the grounds that old people should get places on criteria relating to social needs rather than to wealth.[3] In one authority the welfare officer said: 'The county does persuade people to go into these places if they have some money', but added that the local authority was planning eventually to provide homes for those who were better off.

[1] See Peter Townsend, *The Last Refuge*, Routledge and Kegan Paul, 1962, pp. 200–6, for a discussion of this issue.

[2] See also '£50 million a Year out of the Old Folks', *The People*, February 20, 27, and March 6, 1966.

[3] See Townsend, *op. cit.*, Table 17, p. 58. His figures broadly supported the views of welfare officers in the case study authorities, if it is assumed that higher social class is associated with independent means. However, Townsend also found (pp. 57, 58) that residents in private homes 'display significantly more infirmity than any of the other . . . populations'.

Other authorities described attempts to use their powers of inspection[1] to improve standards of accommodation. The difficulty of applying specific standards was stressed, but one county said that, in terms of space and ratio of facilities to residents, they worked on the same standard as for adapted local authority homes. However, they did not always adopt as high a standard in terms of staff/resident ratio, although trying to ensure that adequate skills were available for care and attention to be provided.

Among these local authorities which expected private homes to be making a contribution to the care of the elderly for a long time to come were three which provided an information and advice service. Two of them said that the service was useful because standards varied a great deal, and the third claimed that standards were high because of the advice the local authority was prepared to give to the registered home as well as to applicants. The potential value of an advisory service covering all matters relating to the structure, equipment and running of both private and voluntary homes has been stressed, and it has been suggested that such a service might be developed on the lines being developed for hospital management committees by the Ministry of Health and the Hospital Centre of the Kind Edward's Hospital Fund.[2]

DOMICILIARY SERVICES

(a) *Home Help*

At least a third of the case study authorities felt that some applicants for home helps should be encouraged to employ private domestic help, since this would reduce the pressure on the local authority's resources. As one organizer remarked: 'We do not bar people from getting this service on grounds of high income, but might try to persuade someone to get it privately, especially the kind of person who is used to having domestic staff.'

Three authorities provided domestic help to meet an immediate emergency for up to a month, but expected this period to be used by the client or the client's relatives to make private arrangements. One of these was a local authority with a voluntarily run service for long-term cases. In another, charges were raised steeply after 4 weeks 'so that we cover short-term illness, but provide a positive incentive to folks paying full charge to make their own arrangements'.

[1] For a discussion of the problem of definition, inspection, and standards in private homes, see National Corporation for the Care of Old People, *Private Homes for Old People*, 1967.

[2] 'Our Old People', *Socialist Commentary*, January 1966.

Some authorities stressed, as one reason for encouraging private arrangements, that it was not a local authority job to run a domestic service agency, but in some authorities: 'The staff do put applicants on to someone who wants a job, if they do not know of anybody themselves.'

At the same time local authorities in certain areas mentioned, as described in Chapter 13, that the existence of 'a lot of fairly affluent old people who can afford to pay for private help' reduced the supply of potential staff for the local authority service.

It has been estimated that in the early sixties, in Britain as a whole, 9% of people aged sixty-five and over were paying for private help compared with 4·5% who were receiving help from a local authority service.[1] More recently, the (then) Ministry of Pensions and National Insurance calculated that, among people of pensionable age in Britain in mid-1965, 6·2% of married couples, 18·5% of single men, and 7·0% of single women obtained paid domestic help from a non-local authority source.[2] The case study authorities did not have figures for their own areas, and the contribution of the private sector was mentioned as a complicating factor in general terms, rather than as something which could be estimated.

Furthermore, there seemed to be little awareness of the fact that some old people might be paying for domestic help privately at considerable hardship to themselves. Although some authorities expressed the view that 'we are offering a service', the practice (see Chapter 10) of operating the service without clearly stated criteria of what constituted 'social need' tended to blind local authorities to the possible existence of people 'in need' by the local authorities' criteria, but who were attempting to meet their own needs without calling on the local authority service.

(b) *Chiropody*

It was argued in some areas that the more affluent applicants for chiropody should make private arrangements and pay commercial charges. This was said to be 'better than going on to the waiting list for the local authority's service'.

However, one medical officer of health pointed out that: 'If you look at the people who go to private chiropodists, it seems to be mainly middle-aged women, but if you stick to the terms of the Ministry circular and priority groups, then the middle-aged would be

[1] P. Townsend and D. Wedderburn, *The Aged in the Welfare State*, G. Bell and Sons, 1965, p. 23.
[2] Ministry of Pensions and National Insurance, *Financial and Other Circumstances of Retirement Pensioners*, H.M.S.O., 1966, Table V.5, p. 70.

excluded from the local authority service.' He thought 'the majority of old people would benefit from chiropody', but was unsure how far to rely on the private sector as an alternative supplier of this service. Evidence from Townsend's study certainly suggested that social class affected the extent to which elderly people paid for private chiropody.[1]

Encouraging all who could pay commercial charges to go to private chiropodists would, to some extent, reduce demand for the local authority service, but at the same time it would help to encourage chiropodists to stay in private practice. This point was raised by one or two of the case study authorities, including one which had found it difficult to recruit chiropodists for a service operated directly by the local authority.

In some areas it was hinted that it was best to operate the service by employing chiropodists who were also in private practice on a sessional basis on the grounds that the Whitley Council scales discouraged chiropodists from entering into full-time contracts. In county areas, employment of private chiropodists on a sessional basis had other advantages: 'If we employed chiropodists directly, they would be travelling round a lot and this would be administratively expensive. This county is well stocked with private chiropodists, so the sessional system works.' In areas with fewer private chiropodists a sessional system did not always work well. It has been estimated that, nationally, it might well be possible to provide a chiropody service on a sessional basis: 'If 20% of old people require chiropody treatment, as seems likely, and if on average they require 6 treatments per year, the average work involved for each chiropodist (assuming 9,000 chiropodists are eligible to register to practise under the National Health Service) would perhaps be about 7 hours per week . . . demand may vary from one area to another, but it seems clear that there would be enough chiropodists to provide a chiropody service for old people once registration of chiropodists has been introduced.'[2] The problem would seem to be the maldistribution of private chiropodists, and the apparent lack of any mechanism for changing this.

(c) *Laundry*

Laundry, for elderly people unable to do it themselves, could be done

---

[1] Townsend and Wedderburn, *op. cit.*, Table 22, p. 54, shows that 20% of people from social class I, 18% from class II, 14% from class III (non-manual), 8% from class III (manual), 9% from class IV and 8% from class V paid for private chiropody treatment.

[2] National Corporation for the Care of Old People, *A Chiropody Service for Old People*, 1960, pp. 4–5.

by home helps, or taken to a municipal laundry, or a laundry in a hospital, old people's home, or housing scheme. About a quarter of the case study authorities mentioned the possibility of using commercial laundries, particularly as the National Assistance Board was empowered to make discretionary additions to grants for laundry costs,[1] so that little or no financial burden would fall on the local authority. Three authorities had a scheme in operation, but 2 of them were not sure it was necessary because use of the service was not high. In no case were local authority funds involved because an off-peak concession rate operated in 2 towns[2] and the client paid in the third. In 2 areas the home helps delivered and collected laundry from commercial premises. Four other authorities liked the idea of using commercial facilities. One had approved a scheme in principle, and approached commercial firms for prices. A second felt that using commercial facilities would lift some of the burden off the home help's shoulders, and that the local health authority and the National Assistance Board could both contribute to the cost. A third, a remote area, was without laundries to use, and a fourth had its plans thwarted by 'a big takeover of laundries'.

However, about half the case study authorities believed there was very little demand for a laundry service[3] or said the problem was solved by the use of disposable pads. These authorities were thinking of a laundry service not to deal with household washing generally but to deal only with bedlinen for the incontinent. The National Labour Women's Advisory Committee believed that commercial laundries 'in the main refuse to take this kind of business'.[4]

(d) *Meals*

The meals-on-wheels service was also sometimes associated with

[1] In 1965, of 2,210,000 additions for special needs met by the Board, 520,000 were for the cost of laundry. Ministry of Pensions and National Insurance, *Report of the National Assistance Board for the year ended 31st December, 1965*, Cmnd. 3042, H.M.S.O., 1966, p. 20.

[2] Of the committees covered by the National Old People's Welfare Council 1965 survey of services for the elderly, under a quarter recorded services for helping old people with their laundry. Of these just under a quarter referred to reductions at launderettes or laundries. National Old People's Welfare Council, *Survey of Services for the Elderly provided by Voluntary Organisations, 1965*, National Council of Social Service, undated, p. 14.

[3] National Labour Women's Advisory Committee, *Care of the Elderly*, Second Interim and Final Report, 1964, p. 22 suggested that 'it may well be that in some areas there has been a failure to publicize the service sufficiently or that old people are reluctant to allow their soiled linen to be collected'.

[4] *Second Interim and Final Report, op. cit.*, p. 20. This belief stemmed at least in part from the Boucher report, p. 43.

commercial organizations. In some areas 'the local authority helps directly by issuing luncheon vouchers to active retired people which secure for them meals at special prices at commercial restaurants'.[1] Taxi and motor-hire firms sometimes provided transport for meals-on-wheels, and some local authorities used profitmaking bodies for the preparation of meals.[2] Just over half the case study authorities used works canteens, local caterers, restaurants, cafés or hotels for the supply of meals in certain areas or at particular times of year, especially school holidays when the school meals service closed down.[3] There were occasional comments only from some of these authorities about the size or suitability of the meal and the difficulties of organizing a service. 'They deliver between 10.30 and 11.00 a.m. because the café or canteen that does it would only provide the meals before their own lunch peak period.'[4]

(e) *Employment*

A few case study authorities co-operated with private firms over employment for older people. Two authorities referred to an organization aiming to provide jobs for the elderly in offices, shops or open industry.[5] One of the bodies operated through the local authority; the other worked independently and was run by retired people themselves.

Two case study authorities had workshops incorporated in a multi-purpose day centre. In one there were 100 people a day working, but the welfare officer did not say whether this satisfied either the demand or need for such facilities. In the other authority, there was a waiting list for places in the workshops, and this guaranteed the labour when additional contracts were obtained and workshop premises were extended.

However, one authority said that contracts could only be obtained for 'jobs which are not profitable for local firms to employ people in. We have to be careful with the trade unions.' Another said that there was little or no light industry to draw on in the area. The younger

---

[1] National Old People's Welfare Council, *Annual Report for the year ending 31st March, 1965*, p. 21.

[2] A. I. Harris, *Meals-on-Wheels for Old People*, National Corporation for the Care of Old People, 1960, found that 20% of the main supply sources were industrial canteens and another 20% private restaurants or cafés. See Table 33, p. 28.

[3] There is still the problem of the supply of meals at week-ends.

[4] Harris, *op. cit.*, Table 46, p. 40, reported five schemes delivering the first meal on or before 10.45 a.m. and over a fifth of all schemes began delivering before 11.30 a.m.

[5] Descriptions of employment placing schemes can be found in *Not Too Old at Sixty*, National Corporation for the Care of Old People, 1963.

341

physically handicapped were already looking for suitable work, and the welfare officer had no time to seek contracts in other areas. The problem of priorities was acute in this context. The National Old People's Welfare Council strongly recommended that opportunities for employment should be made available and did not doubt that full support would be forthcoming for a self-supporting scheme, 'but some people argue that if a workshop needs heavy annual subsidies the money might benefit a larger number of elderly people if it were spent on other services for them'.[1]

Some welfare officers did not consider that there was a demand from the elderly for workshops, and even where the value of employment for old people was accepted, no calculation appeared to have been undertaken of the extent to which this service could usefully develop.

SUMMARY

The importance of the private sector in the provision of housing varied widely. Some authorities saw no point in trying to co-ordinate plans for the development of old people's housing with private developers. Others would have liked to, but said that there was no way of doing so, or implied that it was the planning department's job.

No local authority department knew the extent of owner-occupancy among the elderly, nor how many wished to sell a large house and buy a smaller one. Without such information it would be difficult to convince a private developer that there was a market. In one area the local authority was co-operating with a private developer to provide cost-rent housing, since the private builder was not willing to build speculatively for old people.

Some local authorities commented on the difficulty of knowing how many private old people's homes there were in their area, in spite of the statutory requirement that such homes be registered. There were also criticisms of the standard of accommodation and care in such homes.

Looking to the future, a few authorities planned to provide homes for all old people in need. Other authorities assumed that private homes would continue to meet the needs of some groups of people, and tried to use their powers of inspection to ensure adequate standards. A few provided an advisory service, also with the aim of improving standards.

[1] *Employment and Workshops for the Elderly*, National Old People's Welfare Council, 1963, pp. 12–13.

Many local authorities considered that old people with means should pay for domestic help and chiropody in the private market, and in the case of domestic help positive attempts were made to encourage this. It was thought that this reduced demand for the local authority service, but it was not always realized that it might also divert potential staff away from the local authority service. There had been no attempt to estimate the extent to which old people could satisfy their needs in the private market.

The private sector was also important in some areas as an actual or potential supplier of laundry facilities, and, to a lesser extent, of meals services and employment opportunities.

In general, the case study authorities had very inadequate information about the part played by the private sector, and there seemed to have been little attempt to assess its potential contribution to the development of services.

PART IV

CONCLUSIONS AND RECOMMENDATIONS

CHAPTER 23

CONCLUSIONS

The main purpose of this study was to find out how local authorities plan the provision of services to meet the needs of the elderly in their areas. The ways in which local authorities attempted to plan, and the problems which they faced in formulating and implementing plans were discussed in detail in Parts II and III. In this chapter the position in 1965–6 is summarized, and the reasons for it are examined. In the final chapter, a possible approach to planning is outlined.

THE POSITION IN 1965–6

There was a very considerable growth of local authority services for the elderly between 1945 and 1965 in spite of certain deficiences in the legislation from which local authorities derived their powers, the low priority accorded at national level to the development of health and welfare services throughout the fifties, and the inadequacies of the central government's policy on retirement incomes.

For the most part local health and welfare services evolved piecemeal in response to expressed demand rather than as the result of any plan. The extent to which the home help and home nursing services would be devoted to the care of the elderly was not foreseen when the National Health Service was established, nor were many other needs of the elderly recognized. As understanding of the needs of the elderly increased, services such as chiropody, meals-on-wheels, lunch clubs, warden-schemes and laundry services developed, sometimes at the initiative of a local authority, sometimes at the initiative of a voluntary organization, especially when statutory powers were lacking. These services also evolved in response to expressed demand, or, in the case of new services such as warden-schemes, were simply tried out on a small scale as an experiment.

Since the late fifties local housing policies have taken rather more account of the needs of the elderly than was so in the early fifties, but the change in policy was made by chance rather than design in many cases. Building to meet expressed demand was the most usual practice, and in a few areas even this was an advance on the architect designing schemes without reference to the housing manager's information about sizes of households wanting houses. In some areas the greater emphasis on housing for the elderly was a by-product of slum clearance programmes. Nevertheless, having realized that the elderly tended to be worse housed than the population as a whole, some housing authorities had given a great deal of thought to the provision of suitable housing for them.

The response to the attempt of the central departments to introduce long-term planning in English and Welsh local authorities varied. Scottish authorities had not been required to prepare formal long-term plans, but their approach to planning the development of services was not essentially different from that found in English and Welsh authorities.

A number of officials considered that there was a need for long-term planning, but were not always sure how best to go about it. Those who tried to take the exercise of formulating ten-year plans seriously found that they could do little more than project past trends in the growth of services, adjusted to allow for projected population changes. For residential accommodation and for housing, waiting lists provided some information about needs which were not being met, although only a few of the case study authorities were wholly confident that these waiting lists were of value as a planning tool. For the domiciliary services there were often no waiting lists, because services were supplied on demand even if it meant reducing the level of service to someone already receiving it. Thus local health departments often had not even a waiting list as an indication of unmet need. Comments on the inadequacy of the domiciliary services to meet some of the needs of those already receiving them showed an awareness of a shortfall in present provision, but rarely had any attempt been made to measure the extent of it. It is more difficult to estimate the extent of unmet need among old people not known to the local authority, and such developments as were taking place were aimed more at uncovering individual cases of unmet need, than at estimating the total extent of the problem.

The development of each service was usually considered in isolation, and it could not be said that there was an overall plan for the development of services for the elderly in any of the authorities studied. In a few cases the fragmentation of planning seemed to be as great between sections within the local health department, as between separate health, welfare and housing departments, and between separate welfare and housing authorities. Even in authorities where senior officers from different departments had discussed plans, when it came to the point of framing proposals it had not seemed feasible to do anything else but treat each service separately.

Some officials denied the need for long-term planning, their argument being that the services already did expand to meet the demand for them, and that this would continue to happen in the future. In small authorities, many of which were in Scotland, there was perhaps a greater tendency to believe that there was not much unmet need among old people. Other officials showed greater awareness of the inadequate levels of provision, but doubted the value of trying to estimate the total need for services on the grounds that the extent of unmet need was so great that there would never be enough resources to meet it. To these officials long-term planning was of academic interest only.

All the local authorities studied were deeply concerned about the availability of resources necessary for an expansion of services. There was a tendency to emphasize manpower shortages rather than financial ones, but to some extent manpower shortages were related to problems of finance.

A number of authorities had experienced difficulties in recruiting staff, although some of them seemed insufficiently aware of the extent to which the difficulties were of their own making. Moreover, while officials knew in general terms who were the main local competitors for manpower, there had been no coherent attempt to estimate whether any untapped reserves of labour might be available locally.

Most health and welfare officials claimed that, on the whole, they obtained a reasonable share of finance for the running of existing services, and for a gradual expansion. Some specific problems arose, such as difficulties in convincing elected members, and occasionally even a local authority treasurer, of the desirability of expanding health visiting and social work services because of lack of understanding of the kind of work done by these services. There were also doubts about the extension of financial help to voluntary organizations because of the problems of how to control the development of voluntary services. A disquieting aspect of housing finance, from the point of view of elderly tenants in the context of prevailing pension levels, was the tendency to economize by cutting out help with interior decoration, provision of cookers and other types of fittings.

However, the belief that health and welfare services received a reasonable share of finance must be set in the context of a situation in which purely local sources of finance were not buoyant enough to make major developments practicable, and in which there was strong pressure at national level to keep down the rate of growth of public expenditure financed from exchequer funds.

The rate at which developments involving capital expenditure took place was controlled by central government policy. Thus local authorities could not tell very much in advance what capital finance was likely to be available.

Health and welfare departments also experienced difficulties in obtaining sites for buildings, especially as their needs were small in relation to those of other departments, but they needed sites with special characteristics. Long-term planning was proving to be of positive value in relation to finding sites, but many problems still remained.

In some authorities there were difficulties in obtaining the services of architects for health and welfare projects, and in others it was not always easy to get contractors.

The fact that other statutory bodies had responsibilities for provision for certain needs of the elderly, and that voluntary organizations and private enterprise also provided for the elderly complicated the process of planning for the local authorities. Co-ordination of plans with the Ministry of Social Security could not take place at local level, because local officers of the Ministry of Social Security were not responsible for major policy decisions. There had been some attempts at co-ordination of plans with hospital authorities, and with voluntary organizations, but these attempts had not always been very successful. The question of co-ordination with the private sector was largely unsolved. In general, local authorities assumed that existing provision made by alternative suppliers of services for the elderly would continue to be available, but the possibility of expanding their contribution, or of changes in the balance of provision by different suppliers were not being consciously incorporated into the plans.

In general, it seemed likely that the services would continue to evolve piecemeal in the future as they had in the past, and the attempt to introduce long-term planning had done little to alter this.

THE REASONS FOR THE POSITION IN 1965-6

There were a number of reasons why local authority planning of services for the elderly was still, for the most part, at an embryonic stage. Local authorities did not have much of the information necessary for planning in this field, and it was often difficult for them to acquire it. There were some doubts about the most appropriate methods of providing care for the elderly, and about what part the local authority should try to play in making this provision. Finally, there was a lack of confidence in central government and its policies. These reasons are now considered in more detail.

(a) *Lack of Basic Information*

Local authorities lacked much of the information about the extent of need for help from the social services, about the likely future extent of need among the elderly, about likely available resources, and about what other suppliers of services for the elderly were providing, and were likely to provide in the future.

Local authorities knew approximately the number of elderly people in their population, but did not know how many of them needed help from the social services. Indeed there was not even any clear agreement about what constituted need for social services. As one medical officer of health said: 'Welfare services are as long as a piece of string.' In the absence of any other criterion for an adequate level of provision many local authorities said that they provided up to the level demanded by the public. That the public, particularly the elderly, might not know what services could be available, or might not express their demands, was regarded by some local health and welfare authorities as unimportant because so many of the demands were expressed by an intermediary, such as a general practitioner, health visitor, social worker, home nurse, hospital staff, or voluntary worker. The variation in the criteria for assessing need for services adopted by this varied group of medical and social workers was not always fully realized.

Some information about unmet or inadequately met needs of old people already known to the local authority existed in local authority records, but only rarely was such information collated for use in the planning process. The exceptions were, as already mentioned, waiting lists for housing and for residential accommodation, and these usually only provided a measure of the expressed demands which were not being met, rather than of unmet needs. Information about the possible needs of old people not known to the local authority was difficult to obtain. Local authorities tended to feel that unless there was a survey carried out by a university or a research organization, or unless there was a comprehensive visiting service for all old people in the area, it was not possible to estimate the extent of total need. The idea of extrapolating from the findings of studies, such as Townsend and Wedderburn's, was usually dismissed as too risky because of the difficulty of relating national estimates to local situations.

Thus it was difficult enough to assess the current position, but to estimate the extent to which old people in the future would need help from the social services was thought to be well nigh impossible, since the determinants of needs among the elderly were still imperfectly understood. Even the projections for the elderly population were regarded as suspect by some authorities, especially the counties, because the figures supplied by the Registrar General did not accord with what seemed to be happening locally.

Information was also sadly lacking on the possible supply of resources for the development of the services. No estimates of possible untapped local sources of staff had been made, and in only a few cases had there been a systematic attempt to study the relationships between conditions of employment and the local authorities' ability to recruit and retain staff.

The problems of estimating the likely available finance for development was closely bound up with the relationship between central and local government, and is discussed under that heading.

Information about what other suppliers of services were providing was often incomplete. The population served by a geriatric hospital, or mental hospital, or a voluntary service did not necessarily coincide with that of a local authority, so that it was difficult to judge the contribution of such a service. Some voluntary organizations and some private suppliers of services had no need to be in contact with the local authority, and so their contribution could be unknown, especially in a large authority, or in one where the population was widely scattered.

Of the alternative suppliers of services, only the hospital authorities were known to have long-term plans, although one or two of the larger housing associations had long-term plans as well. Thus the contribution to be made by alternative suppliers in the future was difficult to gauge.

The cumulative effect of all these gaps in the information available to local authorities was to make many officials feel that planning was not a worthwhile exercise.

(b) *Lack of the Means to Obtain Information*

Local authorities could perhaps be criticized for not making a more determined effort to obtain the necessary information. However, there were a number of reasons why such a criticism would be inopportune. Many local authority officials in health, welfare and housing departments had neither the time nor the staff to devote to obtaining information of the kind necessary for planning. In most cases, they also lacked knowledge of the appropriate techniques and methods for obtaining and processing data, and elected members were not always amenable to the idea of paying for the information to be found by some outside body.

Senior officials in local authorities had many calls on their time, and time to devote to planning was often hard to find. The burden of committee work weighed heavily in some areas, especially in the boroughs where local authorities' committees met monthly. The proliferation of co-ordinating committees necessitated by the structure of the National Health Service also imposed a heavy burden, especially on medical officers of health, who were in demand for liaison with hospital boards, local medical committees and for special liaison committees on maternity and mental health as well as geriatric services. When local authority boundaries differed from those for other branches of the health services, the number of committees involved multiplied rapidly. In one of the case study areas the medical officer belonged to no less than 38 committees, and even sharing the honours among other senior officers did little to help.

Furthermore in small authorities the senior officer could be directly involved in the provision of the services to the public. Only in one case study authority did the medical officer of health himself do regular clinic work, and this was partly a matter of personal choice. However, in small welfare authorities it was not uncommon for the chief welfare officer himself to visit old people in response to applications for places in residential accommodation. In one authority the clerk of the council acted as welfare officer in committee work, and the next-in-line was a welfare officer doing practical welfare work. Some small housing authorities had no housing manager, the work being done by the clerk, public health inspector, surveyor, architect or treasurer, or by a combination of these. In some areas, even in larger authorities, the housing manager was very much involved in the day-to-day administrative work of the department. In these circumstances time could not often be spared for planning, and sometimes planning was not even seen as one of the main functions of the senior officer.

In the many authorities in which the need for more information was well enough appreciated, a further problem was the lack of staff who could spend time on collecting and processing information. In many areas the services were working under very great pressure, and senior officials considered that every available member of staff was needed for the provision of services to those whose need for help was already known. It is also important to recognize that senior officials in local authority departments had only rarely had any opportunity of training in survey methods, design of record cards, and data processing. In this respect local health departments were rather better placed than welfare or housing departments, since some medical officers had taken a Diploma in Public Health on a course which included at least some teaching in statistics and survey methodology. Access to mechanical aids for data processing was not often available in smaller authorities, and even in authorities which had card-sorting machinery or computers, the use made of these by health, welfare and housing departments was limited. This was also partly because so many of the staff of these departments had never had the time or the opportunity to learn about the potential uses of mechanical aids to data processing in the social services field.

The officials' limited knowledge of techniques for handling data also helped to explain why census data was not more extensively used, together with the fact that census data was so out-of-date by the time it was published, and that there were formidable problems involved in trying to use census data for local areas, especially since the introduction of sampling for some of the questions.

The possibility of the local authority paying an outside body to provide the basic information needed for planning social services was said by many officials to be very remote, because elected members did not regard this as something on which public money should be spent. Some local authorities had begun to pay firms of management consultants for studies of physical planning problems. Some use was also made of outside bodies for Organization and Methods surveys. However, it seemed that elected members often did not always appreciate the need for better information on which to base plans for the development of the social services.

Thus local authorities, except for some of the larger ones, were not able to do very much to acquire the information needed for planning.

(c) *Doubts about the Best Way to Provide for the Elderly*

A third major reason for the slow development of long-term planning was that there were many doubts about the best ways of providing for the elderly. In some authorities doubts were expressed about the generally advocated policy of caring for old people in their own homes for as long as possible. To some extent this was bound up with the question of deciding how long is 'as long as possible'. Should someone who needs a hot meal delivering 7 days a week continue to live at home? Some medical officers of health considered that it was asking too much of the domiciliary services to provide care at night and at week-ends for very frail, and sometimes bedridden, elderly people living alone. The cost of such provision had not usually been worked out, for it was the difficulty of getting staff to work at week-ends which was thought to be the greater problem. It might be noted here that some hospitals have had to consider closing chronic sick wards at week-ends because of difficulties in staffing them, given the increasing dependence on married women for staff for the services.

There were doubts about how long old people could be cared for in sheltered housing, or by other warden-schemes not involving re-housing. It was extremely difficult to judge this, since warden-schemes were of recent origin in most areas. The problems of deciding which old people needed sheltered housing had not been sorted out in many areas, and tenancies were often allocated solely on the basis of housing need, as defined by the housing authority.

The low overall development of services meant that supporting services such as home helps, night-sitters, and meals-on-wheels were not always available for people in sheltered housing schemes, and as a result, in some areas the whole experiment of sheltered housing was in danger of being wrecked before it had had a fair trial.

Another reason for wondering how far to take the policy of caring for old people in their own homes was that the wishes of old people themselves were not adequately taken into account. Many old people probably would prefer to live independently, but it was difficult to judge how far their views were conditioned by memories of the workhouse, and by the poor quality of some of the residential accom-modation. However, some old people might prefer living with other people to living alone, provided there was reasonable opportunity for privacy.

It was also argued by some welfare staff that adjustment to communal living would be easier if old people made the change while they were still fit enough to maintain links with the community generally, by going out to church, the pub, or the bowls club. In counties, where old people might have to go to residential accommo-dation some distance from their former homes, there was an added reason for arguing that adjustment to a new area might be easier to achieve earlier rather than later in old age.

The need to discover the preferences of old people themselves was also apparent in connection with schemes of grouped dwellings. In densely populated urban areas, and in some rural areas it was thought that rehousing people in grouped dwellings involved separating them too much from younger relatives and from their friends.

There was also some scepticism about the acceptability to the elderly of a comprehensive visiting service aimed at prevention of social problems, and health problems such as malnutrition. It was argued that this might be resented as interference. Yet the corollary, that of waiting until an old person admitted to being in need of help, was to deny the possibility of preventive work.

In one or two authorities the possibility of using services for rehabilitation was mentioned, since some old people could be helped to be independent. The example of home helps teaching elderly widowers how to cook and mend for themselves was a case in point. However, one of the difficulties in such a policy was that some old people expected to be looked after, and resented the gradual reduction of the service.

These doubts expressed about the best ways of providing for the elderly illustrated some of the difficulties which had to be faced before planning could be undertaken with any confidence.

(d) *Lack of Confidence in Central Government*

Confidence, or rather the lack of it, was also the key to understanding the fourth major reason why local authorities were not more enthusiastic about long-term planning. Stated simply, many local authorities lacked confidence in the central government departments. This showed in a variety of ways.

One specific instance was the firm insistence by the Ministry of Health that high priority must be given to the replacement of former public assistance institutions, which was thought by some of the case study authorities to be quite inappropriate, for the reasons detailed in Chapter 5.

The standards of provision for individual services suggested, albeit tentatively, by the Ministry of Health were regarded with great scepticism by many local authorities because they doubted whether the Ministry knew enough about varying social and economic circumstances in different areas, and the needs to which they gave rise, to lay down meaningful standards. In particular, the more astute local authority officials were rightly critical of the assumption that ratios of staff or units of accommodation per thousand elderly population should not be very different in different areas. The principle of setting standards for individual areas was often welcomed; it was the methods of doing it which were regarded as suspect. How naïve the Ministry's suggested standards really were was difficult to judge, since the methods of arriving at them were mentioned only in very general terms, or were derived from the recommendations of reports on various aspects of the health and welfare services.

The Scottish Home and Health Department was less often criticized, both for its policy on the former public assistance institutions, and that on standards of provision, but this was because it had in both cases taken a much less firm stand.

Another aspect of the lack of confidence in central departments showed when the extension of the ten-year plans to cover sheltered housing was discussed. Some of the explanation for this lay in the absence of an agreed terminology for describing different types of housing for the elderly (see Chapter 3), but there was also confusion over whether provision by voluntary organizations other than housing associations should be included. Moreover, by the time of the second revision of the ten-year plans, some authorities were confused by the Ministry's failure to distinguish between housing associations and housing societies. Some housing authorities in counties did not see what sheltered housing had to do with the Ministry of Health, with some justification since district councils in English counties thought of the idea originally, and had done most to develop this form of provision. To the local authorities it looked as though there had been no co-ordination at all between the Ministry of Health and the Ministry of Housing and Local Government.

In Scotland the one or two requests for information about what little sheltered housing there was came from the Scottish Development Department along with the request for details of other housing suitable for and allocated to the elderly. This made rather more sense to the housing authorities, although some of them were not very helpful about providing the information.

However, by far the most important reason for the lack of trust in the central departments was over the question of finance. The immediate cause of trouble was the control exercised by central departments over loan sanction for capital development. The stop-go policies on capital expenditure created difficulties for many health and welfare authorities in obtaining sites, architects' services, and building resources in competition with other local authority departments which were exempted from the deferments, and so able to maintain a smooth flow of work. Housing programmes were less often affected by deferments, but at times housing developments were impeded by the problems of getting loan sanction for roads, or other services under the control of different central departments, at the same time as those for the housing itself.

Moreover, as central departments often had to work on imperfect knowledge about relative priorities as between local authorities, because of the lack of standard criteria for assessing priorities, resources were not necessarily allocated where they were needed most. The central departments were subject to their own pressures of competition with other departments, and at times were anxious to approve schemes quickly. The Ministry of Health, for example, attempt to allow for delays in the preparation of projects and sub-

357

mission of tenders by allowing one project to be substituted for another, and by accepting projects not originally included in the allocation for the year. In these circumstances there was some evidence that authorities which had fewer problems over sites and architectural resources were likely to be able to obtain more than their share of loan sanctions compared with the less fortunate or less well organized authorities.

An indirect effect of central control of capital expenditure was that this was apparently the reason most often given by hospital authorities for their inability to amend their ten-year plans after meeting the local authorities to discuss the needs of the elderly. These criticisms in connection with finance concerned not only the central departments but successive central governments. The long history of intermittent restrictions on health and welfare services had led some local authorities to doubt whether health and welfare services were thought to be important at national level. Repeated exhortations by central governments to keep other local authority expenditure down, and the restraints imposed on wages and salaries for nurses, home helps and chiropodists, whose pay rates were negotiated at national level, also contributed to the impression that the government did not want good health and welfare services. Many elected members at local authority level, as well as believing that their primary responsibility was to keep the local rates down, also tended to feel that they should support the government by trying to limit public expenditure. In these circumstances, planning for growth of the services did not, to some officials, seem worth spending a lot of time on.

There was one further way in which some local authorities had lost faith in the central government over questions of finance. Local authorities were given the power to charge for the home help service, but as most of the users of the service were elderly people with limited incomes the revenue recovered from users of this service was often negligible in relation to the cost of providing it. It was the responsibility of central government to guarantee adequate incomes for those elderly not provided for by income from earnings, investments or occupational pensions, but local authorities had considerable justification for feeling that the central government repeatedly tried to pass on their responsibility to the local authorities.

The issue was likely to grow in importance in the future. The new Health Services and Public Health Act 1968 persisted in the belief that the elderly could pay, not only for home help and laundry services, but for whatever services were provided under the new powers to make arrangements for promoting the welfare of old

358

people. Moreover, if the suggested policy of charging economic rents for local authority housing, with a rebate scheme for low income households, were to be implemented the issue of who should bear the financial responsibility would become of major importance for the elderly.

Lack of basic information, and of the means to obtain it, doubts about what services to develop, and failures in the relationship between central and local government, these then were the reasons which emerged for the limitations of long-term planning by local authorities at the time this study was carried out.

CHAPTER 24

A POSSIBLE APPROACH TO PLANNING— RECOMMENDATIONS

THE NATURE OF THE PLANNING PROCESS

As a first step it is important to be clear about the nature of the planning process. Stripped to its essentials, planning involves the definition of a goal, and the setting of specific objectives as stages towards reaching that ultimate goal. It involves the consideration of methods for achieving the objectives, and this depends on the availability of information about what is involved in reaching the objective and what possible methods are available. In addition it involves the location and mobilization of the resources necessary in order to apply the methods chosen. These steps are not completely independent of each other, and should not be seen as steps to be carried out in a straight time sequence. The definition of objectives may have to be modified in the light of information about what is needed to achieve them and the likely available supply of resources. The methods chosen may have to be modified in the light of the supply of resources. Planning therefore needs to be understood as a process of continuous adjustment of the parts of the system, keeping in mind the ultimate goal. It needs to be recognized also that knowledge of the most appropriate methods will be acquired only as the decisions taken at other stages of planning are implemented and tested. What appears to be a good method may turn out not to be so good in the light of greater knowledge, and the system needs to ensure that methods are evaluated and, if necessary, abandoned and replaced by others.

TOWARDS A SYSTEM OF PLANNING SERVICES FOR THE ELDERLY

Assuming that it is accepted as the general goal that society should ensure that the needs of the elderly are adequately catered for, the next stage is to consider specific objectives to aim for as steps on the road towards that goal.

Specific objectives are, however, difficult to formulate unless there is reasonably good information about the extent and character of needs. This is the stage at which, in the past, the planning process has started to go wrong, mainly because of the failure to distinguish clearly between this stage and the next one, that of selecting methods for meeting needs. To move straight in on estimates of the need for home helps, the need for residential accommodation, and the need for a laundry service is to prejudge the issue about the best methods to use for meeting needs. This can lead to plans to solve the problems of unsuitable housing by expanding the home help service, or plans to combat loneliness by increasing the home nursing and the meals-on-wheels services *without considering whether the services being provided are appropriate to the needs.*

It would be wholly unjust to imply that local authorities are the only ones to slip into this confusion. In so far as the elderly are concerned the central government have a marked tendency to prejudge the issue of methods too, and to let the health and welfare services fill in gaps caused by an inadequate incomes policy for the retired, and the low priority given to housing for the elderly for many years. If this is intentional, it implies one of two things. Either the central government has worked out that it would be cheaper, and/or better, for the elderly to be cared for by the health and welfare services rather than in any other way, or it has decided that the health and welfare services should patch up the present situation as best they can until long-term policies on retirement incomes and housing start to show results. There is no evidence known to the authors that the first alternative is the policy; if it ever was it surely ought to be reconsidered now, if only from the point of view of manpower planning. The second alternative seems rather more likely, and there is some evidence, at least in the history of pensions policy, to support it. If this reasoning is correct, the first essential to any soundly based plan for health and welfare services is for the Department of Health and Social Security to produce estimates based on future pensions policy plans of the rates at which the need for health and welfare services to undertake a patching-up operation is intended to fall off, with a breakdown of the estimates by local areas.

Similar information is needed for housing, but the situation in this case is more complicated because housing policy is partly dependent on incomes policy, and also because local housing authorities and central departments are both involved. What the health and welfare service requires from housing departments and public health inspectors are estimates for each local area of the rate at which it is intended that all elderly households will have hot water, inside lavatories, and the rate at which coal fires are being superseded by central heating. This information is needed in relation to the total stock of housing, not only council housing. The presence or absence of stairs, especially steep stairs, is another factor, although the medical evidence on the importance of this is somewhat equivocal. The now extensive literature on the elderly provides many clues about how inappropriate housing conditions contribute to the inability of some old people to manage to look after themselves. These clues should be assembled, and the weak spots in the evidence strengthened by further enquiries, with the aim of establishing definitions of housing suitable for the elderly. The Scottish Development Department has already made a start (see Chapter 3) in the right direction. The Ministry of Housing and Local Government should follow suit, and the Scottish Department should refine its definition.

The scope for refining definitions should not, however, be allowed to interfere with using an interim definition based on what is already known to be important. It may not be too late to ensure that the 1971 Census provides data and tabulations on the major defects in the housing stock, from the point of view of the elderly.

If staff with time and the appropriate skills can be found to design an inquiry and to collect and analyse the data needed before the 1971 census data are available so much the better, but this is a forlorn hope. Some of the universities might be able to make available the services of people with the skills to design the inquiry, and market research organizations might provide field-workers. Alternatively, students could be paid to do the field-work during a vacation.

The task of seeing that this information is made available is not a task for individual local authorities if there is later to be a distribution of resources related to different degrees of need. It is for central departments to establish what information is to be sought, and for a skilled research worker to work out how it is to be obtained for each area, and how it is to be analysed. If some local authorities are in a position to provide the necessary data for all or part of their total housing stock from existing records, this should be used. Otherwise a survey is necessary.

Once something is known about the present stock of suitable dwellings, and how the elderly are housed in relation to them, the question of the methods to adopt in order to achieve the specific objective of progressively reducing the contribution of bad housing to the inability of some old people to look after themselves can be considered. Some of the answers will be in terms of the relative merits of new building or improvement grants, of arrangements for exchanges, of priorities for allocating vacancies in council properties as they occur, perhaps of buying property from elderly owner-occupiers, using it to house large families, and providing the elderly vendor with a modern dwelling with no stairs. When new building is needed, the contribution which the private sector, and voluntary organizations could make should be considered. No single method will suffice, and the balance between different methods will differ from one local area to another because of the differences in the present stock, different projected rates of change in the number and size of elderly households, local differences in consumer preferences, and differences in the relative costs of implementation of the methods decided on.

In the argument so far the problem of data on old people who cannot manage to look after themselves has been deliberately left on one side. In one sense this problem is irrelevant, since the first definition of 'suitable' housing is going to cover only items like a hot water system, an inside lavatory, ease of access, proximity to shops, which are important to all old people. In later rounds of the planning process more refined definitions of 'suitable' housing may mean that more data on the elderly and their specific needs will be needed.

However, just as housing authorities are urged to move into a position in which they can provide a programme for the rate of reduction in 'unsuitable' housing and thus relieve the burden on the health and welfare services, so the health and welfare services must equip themselves with data about the extent of the inability of the elderly to manage on their own, together with the reasons why they cannot, and also about the attitudes of old people to different sorts of services. This will enable them to provide information to both the Department of Health and Social Security and to housing authorities, and to organize their own services more efficiently, as well as to plan for them.

The Department of Health and Social Security and the Scottish Home and Health Department should establish a working party consisting of experienced staff from the health and welfare services, of experts in the design of records systems, and experts in data processing methods, to work out and pilot a system for defining and recording inability to manage. Townsend has already provided a starting point,[1] but there are some defects in it which need to be ironed out, especially in relation to the *reasons* for inability to manage. It is essential that these are known if the methods of providing care for those who need it are to be appropriate. There is a world of difference between the best ways of providing for an old lady who cannot do personal laundry even though she has a washing

[1] P. Townsend, *The Last Refuge*, Routledge and Kegan Paul, 1962, Chapter 10 and Appendix 2, and (with D. Wedderburn) *The Aged in the Welfare State*, G. Bell and Sons, 1965, Chapter 1.

machine in good working order, an old lady who cannot do it only because she does not have good facilities and an elderly widower who simply lacks the knowledge of how to wash his socks without shrinking them and drifts into not bothering to wash them at all. The records system should also incorporate data about the methods chosen for meeting the need (i.e. the services supplied) under the present system.

Local health and welfare staff should then adopt the system for use when investigating the circumstances of old people referred to them for help. This need not be a particularly difficult step to implement because it would only be a more systematic way of doing what staff such as some health visitors, and all welfare officers and home help organizers do already.

The record would thus provide some basic data about the old people known to the services. In authorities which have already gone a considerable way to provide a visiting service (other than for purely social purposes) for all old people in their area the coverage would soon be fairly comprehensive. In other areas it could perhaps be made complete fairly soon for at least some groups by schemes for visiting the over-eighties or the elderly living alone.

Elsewhere surveys, which could often be on a sample basis, would be needed at intervals to fill the gap. The organization of these presents considerable problems. The central departments, in conjunction with the universities, and with some of the larger local authorities, could provide the expertise necessary for designing the surveys—and it must be remembered that the questionnaire (for want of a better term) will already exist. With the co-operation of local authorities and/or universities which have machinery for data processing, the central departments could then control the analysis of both the survey data and the data on old people already being cared for by the health and welfare services.The central departments should therefore take steps to establish a register of people with appropriate research skills who are willing to provide advice, and of organizations with data processing facilities. Local authorities would then be able to obtain advice and access to facilities.

Methods of payment for facilities provided by other organizations would need to be worked out. Some of the problems in the present situation might become irrelevant with changes in local government, but in the meantime a central fund should be established, since small authorities would have more need of help, and since the information to result from the new approach is as relevant for decisions on national policies as it is for plans for local areas.

The more difficult problem would be to find suitable field-workers.

While questions on housing amenities can be included in the census, or asked by market-research interviewers or students, the kind of assessment of capacity to manage, and the understanding of the reasons for incapacity is a different matter. It is tempting to say that the more recently trained health visitors, with their skills in health, education, nursing, social work, and often their experience of domestic work, are the most suitable people. They probably are, but they are in short supply, and they have skills in child care which should not be wasted. Nevertheless, some of the case study authorities, and not necessarily the better staffed ones, had from time to time managed to spare some health visitor time for helping with surveys, so the possibility should not be ruled out altogether. The other possibility worth considering is that students on social work training courses should help with the field-work as part of their practical training. There would be several advantages in this. The students would have some training in how to talk to people. It would be directly relevant experience for those of them going on to work with the elderly, because they would be using the same 'questionnaire'. It would provide experience which could be used as a basis for discussions about what services they would have recommended had they been taking the decision. Moreover, because they would introduce themselves as people doing a study of old people, the dilemma of how to find out about needs without raising old people's hopes of getting a home help next week would be less acute.

The question of allying a medical assessment and prognosis with this system of social assessment should be considered. The Royal College of General Practitioners could set up a study group, consisting of general practitioners and geriatricians, to create a prototype. This should be linked with the existing system of general practitioners' records so as to minimize the work of record keeping, but also linked with the health and welfare services' records.

General practitioners should then be invited to adopt this way of recording information about those old people who consult them, so that a picture of needs could in time be built up. Help in completing the base-line picture of medical needs more quickly could be made available if ways could be devised of providing refresher training, and finance, for married women doctors whose family commitments prevent them from undertaking any work other than part-time non-emergency work.

The data provided from the health and welfare services' own records, together with the estimates from the sample survey, would be analysed to provide a picture of the total needs of the area, and the reasons for them.

Complementary to this analysis, data from the record cards of people receiving services on what services were being used would be analysed to show what was being used to patch up the holes in income and housing provision, and what for the needs which only the health and welfare services can meet.

This is the point at which the question of methods of meeting needs becomes relevant.[1] The collated information on needs that are due solely to the inadequacies of income and/or housing should be passed to the relevant authorities, and they in turn will be providing their information on the expected rates of removal of the causes of need. The methods chosen will then be the ones which are most suited to the nature of this type of need. For example there would not be much point in putting welfare homes into the programme for 1971 to meet the needs and preferences of a group of people for accommodation with an inside lavatory, no stairs and no coal fires, which the housing authority intends to provide by 1975.

The cost of providing the patching up services should be estimated, and if the authorities responsible for retirement incomes and housing policy fail to meet their deadlines the money cost of patching up services could become a charge on them. This will still leave the health and welfare services with some of its manpower wastefully employed, and perhaps other inefficiencies, but it seems that this cannot be helped.

The health and welfare services will by now be in a better position to set their own objectives, and to select the methods thought to be best for meeting the needs of those who, given adequate income and housing, cannot look after themselves because of some degree of physical or mental disability, some of which may be temporary, but much of which may be permanent. To help in deciding the best methods there will be the data on needs, preferably including the assessments of medical and nursing needs.

Such information as already exists on the available stock of buildings and manpower needs to be supplemented by information on sites and equipment. Furthermore, local authorities need information on the qualitative aspects of existing resources. Only if the expected future life of buildings and equipment is known, and if the rate at which staff will be retiring, or likely to leave for other reasons, is estimated, can plans effectively take account of the need to replace

[1] This must not be taken to mean that old people referred to, or directly approaching the authority in the meantime will not receive any services—health and welfare staff would continue to do their best with what resources and services are available now, and are made available as the result of the normal system of creeping growth plus the effect of the present plans.

existing resources. Steps should be taken now to organize this information systematically, and the Department of Health and Social Security and Scottish Home and Health Department should pilot schemes for doing this in conjunction with health and welfare authorities. More energetic attempts must be made to include similarly classified data on existing voluntary and private provision. There would also have to be data on the probable future supply of resources. The Manpower Research Unit of the Department of Employment and Productivity should, in conjunction with the central departments responsible for health, welfare and housing, try to develop methods of forecasting the likely future supply of staff for local areas. One of the first essentials for the development of techniques for doing this would be the availability of data about existing staff, such as education, their employment history, family circumstances, reasons for wanting the job, reasons for leaving the job. Some case study local authorities already had some of this information in their personnel records. Authorities which do not could start to record at least the basic facts they already ask for when making an appointment, and the reasons for leaving. The system could be refined later.

It would be desirable to have data about the likely future supply of voluntary workers in different local areas. This might be a suitable project for a university department to undertake, although some of the techniques needed will be close to those being developed in the Manpower Research Unit.

Planning departments should consider ways of improving communications with health, welfare and housing officers over the identification of sites suitable for special purposes and expected dates of availability of sites in major developments.

Some or all of this information is likely to affect the decisions on methods of providing for different categories of health and welfare needs of the elderly, as well as consideration of the cost of alternative policies. For example, it may be feasible from the point of view of health and social needs to provide for a group of 50 people by increasing the home help service by 20, but if this is in an area where the social or employment structure is such that the right kind of people are not likely to be available in sufficient quantity, the alternative method of a welfare home with a staff of 8 attendants and domestics (plus senior staff) will have to be considered, even if it costs more.

Once a policy on the methods to be adopted has been worked out and costed the financial implications will be clearer. Estimates for both capital and revenue expenditure can be made. If there are then problems over finance there will be evidence about the way the estimates were arrived at, the reasons why alternative courses which might have been cheaper were rejected, and the implications of not carrying out the plans in terms of the needs which will go unmet.

At the same time, if financial resources are not forthcoming for all the plans, most of the work of establishing priorities and feasible alternative methods will already have been done, so that the task of reconsidering the objectives is easier.

It is hoped that the creation of a system of classifying needs according to *nationally* applied definitions would provide a sound basis for the system for allocating resources between local areas, and for working towards the setting of minimum standards related to the categories of needs being met. The methods by which they are met would vary, as indeed they often do now, according to what makes sense in local circumstances.

Development of techniques for evaluating methods of meeting needs is badly needed, and research designed with this end in mind should be encouraged by bodies such as the Social Science Research Council, the National Institute for Social Work Training and other professional organizations. In the short run more use could be made of what is already known. The central departments could help by publishing abstracts of good quality studies about experiments in different areas and by adding an article drawing together the lessons of recent developments.

This then would be a possible approach to planning. It is complex, but then planning is no simple matter. As it stands, there are many loose ends, but as techniques for planning are developed, the process can be streamlined. These recommendations have been formulated in an attempt to put planning of services for the elderly on a sounder footing. Much of what has been said may, in principle, be equally applicable in relation to planning to meet the medical and social needs of other age groups. The desirability of developing planning machinery and techniques on a wider basis should therefore be considered, since there is also a need for a sound basis for defining objectives in relation to other services, and for deciding priorities between elderly and other users of similar services.

However, it must be realized that putting planning and the definition of objectives on to a sounder basis will do little to help, in the immediate future, with the already pressing problems of caring for old people in some areas. Some suggestions for immediate steps are therefore included in Appendix 1.

THE WIDER PERSPECTIVE

This study was carried out at a time when a great many proposals for change in the structure, organization, management, staffing and finance, of the local health and welfare services, the National Health Service, local government generally, and the civil service were being discussed, and when the restructuring of medical education was also under consideration.

In the long run, many of the activities which it is suggested should be done now by central departments might be done at regional level, if local authorities are reorganized on a regional basis.

Research and intelligence units in regional authorities could, when there are enough suitable people to staff them, take over the functions of designing sample surveys, and processing and analysing data.

Whether or not such units should have staff to work on collecting data is a point which needs careful consideration. If they do not, there are problems involved in incorporating data collection duties into the work of other staff. To contract for the use of the resources of market research organizations may or may not be feasible. It may well be that research and intelligence units should have some staff to work on data collection in fields such as housing, and the health needs of the working age groups, but that health and welfare services would need to rely more on their own staff, and on those training in social work, for data collection on the needs of the elderly. If so, estimates of the extra work involved would need to be incorporated into the planning of staff levels.

The research and intelligence units could provide advice on the organization of data on the existing stock of resources, and could, in the case of capital stock, sites, and equipment, help with some of the investigation work which might be needed in the early days. Once basic data had been checked there should be little need for this kind of investigation, since the records should be up-dated as changes take place. The unit could advise on the organization of personnel records, and would process and analyse data from them.

Some of the manpower forecasting could be done on a regional basis, but it may need to be done using nationally agreed techniques and criteria. There would be a need for projections of population changes and changes in the supply of manpower of different kinds for local areas *within* regions.

If health and welfare services are parted from local government and incorporated into a unified National Health Service, research and intelligence units within the new health service organization could provide the expertise necessary for seeing that the quality of information about needs and resources is improved, and that the necessary analyses are made. However, in that event there would be a need for a close link with whatever institution was responsible for forecasting manpower availability for local areas, and with the institution responsible for land use planning and economic planning.

However, if there are to be research and intelligence units at regional level, regardless of whether they serve a wide range of public services or only the health and welfare services, there is a fundamental question to be answered before their exact function can be determined. Is it acceptable in Britain today for different parts of the country to use different criteria for assessing need for a service? If not, there is simply no alternative to using *nationally* agreed criteria for assessing needs (though methods of meeting similar needs could vary). This would mean that regional research and intelligence units would not design basic records and questionnaires for their own work; these would have to be designed centrally (after consultation in the regions) to ensure that the same descriptive data about needs were available for Inverness as for Worthing. The expertise of the research and intelligence units would still be needed to organize sampling when surveys were needed, and to process and analyse the data.

In the long run it may even be thought preferable that methods of meeting particular types of need should also be standardized over the whole of Britain. If the goal is that of uniformity, which some would call social justice, the means of reaching it must be designed with that end in mind. If the goal is something else, the means of reaching it will need to be different. It must, however, be recognized that local *government* is inconsistent with uniformity of standards of social services. Local *administration* is a different matter, but which is it to be? If the latter, planning must be a central function. The vital need then, is to ensure that there is a good flow of information between those who provide services to the public at a very local level and those who plan at the central level. Details of how to achieve this can be worked out. Policies designed to achieve uniformity in the extent to which social and health needs are met can be formulated on the basis of the information supplied, and resources distributed accordingly. But the first essential is to decide whether uniformity is what is wanted, and whether it is only uniformity of the criteria for assessing the needs to be met, or whether uniformity in ways of meeting the needs is also wanted. At this point, it is perhaps worth emphasizing that the introduction of uniformity in assessing and meeting needs does not affect the individual's choice of whether or not to accept a service. The aim is to make it more likely that the individual will be offered an appropriate service at the appropriate time.

In all the debates about reorganizing the structures of central administration, local government, health services, social services, and finance, the first need is to decide what it is hoped to achieve by the changes to be made. Then, and only then, can useful discussion take place on how to achieve it. If it is hoped to achieve more effective planning for the health and social services it is doubtful how far structural changes of the kind under discussion will help to achieve this aim. Many of the suggested changes might well help to achieve the aim of more efficient administration of the existing services, although even this may be doubted. The separation of social work from local health services under the Social Work (Scotland) Act, 1968, and a possibility, following the Seebohm Report, that the same might happen in England and Wales, seems to replace one set of artificial divisions with another.

Whatever pattern of organization of services finally emerges there will be no sudden miraculous change in the stock of skills and expertise now available for planning among the present staffs of various organizations. Nor can major steps be taken immediately to train people in the techniques of planning in the social services field, since there are few techniques to teach and few who could teach them. Some skills are available, but it is not known whether there are enough people with a sound grasp of, for example, the techniques of designing records systems, or sample surveys, to fill senior posts in research and intelligence units. A lesson can be learned here from the experience of the regional hospital boards. They were established as planning authorities for the hospital services in 1948. Little was known at that time about techniques for planning hospital services, and many of the staff who moved into the hospital boards had little previous experience of how to study needs for hospital care, how to forecast probable future needs for hospital care, how to evaluate hospital care against other alternatives as a method of meeting needs. The regional hospital boards had to start to evolve techniques for planning *after* the structural change had been made. The proposals contained in the first part of this chapter, and summarized at the end, were deliberately framed to try to make a start on the evolution of planning techniques *before* other structural changes take place. They were framed with the intention of making the best possible use of existing resources, on the assumption that little additional finance will be available. They were also framed to be compatible with some possible changes in the day-to-day running of the services which would make for greater efficiency and better services. If implemented, they will involve a number of people in starting to do part of their present job in a different way. Then, by the time the new structures emerge, many of these people will have a more valuable contribution to make to the task of seeing that they can in fact play the role allocated to them. Others will be in a better position to train younger people going into the planning authorities, and to develop and refine techniques.

SUMMARY OF RECOMMENDATIONS

1. Central government should state its policy on the relationship between its policies on retirement pensions, housing, and health and welfare services for the elderly.
2. The Department of Health and Social Security should provide estimates of the expected future levels of retirement incomes in relation to other incomes, including a breakdown by local areas.
3. Central housing departments should develop definitions of what types of housing are *suitable* for old people.
4. (a) Data on the major inadequacies in the present housing stock from the point of view of the needs of the elderly should, if possible, be made available in the 1971 Census.
   (b) Other ways of providing these data sooner might be explored.
   (c) The task of seeing that the data are available is a task for central government.
5. Housing programmes for bringing the housing of the elderly up to the standard of housing generally should then be formulated, and information about the target dates for achieving the objectives set supplied to health and welfare authorities.
6. The Department of Health and Social Security and Scottish Home and Health Department should establish a working party to work out and pilot a system for defining and recording inability to manage among the elderly, the reasons for it, and the methods used to meet the needs under the present system.
7. Local health and welfare staff should then adopt the system for use when visiting old people referred to them for help.
8. The Department of Health and Social Security, Scottish Home and Health Department, and the central housing departments, should create a register of advisers on research and survey methods, and of organizations with data processing facilities.
9. Pending the possible changes in local government and health service structure and finance, a central fund should be established

to meet the costs of using facilities provided by other organizations of the kind mentioned in recommendation 8.

10. Part of the practical training of students on social work courses should be linked with the field work of surveys of old people not known to the social services.

11. The Royal College of General Practitioners should be invited to set up a study group of general practitioners, geriatricians, and experts in records systems, to create a system for linking data based on a medical assessment with the data on social needs.

12. The general practitioners should then be invited to adopt the system, and gradually build up a picture of medical needs.

13. Ways should be found of using the services of married women doctors wanting part-time non-emergency work to help in medical assessment work.

14. Analysis of the data on needs, and the reasons for needs, can then be used as the base-line for discussions on methods of meeting them, and linked with incomes and housing policies.

15. The extent to which existing health and welfare services are being used to make good the deficiencies in incomes and housing policy should be measured and costed.

16. If incomes and housing programmes for removing the deficiencies have not been formulated, or are not carried out on time, the cost of providing the patching up services could become a charge on the authorities responsible for incomes and housing.

17. The Department of Health and Social Security and Scottish Home and Health Department should consult with local authorities, and pilot schemes for organizing data on the quantity and quality of existing stocks of capital (sites, buildings and equipment) and manpower (see also below) in the health and welfare services, including voluntary and private provision.

18. The Manpower Research Unit of the Department of Employment and Productivity should, in conjunction with central departments, try to develop techniques for forecasting the likely future supply of staff for local areas.

19. To help in the implementation of the previous recommendation the present health and welfare authorities should organize and make available whatever data they can from personnel records, especially the data asked for when appointments are made, and data on reasons for staff leaving.

20. The likely future supply of voluntary workers in local areas should be studied either by, or in close conjunction with, the Manpower Research Unit.

21. Planning departments should devise ways of improving their

ways of organizing information on potential sites, and making it available to other departments, and to instructing their colleagues in using the system.

22. The relative costs and feasibility of alternative methods of providing for different categories of needs should be worked out.

23. When the programmes decided on outstrip the financial resources available, decisions on priorities between categories of need, and on the modification of objectives, must be made explicit.

24. National minimum standards should be set in terms of categories of need to be met and *not* in terms of the levels of specific services.

25. Research to help in the development of techniques for evaluating methods of meeting needs should be encouraged.

26. Central departments should publish abstracts of good quality studies of local experiments with ways of meeting needs, together with a review article on the lessons to be learned.

27. Ways must be found of linking the development of techniques which would help to put planning services for the elderly on a sounder footing with the development of similar techniques for planning services for other age groups.

28. The question of how to provide appropriate training in techniques for those who are to be responsible for planning social services when local government, and the health and welfare services are reorganized, should be investigated.

SUGGESTIONS FOR OVERCOMING SOME CURRENT PROBLEMS OF ADMINISTRATION AND DEVELOPMENT OF SERVICES FOR THE ELDERLY

The steps recommended in Chapter 24 would help to improve the quality of planning, and later of policy formulation. They would do little to solve the immediate pressing problems of caring for the present generation of old people. There are, however, a number of practical steps which could be taken to overcome some of the current problems, and some of them are closely linked to the steps needed to help bring about better planning.

In compiling the following list ideas have been culled from many sources, but mainly from the local authorities themselves. The list is by no means exhaustive, but it seemed worth producing in the hope that local authorities, and other interested organizations might find something of use in solving present problems.

DEFINING PRIORITIES

1. Senior officials in health and welfare services should reconsider the criteria for assessing priorities for services between individuals. When demands exceed supply, which is common, it is essential to have agreed criteria for judging between competing claims. Previous definitions of priorities have often only distinguished between broad groups of people, such as maternity cases, problem families, and the aged. There is a need for definitions of priority *within* groups.

   For example, old people living alone have more pressing need for chiropody treatment to keep them mobile than old people living with or near younger relatives. Old people not living near a launderette and not receiving home help may have the greatest need for a laundry service. Such criteria should be reconsidered at regular intervals.

2. Closely allied to the last point, senior officials who have not already done so should draw up guidelines for decisions on how much of a domiciliary service to allocate to an individual. (See Appendix 2 for an example of how this was done by one of the case study authorities for a county home help service at the time of the study.)

3. Housing authorities should re-examine their criteria for eligibility to register on housing waiting lists and for allocating council tenancies to see whether the needs of the elderly are given adequate weight. The possible desirability of setting different criteria for allocating sheltered housing should be considered. More thought should be given to the possibility of abolishing rules on length of residence in the area for those old people who, regardless of whether they have any previous connection with the area, have younger relatives in the area whom they wish to be near. Relaxation of residence rules would also help old people in very rural areas who want to and would be better able to manage in a village or small town.

4. Policies on the under-occupation of council houses should be reconsidered in many areas. Sympathy for the elderly who do not wish to move should not preclude the elderly who do wish to move from having a chance to do so. (See Chapter 9.)

CO-ORDINATION OF SERVICES

5. A master index could be established in each local authority containing name, address, and date of birth of all old people known to the local authority, with a cross-reference to all services involved, including housing. The possibility of introducing a unified records system, on the lines of the unit system for hospital records, also deserves consideration. The advantages of these two measures would be that staff dealing with a referral for help would be able to check quickly whether other services run by different departments, or different sections of the same department, were already involved.

6. Thought should be given to ways of ensuring that the needs of an individual old person for help are not assessed separately by a number of different people, such as home help organizers, welfare officers, voluntary meals-on-wheels organizers, housing visitors.

STAFFING AND TRAINING

7. The possibility of appointing a trained personnel officer for the health and welfare services should be considered. Such a person would publicize vacancies, arrange interviews, share in the selection of staff, provide advice on housing for new staff coming from elsewhere and deal with staff welfare generally.

   In addition such a person would foster relations with the schools and youth employment service, not only to interest school-leavers in careers in the social services, but to interest school-leavers' mothers in coming into this kind of work.

8. If nursery school education is expanded, a quota of places could be reserved for the children of staff working part-time or full-time in the health and welfare services.

9. Consideration should be given to the problem of provision for older children of staff during school holidays, a problem which can cause staffing trouble for the health and welfare services, but which the education authority does not always appreciate. Could voluntary organizations help?

10. Special payments, as for teachers, could be considered for domiciliary nursing and social service workers in areas of desperate staffing shortage; this could be one aspect of a policy of positive area discrimination, linked to the government's recent, special urban programme.

11. Urgent consideration should be given to the pay of staff in residential accommodation and for wardens in sheltered housing schemes.

12. Training facilities for older staff with families, and for married women coming into, or returning to, work in the social services, should be provided as locally as possible. Special grants should be provided by central government for staff in these categories who have to go away from home for all or part of their training to enable them to meet the expense of running two homes.

13. Local authorities and hospital authorities might well consider the possibility of a joint training scheme in basic personal care for nursing auxiliaries in old people's wards, attendants in residential accommodation, and home helps (in areas where they provide some personal care).

14. The possibility of allowing people with some nursing experience but not a midwifery qualification to undertake a health visitor training in in order to work with the elderly should be examined.

15. Adequate arrangements must be made for relief for days off and holidays for wardens of sheltered housing schemes.

PRACTICAL AIDS

(a) *For Staff*

16. Efforts should be made to take as much as possible of the hard physical labour out of much domestic help work. The long-term solution may well be better housing and better incomes for the elderly, so that there are fewer coal fires, more hot water systems and hoovers. However, short-term action is necessary to see that a reasonable minimum of good equipment is available.

17. The adequacy of medical and nursing loans services should be reviewed at regular intervals. To do so would not only help the home nursing service but also the many relatives who nurse elderly people at home.

18. Steps should be taken to ensure that adequate provision is made in all new building and all conversions for the disposal of used disposable equipment and incontinence pads.

(b) *For Clients*

19. The housing authorities which have not already done so should

consider the need for the council to take responsibility for interior decoration in the old people's housing.

20. The question of providing physiotherapy for old people who have had strokes but been nursed at home should be discussed by local authorities and hospital authorities.

FINANCE

21. Grants from welfare authorities to housing authorities for welfare facilities, and the costs of welfare provisions—such as that recommended in point 19—should rank as 'relevant expenditure' for the rate support grant.

SITES AND BUILDINGS

22. Some local authorities could devise better ways of co-ordinating the demands of different departments for sites.

23. Experiments with one or two-day courses designed to give health, welfare and housing officials a better appreciation of the kind of information an architect needs from them would seem to be worth trying.

24. Larger authorities should consider following the example of some of the case study authorities in giving one member of the health and welfare department's staff the job of liaising with the architects on all buildings.

25. The possibilities of developing standard basic briefs for special types of building should be further exploited. Central government departments might well provide an advisory service for small local authorities which build infrequently.

26. The implications of industrialized building and package deals for the design of housing for the elderly should be studied.

27. The problems of getting contractors for one-off jobs, and for building in isolated areas should be investigated.

EXTERNAL RELATIONS

28. General publicity based on modern promotion techniques about the services. Where to enquire about them in the form of leaflets to hand out with pension books, more use of the local press, and of radio and television.

29. More specific education about the problems and the services for local councillors, and for people such as doctors, hospital staff, voluntary organizations, and ministers of religion, who come into frequent contact with old people. It is recognized that the burden on local authority staff of addressing meetings is already considerable in some areas, but more use could be made of films.

30. Descriptions of many visiting and warden-schemes, and of health visitor attachment schemes, are at present published in a wide variety of journals. It would be helpful if the best of these (especially those which give details of organizations, staffing, costs, and the problems which have been overcome) were collected together and published as a handbook by the Department of Health and Social Security and the Scottish Home and Health Department.

31. Having a paid organizer for voluntary services on the local authority staff has proved useful in some areas, especially where the local population did not produce enough leaders, but where volunteers to help run the services seemed to be available.

32. There is scope in some areas for finding ways of encouraging men to help more in voluntary work, in tasks such as visiting elderly men, carrying out small repair jobs, decorating and gardening. To encourage the men could be particularly valuable in areas where many of the women already go out to work as well as running a home.

33. In some areas industrial firms make an important contribution, both by staggering retirement ages, and also by maintaining links between existing staff and their retired workers. This is particularly appropriate in firms in which workers stay with the firm for many years.

34. An advisory service for those running private homes—and perhaps also for voluntary homes—for the elderly has proved useful in some areas.

HOME HELP SERVICE: SCALE FOR GUIDANCE IN DETERMINING THE NUMBER OF HOURS PER WEEK TO BE AUTHORIZED (IN USE IN 1965)

Hours per week	Circumstances and disability
2–4	Patients up all day—no particular complaint but finding heavy household work too great a strain for their advanced years, otherwise active, able to get out, do their shopping, personal washing and light housework.
5–7	Patients up all day but where there is a medium degree of disability—includes such cases as arthritis, asthma, cardiac failure, failing eyesight. Help is given in these cases with personal washing, general cleaning, shopping and fires when needed—recommended in cases where one elderly person is struggling to cope with a bedfast patient or one who is greatly incapacitated.
8–10	Confined to bed for some part of the day—able to get up by dinner time. Recommended in cases of severe disability where patient is living alone and housebound. Also in cases of increasing infirmity and senility of old couples, usually over eighty with no family to help. In these cases, apart from household cleaning, shopping, washing, dinners, fires when needed; general personal care of patients is given under supervision of the district nurse.
11–14	Bedfast patients living alone, no family near. In these cases apart from running the home, keeping it clean, doing cooking, shopping and washing, the help is responsible for the patient's care and well-being. A late evening visit is always essential.
Over 14 hours	Recommended in cases of sudden serious illness, patient living alone and awaiting hospital bed, not normally of long duration.

BASIC BRIEF AGREED BETWEEN A WELFARE DEPARTMENT AND AN ARCHITECT'S DEPARTMENT (IN USE IN 1965)

PROPOSED NEW OLD PEOPLE'S HOME AT:

ARCHITECT'S BRIEF

Except where otherwise stated all requirements to be in accordance with L.A. Building Notes issued by Ministry of Health and with user requirements agreed by Welfare Committee. Reference should also be made to Design Bulletin 1, 'Some Aspects of Designing for Old People' issued by Ministry of Housing and Local Government.

A. RESIDENTS' ACCOMMODATION (for 50 places)

i. Entrance hall		With sitting spaces, sheltered from draughts, which could be used by residents receiving visitors.
ii. Coat hanging space		Off entrance hall.
iii. Sitting-rooms	Minimum total 1,250 square feet	And spaces dispersed through the building mainly on ground floor. Number of small rooms preferred, to include quiet room, smoking room, TV and radio room. (N.B. Sitting rooms to be accessible to service area.)
iv. Dining-rooms	Minimum total 750	Two spaces required, inter-related to permit shows and other functions or two separate spaces with one related to another room (e.g. visitors' room) so as to be enlarged for shows, etc.
v. Store off dining-room	50	For tables, chairs (with doorway off corridor as well as off dining room).

vi. Bed sitting-rooms		6 doubles and 38 singles.
vii. Sanitary accommodation		Baths at 1 to 15 minimum w.c.s at 1 to 6 men and 1 to 6 women minimum (more desirable). Separate provision for each sex. These should be distributed in pairs around the building. It is important to have adequate day toilets (with urinal for men) with coat hanging space nearby, in a suitable position near the the entrance hall and dining-room.
viii. Utility rooms	70–90	One on each floor for use of residents and staff with sink and draining boards for washing small articles of clothing. Point for electric iron.

B. ANCILLARY ACCOMMODATION

i. Office	100–120	With wall safe and cupboard for drugs (double lock).
ii. Combined visitors' and doctor's room	150	With lockable cupboard for library.
iii. Sluice room	50–60	
iv. Laundry	60–80	To accommodate washing machine, spin dryer, ironing machine, table for folding and sink. Laundry to adjoin linen and sewing room and have connecting doors.
v. Dirty linen	50–60	
vi. Linen and sewing room	150	Including linen store 20–40 sq. feet.
vii. Drying cupboard		Heated for drying and airing clothes washed in the home and wet outer garments (sited near laundry).
viii. Box rooms	Total 120	One on each floor. Additional storage space in roof an advantage.

ix. Cleaners' room and store   50–60   With bucket sink and drainer (one on each floor).

x. General storage   Say 100   Including store for (1) wheelchairs in everyday use, (2) linen stocks, (3) linen in everyday use, (4) cleaning materials, and (5) general storage.

xi. Double garage   260

xii. Outside toilet   1 w.c., 1 basin, mainly for use of gardener/handyman.

xiii. Garden and tool store   50–60

C. KITCHEN   Total 850   Including veg. store 40–50
                             Dry store   50–70
                             Larder   50–70
                             Refrigerator and deep freeze.

Bin space   Assume 6 bins, to be under cover.

D. STAFF ACCOMMODATION

i. Flat for Superintendent and Matron   850   Self-contained, 3 bedroom flat (1 double br. and 2 singles).

ii. Flat for Asst. Superintendent and Asst. Matron   550   Self-contained, one bedroom flat.

iii. Extra bedroom   110   This bedroom may be used (a) by visitors to staff or residents or, if it can be suitably sited, (b) by family of Assistant Superintendent and Assistant Matron.

iv. Two staff bed sitting-rooms   140–150 each

v. Resident staff sanitary accommodation   Bathroom and separate w.c.

vi. Staff dining-room   150   For use by resident and non-resident staff. Superintendent, Matron and Assistant Matron may be expected to cook and eat in own flats when off duty.

vii. Cloakroom for non-resident staff   75–85   1 w.c., basin, incinerator and 6 lockers.

viii. Staff cycle store   For 6 bicycles, under cover.

E. BOILER AND FUEL (and
other services)

i. Boiler room	225	
ii. Fuel store	100	Oil.
iii. Switch and meter room	10–15	Cupboard space. One dimension 4 ft. minimum.

F. LIFT   See Building Notes.

EXTERNAL WORKS

1. Car parking space for visitors should be large enough for not less than 6 cars.
2. Vehicular access required
   (a) to kitchen entrance;
   (b) for hearse and ambulance—this should be planned as discreetly as possible away from windows of residents' rooms;
   (c) for staff owned cars;
   (d) for visitors.
3. The grounds should be laid out to provide a pleasant sheltered environment with summer house, spaces for sitting out and paths forming a continuous route or routes. Landscaping should be designed with economy of maintenance in mind. Limited vegetable growing is required. Scented shrubs and flowers are desirable. Provision should be made for growing flowers for cutting.

GENERALLY

It is desired that the residents' accommodation be planned on two floors as a series of groups, preferably four or five groups of bed sitting-rooms conveniently near a sitting space. These groups to be linked to the dining areas and kitchen and to have easy access from the staff accommodation.

It is anticipated that this home will be filled almost entirely with residents from the former public assistance institution. This could affect planning of, for example, the toilet accommodation for men and it is suggested that the Superintendent and Matron of the former public assistance institution should be consulted about problems which have arisen there.

Double rooms should be designed so that furniture can be placed to form two identifiable areas.

Bedroom furniture generally will *not* be built in and rooms should be designed so that furniture can be arranged in various ways.

COST LIMIT   To be agreed with Ministry of Health.

SELECTED BIBLIOGRAPHY

Government Publications

GENERAL REGISTER OFFICE

Census 1961, County Reports (England and Wales).
Morbidity Statistics from General Practice, Vol. 1 (by Logan, W. P. D. and Cushion, A. A.), Studies on Medical and Population Subjects No. 14, 1958.
Registrar General's Quarterly Returns for England and Wales, Births, Deaths and Marriages etc.
Registrar General's Statistical Reviews of England and Wales (especially Part II).

HOUSING CORPORATION

Annual Reports (House of Commons Papers).
Are You Looking for a Modern Home? A Directory of Cost-Rent and Co-Ownership Housing, April 1967.

MINISTRY OF HEALTH

Annual Reports.
Boucher, C. A., *Survey of Services Available to the Chronic Sick and Elderly in 1954–5,* Reports on Public Health and Medical Subjects No. 98, 1957.
The Development of Community Care, Cmnd. 1973, 1963.
The Development of Community Care, Revision to 1973–4, 1964.
The Development of Community Care, Revision to 1975–6, Cmnd. 3022, 1966.
The Field of Work of the Family Doctor (Annis Gillie Report), 1963.
A Hospital Plan for England and Wales, Cmnd. 1604, 1962 (and revisions).
Local Authority Building Note No. 2, Residential Accommodation for Elderly People, 1962.
(Jointly with Department of Health for Scotland), *Report of the Working Party on the Training of District Nurses,* 1955.
(Jointly with Department of Health for Scotland), *Report of the Working Party on Social Workers in Local Authority Health and Welfare Services,* (Younghusband Report), 1959.
(Jointly with Department of Health for Scotland and Ministry of Education), *An Inquiry into Health Visiting,* (Jameson Report), 1956.

Circulars

118/47 National Health Service Act. Health Services to be provided by Local Health Authorities under Part III of the Act. Formulation of Proposals.

N

172/47 National Assistance Bill. Future of Public Assistance Institutions.

15/48 Accommodation for Midwives, District Nurses and Health Visitors.

103/48 National Health Service Act, 1946. Training of Domiciliary Midwives and Nurses.

135/48 National Assistance Act, 1948. National Assistance (Powers of Inspection) Regulations, 1948.

50/49 National Assistance Act. Training Course for Matrons of Old People's Homes.

51/49 Contributions to Old People's Welfare Organizations.

86/49 National Assistance Act, 1948. Registration and Inspection of Disabled and Old Persons' Homes.

11/50 Welfare of Old People. Collaboration between Local Authorities and Voluntary Associations.

29/50 National Assistance Act, 1948. Submission of Proposals for Provision of Premises. Calculation of Exchequer Contributions and Condition and Method of Payment.

25/54 National Health Service. Report of the Standing Nursing Advisory Committee on the position of the Enrolled Assistant Nurse in the National Health Service.

3/55 National Assistance Act, 1948. Residential Accommodation for Old People. Homes for the More Infirm.

3/56 Restriction of Local Government Expenditure. Minister of Health's loan sanctions to be extremely restricted.

14/57 Services for the Chronic Sick and Infirm.

13/58 National Assistance Act, 1948. Authority liable to provide Accommodation.

11/59 National Health Service. Provision of Chiropody Services under s. 28 of the 1946 Act.

14/59 National Assistance (Amendment) Act, 1959. Explains changes in determining ordinary residence for the purposes of provision of residential accommodation.

15/59 National Health Service. Training of District Nurses.

26/59 Health Visiting Service.

10/61 Younghusband Report.

12/61 Services for Old People. Recommends regular review of services provided for old people (joint with Ministry of Housing and Local Government Circular 10/61).

21/61 The Economic Situation: Local Health and Welfare Services.

2/62 Development of Local Authority Health and Welfare Services: Ten-Year Plans.

7/62 Development of Local Authority Health and Welfare Services: Co-operation with Voluntary Organizations.

11/62 Local Authority Health and Welfare Services. Building Notes.

12/62 National Assistance Act, 1948 (Amendment) Act, 1962.

15/62 Admission to Hospital, Hospital Waiting Lists and the Role of Community Services.

18/62 Development of Local Authority Health and Welfare Services: Co-operation with Voluntary Organizations.

21/62 Conduct of Disabled Persons' and Old Persons' Homes.

24/62 Health Visitors and Social Work Training Act, 1962.

26/62 Professions Supplementary to Medicine Act, 1960. Provisions for Registration.

3/63 Discharge of Patients from Hospital and Arrangement for After-Care.

6/63 Development of Local Authority Health and Welfare Services: Ten-Year Plans.

14/63 Incontinence Pads.

18/63 Nursing Homes Act, 1963.

20/63 The Field of Work of the Family Doctor (Annis Gillie Report).

21/63 Development of Local Authority Health and Welfare Services: Ten-Year Plans.

22/63 National Assistance Act, 1948. National Assistance (Powers of Inspection) (Amendment) Regulations, 1963.

9/64 National Health Service Act, 1946. Qualifications of Health Visitors.

10/64 Professions Supplementary to Medicine Act, 1960. New Regulations for Registration.

13/64 Development of Local Authority Health and Welfare Services: Revision of Plans to 1973-4.

18/64 Voluntary Effort in the Health and Welfare Services.

8/65 Training of Health Visitors and Health Visitors' Tutors.

10/65 Development of Local Authority Health and Welfare Services: Ten-Year Plans.

11/65 Fire Precautions in Homes for the Elderly.

12/65 Use of Ancillary Help in Local Authority Nursing Services.

14/65 Development of Local Authority Health and Welfare Services: Revision of Plans to 1975-6.

18/65 Care of the Elderly in Hospitals and Residential Homes.

20/65 Deferment of Expenditure on Capital Projects, etc. by Local Authorities.

25/65 Home Help Service.

4/66 Deferment of Expenditure on Capital Projects, etc. on Health and Welfare Services.

10/66 Development of Local Authority Health and Welfare Services: Ten-Year Plans.

14/66 Facilities for Incontinent People.

23/66 Ministry of Social Security Act, 1966.

10/67 Local Authority Health and Welfare Services: Development Plans and Programme of Capital Projects.

23/67 District Nurse Training.

Planning Local Authority Services for the Elderly

MINISTRY OF HOUSING AND LOCAL GOVERNMENT

Annual Reports.
Design Publications:
  Flatlets for Old People, 1958.
  More Flatlets for Old People, 1960.
  Some Aspects of Designing for Old People, Design Bulletin No. 1, 1962.
  Grouped Flatlets for Old People, Design Bulletin No. 2, 1962.
  Old People's Flatlets at Stevenage, Design Bulletin No. 11, 1966.
Housing Returns for England and Wales.
Housing in England and Wales, Cmnd. 1290, 1961.
Housing Programme 1965 –1970, Cmnd. 2838, 1966.
Housing Subsidies Manual, 1967.
Central Housing Advisory Committee, *Housing for Special Purposes* (1st Supplement to the Housing Manual), 1951.
Central Housing Advisory Committee, *Moving from the Slums*, 1956.
Central Housing Advisory Committee, *Our Older Homes*, 1966.
Report of Committee of Inquiry into the Impact of Rates on Households Cmnd. 2582, (Allen Report), 1965.
Report of the Committee on Housing in Greater London, Cmnd. 2605, (Milner Holland Report), 1965.
Report of the Committee on the Management of Local Government (Maud Report), 1967.
Report of the Committee on the Staffing of Local Government (Mallaby Report), 1967.

Circulars

36/51   Housing for Special Purposes.
69/54   Employment of Older Men and Women.
32/56   Housing of Old People.
18/57   Housing of Old People.
55/57   Housing Accommodation for Old People.
30/58   Flatlets for Old People.
47/60   More Flatlets for Old People.
10/61   Services for Old People. Co-operation between Housing and Welfare Authorities and Voluntary Organizations (joint with Ministry of Health Circular 12/61).
12/62   Housing Associations in England and Wales.
22/64   Rating (Interim Relief) Act, 1964.
23/66   Rating Act, 1966.
46/67   Rent Rebate Schemes.

MINISTRY OF PENSIONS AND NATIONAL INSURANCE

Annual Reports.
Reports of the National Assistance Board.
Financial and other Circumstances of Retirement Pensioners, 1966.

SELECTED BIBLIOGRAPHY

PUBLIC GENERAL ACTS

Housing Acts.
National Assistance Act, 1948.
National Assistance Act, 1948 (Amendment) Act, 1962.
National Health Service Acts.
Health Services and Public Health Act, 1968.
Social Work (Scotland) Act, 1968.

OTHER REPORTS

Report of the Inter-departmental Committee on Social Insurance and the Allied Services, Cmd. 6404, (Beveridge Report), 1942.
First and Second Reports of the National Advisory Committee on the Employment of Older Men and Women, Cmd. 8963 and Cmd. 9628, 1953 and 1955.
Report of the Committee on the Economic and Financial Problems of the Provision for Old Age, Cmd. 9333, (Phillips Report), 1954.
Report of the Committee of Enquiry into the Cost of the National Health Service, Cmd. 9663, (Guillebaud Report), 1956.
Royal Commission on the Law Relating to Mental Illness and Mental Deficiency, Cmnd. 169, 1957.

SCOTLAND

DEPARTMENT OF HEALTH

Annual Reports.
   (From 1958 statistics relating to the health services in Scotland were published separately from the Annual Reports, in a series called *Scottish Health Statistics.*)
Scottish Housing Advisory Committee, *Housing of Special Groups,* 1952.
The Ageing Population, 1953.

Circulars

51/48 National Assistance Act, 1948. Accommodation and Welfare Services to be provided by Local Authorities.
94/48 Charges for Certain Supplies and Services.
65/49 Welfare of Old People.
98/49 National Assistance Act, 1948. Responsibility for Persons in Voluntary Homes.
99/50 Welfare of Old People.
61/53 Care of the Aged.
57/54 Care of the Aged.
88/57 Housing Accommodation for Old People.
60/58 Care of the Elderly.

PLANNING LOCAL AUTHORITY SERVICES FOR THE ELDERLY

75/58   Housing (Repairs and Rents) (Scotland) Act, 1954. Local Authority
        Proposals for dealing with Unfit Houses.
88/58   Old People's Homes. Fire Precautions and Accident Prevention.
90/58   Health Visiting Service.

GENERAL REGISTRY OFFICE (EDINBURGH)

Census 1961, County Reports (Scotland).
*Quarterly Returns of the Registrar General for Scotland, Births, Deaths
and Marriages.*

SCOTTISH DEVELOPMENT DEPARTMENT

Annual Reports.
The Scottish Housing Programme 1965-70, Cmnd. 2837, 1965.
Housing Returns for Scotland.
Returns of Rents of Houses Owned by Local Authorities in Scotland.
Scottish Housing Advisory Committee, *Scotland's Older Houses*, 1967.

Circulars
31/63   Services for Old People.
61/63   Housing of the Elderly—Annual Return.
 4/65   Housing of the Elderly—Return.

COTTISH HOME AND HEALTH DEPARTMENT

Annual Reports.
Hospital Plan for Scotland, Cmnd. 1602, 1962 (and revisions).
*General Medical Services in the Highlands and Islands, Cmnd. 3257, (Birsay
Report),* 1967.
Social Work and the Community, Cmnd. 3065, 1966.

Circulars
  8/62   National Assistance Act, 1948 (Amendment) Act, 1962.
 66/63   Development of Local Authority Health and Welfare Services.
         Co-operation with Voluntary Bodies.
135/63   Services for Old People (joint with Scottish Development Depart-
         ment Circular 31/63).
  3/64   Prevention of Accidents in the Home.
  7/64   Organization of Laundry Service for Elderly and Infirm.
 17/64   Contributions towards Expenditure on the Housing of Elderly or
         Disabled Persons.
 20/66   Ministry of Social Security Act, 1966. Amendment to Circular
         8/62.
 13/67   Facilities for Incontinent People.
 31/67   Homes for Elderly and Disabled—Fire Precautions.
 36/67   Storage and Administration of Drugs in Old People's Homes.

SELECTED BIBLIOGRAPHY

Other Publications

General

ABEL-SMITH, B. and TOWNSEND P., *The Poor and the Poorest*, (Occasional Papers in Social Administration, No. 17), G. Bell and Sons Ltd., 1965.

DAVIES, B. P., 'An Index of Variation in "Need" of County Boroughs for Old People's Homes', *Sociological Review*, Vol. 12, No. 1, March 1964.

— 'Local Health and Welfare Services', *Local Government Chronicle*, No. 5159, January 15, 1966.

— *Social Needs and Resources in Local Services*, Michael Joseph, 1968.

DONNISON, D. V., *Health, Welfare and Democracy in Greater London*, (Greater London Papers No. 5), London School of Economics, 1962.

DONNISON, D. V. and CHAPMAN, V., *Social Policy and Administration*, Allen and Unwin, 1965.

GRIFFITH, J. A. G., *Central Departments and Local Authorities*, Allen and Unwin, 1966.

HALL, M. P., *The Social Services of Modern England*, 6th Edition, Routledge and Kegan Paul, 1963.

JACKSON, R. M., *The Machinery of Local Government*, 2nd Edition, Macmillan, 1965.

MOSER, C. A. and SCOTT, W., *British Towns*, Oliver and Boyd, 1961.

MOSS, J. ed., *Health and Welfare Services Handbook*, 3rd Edition, Hadden, Best and Co., Ltd., 1962.

PAIGE, D. and JONES, K., *Health and Welfare Services in Britain in 1975*, Cambridge University Press, 1966.

PARKER, J., *Local Health and Welfare Services*, Allen and Unwin, 1965.

SLACK, K. M., *Social Administration and the Citizen*, Michael Joseph, 1966.

TITMUSS, R. M., *Essays on the Welfare State*, Allen and Unwin, 1958.

TOWNSEND, P., 'The Timid and the Bold', *New Society*, May 23, 1963.

Elderly

ARKLEY, J., *The Over Sixties*, National Council of Social Service, 1964.

BRACEY, H. E., *In Retirement*, Routledge and Kegan Paul, 1966.

BROCKINGTON, C. F. and LEMPERT, S. M., *The Social Needs of the Over 80s*, Manchester University Press, 1966.

COLE, D. and UTTING, J. E. G., *The Economic Circumstances of Old People*, (Occasional Papers in Social Administration, No. 4), Codicote Press, 1962.

CUMBERLAND COUNTY COUNCIL, *The Needs of the Aged in Cumberland*, Report of the Second Working Party, 1966.

GREENLEES, A. and ADAMS, J., *Old People in Sheffield*, Sheffield Council of Social Service, 1949.

HARRIS, A. I., *Social Welfare for the Elderly*, Government Social Survey, 1968.

391

LIVERPOOL PERSONAL SERVICE SOCIETY, *Social Contacts in Old Age*, University of Liverpool Press, 1953.

LOETHER, H. J., *Problems of Ageing*, Dickenson Publishing Co., 1967.

MCCOUBREY, A. F. and MACQUEEN, I.A. G., 'A Survey of Old People in a Rural Community', *Health Bulletin*, Vol. X, No. 3, 1952, issued by the Chief Medical Officer, Department of Health for Scotland.

MILLER, H. C., *The Ageing Countryman*, National Corporation for the Care of People, 1963.

NATIONAL CORPORATION FOR THE CARE OF OLD PEOPLE, *Annual Reports*.

— *Not Too Old at Sixty*, 1963.

NATIONAL COUNCIL OF SOCIAL SERVICE, *Over Seventy*, 1954.

NATIONAL LABOUR WOMEN'S ADVISORY COMMITTEE, *National Survey into Care of the Elderly*, First Interim Report, 1964.

—*Care of the Elderly*, Second Interim and Final Report, 1964.

NATIONAL OLD PEOPLE'S WELFARE COUNCIL, *Annual Reports*.

—*Ageing—Its Changes and Its Promise*, Report of the 10th National Conference on the Care of the Elderly, National Council of Social Service, 1960.

—*The Elderly Individual in Modern Society*, Report of the 11th National Conference on the Care of the Elderly, National Council of Social Service, 1962.

—*Planning for Ageing*, Report of the 12th National Conference on the Care of the Elderly, National Council of Social Service, 1964.

—*Putting Planning into Practice*, Report of the 13th National Conference on the Care of the Elderly, National Council of Social Service, 1966.

—*Personal Care of the Elderly*, Report of the 14th National Conference on the Care of the Elderly, National Council of Social Service, 1968.

Old People, Report of a Survey Committee on the Problems of Ageing and the Care of Old People (Rowntree Report), Oxford University Press for the Trustees of the Nuffield Foundation, 1947.

'Our Old People', *Socialist Commentary*, January 1966.

RICHARDSON, I. M., *Age and Need*, Livingstone, 1964.

— *Age and Need in the Countryside*, Scottish Council of Social Service, 1965.

ROYAL COLLEGE OF PHYSICIANS (EDINBURGH), *The Care of the Elderly in Scotland*, 1963.

RUCK, S. K., 'A Policy for Old Age', *Political Quarterly*, Vol. 31, No. 2, April/June 1960.

SCOTTISH OLD PEOPLE'S WELFARE COMMITTEE, *Annual Reports*.

—*Handbook of Information on Old People's Welfare in Scotland*, Pergamon Press, 1965.

—*Their Problems Are Our Challenge*, Report of the Conference of the Scottish Old People's Welfare Committee, 1960, Scottish Council of Social Service.

—*Honouring our Heritage*, Report of the Biennial Conference of the

Scottish Old People's Welfare Committee, 1962, Scottish Council of Social Service.

—*Old Age in an Affluent Society*, Report of the Conference of the Scottish Old People's Welfare Committee, 1964, Scottish Council of Social Service.

—*The Elderly: Priorities*, Report of the Biennial Conference of the Scottish Old People's Welfare Committee, 1966, Scottish Council of Social Service.

SHANAS, E., *et al.*, *Old People in Three Industrial Societies*, Routledge and Kegan Paul, 1968.

SHENFIELD, B., *Social Policies for Old Age*, Routledge and Kegan Paul, 1957.

SLACK, K. M., *Councils, Committees and Concern for the Old*, (Occasional Papers on Social Administration, No. 2), Codicote Press, 1960.

SNELLGROVE, D., *Elderly Employed*, White Crescent Press, 1962.

—*Elderly Housebound*, White Crescent Press, 1963.

TOWNSEND, P., *The Family Life of Old People*, Routledge and Kegan Paul, 1957 (Pelican Edition, 1963).

TOWNSEND, P. and WEDDERBURN, D., *The Aged in the Welfare State*, (Occasional Papers on Social Administration, No. 14), G. Bell and Sons Ltd., 1965.

TUNSTALL, J., *Old and Alone*, Routledge and Kegan Paul, 1966.

WILLIAMSON, J., *et al.*, 'Old People at Home: Their Unreported Needs', *Lancet*, 1964, 1, 1117.

Health

AKESTER, J. M. and MACPHAIL, A. N., 'Health Visiting and General Practice', *Lancet*, 1964, 2, 405.

ANDERSON, W. F. and COWAN, N. R., 'A Consultative Health Centre for Older People', *Lancet*, 1955, 2, 239.

BAKER, C. D., 'The Extent in England of Health Visitor Attachment to General Practices', *Journal of the College of General Practitioners*, Vol. 8, No. 46, September 1964.

BRITISH MEDICAL ASSOCIATION, *Accidental Hypothermia in the Elderly*, reprinted from *British Medical Journal*, 1964, 2, 1255.

BUTTERWORTH, J. and MACDONAGH, V. R., 'General Practitioner and Health Visitor', *Lancet*, 1964, 1, 549.

CARTWRIGHT, A., *Patients and Their Doctors*, Routledge and Kegan Paul, 1967.

CARSTAIRS, V., *Home Nursing in Scotland*, Scottish Health Service Studies No. 2, Scottish Home and Health Department, 1966.

DONALDSON, R. J., 'A Multiple Screening Clinic', *Municipal Review*, Vol. 37, No. 435, March 1966.

FARNDALE, J., *The Day Hospital Movement in Great Britain*, Pergamon Press, 1961.

FARNDALE, J., ed., *Trends in the National Health Service*, Pergamon Press, 1964.

FORBES, F. A., 'A Health Visitor Attached to General Practice', *Health Bulletin*, Vol. XXII, No. 1, 1964, issued by the Chief Medical Officer, Scottish Home and Health Department.

FREEMAN, H. and FARNDALE, J. ed., *New Aspects of Mental Health Services*, Pergamon Press, 1968.

— *Trends in the Mental Health Service*, Pergamon Press, 1963.

FRY, J., *et al.*, 'The Evolution of a Health Team: A Successful General Practitioner Health Visitor Association', *British Medical Journal*, 1965, 1, 181.

HADDOW, T. D., 'The Future of Local Authority Health Services', *Health Bulletin*, Vol. XX, No. 1, 1962, issued by the Chief Medical Officer, Department of Health for Scotland.

HOBSON, W. and PEMBERTON, J., *The Health of the Elderly at Home*, Butterworth, 1955.

HOCKEY, L., *Feeling the Pulse*, Queen's Institute of District Nursing, 1966.

MARIE CURIE MEMORIAL FOUNDATION, *Annual Reports*.

MEDICAL SERVICES REVIEW COMMITTEE, *A Review of the Medical Services in Great Britain*, (Porritt Report), Social Assay, 1962.

NATIONAL CORPORATION FOR THE CARE OF OLD PEOPLE, *A Chiropody Service for Old People*, 1959.

— *Chiropody for the Elderly*, 1960.

— *Accommodation for the Mentally Infirm Aged*, 1963.

PETERS R. J. and KINNAIRD, J., *Health Services Administration*, Livingstone, 1965.

REES, W. D. and LUTKINS, S. J., 'Mortality of Bereavement', *British Medical Journal*, 1967, 2, 13.

SCOTTISH OLD PEOPLE'S WELFARE COMMITTEE, *Report of an Enquiry into the Need for Laundry Services for Incontinent Old People Living at Home in Scotland, August 1963*, (duplicated), Scottish Council of Social Service, (undated).

SHELDON, J. H., *The Social Medicine of Old Age*, Oxford University Press for Nuffield Foundation, 1948.

WESTON-SMITH, J. and MOTTRAM, E., 'Extended Use of Nursing Services in General Practice', *British Medical Journal*, 1967, 2, 672.

WOODROFFE, C. and TOWNSEND, P., *Nursing Homes in England and Wales*, National Corporation for the Care of Old People, 1961.

YOUNG, M., BENJAMIN, B. and WALLIS, C., 'The Mortality of Widowers', *Lancet*, 1963, 2, 454.

Welfare

BARAN, S., 'A Friendly Chat is Not Enough,' *New Society*, February 25, 1965.

Caring for People (Williams Committee Report), National Institute for Social Work Training Series No. 11, Allen and Unwin, 1967.

SELECTED BIBLIOGRAPHY

COMMUNITY COUNCIL OF LANCASHIRE, *Lunch Clubs for the Elderly*, revised edition, 1965.

FARNDALE, J., ed., *Trends in Social Welfare*, Pergamon Press, 1965.

HANSON, J., 'Challenge in the Welfare Services', *Municipal Review*, Vol. 36, No. 431, November 1965.

HARRIS, A. I., *Meals on Wheels for Old People*, A Report of an Inquiry by the Government Social Survey, National Corporation for the Care of Old People, 1960.

JEFFERYS, M., *An Anatomy of Social Welfare Services*, Michael Joseph, 1965.

LONDON COUNCIL OF SOCIAL SERVICE, *Day Care Service for the Aged and Infirm in their own Homes*, National Council of Social Service, 1963.

MCMILLAN, R. B., 'Assistance from Local Authorities and Others in the Home Care of the Aged', *Journal of the College of General Practitioners*, Vol. 6, No. 1, February 1963, Supplement No. 1.

NATIONAL ASSOCIATION OF ALMSHOUSES, *An Account of Almshouses*, 1957.

NATIONAL CORPORATION FOR THE CARE OF OLD PEOPLE, *Private Homes for Old People*, 1967.

NATIONAL OLD PEOPLE'S WELFARE COUNCIL, *The Organisation of a Visiting Service by an Old People's Welfare Committee*, National Council of Social Service, 1963.

— *Employment and Workshops for the Elderly*, National Council of Social Service, 1963.

— *Boarding-Out Schemes for Elderly People*, revised edition, National Council of Social Service, 1966.

RAVEN, J. and HAYNES, K. J., 'Social Contact, Loneliness and Clubgoing among Old People', *Journal of the Town Planning Institute*, Vol. 52, No. 3, March 1966.

REDDIN, M., 'The Varying Needs of the Aged', *British Hospital Journal and Social Service Review*, Vol. 76, October 28, 1966.

RODGERS, B. N. and DIXON, J., *Portrait of Social Work*, Oxford University Press, 1960.

RUCK, S. K., *London Government and the Welfare Services*, Routledge and Kegan Paul, 1963.

SAINSBURY, S., 'Home Services for the Aged', *New Society*, April 2, 1964.

SLACK, K. M., ed., *Some Aspects of Residential Care of the Elderly*, National Council of Social Service, 1964.

TOWNSEND, P., *The Last Refuge*, Routledge and Kegan Paul, 1962.

WHITE, E. E., *Clubs for the Elderly*, National Council of Social Service, (no date).

Housing

CRAMOND, R. D., *Housing Policy in Scotland, 1919–1964*, Oliver and Boyd, 1966.

CULLINGWORTH, J. B., *English Housing Trends*, (Occasional Papers in Social Administration, No. 13), G. Bell and Sons Ltd., 1965.
— *Housing and Local Government*, Allen and Unwin, 1966.
— *Scottish Housing in 1965*, Government Social Survey, 1967.
DONNISON, D. V., *Housing Policy Since The War*, (Occasional Papers in Social Administration, No. 1), Codicote Press, 1960.
— *The Government of Housing*, Pelican, 1967.
DONNISON, D. V., *et al.*, *Housing Since the Rent Act*, (Occasional Papers in Social Administration, No. 3), Codicote Press, 1961.
GRAY, P. G. and RUSSELL, R., *The Housing Situation in 1960*, Government Social Survey, 1962.
HOLE, V. and ALLEN, P. G., *A Survey of Housing for Old People*, Building Research Station, Design Series No. 33 (reprinted from *Architect's Journal*, Vol. 135, No. 19, 1963 and Vol. 139, No. 2, 1964).
INSTITUTE OF HOUSING, *A Memorandum on Housing the Aged*, 1958.
INSTITUTE OF HOUSING MANAGERS, *Grouped Dwellings for the Elderly*, 1967.
NATIONAL FEDERATION OF HOUSING SOCIETIES, *Annual Reports*.
— *A Guide to the Formation, Constitution and Purpose of Housing Associations and Societies*, revised edition, November 1964.
— *Housing the Elderly*, Conference Report, 1966.
PARKER, R., *The Rents of Council Houses*, (Occasional Papers on Social Administration, No. 22), G. Bell and Sons Ltd., 1967.
POLLARD, H., 'The Work of the Hanover Housing Association', *Rural District Review*, July 1964.
WEST MIDLANDS OLD PEOPLE'S WELFARE COMMITTEE, *The Warden in Grouped Dwelling Schemes for the Elderly*, Midland Advisory Office of the National Council of Social Service, February 1965.
WILSON, R., *Housing Finance*, Joint Committee of Students' Societies of the Institute of Municipal Treasurers and Accountants, 1967.

Finance

CARTER, T. E., 'Capital Investment by Public Authorities: Local Authorities', *Local Government Finance*, Vol. 68, No. 11, November 1964.
DRUMMOND, J. M., *The Finance of Local Government*, 2nd Edition, Allen and Unwin, 1962.
HARDACRE, W. S., 'The Place of the Finance Committee in this Modern Age', *Local Government Finance*, Vol. 69, No. 4, April 1965.
INSTITUTE OF MUNICIPAL TREASURERS AND ACCOUNTANTS, *Annual Publications:*
Housing Statistics (England and Wales).
Local Health Statistics (England and Wales).
Welfare Services Statistics (England and Wales).
—*The Use of the Revenue Budget as a Means of Financial Control*, 1954.
—*Local Authority Borrowing*, 1957.

SELECTED BIBLIOGRAPHY

INSTITUTE OF MUNICIPAL TREASURERS AND ACCOUNTANTS (SCOTTISH BRANCH), *Annual Publication: Rating Review*.

MARSHALL, A. H., *Financial Administration in Local Government*, Allen and Unwin, 1960.

ROYAL INSTITUTE OF PUBLIC ADMINISTRATION, *Budgeting in Public Authorities*, Allen and Unwin, 1959.

WILSON, A. G., 'Forward Financial Planning in Local Government', *Local Government Finance*, Vol. 71, No. 11, November 1967.

WREFORD, F. C., 'Rationing the Rates', *Local Government Finance*, Vol. 69, No. 11, November 1965.

— 'Rate Rationing—A Postscript', *Local Government Finance*, Vol. 70, No. 5, May 1966.

Voluntary Organizations

MORRIS, M., *Social Enterprise*, National Council of Social Service, 1962.

— *A Study of Halifax*, National Council of Social Service, 1965.

NATIONAL OLD PEOPLE'S WELFARE COUNCIL, *Recruiting Volunteers to Help the Elderly*, National Council of Social Service, 1963.

— *Survey of Services for the Elderly provided by Voluntary Organizations, 1965*, National Council of Social Service, (undated).

— *A Manual of Voluntary Visiting*, National Council of Social Service, 1967.

ROOFF, M., *Voluntary Societies and Social Policy*, Routledge and Kegan Paul, 1957.

SCOTTISH OLD PEOPLE'S WELFARE COMMITTEE, *Results of National Questionnaire in Scotland, November 1962*, (duplicated), Scottish Council of Social Service, (undated).

— *Summary of Services provided by Old People's Welfare Committees in Scottish Counties, 1965*, Scottish Council of Social Service, (undated).

INDEX

(Summaries to chapters excluded)

Abbeyfield societies, 81, 318
Aberdeen, 29, 174, 192
Advice services, 337, 364, 379
Allen Report, 270, 273
Almshouses, 45 f., 77, 80–2
Ambulances, 94 f., 206
Architects, 16, 20, 136, 140, 150, 161, 210, 212, 254, 285–6, 289–306, 319, 348, 350, 353, 357–8, 378
Arkley, J., 197, 335
Attachment schemes, 190–2, 199, 207, 240

Bacon, Alice, 24
Bathing attendants, 231, 316
Bereavement, 197, 207
Bethnal Green, 173
Bevan, Aneurin, 23–4, 29
Birmingham, 206, 335
Birsay Report, 58
Blind, 14, 85, 198, 322
Boarding-out schemes, 101, 109, 118
Boucher Report, 26–8, 116
Bristol, 312
British Medical Association (local), 312
Brockington, F. M., and Lempert, S. M., 334
Budget rationing systems, 262–5
Building contractors, 288, 293, 302, 304–5, 350, 378
Building—industrialized, 288, 297, 304, 378
Building industry—capacity, 248, 293, 357
Building materials—control, 25, 34, 251–2
Building societies, 154
Bulletins for general practitioners, 187
Bus services, 47, 178, 193, 240–1, 288

Call-bell systems, 40, 142, 145–6, 281
'Care and attention', 24, 27, 122, 128, 132, 337
Caretakers, 71, 146
Carstairs, V., 174, 231
Carter, T. E., 250
Cartwright, A., 184
Census, see Planning
Central departments, see also Ministry of Health, etc., 15, 19, 23, 37, 49, 125, 129, 135, 158–9, 248, 290–1, 294–6, 304–5, 326 f., 348, 356–8, 364, 368

Central Housing Advisory Committees, 34
Charges, see Home help, etc., also Retirement incomes
Chiropody, see also Foot hygiene
  charges, 187, 338–9
  needs, 43, 166–7, 182, 184, 199, 201, 218, 261, 338–9, 347
  provision, 14, 25, 29, 33, 37, 98–9, 166–7, 176, 188, 201, 218, 261–2, 309–10, 323, 325–6, 329–30
  staff, 39, 98–9, 167, 176, 218, 222, 231, 235, 241, 338–9, 358
Church Army Housing Ltd., 81
Clerk (town, county, etc.),
  co-ordinating role, 135, 137–8, 140, 247, 289–90
  housing role, 16, 155, 158, 281, 353
  legal, 336
Clinics, 98–9, 187, 237, 252, 254, 286–7, 289, 297–8, 313
  advisory for old people, 101, 184, 312–13
Clubs, see also Lunch clubs, etc., 101, 178, 199, 207, 314, 327
Combined duty nurses, 86–8, 94–7, 172, 190, 204, 233, 237
Community care, 24, 27, 37, 42, 48, 108, 114–15, 120, 128, 253, 280, 308, 354–5
Community centres, 141, 303, 314
Compulsory purchase orders, 286–7
Concession prices for old people
  cafes, 341
  council rents, 268–71, 282
  laundries, 100–1, 340
  travel, 47, 178, 193
Convalescent homes, 116, 198
Conversion of property, see also under Residential accommodation, 35, 40, 71, 81–2, 126, 156–7, 237, 256, 319
Councils of Social Service (local), 177–8, 201, 324
Cullingworth, J. B., 75–6
Cumberland County Council, 71–2

Daughters of old people, see Relatives
Davies, B. P., 23, 206 f.
Day centres for old people, 126–7, 206–7, 254, 311–12, 341
Day hospitals for old people, 42, 172, 311

Deaf, 14, 198
Decoration services, 195, 206, 377–8
Dental services, 313
Department of Education and Science, 253, 294–5
Department of Health and Social Security, *see also* Ministry of Health, etc., 48n, 361, 363, 367
Department of Health for Scotland, *see also* Scottish Home and Health Department, etc., 26, 31, 44–5, 135
District nursing, *see* Home nursing
District Valuers, 110
Domestic help, *see* Home help
Domiciliary midwifery, 95, 190, 204
Domiciliary services, *see also* Home help, etc., 20, 24–5, 27–33, 37–9, 43–4, 46, 84–103, 117–20, 126–7, 145, 164–213, 243, 252, 254, 323–30, 337–42, 348, 354–5
Donations, 278

Education departments, 174, 249–50, 253–4, 260–1, 264, 286, 294, 296, 298, 314–15, 336
Elected members, *see under* Local councils
Employment of old people, 14, 23, 38, 102, 341–2, 379
Engineers, 16, 140
Estates surveyor, 286, 290

Families of old people, *see* Relatives
Farndale, J., 311
Finance, *see also* Grants, etc., 20, 23, 25, 308–10, 352, 357–9, 367–8, 371
capital programmes, 247–51, 254–5, 280, 287, 289–90, 293–6, 298, 350
revenue account, 28–30, 44, 108, 167, 177, 215–16, 236, 238–42, 248, 258–66, 278–83, 326, 329
revenue contributions to capital, 254–6
Finance officer, *see* Treasurer
Flashing-light schemes, 146–7
Foot hygiene services, 176, 231
Fringe benefits, 236, 241
Fry, J., 190

Gas Board, 193
General medical services, *see also* General practitioners, 14, 27, 101, 280, 312–13
General Nursing Council, 38–9

General Practitioners
attachment schemes, 190–2
referral to services, 114, 131–2, 138, 143, 168, 182–4, 188–9, 199, 351
planning, 286, 307, 309, 312–13, 365
Geriatricians, 101, 108, 116, 119, 171, 177, 189, 310–11, 365
Geriatric beds, *see also* Hospital service, 27, 54–5, 120, 171, 177
hospitals, 189, 352
Geriatric health visitor, 171, 198, 242, 328
Gifts, 193
Glasgow, 101
Good neighbour schemes, 99, 172–3
Grants
exchequer, 23, 37, 129, 250, 252, 255, 263, 272, 283, 308
local authority to
housing associations, 35, 40–1, 319–20
housing authorities, 36, 40, 69–70, 134–5, 139, 144, 154, 269, 278–83, 302–3, 378
voluntary organizations, 25, 235, 311, 325–7, 329, 349
Griffith, J. A. G., 15, 75, 249–50
Grouped dwellings, *see* Sheltered housing
Guillebaud Report, 27–8

Hampshire County Council, 115–16
Handbooks of local services, 187
Hanover Housing Association, 81
Harris, A. I., 166, 168
Health centres, *see* clinics
Health departments (*see also* Priorities —resource allocation), 158, 168, 189, 198, 200–1, 233, 298, 311, 352
Health and welfare (combined) departments, 16, 136, 144–5, 208, 299
Health Services and Public Health Act 1968, 198 f., 323 f., 358–9
Health Visiting and Social Work Training Act 1962, 38
Health Visitors, *see also* Combined-duty nurses, 14, 24–5, 32–3, 38, 84–9, 91–6, 216–17, 226–9, 231–3, 236–7, 240, 242, 259, 349, 351, 364–5
work with old people, 25, 32, 93–4, 168–9, 189–92, 194–5, 197–200, 202, 226–7, 313, 351, 364–5
Holiday schemes, 102
Home help
charges, 29, 47, 95, 186–7, 202, 313–14, 337–8, 358

Home help—*continued*
  need for, 24–5, 43, 90–1, 118, 145,
    164–5, 167–9, 172–5, 181–9,
    195, 199, 201–2, 205, 209, 347,
    355, 361
  provision, 14, 24–5, 28, 33, 45,
    84–6, 89–97, 164–5, 167–75,
    181, 188, 201, 206, 215–16,
    221–2, 226–7, 229, 234–5, 241–3,
    258–9, 326, 337–8, 355, 358, 367
    private, 186, 205, 221, 337–8
    voluntary, 326, 337
  scope of duties, 30, 45, 97, 99, 100,
    147, 164–5, 172–3, 175–6, 194,
    221–2, 231, 234–5, 242–3, 283,
    340, 356
Home help organizer, 16, 84–5, 119,
    131, 164–5, 167–9, 182–3, 186–8,
    208, 234–5, 364
Home nursing, *see also* Combined
    duty nurses
  need for, 43, 145, 171–2, 176–7,
    182–3, 190, 206, 230–1, 307,
    309, 347, 361
  provision, 14, 24, 28, 31, 33, 39, 43,
    84–8, 91–7, 145, 171–2, 176,
    182–3, 195, 204, 217–18, 222–3,
    226, 228–32, 236–8, 240, 252, 305
  referrals to services, 138, 143, 168–9,
    177, 195, 199, 201–2, 351
Home-wardens, 147, 194
Hospital service, *see also* Regional
    Hospital Boards, Geriatric beds,
    etc., 14, 42–3, 45, 307–12, 350,
    352, 358, 371
  and local health services, 27, 42, 101,
    171, 174–5, 182, 186, 188–90,
    307, 309–12, 340, 351, 354–5
  and residential accommodation, 27,
    42, 108–9, 114–18, 125, 131–2,
    208–9, 251, 253, 293, 307–9
  staff, 31, 42, 222–3, 228, 235, 355
Hotels, etc., 336, 341
Housekeepers, 81
Housing Acts, 14, 23, 34–5, 39–41,
    45–6, 77, 135, 141, 272
Housing associations and societies, 35,
    40–1, 45, 76–7, 80–2, 318–21,
    352, 357
Housing conditions—old people, 19,
    34, 75–6, 138, 143, 155, 157–8,
    162, 204, 277, 316, 348, 361–3
Housing Corporation, The, 41, 77, 319
Housing departments, 16, 119, 144,
    195–6, 198, 298–300, 334, 353
Housing managers, 16, 137–8, 140,
    144, 146, 149–50, 155–6, 158–61,
    188, 227, 233, 273, 277, 290,
    300–2, 348, 353

Housing mobility—old people, 143,
    154, 159–60, 275, 278, 319,
    334–5, 376
Housing for old people, *see also*
    sheltered housing, private etc.,
    14–20, 24, 27, 34–7, 39–41,
    45–8, 67–83, 138–43, 149–63,
    176, 195–6, 251, 253, 267–84,
    314–15, 340, 347–50, 353, 357,
    361–3, 366
  architects for, 299–304
  contracts, 304–5
  sites, 295–7
Housing Revenue Account, 39, 268–72,
    275–9, 282–3
Housing—staff, 28, 236–9, 252, 305
Housing subsidies, 34–5, 39–40, 46, 70,
    150, 267–8, 272, 278, 280
Housing tenure—old people, 75–6, 78,
    80, 162, 334–5
Housing visitors, 196
Huws Jones, R. 118, 129

Improvement grants, 35, 40, 362
Institute of Housing Memorandum on
    Housing the Aged, 37
Institute of Municipal Treasurers and
    Accountants, 62–4, 69–70, 79,
    96–7, 248
Intercommunication systems, 141, 145,
    281

Jackson, R. M., 249
Jameson Report, 32, 38, 92, 205–6,
    231, 259
Jefferys, M., 196 f., 224, 325
Joint Industrial Council, 235, 239 f.
Joint-user institutions, *see also* Resi-
    dential accommodation, 52, 57,
    110, 260
Jones, G. C., 263–4
Joseph, Keith, 73, 321

Keighley, 192
King Edward's Hospital Fund, 337

Laundry
  charges, 100–1, 187, 202, 340, 358
  incontinent, 100, 176, 242, 309, 340
  needs, 24, 167, 175–6, 199, 201–2,
    243, 277, 340, 347, 361, 363–4
  provision, 14, 25, 30, 100–1, 175–6,
    243, 309, 339–40
Leeds, 192
Liaison committees, 353
Libraries, 195, 263, 273, 295
Loan charges, 251, 255, 264

Loan sanction, 26, 41, 109, 137, 247, 251–5, 264, 290, 294–5, 302, 357–8
Local Acts of Parliament, 30, 147, 194
Local authorities
boundary changes, 110, 128, 136, 324
size of, 18, 109–10, 129–30, 151, 160, 185, 195, 200–1
structure (county council, etc.), 15–17, 36–7, 39, 52, 60–1, 68–70, 79, 86–90, 95–7, 134–6, 138–40, 144–5, 153–4, 167–9, 170, 187–8, 196, 198–9, 207–9, 237–8, 248, 268–9, 278–83, 288–9, 302, 310, 348–9, 353
reorganization, 201, 364, 369–72
type of area
commuter, 216, 223, 325
holiday, see also retirement, 18, 221
industrial, 18–19, 31, 204–5, 221, 236, 240–1, 291, 325, 341–2
mining, 185, 221
new town, 125, 220
retirement, 52, 87, 109, 127, 153, 165, 171, 177, 205, 243, 309, 311, 324–5, 332–4, 336
rural, 18, 52, 58, 87, 97, 99, 109, 125, 132, 135, 138–9, 165–6, 183, 192, 204–5, 221–4, 230–1, 240, 273, 286–8, 311, 339–40, 355
scheduled development, 223, 253–4, 332
slum clearance, 158–9, 221, 285–6, 290, 320, 348
sparsely populated, 18–19, 86, 89–90, 97, 130–1, 151, 158, 169, 171–2, 181, 215–16, 226–7, 229–30, 254, 304–5, 325, 352
urban, 18, 26, 28, 60–1, 80, 89, 141, 146, 168–9, 173, 178, 183, 185, 210, 215–16, 221–4, 233, 285, 298, 312, 315, 336, 355
Local authority associations, 27, 29, 45, 116, 308
Local Councils, 149, 154, 156, 159, 160–1, 318–19, 325, 332–3
committees
capital priorities, 248, 293
establishment, 217, 233–4, 259
finance, 112, 248–9, 251, 259, 260–2, 288, 314
health, 132, 192, 199, 201–2, 210, 215–17, 309
housing, 136, 155
planning, 112, 288
welfare, 16, 111–12, 114, 136, 150, 298, 302–3, 308

committee chairmen, 128, 135, 250, 260, 299
councillors, 16, 80, 111–12, 132, 134–5, 140–1, 146, 158, 160–1, 163, 233–4, 236, 250–1, 259–62, 264, 269, 323, 325, 349, 353–4, 358
Local Government Acts, 36–7, 135, 275, 278
Local medical committees, see also National Health Service Executive Councils, 45, 312, 323, 353
London, 16, 72–3, 128, 316
Lord Mayor's Fund, 81
Lunch clubs, 30–1, 33, 97–8, 166, 178, 187, 201, 314, 327–8, 347

Mallaby Report, 232, 292
Malnutrition, 23, 114, 169 f., 178, 200, 355
Management consultants, 354
Manpower Research Unit, 367
Marie Curie schemes, 99–100, 174
Market research organizations, 362, 369
Marshall, A. H., 261 f., 265
Matrons, 16, 145, 219, 234, 236, 238, 244, 283, 299–300
Maud Report, 248–9
Mayor, 324
Meals-on-wheels, 14, 24–5, 30–1, 33, 37, 97–8, 119, 145, 165–6, 168–9, 174–8, 184–5, 187, 195, 199, 314–15, 323–7, 330, 340–1, 347, 354–5, 361
Medical loans depot, 329, 377
Medical officers of health, 16, 353–4
and capital projects, 254–5, 292–4, 298, 312–13
and domiciliary services, 167, 170–6, 183–7, 190, 198–202, 205–11, 215–19, 222–4, 228–30, 232, 234, 236, 240–3, 259–62, 338
and housing, 143, 145, 161–2
and residential accommodation, 109, 131, 210, 309
and voluntary organizations, 323–5, 327, 329
Medical officers—area, division, 16, 167, 196, 208, 232
Mental Health Acts, 14, 109, 198
Mental health officers, 198, 206
Mental health services, 37, 94–5, 198, 237, 262, 296, 353
Mental hospitals, 41, 189, 309, 352
Mentally handicapped, 25, 110, 112, 198, 206

Migration, 117, 124–5, 152–4, 205, 208
Milkmen, 132
Milner Holland Report, 270
Ministers of religion, 182, 187, 378
Ministerial approval, 25, 29, 32, 36–8, 135, 252, 278
Ministry of Health, *see also* Department of Health and Social Security
information services, 26–7, 62, 87–8, 98–9, 120, 123, 301, 337
norms (standards), 44, 50–1, 90–2, 124–5, 207,
policy on old people, 23–4, 28–31, 37–9, 42–5, 56–7, 107–9, 127, 137–9, 210, 232, 238, 307–8, 310, 320–1, 323, 338
restrictions, 29, 31–2, 36–8, 137, 176, 237, 247, 251–5, 290–1, 294–6, 297, 356–8
Ministry of Housing and Local Government, 35–6, 45–6, 75, 139, 251–2, 263, 294
and housing old people, 35–6, 39–40, 136–7, 139, 142, 288, 302–4, 357, 362
Ministry of Pensions and National Insurance, *see also* Ministry of Social Security, 47, 187, 193, 313–14, 338
Ministry of Social Security, 47–8, 195, 269–71, 275–8, 280, 313–14, 350
Morris, M., 323
Mothers and young children—care of, 25, 32, 94–5, 112, 252

National Assistance Act 1948, 14, 23, 25, 29, 30, 36, 38, 50, 56, 109–10, 131, 198
Amendment Act 1962, 37
National Assistance Board, *see also* Supplementary Benefits Commission
income supplementation, 24, 29, 47, 95, 101, 186, 242, 269–71, 275–8, 313–14, 340
welfare functions, 168, 199, 233, 314
National Association of Almshouses, 77
National Corporation for the Care of Old People, 29, 74–5, 81, 329
National Council of Social Service, 42, 219
National Federation of Housing Societies, 76–7
National Health Service, *see also* Regional Hospital boards, etc., 39, 191, 310, 339, 347, 353, 368
Acts, 14, 23–5, 28–30, 32

executive councils, 45, 193, 286, 312–13
National Institute of Social Work Training, 368
National Insurance Acts, 23, 47
National Labour Women's Advisory Committee, 74, 178, 340
National Old People's Welfare Council 33, 100, 102, 118, 234, 236, 342
National policy
economic, 25–8, 35, 41, 43–4, 48, 125, 150, 158, 237, 248, 251–5, 258–9, 264, 290, 304, 316, 350, 356–8
education, 260–1
housing, 34–6, 39–41, 150, 267–8, 271–2, 281
old people, 19, 23–48, 193, 270–1, 361, 364
National Plan, The, 262–3
Neighbours, 132, 143, 172–3, 183, 185, 193, 315
New services, 201, 260–1, 311, 329, 347
Newspapers—local, 189, 208, 227, 273–4, 287, 335, 378
Night-sitters, 99, 145, 173–4, 184, 187, 199, 355
Norms, *see* Planning-standards
Nuffield Foundation Survey, 1947, 23, 34
Nursing care, 27, 42, 332
Nursing Homes Act, 1963, 42
Nursing homes, 42, 99–100, 116
Nursing officers—area, division, 16, 208, 328–9
Nursing officers—chief, 16, 167, 172, 176, 182–3, 187, 190, 193, 195, 206–8, 217, 223–4, 228–32, 259, 294, 309, 312, 323, 328–9

Occupational therapy, 85, 311
Old people
apathy, 169 f., 207
capacity for self-care, 127, 363–5
clothing, 167, 195, 198
housebound, 101–2, 164–5, 168–9 f., 207, 312, 354, 380
independence, 24, 27–8, 130, 156, 185–7, 205, 274, 370–1
living alone, 125–6, 128 f., 169 f., 197, 205, 335, 380
loneliness, 178, 195, 198, 361
mentally infirm, *see* residential accommodation
preferences, 156–7, 355–6, 363
privacy, 24, 193–4, 355
Old people's homes, *see* residential accommodation

Old People's Welfare Committees, 30, 97–8, 101, 199, 235, 273, 323
Ophthalmic services, 313
Organization and Methods, 172, 200–1, 234, 354
Owner occupiers—elderly, 35, 75–6, 81, 155, 274, 319, 333–5, 362
Overcrowding, 34–5, 76, 155, 157, 355

Paid organizers of voluntary work, 327–8, 379
Parish councils, 137–8, 156
Parker, R., 270–2
Parks department, 146, 277, 315
Pensions, see retirement incomes
books (cards in), 187, 193, 378
collection of, 142, 146, 175, 195
Pharmaceutical services, 230, 313
Phillips Committee, 27, 46, 113
Physically handicapped, 14, 50, 178, 342
Physiotherapy, 177, 310–11, 378
Planning, see also Ten-year plans
  attitudes to, 127–9, 201, 209–11, 348–50
  co-ordination
    in departments, 167–70, 207–9, 348–9
    in local authorities, 118–19, 127, 135–6, 150, 208–9, 290, 314–16, 348–9
    between local authorities, 135–6, 138–40, 170, 279, 289, 348–9
    with hospitals, 108, 115–17, 209, 307–12, 350
    with other bodies, 125, 127, 190, 209, 312–13, 318–31, 332–42, 350, 367
  estimating needs, 109, 113–16, 118, 123–32, 134–5, 137–43, 150, 158–6, 204–7, 209, 348–51, 360–6, 368
    from census date, 13, 127–8, 162, 225, 334, 354, 365, 369
    from records, 118–21, 123, 131, 170, 182–3, 188, 193, 199, 363–4
    surveys, see surveys
    from waiting lists, 122–6, 131–2, 149, 151–7, 167, 182, 201, 338, 348, 351
  estimating resources, 126, 130, 192, 210–11, 224–5, 247–51, 262–5, 267–9, 275–83, 286, 288–90, 293–4, 349–54, 360–1, 366–70
  evaluation and feedback, 143–6, 186–7, 190, 199, 226–44, 298–302, 360, 368
  forecasting needs, see also population projections, 119, 123–8, 132, 161–2, 205, 352

standards (norms), 44–5, 50–1, 71–2, 74–5, 90–2, 124, 139, 205–7, 262–5, 356, 368, 370
techniques—lack of, 117, 161–3, 170, 199–201, 206, 352–4, 360–71
Planning departments, 150, 285–90, 334–5, 367
Police, 182, 227, 294, 336
Poor Law, 24, 57
Population
  ageing, 13, 17–18, 28, 90–1, 97, 123, 125, 132, 138–9, 204, 208–9
  projections, 13, 123–4, 161–2, 205, 209, 348, 352, 369
  socio-economic, 151, 204–5, 221–4, 265, 325, 332–3, 335, 367
Postmen, 132
Poverty, 46–7, 204, 269–70, 273, 275
Preston, 30
Preventive, work, 25, 28–9, 128, 193–4 200, 207, 313, 355–6
Priorities
  criteria for assessing needs, 25, 125–6, 152, 155, 167–70, 181, 189, 197, 202, 326, 338, 342, 351, 363–6, 370, 375–6, 380
  in resource allocation, 23, 25, 210, 249–55, 258–65, 285–90, 292–9, 307, 333, 357–8, 368, 370–1
Private provision
  architects, 293, 296–7, 303
  domiciliary services, 97–101, 186, 205, 221–2, 235, 337–42
  housing, 35, 75–6, 78–80, 139, 146–7, 319, 332–5, 363
  industry, 341–2, 379
  residential accommodation, 50–1, 109, 125, 127, 335–7
Private rented housing, 75–6, 155–7, 162, 318
Problem families, 242
Professional associations and journals, 49, 236, 368
Professions Supplementary to Medicine Act, 1960, 39
Public baths and washouses, 243, 315–16
Public health inspector, 16, 138, 161, 258, 290, 336, 353
Public Works Loan Board, 319
Publicity, 144, 160, 188, 378

Quantity surveyors, 254, 292–3, 295
Queen's Institute of District Nursing, 31, 205, 209, 230

Rates—local, 248, 255–6, 265, 273, 308, 358
Ratepayers, 108, 272, 281–3

Rate relief, 273-5
Rating Acts, 47, 273-5
Reading, 197, 335
Records systems, see also under Planning, 363-5, 369, 371, 378
Red Cross, 98, 100 f., 171-2, 176, 231
Reddin, M., 120 f.
Regional hospital boards, 43, 53-6, 109-10, 115, 293, 307-12, 353, 371
Registers of old people, 128, 193-4, 197, 207
Rehabilitation of old people, 177, 310-11, 356
Reid, E. Neil, 71, 75
Relatives of old people, 129, 224
    and domiciliary services, 126, 145-6, 171, 173-5, 182, 184-5, 204-5, 207, 231, 277
    and housing policies, 119, 141-3, 152-4, 158, 160, 355
Removal expenses, 160, 236
Rent Act, 1957, 35
Rents
    club premises, 314
    council houses, 157, 160, 267-72, 275-7, 282, 332-3, 335
    for staff, 232, 237-9
    voluntary housing, 41, 77, 81, 319-20
Rent collection, 195-6
Rent rebates, 48, 268-71, 273
    for staff, 232
Research facilities—need for, 126, 200-1, 351, 369-71
Residential accommodation, 16, 20, 24-8, 41-3, 46, 49-66, 107-33, 139, 193, 208, 210, 281, 301-2, 307-9, 320-1, 361, 367
    adapted homes, 25-7, 111-12, 337
    charges, 24, 125, 255-6, 322
    elderly mentally infirm, 41, 108-9, 206, 254, 309
    finance, 26, 62-3, 250-6, 260, 263, 281
    frail ambulant, 116, 131-2, 301
    hidden need, 113-14, 119-20, 122-3, 125, 127, 131
    linked with sheltered housing, 71, 81, 136-7, 142, 145
    location, 25-6, 129, 131, 295-302, 304
    See private
    public assistance institutions (ex), 27, 43, 52-3, 56-8, 107-10, 120, 128-9, 131, 137, 141, 255, 289, 356
    purpose-built, 25-6, 129, 131, 295-302, 304, 311-12, 340

quality of, 26, 42, 57, 107-12, 114, 130, 332, 336-7, 355
    replacement of, 56-8, 107-12, 121-2, 128-9, 131, 137, 210, 260, 356
    residents, 59-61, 108-11, 114, 119-23, 125-6, 131, 138, 322
    short-stay, 43, 114, 174-5, 301-2
    size of home, 24, 26, 41, 55-9, 130-1
    staff for, 42, 62, 108, 111, 131, 219-21, 223, 225, 235, 238, 241-2, 244, 309, 337
    See voluntary,
    waiting lists, 26, 114, 116, 122-3, 125, 131-2, 348, 351
Retirement areas, see Local authorities, type of area
Retirement incomes, 14, 23, 24, 46-7, 336, 338, 347, 361, 366, 372
    and charges for local health and welfare services, 24, 29, 47, 186-7, 313-14, 358
    and rents, 47-8, 157, 195, 270-1, 274-7, 349, 359
Richardson, I. M., 184, 205, 335
Roads department, 249-51, 293
Rotherham, 312
Royal College of General Practitioners, 365
Royal College of Physicians Edinburgh, 53, 99, 101, 193
Royal Commission on Local Government, 201, 369-72
Royal Commission on the Law Relating to Mental Illness, 37, 309
Royal Institute of Public Administration, 248-9, 255, 261
Ruck, S. K., 72-3, 128
Rural areas, see Local authorities type of area
Rutherglen, 29, 101, 312

Salford, 312
Schools, see also Education,
    and domiciliary services, 177, 228, 315, 341
Scotland (special points from Parts II and III only)
    domiciliary services, 166, 168, 170, 174, 178, 182-7, 191, 194-6, 200, 209, 311-12, 323
    finance, 248, 250-1, 254, 261, 268-9, 271-2, 275, 278, 282
    housing, 135-6, 140-3, 146-7, 319, 321, 333-5
    residential accommodation, 110, 114, 116-18, 129-32, 290-1, 309, 322
    staff, 215, 220, 224, 229-31, 233

Scottish Development Department, *see also* Department of Health for Scotland, 40, 67–8, 73–4, 85, 96 f., 99, 321, 357, 362

Scottish Home and Health Department, *see also* Department of Health for Scotland, 26, 29, 32, 43, 50, 88, 92, 96 f., 130–2 200, 209 f., 231, 323, 356, 363, 367

and replacement policy, 43, 57–8, 107, 110, 356

Scottish Old People's Welfare Committee, 31, 98, 100

Secretary of State for Scotland, 31, 38, 40, 56, 135, 272

Seebohm Report, 371

Sheldon, J. H., 29, 184

Sheltered housing, 36, 42, 45–6, 61, 67–72, 78–80, 134–48, 155, 158, 160, 194, 269, 278–83, 288, 302–4, 315, 355, 357

and domiciliary services, 42, 144–5, 170, 173, 194, 208, 231, 243, 315, 349, 355

linked with residential accommodation, 71, 81, 136–7, 142, 145

and need for residential accommodation, 42, 46, 61, 117–20, 131, 208, 320–1

Shenfield, B., 335

Sites, 20, 26, 136, 140, 210, 212, 254, 285–91, 297, 313, 320, 332–4, 350, 357–8, 366–7, 378

Slack, K. M., 117, 329

Slum clearance programmes, 34–5, 45, 150–1, 158–9, 221, 272, 285–6, 290, 320, 348

Social centres, 101, 178, 181, 312

Social Science Research Council, 368

Social Work (Scotland) Act, 1968, 371

Social Workers, 32–3, 38, 84–5, 138, 197–8, 200, 231, 233–4, 237, 240, 259, 325, 349, 351, 365

geriatric, 189 f.

medical, 189

organization of, 126, 183, 198, 371, 376

Staff

recruitment, 20, 25, 27–8, 31–2, 167, 172, 176, 198, 200–1, 215–25, 226–46, 310–11, 315, 324–5, 328, 338–9, 349, 352, 354–6, 365, 376–7

turnover, 216, 223–5, 229, 258, 293, 298, 367

Standard plans, 297–9, 381–4

Standards for provision, *see* Planning

State enrolled nurses, 31, 39, 176, 230–1

Stockport, 334

Street-wardens, 146, 193–4

Sunderland Old People's Welfare Committee, 128 f.

Supplementary Benefits Commission, *see also* National Assistance Board, 48n, 313–14

Surveyors, 16, 141, 144, 248, 353

Surveys

local authority, 79, 109, 126, 128, 130–2, 138, 141, 159–62, 184, 197, 199–202, 206, 230, 242–3, 261, 299–301, 351–4, 364–5, 371

research in local areas, 29, 72, 128, 173, 183–6, 196–7, 205, 224, 316, 325, 334–5

Sutton Dwellings Trust, 81

Ten-year plans, *see also* Planning, 43–5, 54–5, 67–8, 88, 90–2, 107–9, 115–18, 122–9, 136–40, 204–12, 247, 251, 259–60, 293, 307–8, 313, 320–1, 323, 348–50, 358

Toc H, 276

Townsend, P., 45, 50, 71, 108, 121, 123, 173, 363

Townsend, P., and Wedderburn, D., 13, 71, 91, 183–4, 338–9, 351, 363

Trade unions, 341

Training, 31–3, 38–9, 146, 167, 177, 211, 231–5, 237, 244, 258, 328, 339, 353–4, 365, 376–7

Transport, 166, 178, 311, 341

Travel Concessions Act, 1964, *see also* Concessions, 47

Travel Expenses (Staff), 169, 192, 240–2, 258

Treasurers, 16, 191, 210, 218, 247–9, 256, 261–5, 280, 282–3, 290, 349, 353

Twickenham, 101, 312

Underoccupation

council houses, 138, 159–62, 376

private, 155, 159, 275

Universities, 184, 351, 362, 364, 367

Urban areas, *see* Local authorities—type of area

Valuation of property, 267–9

Visiting services, 33, 102, 119, 170, 194–9, 207, 231, 323–4, 351, 355, 364, 379

Voluntary organizations, 14, 37–9, 188, 200, 280, 318–3, 347, 349

Voluntary organizations—*continued*
  domiciliary services, 25, 29–30, 33,
    37, 97–102, 118, 147, 166, 178,
    194, 197–9, 235, 278, 311–12,
    315, 323–30, 337, 379
  housing, 35, 40, 71, 76–7, 80–2,
    318–22, 357, 363
  residential accommodation, 49–53,
    123–4, 127, 321–3, 337
  and planning, 35, 45, 123–4, 138,
    209, 320–1, 350, 352, 357, 367
Volunteers, 31, 165–6, 169, 194, 199,
  324–5, 328, 351, 379

Wages and salaries, 145, 174–5,
  181–2, 211, 221–3, 235–9, 241,
  264, 293, 326, 339, 358, 377
Wales, 18, 73, 86, 135
Warden — schemes, *see* Sheltered
  housing
Wardens, *see also* Caretaker, Home-
  warden, Housekeeper, Street-
  warden, 36, 40, 43, 68, 71, 142–3
  146–7, 194, 281, 283, 347, 355
  duties, 36, 78, 118, 144–6, 170, 173,
    243
  pay, 238–9, 377
  recruitment, 144–6, 220, 223, 243–4
  training, 146, 234
Welfare assistants, 33, 218–19, 231, 233
Welfare departments, *see also* Priorities—resource allocation, 109,
    115, 142, 168, 182, 187, 189,
    193, 196, 198, 233–4, 298–301,
    327, 352
Welfare homes, *see* Residential accommodation

Welfare officers, 85, 168–70, 182, 193,
  196–9, 218–19, 226–7, 232–4,
  237, 242, 244, 355, 364
  area, 17, 196
  chief, 16, 353–4
    and domiciliary services, 165–6,
      168–70, 177, 181, 183, 185, 187,
      193–8, 206–7, 311–12, 314–15,
      323–4, 342
    and finance, 250–1, 254–6, 259–61,
      263
    and housing, 135–40, 142, 144,
      146, 150, 282
    and residential accommodation,
      110–33, 210, 285–90, 298–300,
      308, 311–12, 336
    and staff, 218–20, 238, 259, 309,
      328
Weston-Smith, J., and Mottram, E.,
  190
White, E. E., 178, 197
Whitley Councils, 235, 237–9, 339
Williams Committee, 42, 62 f., 219
Williamson, J., 184
Wilson, A. G., 265, 277
Women's Royal Voluntary Service,
  81, 97–8, 168, 243
Work centres for old people, 38, 102,
  341–2
Works canteens, 174, 341
Wreford, F. C., 263–4

Yardsticks, 127, 249, 277
Younghusband Report, 32, 38, 92, 113
  training courses, 218–19, 232, 234
Youth employment offices, 228